Reason, Religion, and Natural Law

Reason, Religion, and Natural Law

FROM PLATO TO SPINOZA

Edited by Jonathan A. Jacobs

OXFORD
UNIVERSITY PRESS

OXFORD
UNIVERSITY PRESS

Oxford University Press is a department of the University of Oxford.
It furthers the University's objective of excellence in research,
scholarship, and education by publishing worldwide.

Oxford New York
Auckland Cape Town Dar es Salaam Hong Kong Karachi
Kuala Lumpur Madrid Melbourne Mexico City Nairobi
New Delhi Shanghai Taipei Toronto

With offices in
Argentina Austria Brazil Chile Czech Republic France Greece
Guatemala Hungary Italy Japan Poland Portugal Singapore
South Korea Switzerland Thailand Turkey Ukraine Vietnam

Published in the United States of America by
Oxford University Press
198 Madison Avenue, New York, NY 10016

Library of Congress Cataloging-in-Publication Data
Reason, religion, and natural law : from Plato to Spinoza / edited by Jonathan A. Jacobs.
p. cm.
Includes bibliographical references (p.) and index.
ISBN 978-0-19-976717-5 (alk. paper)
1. Natural law—History. 2. Natural law—Philosophy. I. Jacobs, Jonathan A.
K428.R43 2012
340′.112—dc23 2012001316

1 3 5 7 9 8 6 4 2

Printed in the United States of America
on acid-free paper

{ CONTENTS }

{ ACKNOWLEDGMENTS }

First and foremost I would like to thank the contributors to this volume. Each was generous in making the commitment to participate in the project, and I have learned much from them. The authors have combined the study of the history of philosophy with analysis, argumentation, and theorizing in ways that illuminate important texts from the past and explicate their relevance to important, enduring debates and issues. In asking them to contribute to a volume exploring the relation between natural law theorizing and theistic considerations from antiquity to the early modern period, I was suggesting a focus not all might have selected on their own. For that reason I am especially grateful for their contributions.

A grant from the Earhart Foundation funded a two-day seminar of the contributors in June 2010. That opportunity for conversation and criticism enabled us to shape the project and consider how to fit together its various elements. The Earhart Foundation's generous support has been a great help to me with regard to a number of scholarly projects and that support is much appreciated. The seminar was held in Granville, Ohio. Tony Lisska—a contributor to the volume—helped organize it, and he arranged for the use of some of the resources of Denison University, as well as helped in several other ways. He and Denison were excellent hosts and were instrumental in making the seminar both enjoyable and successful.

During part of 2011 I was a Visiting Scholar at the Social Philosophy & Policy Center at Bowling Green State University. In regard to the resources available and the atmosphere created by the Directors—Fred Miller (a contributor to this volume), Ellen Frankel Paul, and Jeffrey Paul—the Center is an ideal place for scholarship. I am very grateful to the Center and its staff. This was my second opportunity to spend a period of time at the Center and I have enjoyed and benefited greatly from both periods there.

The referees selected by Peter Ohlin, Philosophy Editor at Oxford University Press, made numerous helpful suggestions and critical observations. Peter's guidance and patience throughout the process of developing and producing the book are much appreciated. In addition, Assistant Editor Lucy Randall and members of the Production Staff were helpful, responsive, and tolerated my slips and errors with impressive equanimity. Robert Swanson prepared the Index and is owed thanks for that important task.

{ NOTES ON CONTRIBUTORS }

Richard Cross is John A. O'Brien Professor of Philosophy at the University of Notre Dame. He is the author of *The Metaphysics of the Incarnation: Thomas Aquinas to Duns Scotus* (Oxford University Press, 2002), *Duns Scotus on God* (Ashgate, 2005), as well as other books and articles on medieval philosophy and theology.

Douglas J. Den Uyl is Vice President of Educational Programs at Liberty Fund Inc. and former Professor of Philosophy at Bellarmine University. Among his published works are *Power, State and Freedom: An Interpretation of Spinoza's Political Philosophy* and *God, Man, & Well-Being: Spinoza's Modern Humanism.*

Jonathan A. Jacobs is Presidential Scholar, Director of the Institute for Criminal Justice Ethics, Chair of the Department of Philosophy at John Jay College of Criminal Justice, and a member of the Doctoral Faculty of Philosophy at the CUNY Graduate Center. Author of nine books and editor of two, he works primarily in moral philosophy, moral psychology, and philosophy of law and punishment. Among his books are *Law, Reason, and Morality in Medieval Jewish Philosophy* (2010), *Dimensions of Moral Theory*: *An Introduction to Metaethics and Moral Psychology* (2002), and *Aristotle's Virtues*: *Nature*, *Knowledge*, and *Human Good* (2004). He is currently writing *Liberalism and Criminal Sanction.*

Jacob Klein received his Ph.D from Cornell. He is Assistant Professor of Philosophy at Colgate University, and is completing a book on the Stoic theory of practical reason.

Anthony J. Lisska is Maria Theresa Barney Professor of Philosophy at Denison University. His *Aquinas's Theory of Natural Law* was published by Oxford University Press. Lisska published several articles and book chapters recently on both medieval and contemporary theories of natural law. He was the 2006 president of the American Catholic Philosophical Association, served as Denison's Academic Dean of the College, and was the 1994 Carnegie Foundation United States Baccalaureate Colleges Professor of the Year.

Fred D. Miller, Jr. is Professor of Philosophy and Executive Director of the Social Philosophy and Policy Center at Bowling Green State University. He is the author of *Nature, Justice, and Rights in Aristotle's Politics* (1995) and co-editor of numerous collections, including *A Companion to Aristotle's Politics*

(1991), of *Freedom, Reason, and the Polis: Essays in Ancient Greek Political Philosophy* (2007), and *A History of the Philosophy of Law from the Ancient Greeks to the Scholastics* (2007).

Jon Miller is an associate professor of philosophy at Queen's University (Canada). He works in both early modern and ancient philosophy, with his special interest centering on the reception of ancient philosophy by the early moderns. His publications include *Aristotle's Nicomachean Ethics: A Critical Guide* (Cambridge University Press, 2011) and *Spinoza and the Stoics* (Cambridge University Press, forthcoming).

Douglas B. Rasmussen is Professor of Philosophy at St. John's University in New York City. He is coauthor (with Douglas J. Den Uyl) of *Liberty and Nature: An Aristotelian Defense of Liberal Order* (1991) and *Norms of Liberty: A Perfectionist Basis for Non-Perfectionist Politics* (2005). He is also author of numerous articles in various philosophical journals and scholarly anthologies, including "Perfectionism," an entry in the 2012 *Encyclopedia of Applied Ethics* 2nd ed., Vol. 3. He earned his Ph.D. from Marquette University.

T. M. Rudavsky is Professor of Philosophy at The Ohio State University. She specializes in medieval Jewish philosophy and has edited three volumes: *Divine Omniscience and Omnipotence in Medieval Philosophy: Islamic, Jewish, and Christian Perspectives* (1984), *Gender and Judaism: The Transformation of Tradition* (1995) and with Steven Nadler, she co-edited the *Cambridge History of Jewish Philosophy: From Antiquity through the Seventeenth Century* (2009). Her *Time Matters: Time, Creation and Cosmology in Medieval Jewish Philosophy* appeared in 2000. *Maimonides,* in the "Great Minds" series with Wiley-Blackwell, is her most recent book.

Eileen C. Sweeney is Professor of Philosophy at Boston College. She is the author of *Logic, Theology, and Poetry in Boethius, Abelard and Alan of Lille: Words in the Absence of Things* (2006) and *Anselm of Canterbury and the Desire for the Word* (Spring 2012), as well as a number of articles on Thomas Aquinas in the areas of metaphysics, natural theology, and ethics.

Reason, Religion, and Natural Law

Introduction

This volume is a collection of new essays exploring relations between natural law theorizing and theological considerations, from antiquity to the seventeenth century. This introduction presents the rationale for the book's focus, places the essays in a broader philosophical context, and summarizes key claims of the essays. That three-fold purpose has made this is a rather lengthy introduction. The reader is welcome to go directly to the essays, but the introduction addresses conceptual and historical matters in ways that could help illuminate important topical relations between the essays and the philosophical significance of the concerns addressed.

The Project's Rationale and Character

During the last few decades there has been steadily increasing interest in the history of philosophy. In the English-speaking world, the study of the history of philosophy is much more a part of philosophy proper than it was, say, forty or fifty years ago. At that time the history of philosophy was widely regarded as scholarship but not philosophy. In recent years it is much more widely thought that many philosophical issues are best approached in ways that involve considerable attention to the history of philosophy. In ethics, for example, there is extensive employment of resources from Aristotle, Hume, and Kant's philosophies. There is broader interest in Spinoza than there was some decades ago, and the same is true of Hegel, the Stoics, thinkers of the Scottish Enlightenment, and many medieval philosophers. More and more thinkers are being recognized as important and interesting in ways that both enlarge current debates and fill gaps in our understanding of the history of philosophy.

There are several reasons for this development. Modes of analytic philosophy that had been dominant for several decades were subjected to extensive critical attention, both from within and without that tradition. That attention exerted enormous pressure on an approach to philosophy that held that a specific method of philosophical analysis defined philosophy as an intellectual undertaking, even as there were some disagreements over exactly what the method was. In the view of many influential philosophers this approach was tied to a specific conception of meaningfulness. The associated conception(s) of meaningfulness yielded a well-defined but also narrow, limited form of philosophy. Moreover, according to it, there is no substantive philosophical knowledge; philosophy is a method for the explication of other kinds of knowledge, themselves small in number. Gradually, decades of internal and external criticism created opportunities for philosophical insights and approaches not confined by fixed criteria. It also motivated willingness to look again—or for the first time—at the history of philosophy. Willingness to look to historical sources for their conceptual resources, formulations of issues, and strategies of addressing them grew discernibly.

If by 'analytic philosophy' one means a specific approach to philosophy dominated by concerns with language, meaning, and logical analysis, it is not so surprising that many (especially English and German language) philosophers did not think that there was much important history of philosophy before Frege in the last third of the nineteenth century or, at least, before Hume and Kant, at the earliest. Developments in logic and the philosophy of language set many philosophers on a course that took logical analysis and semantic considerations to be definitive of philosophy. However, if by 'analytic philosophy' one means philosophical theorizing that takes argumentative responsibility, clarity of distinctions, and precision in articulation very seriously, then Aristotle, Aquinas, Ockham, Descartes, and Kant (among several others) are important philosophers of analytic disposition despite the fact that they did not take a "method of analysis" to be what philosophy *is*. Post-positivist analytic philosophy has looked more widely and more closely at the history of philosophy as it enlarges its conception of philosophical method and theorizing. While the study of the history of philosophy is distinguishable from theorizing about one or another specific philosophical issue, the two projects are more collaborative and complementary than they had been.

In addition, normative theorizing in ethics, politics, and philosophy of law are more vibrant and prominent areas of philosophical theorizing than they were a few decades ago. They are also areas in which deep, substantial connections with the history of philosophy are increasingly evident and significant. In addition, figures such as Smith, Sidgwick, and Thomas Reid, who had been less widely studied than say, Hume and Kant, are now garnering more attention both as resources for current debates and in regard to reconsideration of the history of philosophy. Moreover, some of the most important recent metaethical debates are, to a large extent, developments of Aristotle vs. Hume vs. Kant debates, often influenced by the work of the later Wittgenstein and other developments in the philosophy of language.

In the late 1950s philosophers such as G.E.M. Anscombe and Philippa Foot began a retrieval and reconstruction of virtue-centered ethics, which, after some delay in its effects, has become a very important aspect of contemporary ethical theory, moral psychology, and metaethics. An example of this is the 'mainstreaming' of Aquinas, who is being studied outside of Catholic philosophy much more than in the past. His thought on ethics, the virtues, and natural law is increasingly acknowledged as strongly relevant to several current debates. The striking increase in attention to natural law theorizing in general is fueled by several sources, including enlarged interest in the history of philosophy, normative issues, and the ways that historical roots such as Aristotle, Plato, and Aquinas are relevant to later philosophy.

During the last few decades, interest in natural law theorizing has grown steadily. In addition to scholarly interest in historically influential theories of natural law there has been important work defending and elaborating natural law as a contemporary approach to fundamental issues of moral and political theory. For example, consider works during roughly the last three decades either by or about Lon Fuller, John Finnis, Robert George, and Germain Grisez. In very recent years works by Knud Haakonssen, Mark Murphy, Jean Porter, and Anthony Lisska (a contributor to this volume) have both given attention to natural law and drawn attention to it. Indeed, in many cases, the two projects—historical scholarship and expounding natural law—are combined, in some cases, with roots in medieval natural law theorizing, and in some cases with roots in early modern thought, and thinkers such as Hobbes, Locke, and Grotius.

Outside of the work of specialists and outside of Catholic institutions, medieval natural law theorizing had garnered very modest attention until the last few decades. In addition, early modern natural law thinkers who had been more or less neglected—at least in comparison with Hobbes and Locke—are being retrieved and explored. This is certainly true of Grotius and Pufendorf, but also of less influential but still notable thinkers such as Gershom Carmichael and James Dalrymple (Viscount Stair).

There are surely several reasons for the increased interest in natural law and it is doubtful that some single consideration has motivated the diversity of approaches contributing to the growing literature on natural law. Still, there is little doubt that dissatisfaction with some of the more prevalent currents of recent philosophy, especially in regard to theorizing about morality, has motivated interest in natural law and interest in ensuring that it is part of the debates about moral and political theory. For several decades diverse versions of non-cognitivism, ranging from 'thin' types of emotivism to more complex conceptions of projectivism and norm-expressivism, have had a prominent place in metaethics. At the very least, the number and sophistication of critiques of moral realism, cognitivism, and objectivism have been impressive, and they have sometimes been conjoined with barely disguised condescension toward the objects of their critiques. Interest in natural law has been part of the philosophical response to those critiques, and that interest is, at the same time, part of broader interest in the history of philosophy and the willingness to employ extensive resources from the history of philosophy in current debates. Some of those resources have been deployed in responding to non-cognitivism and the diverse versions of antirealism developed in recent decades.

Of course, resources from the history of philosophy are deployed in the defense of non-cognitivism and antirealism, too. Nominalism and skepticism have ancient roots. But the way in which the history of philosophy is now more widely and more fully appreciated—and the reasons for that appreciation—have been notably helpful to what we might call a 'realist disposition' and to responses to nominalist, antirealist, and skeptical arguments and positions.

Plato and Spinoza are the historical bookends of this volume, which is chiefly concerned with thinkers from antiquity and the Middle Ages, and which extends into the early modern period via Spinoza. That might seem surprising, given the crucially important natural law theorizing undertaken by other early modern thinkers. The period and the figures have been chosen in order to highlight certain elements of the history of natural law theorizing just up to the point at which what we might call 'the modern turn' becomes fully visible. This is not to suggest that 'pre-modern' connotes anachronism or what is of only specialized scholarly interest. The contributors to the volume regard pre-modern natural law theorizing as highly significant, as well as historically interesting. A distinction between pre-modern and modern here is not meant to connote a difference regarding importance, depth, or relevance. At the same time, there is a sense in which modern natural law theorizing involves some significant changes in orientation, and the essays in this book focus on some crucial issues of moral theorizing in ancient thought and in the medieval philosophies of key figures in the Abrahamic faith-traditions, along with Spinoza's important and complex relation to earlier philosophers and those religious tradition.

In the work of thinkers such as Hobbes, Locke, and Grotius there is much more emphasis on what a rational agent would agree to, and on fundamental issues concerning political legitimacy, than in earlier natural law theorizing. It had different, if no less important, emphases. In both periods what it is for man to be a political being was a central concern. Also, theological considerations and the relation between reason and religion had a central place in the thought of most of the early modern natural law theorists. However, they were less centrally concerned with the relation between reason and revelation than their predecessors, or rather, they addressed it in ways that made it less central to moral theory. For the medievals the respective roles of reason and revelation and their authority were crucial. With many important thinkers from the seventeenth century on, the concern with the relation between divine law and natural law was less pronounced.

The periods and thinkers discussed in this volume represent crucial formative developments in natural law theorizing. The essays are mainly concerned with roots of natural law theorizing and with different understandings of the character and authority of theistic considerations in it. By looking at some rationalistically disposed thinkers from antiquity to Spinoza, we can explicate some of the most significant philosophical issues concerning relations between the claims of reason and theistic considerations prior to a period of some significant changes in the orientation of natural law theorizing and the understanding of politics.

In antiquity and the Middle Ages 'man is a political being' was understood by many important thinkers to mean that human beings are able to develop and can best exercise their distinctive nature and its proper excellences only in political community. Political life was thought to be essential to practical and ethical perfection, in large part because it is in political life that our capacities as rational, deliberating, acting agents are developed. Moreover, political order was often thought of in terms of the rule of law understood as the rule of reason. Reason has authority to rule both the individual and the political community. This notion of the rule of law as the rule of reason, along with the conception of human beings as rational beings, had a crucial role in shaping ancient and medieval natural law theorizing. There was a basic contrast between what reason ascertains as right and what is underwritten by the will of the strong or the weight of custom and convention. In the Stoics there is an especially vivid identification of the rational, the natural, and the divine.

Developments in the early modern period shifted the focus of much political theorizing to questions of the conditions under which political rule is legitimate and what it is rational for an individual to agree to in regard to trading natural liberty for the civil condition. Hobbes is a hugely significant figure for a number of reasons, one of them being the boldness and clarity with which he explained how and why the state is an artifact even though it is sanctioned by considerations of natural law. Hobbes's understanding of the relation between natural law and the civil condition differs quite sharply from most conceptions before his time. (Whether or not modern natural law theorizing in general *endorses* Hobbes's views, his insights have been enormously significant to the history of political thought.) In addition, early modern thought put much more explicit emphasis on the rights of individuals, in contrast to earlier emphases on what makes political rule right.

The notion of 'right reason' has a pronounced presence in much medieval thought concerning natural law. The role of rationality in contract theory, for example, is different in important ways. It is worth mentioning that when medievals spoke of 'right reason' they typically had ethics *and* politics in mind, while many early modern theorists saw the relations between ethics and politics differently. Because of how they conceptualized the main issues of political theory, those issues had a character distinguishable in some ways from theorizing about ethics.

The transition from pre-modern to modern emphases should not be regarded uncritically as a process of obsolescent ways of thought being superseded, the role of theistic considerations in medieval natural law theorizing having rendered it unsuited to modern liberal-democratic polities. Actually, the role and relevance of religious considerations in regard to politics is very much alive and important. However, this volume is meant to contribute to understanding crucial developments in the history of natural law theorizing rather than the place and the authority of religious considerations in political life. There is a rich, complex history of thought in which conceptions of nature, reason, the authority of reason, God, and (in the Abrahamic faith-traditions) revelation are related to each other in integral ways. Theistic considerations were not merely accessories to natural law theorizing, and that is especially evident in revealed religion. Some of the most fundamental features of the understanding of reason, nature, and ethical requirements were intimately interrelated with theistic commitments.

Whatever one's view of religion, it is clear that, in natural law theorizing from antiquity to early modern times, the role of theistic considerations is a crucial matter. Medieval Christian thinkers' beliefs concerning creation, revelation, and providence shaped their conceptions of the scope and power of unaided human reason, the relation of natural law to divine wisdom and divine will, and how 'right reason' is to be understood. Revealed religion differed markedly from Stoic theism, but in both traditions theistic metaphysics is a core commitment. The combination of Stoic resonances and the critique of revealed religion make Spinoza an especially apt figure to be one of the 'bookends' of this study. Spinoza is someone for whom theism is front and center but in ways that were a shock to orthodoxy.

In regard to the general philosophical character of the essays in this volume it would be fair to say that they all reflect an aspiration to attain analytical clarity while also being historically informed. They are not exercises in 'pure' theorizing but neither are they strictly historical scholarship. Their contents and concerns include matters of ethics, political theory, metaphysics, epistemology, and theology without being confined to one or another of them. The essays reflect a shared sense of the importance of certain issues but do not jointly defend one or another specific position. Readers will, we hope, find that the essays persuade them of the value of examining natural law theorizing in the thematic way it is approached here.

In Abrahamic monotheism there are important questions concerning the rationality of what is revealed and questions concerning the epistemic authority of rational justification, revelation, and tradition. It is notable that while there are rationalistic currents of medieval Jewish, Christian, and Islamic thought, only in the Christian tradition do we find natural law theorizing, not only present explicitly, but also with high importance. In the Jewish and Islamic traditions there were thinkers who maintained that ethical requirements are rational and that human reason can ascertain the justifications for them though they did not formulate their views in the conceptual idiom of natural law. Two of the essays discuss whether the absence of natural law language in Jewish philosophy was mainly a matter of not using the idiom or mainly a matter of maintaining views that are importantly different from natural law views.

Of course, in addition to the rationalistic currents in medieval thought there were anti-rationalists and mystics as well. However, many medieval philosophers regarded reason and revelation as modes of approach to a single body of truth. They held that there is nothing contrary to reason in faith, and in some instances, maintained intellectualist conceptions of human perfection. For them, much of what is revealed is to be studied and understood by reason, and reason is that through the exercise of which, closeness to God is possible. Reason enables human beings to be responsive to the normative authority of law, and to pursue the good on the basis of an understanding of it. That is part of the explanation of why medieval philosophy is so rich with conceptions of law in which 'right reason' has a central place.

The present volume focuses on Judaism and Christianity because of the manifest influence of Jewish and Christian thought in the West. Medieval Islamic philosophy powerfully influenced Jewish and Christian thought in several ways. An enlarged understanding of Islamic thought is highly important to understanding medieval thought and there is a formidable tradition of jurisprudential reasoning in Islam. However, Islamic thought has not figured directly in Western ethical and political theorizing as powerfully as Christianity and Judaism. Medieval thinkers in those two faith-traditions had insightful, complex views of the relations between reason, law, nature, and revelation and in important respects those views continue to resonate through some contemporary debates. That is not so, in the same way, with respect to Islam, at least in Western thought.

Given that modern natural law has developed in ways differing from its antecedents, what interest is there besides historical, scholarly interest in ancient and medieval natural law? If we think that the notion of the rule of law—understood to centrally involve reason—is important, that alone is reason enough for taking ancient and medieval natural law theorizing seriously. Some of the most significant conceptions of the rule of law are, at the same time, conceptions of the rule of reason. There are important connections between concepts of law, reason, and nature. Again, mere mention of the Stoics illustrates the point.

Even in Scotus's case, wherein natural law concerns what is owed to God, the account of what is owed to God is explicated in terms of what is rationally necessary. It is evident to reason (Scotus argued) that we are to love and obey God. Given the divine nature, there are necessary truths concerning our relation to God and God's authority. Moreover, while philosophers are much less likely to share the medievals' faith-commitments, the study of medieval thought helps us understand the implications for ethics and politics of the relations between faith-commitments and reason. Our time may not share some of the commitments of the medievals, but we face issues and difficulties about which the medievals were subtle, sophisticated thinkers.

Natural law theorizing concerns the metaphysical, explanatory, and normative relations between nature and reason, and in consequence, chief characteristics of right human action. The study of natural law theorizing in the periods covered by these essays is an exploration of how normative authority is related to accounts of what is rationally necessary, especially in regard to practical rationality. The contributions do not make a case for some single, best way of conceptualizing natural law. Indeed, part of the point of the project is to exhibit the conceptual texture of natural law theorizing and the different ways in which relations between rationality, law, and nature have been understood and have shaped conceptions of normativity. For instance, there are essays in this volume arguing that aesthetic considerations (Richard Cross's essay on Scotus) and tradition (Jonathan Jacobs's essay on Jewish thinkers) are especially important to understanding the relevant types of normativity.

When looking at philosophical theorizing over a long period, tracing philosophical influences and resonances, much can depend upon the level of generalization and detail employed. There are ways of characterizing positions that highlight likenesses and yet, if one wants to foreground contrasts, that can be done just as effectively. Creation, revelation, and redemption are examples of respects in which the Abrahamic traditions are similar; those are essential elements of each tradition. Yet, specification of each tradition's conception of these elements indicates some of the most significant ways in which these traditions differ from each other. For example, Judaism and Christianity share the story of the Garden of Eden but 'original sin,' a fallen, wounded condition of human nature, reparable only by being remade by the agency of supernatural grace, is not part of Judaism. The 'fall' and what is required for redemption are interpreted differently. In making comparisons and general claims about the faith-traditions a great deal can depend upon the level of abstraction selected.

Nevertheless, it is safe to say that among the fundamental notions shared by Judaism and Christianity we can include the notion that the world is a created order and that through revelation mankind has been graciously offered the way to redemption. Those claims are the basis for many of the most important contrasts between ancient philosophy and the way in which it was appropriated and developed by theistic thinkers. The differences between, for example, Aristotle's First Cause on the one hand, and the creator-God of the faith-traditions on the other, make for pervasive differences between Aristotle's thought and even the most Aristotelian medievals. Creation is not just an additional event that is not found in Aristotle's cosmos. It reverberates through metaethics, moral epistemology, and moral psychology. Creation has important connections with revelation, the nature of human perfection, and the virtues.

In addition, the question of the relation between divine volition and ethical requirements is an important issue in medieval moral philosophy. Rationalistic thinkers argued that divine commands are in accord with divine wisdom and, on that basis, ethical requirements are to be understood in rational rather than voluntarist terms. That did not fully resolve the matter because, after all, divine will is not distinct from divine reason and thus, what is required could still be interpreted as reflective of God's will. Voluntarists emphasized divine will as the source of requirements, to protect divine sovereignty from any constraints. They then had to meet objections motivated by concerns about whether God could make something right and obligatory simply by willing it, whatever *it* is. Neither rationalists nor voluntarists could confidently conclude that they had once for all solved the Euthyphro problem.

Notwithstanding how different our way of understanding the world is from that of the ancients and medievals, there are ways in which conceptual architecture, including the conceptual architecture of disputes formulated long ago, remains illuminating, helping us negotiate enduring philosophical issues, recognizable across many centuries.

The Essays

The essays are organized into four groups, reflecting historical periods and major currents of thought. The first group includes essays on Plato and the Stoics. The second includes essays on medieval Jewish philosophy. The third explores the thought of Aquinas, Ockham, and Scotus. The final group of essays focuses on Spinoza. Those two essays examine his thought in relation to antecedents, the Stoics in one case, and Aquinas in the other, and they also relate Spinoza's thought to contemporary aspects of moral theorizing. By concluding with Spinoza the volume completes its discussion, examining the thought of someone who at the same time looked back to the past and broke from it in an intellectually courageous manner.

The first essay, Fred Miller's "The Rule of Reason in Plato's Laws," explains the ways in which, as he puts it, "If Aristotle can be called 'the father of natural law,' Plato might well be called its grandfather." The claim on behalf of Plato's role in the ancestry of natural law is supported by evidence from the *Republic*, the *Statesman*, and most of all, the *Laws*.

Miller examines Plato's answers to the question of whose good is the good sought, the correct aim of the statesman, and how the good is to be sought. Plato's answer is that the legislator is to legislate for the common good and that "intelligence is the sovereign principle for the soul, the city, and the cosmos." The intelligence that has authority to rule is identified with a god; man is *not* the measure of all things, not even political rule. The Platonic conception of reason having the authority to rule is an important anchor for conceptions of natural law developed by later thinkers. One respect in which it is an anchor is that it is an alternative to the view that political rule and morality are grounded on convention or that politics and morality can only reflect power, volition, or some other basis separate from objective normative considerations.

Miller explains how Plato's conception exhibits "trickle-down rationality" as a significant feature of the rule of law. Governance by regulations aimed at virtue and reflecting reason is the best constitution. In the absence of an absolutely wise ruler this is the best humans can do. If, as part of the rule of reason, citizens can be brought to understand that their good is attainable by following the laws, then they will have a reason to obey the law and its intelligence will shape their lives. Thus, the rule of law, as the rule of reason, includes reasons for obedience to it. Ordinary citizens cannot be expected to know what is in the common interest or how to attain it and indeed, they do not reliably understand their own individual good. But they can be brought to obey the rule of law by means other than coercion.

This leaves difficult questions concerning the limits of the obligation to obey the law. Nonetheless, the Platonic legacy regarding the conception of the rule of law as the rule of reason, and the rule of reason as transcending convention and volition—regarded as divine, even—went on to have profound influence. This is evident in the thought of the Stoics, Christians, and Jewish thinkers, though the evidence of the influence is different in each case. For example, as Miller points out near the close of his essay, Augustine's commitment to the Christian doctrine of original sin meant that, in his view, no political order shaped by human efforts—even human *rational* efforts—could attain and maintain rational order. For Augustine, reason and law were related to the divine in manner quite different from Plato's conception, though the Platonism of Augustine's thought is unmistakable. While departing from Plato in important respects, the Stoics took up the notion of the rule of reason and they were happy to credit Plato as a vital source. The Stoic metaphysics of "right reason in agreement with nature" contrasts sharply with Plato's metaphysics, but there is still an important affinity with Plato at the normative core of Stoic thought.

In the second essay in the volume Jacob Klein argues that *eudaimonism* is the most important justificatory concept in Stoic ethical theory. The Stoics have certainly garnered enlarged attention in recent years and they are steadily being more carefully and fully integrated into the history of ethical thought. There are significant Platonic and Aristotelian resonances in the Stoics and there are significant Stoic resonances in later moral philosophy. That Klein argues for understanding the Stoics as *eudaimonists* is significant, given that they are often regarded as being early, highly important developers of deontological ethics and also that they are often seen primarily in terms of expounding an explicitly cosmopolitan natural law approach. *Eudaimonism* is not logically excluded by such commitments but interpreting the Stoics as *eudaimonistic* thinkers does represent a departure from some long and widely held characterizations of them.

Klein's "Stoic *Eudaimonism* and the Natural Law Tradition" explicates some key features of Stoic ethical thought and explicates respects in which later resonances of Stoic thought depart from their sources. He writes, "Questions about the relation of Stoic theory to later views must be distinguished carefully from the question of how later thinkers received and understood the available sources." Klein argues that the Stoics are best understood as having developed a conception of 'rational *eudaimonism*,' a view comprising both natural law and *eudaimonism*. Their *eudaimonism* differs from Aristotle's in that, for the Stoics, the best life is structured by a grasp of the rationality that orders the cosmos as a whole, rather than being structured by comprehension of human good. Thus, what is beneficial to human beings is not the sole criterion of *eudaimonism* or human wellbeing. Instead, "The rational principles expressed in the cosmos as a whole apply to human beings, in the Stoics' view, in virtue of what is good for them as rational agents" and, in being rational agents, human beings are able to understand the principles of reason ordering the cosmos.

Thus, in Stoic thought, there is an end human beings are to pursue. If one insists that natural law theorizing requires obligations to act according to certain principles independent of any end, then the Stoics are not natural law thinkers. However, their conception of the end to be pursued, and their conception of human well-being is shaped by their conception of the rational principles of the cosmos. In that sense, they clearly are natural law thinkers. The substantive norms of cosmic rationality determine what constitutes human well-being. Like Plato and Aristotle they regard what is beneficial to human beings as such, as central to ethics. Yet, they also hold that what is beneficial to human beings depends upon the rationality of cosmic nature, to be instantiated in our own (virtuous) dispositions.

The Stoics identified natural law with right reason, and right reason with the will of Zeus but they did so in a way that should not be interpreted as voluntarism. Zeus is not a creator-First Cause and natural law is not an artifact attributable to Zeus. The significance of the identification of Zeus's will with reason is that, for the Stoics, the rationality of right practical reason depends upon knowledge or comprehension of the rationality ordering the cosmos. Right practical reason is right through knowledge of what is good, and Zeus possesses that to a perfect degree. Klein notes that no Stoic sources affirm that, "natural law is rational and authoritative because Zeus wills it."

The Stoic conception of nature is normative through and through. They did not hold that appeals to nature supply value-neutral starting points or premises from which normative claims can be derived. Klein argues that the Stoics collapsed the dichotomy of *nomos* and *phusis*, with the result that "social forms and conventions may be regarded as rational only to the extent to which they accord with nature." In their view, law and artifice express what is natural in the fundamental sense that nature is understood as a rational artisan.

Stoic theology differed from the theology of the Abrahamic traditions in significant ways and the differences explain why, for the Stoics, there was no basis for interpreting natural law in voluntarist terms. Even Stoic world conflagration does not provide conceptual space for a divine voluntaristic reordering of the cosmos. Indeed, the Stoics held that the cosmic pattern recurs eternally. The notions of creation, providence, and redemption—notions very nearly definitive of Abrahamic monotheism—are not elements of the Stoic conception of the world or Zeus.

The theism of the Abrahamic traditions almost instantly raises difficult questions about the relation between reason and revelation, and also epistemological questions about the powers of unaided human reason versus what is known by revelation. The second group of essays focuses on the question of whether there are natural law elements in medieval Jewish thought, and in Saadia and Maimonides's, in particular.[1]

Given the extensive Neoplatonic and Aristotelian influences on Jewish philosophy we might expect Jewish philosophers of the twelfth and thirteenth centuries to articulate natural law conceptions or at least conceptions reflecting considerations with affinity to natural law. Actually, that is the crux of one of the important interpretative debates about medieval Jewish philosophy. Some scholars argue that, though the idiom of natural law is absent from medieval Jewish philosophy, the basic principles of natural law theorizing are present in it. Tamar Rudavsky's essay in this volume, "Natural Law in Judaism: A Reconsideration" develops an argument along those lines. One way to make this case is by arguing that the more rationalistically disposed Jewish philosophers (e.g., Saadia and Maimonides, among others) held that there are principles of right action accessible to reason and thereby applicable to all human beings. That those principles are also among the commandments means that, for Jews, those principles are also obligatory as divine commands; but human reason could ascertain their rightness unaided by revelation. This is how the Noachide commandments are often understood; namely, ascertainable by reason and universally applicable.

Thus, for Jewish thinkers eager to show that there are rational justifications for the commandments concerning moral matters (in contrast to commandments

[1] Saadia Gaon (882–942) is a key figure in medieval Jewish philosophy. He was 'Gaon,' i.e., head of the Babylonian Talmudic academy in Sura. In important respects he set the agenda of medieval Jewish philosophy. His work, *The Book of Beliefs and Opinions* presented arguments on all the main topics of Jewish philosophy and it opened with a treatise on epistemology in which Saadia sought to show that Judaism was a religion of reason. His philosophical thought is particularly notable in that it exhibits considerable sophistication though showing almost no signs of being influenced by particular philosophical doctrines or schools. It did show the influence of Islamic *kalam*, dialectical (rational) theology, but Saadia was not clearly a neoAristotelian or a neoPlatonist, for instance. Three centuries later Maimonides's *The Guide of the Perplexed* and other works exhibited knowledge of Saadia's thought and criticism of it.

concerning ritual and ceremonial matters) it might seem that natural law theorizing would be quite congenial. Rudavsky argues that while it is true that prior to Joseph Albo (1380–1444) no Jewish philosopher used the term "natural law," there are "natural law sentiments" in some important medieval Jewish thought. The two most important sources are the works of Saadia and Maimonides. Both thinkers, Rudavsky argues, elaborate views in which at least some commandments are grasped by reason as objectively sound and applying to all human beings. Rudavsky explains some of the main differences between Saadia and Maimonides's views of just how this rational comprehension is explicated but also emphasizes that both thinkers sought to show that, with regard to ethically important commandments, unaided human rationality is able to ascertain reasons for them. (In addition, Rudavsky argues, there are other Jewish thinkers, such as Ibn Ezra, in whose work we find views reflecting commitments much like natural law commitments.)

Saadia's account of how the reasons for some commandments are ascertained has intuitionist features. He thought that at least in some cases, the rationales are *evident* to reason. Maimonides held that ethical requirements are never demonstrative or strictly self-evident but he was clear that he did not take them to be matters of convention. He argued that, unlike *true* and *false*, *good* and *evil* are not intellectual concepts. They are notions arising from imagination and, accordingly, they are not measured by standards of demonstration or rational self-evidence. (This is an important point that helps explain why Marvin Fox's argument for why Jewish moral thought *could not* contain natural law elements seems wide of the mark. As Rudavsky explains, Fox failed to acknowledge a category of rational justification other than the self-evident or demonstrative. He argued that either the commandments are rationally evident or fully and exclusively dependent upon divine will; thus, they must be the latter because it is plain that they are not the former.)

Rudavsky examines some of the key components of Maimonides's moral epistemology and moral psychology, highlighting different ways ethical requirements and ceremonial requirements figure in virtue and the different bases for praising and admiring individuals for fulfilling the different classes of commandments. It is more praiseworthy to fulfill ceremonial commandments while wanting to violate them than to have a temperament making it easy or 'second nature' to fulfill them. Those commandments are different sorts of requirements and challenges than the more clearly ethical commandments. In regard to the latter, Maimonides agrees with Aristotle that it is better to have desires and passions that do not conflict with them. Thus, Maimonides preserves the grounds for the praiseworthiness of the *pious* man who works hard at fulfilling the commandments while also having grounds to praise the *virtuous* man for whom doing what courage, temperance, and justice require does not involve conflicts of motivation.

Moreover, Rudavsky notes that Maimonides argued that, for the Jewish people to be recognized as a wise and understanding people by the nations, it is crucial that Jewish law should be rational. One way this is exhibited is the importance Maimonides attached to the reasons for the commandments and to the Jewish people grasping those reasons. Both Saadia and Maimonides provided explanations for why so many (rationally justifiable) commandments were revealed. In doing so they were demonstrating how important it was to them to place the commandments—the giving of them as well as the content of many of them—in an overall rational conception of the world and divine activity.

Given the role of reason in regard to the commandments, Rudavsky argues that there are indeed natural law elements in several Jewish thinkers' views, despite the absence of the idiom. The respects in which Jewish philosophers explained the particularism of Judaism involved contrasting some elements of the Sinaitic covenant with God with other elements, the latter having universal application in much the same terms as a natural law theory would involve. A key point of Rudavsky's argument is that there are significant, universal elements of the covenant and that, at least some Jewish philosophers sought to reconcile the objective rationality of those with the elements of the covenant uniquely applicable to the Jewish people.

Jonathan Jacobs, in his essay in this volume, elaborates a different view of some of the same thinkers, while also emphasizing the respects in which rational justification was crucial to their conception of the commandments. He acknowledges overlap between the views of medieval Jewish philosophers and natural law theorists, but focuses on the role of tradition in Jewish moral thought and the ways in which that grounds a contrast with natural law theorizing. Jacobs argues (the main, but not exclusive focus of his essay) that Maimonides developed a view of the "non-evident rationality" of tradition. Furthermore, Jacobs argues that Maimonides (and other rationalistically disposed Jewish philosophers) held that ethical requirements are based upon objective considerations of human good but that those considerations are not self-evident or demonstrable. That is one of the reasons tradition is so important. Tradition supplies a stable, public basis and guidance for ethical life. That is also helpful in regard to coming to understand the reasons of the commandments, by keeping in view what is required even when the justifications for what is required are not (yet) clear. In Maimonides's view tradition is not a substitute for objectivity; it (when it is tradition of a certain kind) is a mode of access to objective considerations.

In this view tradition is rational in that what is required by the commandments is rationally justified, though many of the justifications can only be ascertained clearly by people who fulfill the requirements commanded by tradition. Living in accord with tradition enables a person to comprehend the ways in which doing so shapes and encourages virtue. The combination of practice with transmission of interpretation and ongoing study of the commandments and how they are to figure in leading a life enables a person to understand the reasons for them.[2] In turn, that understanding motivates commitment to practice and there is thereby a spiral of mutual reinforcement of ethical and intellectual virtue. Tradition has a crucial role in medieval Jewish moral epistemology. Saadia is a key early figure in formulating this view, later elaborated in a more complete and sophisticated form by Maimonides.

Jacobs and Rudavsky both draw attention to Maimonides's view that many ethical matters have the status of being "generally accepted" and are neither self-evident nor merely conventional. Rudavsky argues that there are grounds for interpreting such claims as having a status similar to the claims one would include in a theory of natural law. Jacobs argues that, while there is some likeness between the "generally accepted" and Aquinas's view of the determinations of natural law (i.e., some of its specific requirements arrived at by reason though not formally derivable from natural law principles) there is still an important reason to withhold natural law status from the former. For Jewish thinkers tradition was crucial to shaping the way of life of the covenanted community and necessary for attaining human perfection. Jacobs argues that while it is true that there is overlap between natural law approaches and the conception of tradition developed by medieval Jewish thinkers, that conception involves elements and features distinguishing it from natural law. We might say that natural law and tradition are rival conceptions of the rational ground and authority of ethical requirements, even if they are also revealed.

Jacobs argues that Maimonides understood tradition as a guide to human comprehension of the wisdom of the created order as well as a guide to virtuous conduct. The more fully people understand the reasons for the commandments the more fully they can grasp divine wisdom. Jacobs suggests that there are resources in medieval Jewish thought for a conception of the moral epistemology of tradition relevant to some enduring issues of moral thought. In making the case for this he discusses some of MacIntyre's recent work on tradition, noting some of the differences between it and the medieval Jewish view.

The next group of essays focuses on medieval Christian philosophy. Aquinas is a central figure in the first two of the three essays. He is a major figure

---

[2] Exodus 4:5–8 figures prominently in Jewish philosophy. The passage reads:

> Behold, I have taught you statutes and ordinances, even as the LORD my God commanded me, that ye should do so in the midst of the land whither ye go in to possess it. Observe therefore and do them; for this is your wisdom and your understanding in the sight of the peoples, that, when they hear all these statutes, shall say: "Surely this great nation is a wise and understanding people." For what great nation is there, that hath God so nigh unto them, as the LORD our God is whensoever we call upon Him? And what great nation is there, that hath statutes and ordinances so righteous as all this law, which I set before you this day?

Many Jewish thinkers interpreted the passage as expressing a command to study the Law and to perfect oneself through enlarging and deepening one's understanding. For Maimonides, for example, the passage was read as pointing to a perfectionism in which the virtues of study and practice are mutually reinforcing elements in the activity of actualizing one's intellect.

in the history of natural law theorizing, his thought having a prominent role in the Catholic natural law tradition and also in recent secular theorizing. As Eileen Sweeney mentions in her "Thomas Aquinas on Reading the Natural Law Written on our Hearts," some important contemporary natural law theorists arrive at normative results congenial to the Catholic tradition, even though they argue that their views do not depend upon Catholic theological commitments. While taking different approaches, Sweeney and Lisska's essays both probe the issue of how we are to understand the naturalness of Aquinas's natural law theorizing and its relation to some of Aquinas's most fundamental theistic commitments.

Sweeney argues that debates about the role of theistic considerations in Aquinas's theory are fueled by the fact that "it is Aquinas himself who is responsible for this divergence of interpretations, . . . they flow out of tensions, ambivalences and the methodological assumptions of his writing." Thus, some of the differing emphases various interpreters have selected are not mistaken; they are based upon elements of Aquinas's thought, which highlights different considerations in different places throughout his work. Sweeney examines complexities of the notion of nature when it includes the Christian story of paradise, fall, and redemption. She examines complexities arising from the way in which Aquinas's discussion of law fits into the larger, explicitly theological context of the *Summa Theologiae* and Aquinas's thought overall. One way to get to the core of the issue is to ask whether the nature referred to by the term 'natural law' can be considered not only in abstraction from grace and a supernatural end for human beings, but whether it can *actually be realized* independent of grace and a supernatural end for human beings.

Sweeney notes the respects in which the *Summa* appears to make a case for the 'independent nature' view, while *Commentary on Romans* seems to point in a different direction, one in which (as Eugene Rogers has argued) the nature discussed in the *Summa* must be thought of as nature reformed by grace. Human nature altogether independent of grace would (on account of the fallenness of human nature) fail both in regard to attaining knowledge of what is good and in regard to achieving excellent activity actualizing human good. Without reformation by grace the practical reasoning and *praxis* of human beings would be corrupted by ignorance and injustice. Sweeney notes that if the notion of nature in the *Summa* is nature abstracted from the context of grace and sin then "the nature which grounds Aquinas's whole morality, his entire anthropology never existed in the past, does not exist in the present, and will not exist in the future in the form in which he more or less constantly refers to it, integral or whole, that is, nature without sin or grace." Are we to regard Aquinas as holding that human nature abstracted from sin and grace is a real nature, and the core conception of his anthropology? (Several recent commentators and theorists have done this.) Or, would it be more correct to regard the nature described in the "Questions on Law" as an abstraction, which, in its actuality, is inseparable from the metaphysics and history of sin and grace and man's supernatural end?

Answering that question involves ascertaining how we are to regard the "fomes of sin" (the inclination of sensuality disposing us to deviate from the law of reason that is the result of original sin for Aquinas). Does it *not* belong to the human nature Aquinas has in mind in the "Questions on Law," and should we interpret that nature as a rational nature with an actuality distinct from sin and fallenness? Aquinas does say, "by his natural endowments [a human being] could will and do the good proportionate to his nature, such as the good of acquired virtue." (II–II, *ST*, 109, 2) However, human nature is, according to Aquinas, fallen, and the integral state of human nature is not found anywhere other than in Paradise before the Fall. (Actually, to be precise, Adam's state before the Fall is not pure or integral nature because Adam has, in addition to integral nature, the gift of original justice, which is *not* part of his nature but a supernatural gift to that nature, according to Aquinas.

Sweeney notes that "As Aquinas considers whether one can know truth without grace, will and do good, love God, fulfill the law, merit eternal life, or prepare oneself for grace, Aquinas rather carefully and gradually turns from the emphasis on nature to grace." In Aquinas's discussion of the role of grace in regard to both knowledge and ethical virtue a more Pauline/Augustinian disposition of thought—that is, one that is less optimistic about human nature apart from grace—is in evidence in his thought. Sweeney summarizes Aquinas's view namely, that "[w]ith healing grace, which heals the mind but not the appetite, one can avoid all mortal sin and each but not all venial sin. Without justifying grace, one can avoid each mortal sin though not every one and not for long."

There is a second locus of interpretative ambiguity in Aquinas's conception of natural law. This one has to do with the determination of nature versus the openness or freedom grounded in reason. "Having a rational nature means having a nature not determined by inclination or any particular ends, moved only necessarily by the universal and perfect good." By virtue of possessing rational capacities, human beings are not limited in their activities to governance by biological and physical imperatives.

> Rational beings are not satisfied with a single or finite good because they are able to consider all things under the aspect of good and able to desire a universal and perfect good. Thus we arrive at another paradox, that human nature, because it is rational, exceeds its nature, desiring more than the good merely proportionate to its nature.

Philosophical defenses of the 'independent' view of natural law will emphasize Aquinas's characterization of law, *synderesis*, and the way in which human reason can comprehend rational principles of action, with a view to realizing human good. Theologians and others have drawn attention to Aquinas's view both that human beings regularly fail to realize the good proportionate to nature and that human beings have an end that transcends our nature and, as Sweeney puts it, "reason, freedom and history place humanity outside the constraints of nature," freeing human beings from the confines of a determinate natural end. Thus, in regard to nature and even in regard to reason Aquinas's thought presents rich resources for rival interpretations.

Granted, contemporary exponents of natural law are free to borrow selectively from Aquinas in elaborating a theory of natural law that maintains that facts about human nature, accessible to human reason, are the basis of natural law in a way that does not require or imply any specific theological commitments. However, Sweeney's essay shows how, in Aquinas's works, his commitments concerning grace and the supernatural end of human reason place his theory of natural law in a theological context. The key features of the latter are not just accessories or supplements to his theory of natural law. While Aquinas says that the primary principles of natural law cannot be blotted out of one's heart (I–II *ST* 94, 6) he also gives four explicit reasons for why there is a need for divine law as well as natural law. (See I–II *ST* 91, 4.) Moreover, the ways in which even the primary principles can be obscured—through bad habits and the distractions of powerful, unruly passions—are grounded in sensuality, which is the other law of our nature besides reason. That reflects fallenness.

Sweeney's essay explicates Aquinas's integration of elements of what we might call 'Aristotelian naturalism' with Christian doctrine in his conception of natural law. In doing so the essay draws attention to the relevance of *other* parts of Aquinas's work to his conception of natural law. That helps us see more clearly both the sophistication and the inner tensions in Aquinas, tensions that resonate in ways that make possible diverse interpretations of his ethical and political thought. Sweeney concludes with discussion of some implications of those tensions for nature, knowledge, for human rational agency in the political context, and for the bindingness of law and the relation between reason and custom.

Part of what is so striking about the influence of Aquinas's treatment of natural law is that he devotes a relatively small amount of text to it. Often, his discussion and developments of it proceed without acknowledging the ways in which it is explicitly or implicitly connected with his thought on several other issues. Sweeney's essay highlights some of those connections in ways that encourage reconsideration of interpretations of Aquinas and views claiming to elaborate a Thomistic conception of natural law. For Aquinas, natural law is connected with a complex conception of nature, one which can rise (or be raised) above the natural order while also admitting of an explanatorily significant rendering in terms that do not involve supernatural ends, agency, and aid. Yet, many defenders of Aquinas and perhaps even Aquinas himself seem not to realize the extent to which moral blindness and self-deception derail human morality and obscure the natural knowledge of the good, which is natural law. For Sweeney, on Aquinas's own principles, and assuming ethical realism, there is no guaranteed access to ethical truth.

Anthony Lisska's "Right Reason in Natural Law Moral Theory: Thomas Aquinas and William of Ockham" explicates the chief differences between Aquinas's conception of natural law as grounded in a view of right reason reflecting dispositions constitutive of human nature, which is teleologically ordered, and Ockham's theologically definist conception of natural law. Lisska regards the contrast between Aquinas and Ockham as indicating the main differences between a realist conception of natural law and a voluntarist conception. The contrast remains relevant, appearing in contemporary political philosophy as the contrast between a 'good reasons' (nominalist) approach and a naturalistic-realist approach, in which there are goods grounded in features of human nature, accessible to the understanding, and properly directive of practical reason.

Lisska employs Aquinas's distinction between four different notions of 'right reason,' i.e., four different ways in which order is related to reason, and sets off those four in contrast to Ockham's notion of right reason, which is a version of divine prescriptivism. It is crucial to Lisska's discussion of the comparative merits of Aquinas and Ockham's views that "Ockham's nominalist analysis of human nature apparently unfettered by any Divine archetype eliminates a role for final cause in his philosophical anthropology." Lisska argues that Ockham's metaethics creates space for a type of 'liberty of indifference' on the part of the volitional agent—even if it is God—and that is seriously problematic for natural law and ethics because there is no real, substantive good by which the rightness of willing is to be measured.

A defender of Ockham could claim that there is indeed such a good, namely, willing in accord with what God has commanded. That is what right reason *is*; when a human being does what God has commanded that person acts in accord with what is good, by definition. Ockham writes, "Every will is right through its conformity with right reason." [*I Sent.* D. 41, Q. 1:K.] But, given the divine voluntarism of Ockham's view, there is no real connection with good as grounded in substantive features of the created order or an end proper to human nature. That is not an embarrassment to a philosopher defending nominalism, as Ockham was and, as Lisska notes, this general approach resonates in numerous later approaches. It was important to Ockham (as it was to Scotus) to defend the sovereignty of the divine will, and the abandonment of real natures with metaphysically grounded ends proper to them was part of that defense, whereas for Aquinas, what the intellect understands is centrally important to what it is right to will.

According to Aquinas, natural law has a realist basis and practical reason is well ordered when it is exercised in accord with principles of right reason reflecting that basis and thereby realizing objective human good. Lisska claims that Ockham's view is implausible inasmuch as the distinction Aquinas drew between natural law and divine law has no role in Ockham's view because it renders natural law identical to divine law, to what God has revealed as obligatory. In so doing, it undermines the possibility of substantive practical wisdom. Lisska sees in Ockham the precursor of modern prescriptivist and 'good reasons' approaches to ethics, despite the essential role of God in Ockham's view. Once the rightness of an action is detached from realist considerations of human good, the result is voluntarism with no scope for any further grounding of the rightness of what is required. That is what Lisska finds objectionable. It is also precisely that feature of Ockham's thought that presages a great deal of modern thought, from Kant's rationalist prescriptivism, to Hare's prescriptivism, to 'thin theories of the good' in political philosophy.

Aquinas's theory has remained a model for approaches in which objective considerations of human good are the basis for the conception of natural law, and there are important contemporary conceptions of natural law inspired by Aquinas. One of them, the view Lisska supports, holds that, given our knowledge of the capacities constitutive of human nature, we come to understand that there are goods realizable through the well-ordered exercise of practical reason. The principles of natural law have their basis in the understanding of the formal and final cause of human beings' kind-specific nature. Facts about human nature (intelligible to theoretical reason) supply guidance for practical reason, along lines shaped by the human *telos*. A second interpretation of Aquinas maintains that the principles of natural law are *evident to practical reason*. Rather than explaining the principles (and the specific determinations) of natural law as based upon facts about human nature, the understanding of which then guides practical rationality, the principles are known directly by practical reason without the mediation of the exercise of theoretical reason. (Some of the most influential versions of "New Natural Law" theories include this view.) Lisska's explication and defense of Aquinas highlights the key features of the former of the two main interpretations of Thomistic natural law and the chief elements of Ockamist conceptions of natural law theorizing.

Richard Cross's "Natural Law, Moral Constructivism, and Duns Scotus's Metaethics: The Centrality of Aesthetic Explanation" explicates Scotus's conception of natural law in terms of aesthetic reasons God has for favoring certain moral norms. The view analyzes some of the main contrasts between Aquinas and Scotus in terms of the former maintaining that God necessarily acts in ways that would represent moral duties for a moral agent, while Scotus focuses on the divine motivation, to which the aesthetic qualities of moral norms are central.

Scotus's view is not what we might call 'simple' voluntarism and Cross indicates important respects in which Scotus's view differs from Ockham's divine command theory.

It is not as though there are no constraints on what God wills to be moral norms and requirements. Cross does not think that Scotus rejects teleological considerations or that he articulated a simple divine command theory of morality. Rather, the view is that God's reasons for endorsing what he endorses are aesthetic reasons rather than moral reasons, and divine motivation is necessarily good. While God is not bound by antecedent independent moral norms or reasons, we know that moral goodness is a matter of conformity with right reason, and God's acts satisfy this condition. God is necessarily just or virtuous, and we should understand God's goodness in terms of his necessarily good motivation, rather than in terms of God doing what he ought to do because it is right. Cross argues that this is how Scotus formulates a moral theory that succeeds in reflecting both divine goodness and freedom.

Though God's freedom is unconstrained, and God's willing is contingent, that does not mean that God can will just any norms. There are many different possible sets of moral norms, each incompatible with the others. Still, what God wills is in accord with right reason. While he could have willed different norms than the ones in fact willed, aesthetic requirements, especially concerning the fit of means to ends and the consonance of norms with natural law, shape what can count as right reason. God's willing constructs norms in harmony with "the divine will [which] has no rectitude inclining it determinately to anything other than its goodness as other, as it were . . . it follows that it has no justice other than for paying to his goodness what suits (*condecet*) it." Cross writes, "Scotus takes it for granted that God's necessary goodness means that his endorsing the relevant norms is in accordance with his motivations." God wills in accord with his good motivations.

One of the most distinctive features of Scotus's view is that what is willed on the second table of the Decalogue is willed for aesthetic reasons having to do with the harmonious character of the relation between those requirements and those on the first table. According to Scotus, that God is to be loved is the first principle of natural law; hence, human beings have a reason to regard the norms of the second table as requirements. Though Scotus does not eliminate teleological considerations from his conception of things, what is included in the second table is not included *because* those norms express necessary conditions for the attainment of human perfection or the realization of the human *telos*. Rather, it is God's attitude to them, based upon non-moral reasons, that makes them moral duties. That is how divine freedom is preserved and how it is related to what is right reason for human beings.

We noted above that natural law theorizing with Thomistic roots has undergone a considerable renaissance recently. However, looking at early modern natural law theorizing we can find what appears to be Scotist influence. The metaphysics associated with Aquinas (leaving aside the question of whether it was fairly and accurately understood) was by and large rejected in the early modern era, and with it, much of the Thomistic conception of natural law. Conceptions of law—and natural law—were developed with centrally important roles for notions of command and sanction (the two powers being closely related). Some were grounded in voluntaristic views with a diminished role for the teleological considerations so significant in Thomistic thought. It is not difficult to see how Scotist thought supplied conceptual resources that were then developed into divine command theories, and theories of natural law in which command and sanction were highlighted. Though the aesthetic aspects of Scotus's view may not have had a significant influence, the sophistication and subtlety of Scotus's thought regarding divine freedom, goodness, and motivation did have a role in shaping later views. Cross's discussion explains how much more there is to Scotus's view than is captured by many of the most familiar characterizations of it as voluntarist. There is a conception at work that is much more complex and carefully integrated than simply divine prescriptivism.

The final two essays in the volume focus on Spinoza. Very significant natural law theorizing was elaborated during Spinoza's lifetime and the decades following it. There are important ancient and medieval resonances in his thought, and at the same time it has distinctively modern features. Spinoza is a complex and difficult thinker to interpret. How to understand the role of theistic considerations in his thought is a particularly challenging issue. These two essays point in some new directions for negotiating it.

Jon Miller's "Spinoza and Natural Law" connects key elements of natural law theorizing with examination of metaethical aspects of Spinoza's thought in order to ascertain whether it is correct to regard Spinoza as a natural law theorist. In particular, Miller is interested in looking at affinities between Spinoza and Stoic thought. This is a way of drawing some limits around the very considerable expanse of possible conceptions of natural law while acknowledging the widely held view that there are Stoic features to Spinoza's thought.

One of the interpretive difficulties concerning Spinoza and natural law is that it can seem as though Spinoza's metaphysical views do not include a basis for normativity or prescriptivity above and beyond descriptive necessity. Is there a place in Spinoza's thought for nature being a basis for what we ought to do? That "everyone is to seek his own advantage" is, in Spinoza's view, the foundation of "virtue and morality." This sounds like a notion of what one does 'anyway,' as a matter of natural necessity, rather than being an action guiding normative principle. Miller argues that Spinoza held that divine laws are end-oriented rules of conduct, that divine laws must be followed if human beings are to attain their *summum bonum*, and that divine laws—which, for Spinoza, are not volitionally grounded commands but natural laws—have an intrinsically practical nature. In this aspect of his thought, Spinoza is indeed much like the Stoics.

Moreover, Miller argues that in his account of moral experience and moral value Spinoza held something like a quasi-realist view but in such a way that it is nonetheless appropriate to interpret him as a natural law theorist. The 'quasi' aspect is based upon Spinoza's denial that moral judgments are literally true or false, and his view that good and evil "indicate nothing positive in things, considered in themselves." They are not anything "other than modes of thinking." Still, Spinoza argued that, even though moral judgments are not cognitive judgments, the basis of their prescriptivity is that we are to conform to our natures. Hence, without a realist ontology or epistemology for morality Spinoza was able to retain the form and force of moral judgments and the realist-seeming features of moral discourse. Thus, Spinoza's thought manages to connect a non-cognitivist account of moral value and moral judgment with a Stoic-like conception of the imperatives enjoining us to act in conformity with our nature as imperatives expressing a moral *ought*.

Miller argues that one respect in which Spinoza diverges from the Stoics is in his account of providence. Spinoza rejected the idea that providence reflects God's concern for the world, and the idea that providence reflects divine decrees or commands. For the Stoics, Miller says, natural law is an expression of God's will. This is a position Spinoza could not accept and by the end of his life Spinoza ceased to connect providence with natural law. Miller interprets Spinoza as steadily moving to the view that providence is little more than wishful thinking, rather than governance and command grounded in concern for the world. It is really nothing more than God's conatus, his striving to remain in existence. The overall upshot is that Miller explicates Spinoza as a natural law thinker yet one whose metaethics denies natural law the realist and cognitivist status typically attributed to it. Miller's discussion links Spinoza with ancient antecedents and with contemporary (for us) metaethical issues and insights.

The final essay in the volume is Douglas Rasmussen and Douglas Den Uyl's "Agent Centeredness and Natural Law: Perfectionism, Immanence, and Transcendence." In it, the authors look at Aquinas and Spinoza's metaethical thought in order to show how the notion of agent centeredness can be centrally important in regard to recognizing different, basic orientations in natural law theorizing. In focusing on agent centeredness their approach also includes some contemporary concerns of ethical theorizing. Their formulation of the issues directs attention to aspects of Aquinas's and Spinoza's thought in ways that could motivate a reconsideration of how those thinkers are often interpreted. Their view motivates some reconsideration of the interpretation of the role and significance of the individual person's perfective agency.

By 'agent centeredness' they mean "[t]he idea of grounding moral norms generally, and thus natural law in particular, in terms of what is perfecting of the agent's own nature alone . . ." They note that Aquinas is widely regarded as a paradigmatic example of an agent-centered natural law theorist but they argue that there are significant reasons to revise that view. In addition, they argue that Spinoza is especially important and interesting for the following two-fold reason: on the one hand, he disavowed the teleological perfectionism that appeared to underwrite much classical agent centeredness, while on the other, "Spinoza gives us agent centeredness through immanence" and that, natural law, for Spinoza, "culminates in a rather extreme form of agent centeredness." Rasmussen and Den Uyl carry out an interpretive analysis of natural law using the notion of agent-centeredness as a key to explicating significant features of it and important contrasts to be found in different approaches to it.

This use of 'agent centeredness' is a somewhat untypical idiom for discussing natural law. We should say a bit about it here. Rasmussen and Den Uyl's use of the idiom primarily concerns perfectionist features of human agency. In this sense, an ethical theory is *agent centered* if virtuous activity is explicated in terms grounded in the nature and activity of the individual agent. Accordingly, there is an important respect in which 'agent centered' ethical considerations are person-relative but, at the same time, objective. They are not to be explained in volitional, projectivist, or expressivist terms. An important result of the analysis is that Spinoza elaborates an agent centered approach to ethics while there is at least one important sense in which Aquinas does *not*. That is because, for Aquinas, "the norms of natural law derive not from the nature of the individual agent, but from God, though they may be applied *to* the agent."

To be sure, Rasmussen and Den Uyl acknowledge the ways in which Aquinas's ethics is perfectionist and centrally involves the individual agent's rational self-determination. Also, they acknowledge the ways in which Spinoza's theory is a God-centered monism. Nonetheless, they argue that there are good reasons for reconsidering the widely held view that 'classical' natural law theorizing is (in its most influential versions) agent-centered. Moreover, in their interpretation there is an important version of modern natural law theorizing—Spinoza's—which does *not* ground moral principles primarily in rational rules and principles governing the *social* world. They maintain that Spinoza can be interpreted as developing a robust conception of agent centeredness. Overall, their examination of Aquinas and Spinoza's views in terms of agent-centeredness is meant to focus attention on the metaethics of natural law theorizing in new, both historically and analytically instructive ways.

Stated in compressed form, they hold that the way in which Aquinas's conception of natural law is related to his theistic commitments gives us reason to heavily qualify the agent centeredness of his conception of natural law. Ultimately, "Aquinas' doctrine is not agent centered, but rather, God centered." At the same time, while Spinoza's rejection of teleology in conjunction with his endorsement of monism and determinism might seem to shut out agent centered morality, "the good is finally found in agents who are active, rather than passive, and the degree of activity is a function of the degree to which one acts from one's nature alone." Spinoza "gives us agent centeredness through immanence."

They acknowledge that Spinoza elaborates a conception of a "God centered universe" but there is an important sense in which Spinoza's conception of natural law can be said to be individually agent centered in a more robust sense than Aquinas's. This holds, despite Spinoza's monism and rejection of teleology. Rasmussen and Den Uyl argue that Spinoza's philosophical anthropology and ethics contrast sharply with "the transcendent turn in natural law, and its inevitable movement away from the agent, by his insistence on immanence." Each person has a distinct conatus, and self-directedness shapes each of us in a more thoroughgoing way than in the Thomistic view. Despite the fact that in Spinoza's view, particulars are affections of an attribute of God, "God centeredness in Spinoza has fewer *normative* implications than it does for Aquinas."

Their essay negotiates metaethical issues in a way intended to motivate a reconsideration of some of the most familiar readings of Aquinas, Spinoza, and natural law. In particular, they encourage some new questions about the relation between immanence and transcendence on the one hand, and agent centeredness and perfection on the other. They suggest that a theory that includes a grounding role for divine transcendence can thereby diminish the extent to which the individual person is both the agent and the object of perfective activity. In contrast, "God does not pull us out of ourselves for Spinoza but rather more into ourselves, thus emphasizing a kind of agent centeredness."

The interpretation of Spinoza is a complex business and there is room for diverse plausible approaches, especially when exploring how his thought is related to what came before and what came after. Miller's essay and Rasmussen and Den Uyl's essay present Spinoza in ways that encourage reconsideration of some widely held views of his thought and they place it in relation to important contemporary issues in moral theorizing in some new ways.

The essays in this volume point to some new ways of understanding the thinkers and theories discussed. They do this through a combination of attention to the history of philosophy, alertness to metaethical concerns, and the disentangling of threads in the fabric of normativity. As indicated above, the authors did not aim at fashioning some single, overall interpretation of natural law or the relation between reason and religion in natural law. Instead, the guiding concern was to illuminate ways in which natural law has been understood, how it has been present in important thinkers' works, and why it may be absent from others' when they, too, were influenced by, and borrowed from, some of the same sources and addressed similar issues. The relation between natural law and religion is a relation of longstanding and enduring significance. If these essays encourage readers to take a fresh look or, in some cases, a first look, at the thinkers and topics discussed, that will be welcome confirmation of the continuing relevance of the complex relations between reason, religion, and natural law.

{ PART I }

Ancient Origins

{ 1 }

The Rule of Reason in Plato's *Laws*

Fred D. Miller, Jr.

If Aristotle has been called "the father of natural law," Plato might well be called its grandfather.[1] For the idea that laws can be natural rather than merely conventional was already adumbrated in Plato's *Laws*: "Law . . . is by nature (*phusei*) or not inferior to nature if it is the offspring of intelligence (*nous*)" (X.890d).[2] This passage suggests that natural law is a corollary of a deeper principle in Plato's thought: *the rule of reason*. Although this principle was anticipated by earlier Greek thinkers, Plato was the first to articulate it clearly,

[1]On Aristotle see Max Shellens, "Aristotle on Natural Law," *Natural Law Forum* 4 (1959), 72–100; and Fred D. Miller, Jr., "Aristotle's Philosophy of Law," in *A History of the Philosophy of Law from the Ancient Greeks to the Scholastics*, eds. Fred D. Miller, Jr., and Carrie-Ann Biondi (Dordrecht: Springer, 2007), 79–110. On Plato see J. P. Maguire, "Plato's Theory of Natural Law," *Yale Classical Studies* 10 (1947), 151–78; Glenn R. Morrow, "Plato and the Law of Nature," in *Essays in Political Theory Presented to George H. Sabine*, eds. M. R. Konvitz and A. E. Murphy (Ithaca, NY: Cornell University Press, 1948), 17–44; J. Hall, "Plato's Legal Philosophy," *Indiana Law Journal* 31 (1956), 171–206; Susan Sauvé Meyer, "Plato on the Law," in *A Companion to Plato*, ed. Hugh H. Benson (Oxford: Blackwell, 2006), 373–87; Richard F. Stalley, "Platonic Philosophy of Law," in Miller and Biondi 2007, 57–77; and Terence Irwin, "Morality as Law and Morality in the *Laws*," in *Plato's Laws: A Critical Guide*, ed. Christopher Bobonich (Cambridge: Cambridge University Press, 2010), 92–107.

[2]See *Laws* VIII.839a: the law against incest is "laid down according to nature" (*kata phusin . . . keitai*). Cf. also 836c where legislating against homosexual intercourse is "to follow nature." In 839a Trevor J. Saunders translates "it is a natural law" (in John M. Cooper, ed., *Plato: Complete Works* (Indianapolis: Hackett, 1997), 1318–1616). Here, as in many passages, Saunders tries to convey the general meaning more explicitly to the Greekless reader, but the result is often misleading. In contrast, Thomas Pangle aims at a more literal, precise, and consistent translation. Therefore, throughout this chapter all translations of the *Laws* are from Pangle, *The Laws of Plato* (Chicago: University of Chicago Press, 1988), unless otherwise indicated. All subsequent references to Plato are to the *Laws* unless another of his works is cited.

offer a justification for it, and investigate its political applications in detail.[3] This chapter will examine the rule of reason, which is, for Plato, a central theme in cosmology, theology, and psychology, as well as in ethics and politics.

The rule of reason appears in the *Republic* in connection with the distinction of the soul into three parts: rational, spirited, and appetitive (*Rep.* IV,441e–444d).[4] Socrates asks whether it is "not appropriate for the rational part to rule, since it is really wise and exercises foresight on behalf of the whole soul." A soul is wise when it issues commands based on its knowledge of what is advantageous for each part of the soul and for the soul as an integrated whole. The other three cardinal virtues are also defined in terms of the rule of reason: courage is present when the spirited part "preserves through pains and pleasures the declarations of reason about what is to be feared and what isn't." Temperance is present when all three elements concur that the rational part should rule and the non-rational elements do not rebel against the rational. Finally, justice is found in the soul when reason rules over appetite, because the former is a natural ruler and the latter its natural subject, and it is assisted by spirit, its natural ally and helper. This implies that justice is natural and injustice unnatural, thus paving the way for the doctrine of natural law.

Socrates's political application of the rule of reason in the *Republic* seems problematic. Although he asserts that "our city, if indeed it has been correctly founded, is completely good" (IV.427e6–8), he prescribes controversial policies for his Callipolis or "beautiful city" (cf. VII.527c2), involving intellectual elitism (a segregated class of philosopher rulers with the aid of warriors dominating a disenfranchised class of workers), communism of property and of spouses and children, and authoritarianism (extensive use of deception, manipulation, propaganda, surveillance, censorship, and coercion). Socrates himself winsomely depicts his proposals as greeted by waves of laughter that threaten to drown him in ridicule and contempt (V.473c6–9). Aside from his radical utopian agenda (or dystopian, depending on one's point of view), Socrates also concedes that his city "in speech" may never exist anywhere on earth but may only

---

[3]The rule of reason emerges as a cosmological theme before Plato. Xenophanes (c. 570–c. 478 BC) says there is one god who "shakes everything with the thought of his intelligence (*noou phreni*) (DK 21B23). Anaxagoras (c. 500–428 BC) says that "intelligence (*nous*) controls all things that have soul" (DK 59B12), and Diogenes of Apollonia (mid-fifth century BC) that "all things are governed by thinking (*noêsis*)" (DK 64B5). Some commentators see this idea as implied by Heraclitus (fl. 500 BC) when he says that "all things come into being in accordance with the *logos* (reason or account)" and that "all human laws are nourished by the one divine; for it controls as far as it wants, and it suffices for all, and it prevails" (DK 22B1 and 114).

[4]For fuller discussion of the *Republic*, see my essay, "Plato on the Rule of Reason," *The Southern Journal of Philosophy* 43 (2005), 50–83. Translations of *Republic* are by G. M. A. Grube, rev. C. D. C. Reeve, in Cooper, *Plato: Complete Works*, 971–1223.

be "a model in heaven" (IX.592a–b). This raises the question, not pursued in the *Republic*, of whether the principle of the rule of reason could have any bearing on practical politics.

The rule of reason is also a central theme of the *Statesman*.[5] This dialogue presents the doctrine abstractly and focuses on the role of the statesman as legislator. The most controversial political applications of the *Republic*—in particular, a ruling class of philosophers—are generally missing or muted. Nonetheless, an unnamed Eleatic stranger (henceforth "the Eleatic") contends that the ideal constitution "is the one in which the rulers would be found truly possessing knowledge, and not merely seeming to do so, whether they rule according to laws or without laws, over willing or unwilling subjects, and whether the rulers are poor or wealthy" (293c–d). Even so, this dialogue makes important theoretical contributions, perhaps most notably in the recognition of unavoidable necessity in politics, owing to the fact that flawless scientific rulers are not in evidence (301d–e), and that humans are mostly fallible and corruptible and often fail to act rationally, especially when the possession of political power permits them to satisfy their desires. Thus the legislator must contrive a "second sailing for those who establish laws and written rules," that is, a system in which all the citizens abide by the laws (300c).[6] In second-best theory the best constitution serves as a regulative ideal for comparing and evaluating inferior constitutions. The better imitations of the ideal constitution are characterized as "law abiding" as opposed to "lawless" (297d–303d).

Plato's *Statesman* is not immune to criticism. The Eleatic's argument remains sketchy and programmatic. Though promising, his comparison of the science of statecraft to the arts of measurement and weaving (305e, 311b–c) is not developed in much detail. How, for example, might a diverse citizenry be "woven" into a fully integrated city? The Eleatic seems biased in favor of top-down rule; he simply dismisses the possibility (seriously entertained by Aristotle in *Politics* III.11) that a citizen body could manifest rationality from the bottom up. He does not explain why lawful constitutions are better imitations of the ideal than lawless ones. Presumably it is because a law-abiding constitution more closely approximates the rule of reason. But why suppose that this is the case? Nor does the Eleatic consider whether the law as such has normative force: that is, do citizens have a moral obligation to obey the laws of the city in which they happen to reside?—a question at the heart of Plato's *Crito*.

---

[5]For fuller discussion of the *Statesman*, see my essay, "The Rule of Reason in Plato's *Statesman* and the American *Federalist*," *Social Philosophy & Policy* 24:2 (2007) 90–129. Translations of *Statesman* are by C. J. Rowe in Cooper, *Plato: Complete Works*, 294–358.

[6]"Second sailing" (*deuteros plous*), a nautical euphemism for hauling out the oars when the wind has failed, is a metaphor for the second-best method of proceeding (cf. *Phaedo* 99c9–d1).

Valuable light is shed on these concerns by Plato's *Laws*, traditionally viewed as his last work, in which he expressed his final thoughts about politics. In this dialogue an unnamed Athenian stranger (henceforth "the Athenian") and two other elderly men, Clinias of Crete and Megillus of Sparta, discuss issues concerning legislation while they make a pilgrimage on Crete. En route Clinias announces that he has been appointed to a constitutional commission for a future colony in Magnesia and proposes that they "construct a city in speech," as if they were its legislators (III.702d). The *Laws* is a veritable trove of ideas concerning statecraft, legislation, the concept of law, and the relation of ideal theory to practical politics, as will hopefully be evident in the following discussion. At the same time, this dialogue presents serious difficulties of interpretation, beginning with the Athenian himself, about whom little is revealed except that he hails from Athens.[7] Moreover, his two interlocutors are nonphilosophers and sometimes out of their depth (see X.892e). If the Athenian relies often on theological arguments[8] and eschews the theory of Forms, central to the *Republic*, is this due to the fact that he does not accept this theory, or merely that Clinias and Megillus are too benighted to follow an argument unless it is couched in religious terms?[9] Another impediment to interpretation is the absence of a continuous argument of the sort that dominates the *Republic*. Since the Athenian's main task is legislating, theoretical discussions play a subsidiary structural role. They are interspersed throughout the dialogue, in "preambles" to the constitution as a whole or to groups of laws, in "digressions," in dialogues with imaginary interlocutors, and in myths and playful asides. However, it is possible to reassemble these scattered materials into an intriguing unitary argument.

This chapter will treat the rule of reason as a fundamental principle undergirding the argument of Plato's *Laws*. The discussion will consider how the Athenian answers five sets of questions: first, if a city should be ruled by reason, what will be reason's proper function? If it is claimed that reason should promote "the common good" or "the public interest," how should these expressions be understood? Second, what entitles the rational factor to rule over the nonrational? Why suppose that the city is ruled in a rational manner

---

[7]Aristotle (*Politics* II.6) identifies him with Socrates of the *Republic* without any basis, prompting questions about the relation between these two characters.

[8]It seems no accident that the first word of the *Laws* is *theos*, "god" (I.624a1).

[9]The apparent discrepancies between the *Republic* and *Laws* are seen by commentators as evidence of a development in Plato's political thought, possibly in a more "liberal" direction; for example, George Klosko, *The Development of Plato's Political Theory* (London: Methuen, 1986) and Christopher Bobonich, *Utopia Recast: Plato's Later Political Philosophy* (Oxford: Oxford University Press, 2002). This chapter will, as far as possible, sidestep developmental issues except where they bear directly on the understanding of the rule of reason in the different dialogues.

just in case the *rulers* are rational? If it is alleged that the rational part alone can possess the "wisdom" that confers political legitimacy, what sort of wisdom is this, and who has it? And what if nobody in the city possesses such wisdom? Third, how is rational rule embodied in the city? Is it dispersed throughout the entire citizenry, or is it confined to an elite group as in the *Republic*? Fourth, by what means is it appropriate for the rational part to rule over the nonrational part? What policies should be in force? In particular, do they include the rule of law? Finally, if the rule of reason must be implemented by means of a legal system, do all the citizens have a moral obligation to obey the law, and, if so, is this obligation qualified in any way?

By considering these questions in turn, it will become evident that the *Laws* breaks important new ground in the philosophy of law.

The Aim of Rational Rule

The key to understanding the role of reason in politics is, for Plato, the analogy between the statesman and a craftsman such as a doctor, a general, or a captain of a ship.[10] Just as each craftsman has a unique aim—for example, health for the patient, victory for the army, or safe passage for the crew—which requires a specialized kind of intelligence (*nous*), the statesman or legislator also has a specific goal or end, the achievement of which requires political intelligence (*politikos nous*) (XII.961e–962a, 963a–b).[11] Since politics is a goal-directed craft, there are two criteria for evaluating the practitioner: is the aim correct? And are the correct means used to achieve it? (V.744a, XII.962b). This raises further questions. How do we determine whether the statesman has a correct aim? This is not merely a matter of whatever goals people happen to pursue, for example, wealth, or freedom, or power over others (XII.962d–e). These are the aims of regimes such as oligarchy, democracy, and tyranny, which Aristotle called "deviant" (*Politics* III.7) and which the Athenian denies even qualify as constitutions (IV.712e). Thus political intelligence does not play a merely

---

[10]The guardians in the *Republic* are called "craftsmen" (*dêmiourgoi*) (III.395b9–c1, IV.421c2), and the legislator is compared to a statue painter (IV.420c). The craftsman analogy enjoys more elaborate development in the *Timaeus*'s "likely story" about the origin of the empirical world, with an immaterial intelligent demiurge looking to transcendent Forms as models, and shaping preexisting matter into an orderly cosmos (30a, c, 37d, 50d, 53a–b, 69b–c). On the parallels between the cosmic demiurge and the human legislator, see Glenn R. Morrow, "The Demiurge in Politics: The *Timaeus* and the *Laws*." *Proceedings of the American Philosophical Association* 27 (1953–4), 5–23; and André Laks, "Legislation and Demiurgy: On the Relationship between Plato's *Republic* and *Laws*," *Classical Antiquity* 9 (1990), 209–29.

[11]A statesman (*politikos*) engaged in framing the constitution and laws is called a legislator or lawgiver (*nomosthetês*).

instrumental role, finding the most efficient means to attaining the goals that seem good to whoever holds sway: rather, it seeks the goal which is truly good (I.646c–d, II.664a). The Athenian claims that the legislator should have a single goal, which is "honored preeminently and toward which their other affairs should look" (cf. XII.962d–963b).

What is the unique good at which the legislator should aim? There are two issues here. First, *what kind* of good is it? Repeatedly the Athenian offers a plethora of aims for the legislator, including happiness, virtue, justice, friendship, freedom, unity, and concord.[12] However, he also indicates that these goods should form a hierarchy:

> [C]orrect laws . . . make those who use them happy. For they provide all the good things. Now the good things are twofold, some human and some divine. The former depend on the divine goods, and if a city receives the greater it will also acquire the lesser. If not, it will lack both. Health leads the lesser goods; in the second place is beauty; third is strength . . .; and fourth is wealth—not blind but sharp-sighted insofar as it follows prudence. Prudence, in turn, is first and leader among the divine goods. Second after intelligence[13] comes a moderate disposition of the soul, and from these two mixed with courage comes justice, in third place. Courage is fourth. All of these last goods are by nature placed prior in rank to the first, and this is the rank they should be placed by the legislator. . . .
>
> Looking back over all these things, the one who frames the laws will set up guards—some grounded in prudence, others in true opinion—so that intelligence will knit together all things and may declare that they follow moderation and justice but not wealth or love of honor. [I.631b–d, 632a]

This passage implies that the virtue of prudence (*phronêsis*) is distinguished from true opinion (*alêthê doxa*), though both are associated with intelligence (*nous*). But the explanation of how prudence, temperance, courage, and justice constitute a single virtue, is in the end left by the Athenian as a task for the legislators who will succeed him (XII.965b–d).

---

[12]Happiness: III.683b, 697b, IV.709c, V.743c, VIII.828d–829a. Virtue: I.630c, 631c–d; III.688a–b, 688a–689e, 693b–d, 697b–c; III.701d; IV.705d–706a, 707d; VI.770c–d; VII.807c–d; VIII.829a, 836a–d; IX.853b; XII.963a–967a. Friendship: III.693b–c, 697c, 701d, V.738b–e, 742c, VI.759b, 771d, VIII.828a–d. Unity: V.739d. Concord: III.691b, 695d, 697c. Freedom: III.693b, 694a–b, 695d, 701d; V.738e, 743c; VI.757a, IX.880d. Justice: VI.757d, XII.962d–e.

[13]Pangle reads *meta noun* following the manuscripts and Stobaeus. Saunders translates "the habitual self-control of a soul that uses reason," reading *meta nou* following Eusebius and Theodoret and most modern editors.

The second issue is, *whose* good is it? The short answer is that it is the *common* good. The Athenian offers a medical analogy: "every doctor and every artful craftsman does everything for the sake of a whole, creating a part which strives for what is best in common, for the sake of the whole, and not for the sake of the part" (X.903c). The same holds for the political craft, according to the Athenian: "I will legislate with a view to what is best for the entire city and family, and with a view to all this, will justly assign a lower rank to what belongs to each individual" (XI.923b). But questions remain: is the good of the city an organic whole that transcends and supersedes the good of the parts, or is it a mere aggregation of the goods of its individual citizens? And what if the individual good and common good come into conflict? Should the legislator sacrifice individual citizens in order to benefit the whole city, if necessary, just as a doctor would amputate a limb to save a patient? We shall return to these questions below.

Rational Ruler and Nonrational Subject

The "rule of reason" might be understood in two different ways: that the city must be ruled in a rational manner, or that the *rulers* must be rational. Plato views these two requirements as equivalent. This explains why the rational factor is entitled to rule over the nonrational. But what accounts for this equivalence? The Athenian's answer involves the analogy between the city and the individual soul familiar from the *Republic* (III.689b). A soul lacks intelligence when it resists the states of knowledge and belief which are its "natural ruling capacities." A state is foolish when the multitude disobeys the rulers and laws, like an individual man in whom "noble reasons (*logoi*)" fail to rule over the appetites (cf. VIII.835e).[14]

The Athenian goes on to discuss "worthy claims" (*axiômata*) to rule and be ruled in cities and households (III.690a–c). These claims are based on different relations between the ruler and ruled: (1) parent and offspring; (2) high born and low born; (3) master and slave; (4) old and young; (5) strong and weak; (6) prudent and lacking knowledge; (7) lucky and unfortunate. Although Pindar had favored the fifth as "according to nature" (*kata phusin*),[15] the Athenian contends that the sixth provides the worthiest claim: "the natural rule (*archên pephukuian*) exercised by the law over voluntary subjects without violence."[16] As noted above, he calls prudence the leading virtue and describes it as the

---

[14]I depart from Pangle by translating *archikois* as "ruling capacities" and *logoi* as "reasons."

[15]Compare *Gorgias* 483e where Callicles exclaims that the rule of the stronger over the weak is naturally just and "yes, by Zeus, in accordance with the law, at any rate, the law of nature (*kata nomon ge ton tês phuseôs*)!"

[16]I depart from Pangle by translating forms of *hekôn* and *akôn*, as "voluntary" and "involuntary."

virtue exemplifying intelligence (*nous*) and reason (*logos*) (III.687e, 689d, XII.963e).[17] Again, he claims that it is not "right for intelligence to be subordinate, or a slave, to anyone, but it should be ruler over everything, if indeed it is true and really free according to nature" (IX.875d). What is the source of the authority of intelligence or reason? In the *Republic*, Socrates reveals the source in the theory of Forms, and in particular the Form of the Good, which enables the mind to grasp what is objectively good for the individual soul and for the city.[18] The Athenian advances no such theory in the *Laws*. Indeed, scholars disagree over whether the Forms are even presupposed by the Athenian. What is clear, however, is that the Athenian amplifies Socrates's central analogy into a *threefold* analogy comparing soul and city and cosmos.

The analogy is developed in the Athenian's proof that the gods exist, which occurs in a lengthy preamble to his laws against impiety (X.884a–907d). After arguing that all motion must be due to a first cause, namely, a self-moving entity identified with the soul, the Athenian adds that the soul comes into being before the body and is its natural ruler (895e–896c). Noting that the states of the soul, including its acts of reasoning and beliefs, precede the states of the body, such as its magnitude and strength, he concludes that the soul is the cause of all things, whether they are good or bad (896d). The same argument applies to the motions of the heavens: they must be due to one or more self-moving souls. The Athenian speculates that these celestial souls have motions of their own—cognitive motions such as investigating, deliberating, and believing, and emotions such rejoicing, grieving, fearing, hating, and desiring—which result in corporeal motions that produce qualities such as hot and cold, heavy and light, hard and soft, etc. "Soul makes use of these and every time it takes as a helper intelligence—god, in the correct sense, for the gods[19]–it guides all things toward what is correct and happy, while when it associates

[17]The Athenian uses "prudence" (*phronesis*) to correspond to the particular virtue which Socrates calls "wisdom" (*sophia*) in the *Republic*. Although he associates prudence with wisdom on at least one occasion (III.686d), the Athenian generally uses the word "wise" in a less technical sense, ironically or as paraphrasing misguided claims to divine wisdom. It is implied at XII.965a that prudence is a copy of intelligence (*nous*). The connection between prudence and law, assumed here, is explained later in the *Laws* and is discussed later in this chapter.

[18]In the *Republic* it is through dialectical reasoning that we come to grasp the Form of the Good, a.k.a. the good itself, and "it's by their relation to it that just things and the others become useful and beneficial" (*Rep*. VI.505a2–4, cf. VII.534b3–d1).

[19]The words between the dashes translate an uncertain text: *theon* is in manuscripts A and O, and *theion* in manuscript L, the margin of O, and Eusebius. Pangle's "god, in the correct sense, for the gods," renders *theon orthôs theois* with Burnet's text. Saunders's "soul being, if truth were told, a divinity" translates *theion orthôs theos ousa* with Diès's text. A problem with the latter reading is that soul is not identified with god until 899a as noted by Klaus Schöpsdau, ed., Platon *Werke* 8/2 (Darmstadt: Wisseschaftliche Buchgesellschaft, 1977). For various attempts to repair the text see the note in E. B. England, *The Laws of Plato* (Manchester: Manchester University Press, 1921).

with lack of intelligence it produces in all things just the opposite to these." When the soul is full of prudence and virtue, its motions have the same nature as the motions of intelligence, that is, orderly motions, while when it is bad the motions are mad and disorderly (897b–d). The intelligent motions are as regular as possible, moving in the same way, in the same place, around the same thing, in the same proportion and order (898a–b). Since this describes the observable motions of the sun, moon, and stars, the celestial motions must be caused by intelligent and virtuous souls, which the Athenian declares to be gods (899b).

The implication of the threefold analogy is that intelligence is the sovereign principle for the soul, the city, and the cosmos. As André Laks observes, the ideal constitution of the *Laws* is not a monarchy or a democracy but a *noocracy*.[20] He goes so far as to suggest that, insofar as *nous* is identified with a god (897b1–2) the constitution can be called a "theocracy." He notes that the ideal at which the legislator aims is a city populated by gods or children of gods (V.739d–e). There are theological overtones to the Athenian's legislation, beginning with his proposed introductory address to the new colonists, "The god, just as the ancient saying has it, holding the beginning and the end and middle of all things . . . " (IV.715e–716a). He continues, "For us, the god would be the measure of all things in the highest degree, and far more so than some 'human being', as they assert" (716c)—an implicit repudiation of Protagoras's relativistic dictum that man is the measure of all things. Moreover, if the citizens dutifully worship the gods and revere them along with spirits, heroes, ancestors, and living parents, "each of us will on each occasion reap what we deserve from the gods and from those who are stronger than we are, and we will pass most of life in good hopes." (718a) Despite these religious themes, however, it is somewhat misleading to describe this constitution as a "theocracy." For it does not consist of a set of ordinances promulgated by the gods and revealed to a prophet with a priestly class wielding legal and political power.[21] The intelligence which governs Magnesia may have a divine nature, but it is exercised by human legislators and officials.

---

[20]The constitution of the *Laws* could be called a "noocracy" if *nous* were identified with the unnamed god said to rule as a master over rational men at IV.713a. Alternatively, it could be called a "nomocracy" if the ruler was identified with *nomos* (law), which derives its name from *nous*, according to 713e–714a. See the discussion in André Laks, "The *Laws*," in *The Cambridge History of Greek and Roman Political Thought*, eds. Christopher Rowe and Malcolm Schofield (Cambridge: Cambridge University Press, 2000), 260–61, 271, 281.

[21]The term "theocracy" was coined by Josephus, who stated that Moses ordained the Jewish government to be "what, by a strained expression, may be termed a theocracy, by ascribing the authority and power to God . . . " (*Against Apion* II. 17, trans. William Whiston).

The Rational Elite

This leads to the next question: how is rational rule properly exercised in the city? The general answer (VIII.846d–847b) involves *the principle of specialization*: each person must exercise one and only one craft. This is given a political application: a citizen as such has as a craft preserving and holding the common order of the city. (The latter is implied by the analogy between politics and other crafts.) It follows that the citizens must all devote themselves to politics and not become craftsmen or merchants or engage in any other activity that would divert them from their political duties and what that entails, namely, maintaining their households and cultivating their own virtue and that of their family and servants.[22]

Magnesia is to have 5040 citizen-households with political rights. At first blush the contrast between the philosopher-rulers in the *Republic* and the governance-sharing citizens in the *Laws* could not be more striking. The empowerment of the citizens in the *Laws* is, however, an application of what might be called a *policy of approximism*. The Athenian compares legislation to a game of draughts in which a player is unable to accomplish the goal of keeping his pieces on the "sacred line" and opts instead to keep them as close as possible to the line. Likewise, in politics, "the best procedure is to state what the best constitution is, and the second and the third, and after stating this, to give the choice among them to whoever is to be in charge of the founding in each case." The founder should use the best city as his model (*paradeigma*) "and seek with all one's might the constitution that comes as close as possible to such a constitution" (V.739a–e).[23] For the ideal constitution would involve a gifted tyrant in collaboration with a praiseworthy lawgiver (IV.710c–d): "when the greatest power coincides in a human being with prudence and moderation, then occurs the natural genesis of the best constitution, and laws to match" (712a, compare *Rep*. V.473c–d). Such an ideal is not attainable because "human nature is not at all capable of regulating human things, when it possesses autocratic authority over everything, without becoming swollen with insolence and injustice" (713c, cf. IV.691b–c and *Statesman* 275c).

Although all the citizens will have political rights and duties in Magnesia's constitution, it is still a far cry from an egalitarian democracy like ancient Athens, since the more important officials are chosen on the basis of merit. An important standard for selecting officials is *proportionate equality*, which is described as follows:

---

[22] A further implication of the principle of specialization is that productive and commercial crafts are to be left to non-citizens, resident aliens, or slaves, and that these, too, are confined to a single craft.

[23] For consistency with the main text, I depart from Pangle, here and elsewhere, by translating *politeia* as "constitution." The term *paradeigma*, "model" or "pattern," is also applied to the ideal city in the *Republic*: V.472b–473a, IX.592a–b.

> By distributing more to what is greater and smaller amounts to what is lesser, it gives due measure to each according to their nature: this includes greater honors always to those who are greater as regards virtue, and what is fitting—in due proportion—to those who are just the opposite as regards virtue and education. Presumably this is what constitutes for us political justice. (VI.757c.)[24]

Taken together, the principles of the rule of reason, of specialization, and of proportionate equality imply that the constitution of Magnesia will exhibit a kind of trickle-down rationality. Higher officials must meet stricter qualifications, and the highest offices must meet the most stringent qualifications of all. This includes the Guardians of the Laws, who play a vital role in the city's founding and operate as chief executive officers (752d–755b). The Guardians are selected for their age and virtue and must be carefully scrutinized before they can take office. This elitist interpretation, based on the rule of reason, is supported by a simile of the city to a "trunk" surmounted by guardians chosen for their superior natures and mental capacities: the younger ones use their perception and memory to survey the city and relay information to the older guardians who are comparable to intelligence due to their superior prudence (XII.964e–965a, cf. 961d).

As the *Laws* draws to a close, a body called the Nocturnal Council assumes an increasingly prominent status. Although it goes unmentioned in the initial inventory of officials (VI.751a–768e), we learn later on that it is authorized to visit criminals convicted of impiety for the purpose of admonishing them and saving their souls (X.909a) and to supervise official Observers of foreign countries (XII.951d–952d). In the end (960b–969d) the Nocturnal Council is revealed as the body responsible for interpreting, explaining, and preserving the constitution and the legal code. Its members include the ten most senior Guardians of the Laws, the most distinguished priests, the Minister of Education, selected official observers, and junior candidates who pass muster. The Nocturnal Council is compared to a soul and head. Just as an animal is preserved by the presence of intelligence in the soul and the presence of sight and hearing in the head, the city is preserved by the guardians who possess knowledge of virtue (961d, 964c–d). The Nocturnal Council's privileged role as safeguard of religious, moral, and cultural orthodoxy may be warranted by the aforementioned principle of specialization. It is tempting to view it as a stalking horse for the *Republic*'s philosopher-kings.[25] Its existence is foreshadowed in a passage which distinguishes an educated minority from the many (*hoi polloi*):

---

[24]The Athenian contrasts this kind of equality with arithmetical equality. Aristotle makes a similar distinction between arithmetical and geometrical equality in *Nicomachean Ethics* V.3–4. Aristotle also identifies political justice with proportionate equality in *Politics* III.9.

[25]See for example Glenn Morrow, *Plato's Cretan City* (Princeton: Princeton University Press, 1960; repr. 1993), ch. 12; and Pangle 1988, 504.

> For the free men there are . . . three subjects to be learned. One subject is calculation and what pertains to numbers; second is measurement of length, surface, and volume, considered as one subject; third is the way the stars revolve, in their natural relation to one another as they move. The many need not labor at all these things to the point of precise accuracy; that will be required of a certain few (who they are we will explain when we get to the end, for that would be fitting). (VII.817e–818a.)

At the end of the dialogue it is revealed that the educated elite class must understand that the soul is the eldest and most divine of ever-moving things and that intelligence is the cause of the whole cosmic order. The pious man "should be able to give the reason for as many of these as have a reason. He who is incapable of acquiring these attributes in addition to the popular virtues would almost never become an adequate ruler of the city as a whole, but would be an assistant for the other rulers" (XII.961c–968a). As noted above, the Nocturnal Council also includes distinguished priests and selected official Observers of foreign laws and customs, so that it will have expertise in religion and jurisprudence as well as theoretical subjects including mathematics, astronomy, biology, and ethics.[26] The Council's primary role is judicial, as Glenn Morrow describes:

> The members of Plato's Council will be in fact jurists, not mere empiricists, but scientific and philosophical students of the law. Projected on the plane of history, [the role of philosophy] means the rule of law, when this law has been scientifically formulated, and when its later interpretation and revision are guided by competently trained experts.[27]

The Rule of Law

Given that the Magnesian constitution has a hierarchical structure with an educated elite at the head, by what means is it appropriate for rational rule to be exercised? The *Laws* contains many echoes of the *Republic*. The Athenian emphasizes the role of music and the arts in moral education, and he calls for censorship and a prohibition against innovation or nonconformity in musical performances or religion rites (II.660c–663d; VII.797d–e, 799b, 802a–e, X.909d–910d).[28] He advocates telling "profitable lies" to children in order to

---

[26]See I.632c, VII.817e–818a, VIII.837d–839e, XII.961c–968e.

[27]Morrow, 1960, ch. 9.

[28]How different is this from the crime of impiety for which Socrates was prosecuted? Cf. *Apology* 24b.

encourage virtuous conduct (II.663e–664a). Finally he recommends the thoroughgoing regulation of the personal conduct of all citizens (VII.780a, 784c–d, XII.942a–c). These prescriptions suggest the sort of static, strictly regulated regime that Karl Popper condemned as inimical to the "open society."

In other respects the *Laws* diverges from the *Republic*, most importantly in endorsing *the rule of law*: "it's necessary for human beings to establish laws for themselves and live according to the laws, or they differ in no way from the beasts that are most savage in every way" (IX.874e–875a). Although the rule of law was already recognized in classical Athenian politics, it is grounded in the rule of reason in Plato's *Laws*.[29] The ideas of law and reason are linked in a passage (I.644d–645c) comparing a human being to a "divine puppet" pulled toward different deeds by opposing cords or motives. The most important "cord is the golden and sacred pull of calculation (*logismos*) and is called the common law (*koinos nomos*) of the city." The derivation of the rule of law has the following general structure:

Derivation 1. The rule of law

1.1. The best constitution has as its aim the virtuous life, which is achieved through the direct and unimpeded rule of reason over the passions.
1.2. The constitution in which a human being rules absolutely and unimpeded according to reason is not attainable.
1.3. If the best constitution is not attainable, the intelligent legislator will pursue the same aim through the constitution most closely resembling the best.
1.4. A correct system of laws will be established by an intelligent legislator aiming at the virtuous life.
1.5. Ruling in accordance with a correct system of laws will most closely resemble the direct and unimpeded rule of reason.
1.6. Therefore, the best attainable constitution has the rule of law.

The argument for Premise 1.1 follows the *Republic* and is discussed above.

The rationale for Premise 1.2 is discussed above: ordinary human beings are not qualified to serve as absolute rulers because power corrupts.[30] If humans are

[29]On the rule of law in Athenian politics, see Martin Ostwald, *From Popular Sovereignty to the Sovereignty of Law* (Berkeley, CA: University of California Press, 1986); Josiah Ober, *Mass and Elite in Democratic Athens: Rhetoric, Ideology, and the Power of the People* (Princeton, NJ: Princeton University Press, 1989); and Mogens Herman Hansen, *The Athenian Democracy in the Age of Demosthenes* (Oxford: Blackwell, 1991). On the rule of law in Plato see Zena Hitz, "Plato on the Sovereignty of Law," *A Companion to Greek and Roman Political Thought*, ed. Ryan K. Balot (Malden, MA: Wiley-Blackwell, 2009), 367–81.

[30]The theme that power corrupts is already sounded in *Statesman* 301d–e: tyrants are feared because people "think that a person in such a position always mutilates, kills and generally maltreats whichever of us he wishes." Although a truly scientific ruler could govern a constitution correctly and steer it to happiness, laws are necessary "when a king does not come to be in cities as a king-bee is born in a hive, one individual immediately superior in body and mind."

granted autocratic power, they manifest "insolence and the injustice that is born from insolence" so that their "thought becomes filled with the greatest sickness, namely lack of intelligence" (IV.691c, cf. 713c). A human absolute ruler faces two difficulties: the first is that it is difficult to know that "the true political art" must aim at the common interest and see how the private and common interest are interconnected; the second is that even if the ruler had such knowledge, "he would never be able to adhere to this conviction and spend his life giving priority to nourishing what is common in the city . . .; mortal nature will always urge him toward getting more than his share and toward private business, irrationally fleeing pain and pursing pleasure, and putting both of these before what is more just and better." Ideally it would be best to have an intelligent ruler unencumbered by laws:

> Of course, if ever some human being who was born adequate in nature, with a divine dispensation, were able to attain these things, he wouldn't need any laws ruling over him. For no law or order is stronger than knowledge, nor is it right for intelligence to be subordinate, or a slave, to anyone, but it should be ruler over everything, if indeed it is true and really free according to nature. But now, in fact, it is so nowhere or in any way, except to a small extent.[31] (IX.875c–d.)

The legislator cannot assume that fully rational rulers will be forthcoming and must therefore seek a realistic alternative.

Premise 1.3 proposes such an alternative, which involves his aforementioned policy of approximism. In this case the best policy is to rely on order and law when the intelligent ruler is not available. The Athenian is fond of reminding his interlocutors that they are laying down laws for human beings not gods (V.732e, IX.853c). This anticipates James Madison's observation that "if men were angels, no government would be necessary" (*Federalist* no. 51). The legislator is like the divine demiurge who cannot fight with necessity (V.741a, VII.818b). Hence the Athenian promulgates a policy of approximism for legislation: in this instance, the laws governing property are to aim at making the city come as close as possible to unity.[32] He compares legislators to tragic poets: "our political constitution is constructed as the imitation of the most beautiful and best way of life, which we at least assert to be really the truest tragedy . . . We are . . . artists and performers of the most beautiful drama, which true law alone can by nature bring to perfection—as we hope" (VII.817b–c).

---

[31] Although the final clause leaves a loophole, how much it might let through is a matter of speculation.

[32] Elsewhere, he prescribes approximism in connection with legislation concerning drinking wine (II.673e–674c), organization of the city (V.745e–746d), regulation of sexual conduct (VIII.839e–842a), and punishment (IX.853b–c, 858a).

Premise 1.4 is anticipated by the Athenian's remark that a law is "rightly laid down" only if it constantly aims at the right end, which is the whole of virtue (IV.705d-706a). This premise is also foreshadowed in the description of the mythical age of Cronus. Because Cronus did not trust humans to rule over themselves, he set up divine spirits (*daimones*) as rulers over human beings, just as we now have human beings in charge of tame animals. The moral is that "there can be no rest from evils and toils for those cities in which some mortal rules rather than a god." Therefore, "we should imitate by every device the way of life that is said to have existed under Cronus; in public life and in private life—in the arrangement of our households and our cities—we should obey whatever within us partakes of immortality, giving the name *nomos* (law) to the name of distribution (*dianomê*) ordained by *nous* (intelligence)" (IV.713c–714a; cf. *Rep*. IX.590c–e).

Given what has preceded, Premise 1.5 seems reasonable: failing an absolute wise ruler "one must choose what comes second, order and law—which see and look to most things, but are incapable of seeing everything" (IX.875d). The laws express the legislator's judgment that acts of a certain type befit a virtuous life or a vicious life and thus should be, respectively, commanded or forbidden. But there can be exceptions to any rule: for example, it is just to return what one has borrowed, but not if it is a sword belonging to someone who has gone mad (cf. *Rep*. I.331c). Hence, the reliance on law is only second best; it would be better if the legislator could decide on the spot whether a particular act should or not be performed (cf. *Statesman* 294a–297a). Thus "reason (*logos*), striving to become law," orders the citizens to avoid the desires that cast them into the depths (VIII.835e).[33] Again, "Of all branches of learning, those which have the most sovereign influence in making the learner become better are the ones that pertain to the laws—if, that is, they should be correctly set up; and they would be, or else our divine and marvelous *nomos* (law) would in vain possess a name akin to *nous* (intelligence)" (XII.957c).

This derivation of the rule of law has two important implications: the first is that the citizens must be "voluntarily enslaved, in a certain sense, to the laws" (III.700a).[34] That is, all the citizens, including even the highest officials or rulers, are subject to the law (cf. VI.762e). "Where the law is itself ruled over and lacks sovereign authority, I see destruction at hand for such a place. But where it is a despot over the rulers and the rulers are slaves of the law, there I foresee safety

[33]These are the unnatural desires, for example, for homosexual intercourse with men or boys "bringing as a witness the nature of the beasts and demonstrating that males don't touch males with a view to such things because it is not according to nature to do so" (VIII.836c, 841d) "The natural use of sexual intercourse" aims at "the production of children" (838e); cf. note 2 above.

[34]This is the Athenian's description of the Athenian people (*dêmos*) in the good old days before it became corrupted under the influence of demagogues.

and all the good things which the gods have given to cities" (IV.715d). Officials including judges are required to enforce the law strictly and are subject to prosecution themselves if they fail in their duties (VI.761d–762e). A city with unreliable officials is at risk for dissolution like a ship with defective stays and bracing ropes, or an animal with weakened tendons and sinews. Hence there is a need for special officials called auditors (*euthunoi*, literally "straighteners"), who are tasked with scrutinizing all office holders. The auditors, who are held in the highest esteem, must be selected with care to ensure that they are virtuous. Moreover, they are themselves subject to the law and to scrutiny and they can be indicted for misconduct and removed and dishonored if found guilty (XII.945b–948b).

The second implication concerns the crucial role of the legislator, who must possess moral courage as well as knowledge in order to design a legal code, for example concerning sexual conduct. This is "in fact the task of a god, if it were possible somehow possible to get the orders from him." Failing this they must turn to some human being who is daring enough to "say what in his opinion is best for the city and the citizens." Before an audience of corrupt souls, he will order them to abide by rules which are appropriate for a political constitution. "[O]pposing the greatest desires and having no human ally, all alone he will follow reason (*logos*) alone" (VIII.835c). The Athenian distinguishes between the job of legislator and that of judge.[35] The legislator lays down laws "which see and look to most things, but are incapable of seeing everything" (IX.875d). For example, in cases where someone wounds another there are thousands of different possible varieties depending on who was wounded in what way and when and under what circumstances. Some decisions must be left to judicial courts: whether or not the alleged act in fact occurred, and what fine or other punishment is appropriate. The latitude accorded to judges must depend on their reliability. If it is expected that they will be unruly or biased the legal code should be as detailed and explicit as possible. But if the courts will be well-managed and the judges properly educated and vetted before assuming office, they may be allowed greater discretion. Even so, the legislator must provide clear guidelines so that the judges do not exceed the bounds of justice (876a–e). The legislator's work is not confined to prescribing laws and punishments. "What is really required of a lawgiver is that he write not only laws, but in addition to laws, things interwoven with the laws, writings that reveal what seems noble and ignoble to him" (VII.823a). The legislator's writings should provide edifying guidance for the citizens by revealing what sort of conduct is worthy of praise and blame. For example, in the case of hunting, the wise legislator will exhort young citizens to hunt strong and fast beasts in ways that will challenge and promote their virtue; he will admonish them against the idle

---

[35]The word *dikastês* can mean either "judge" or "juror." In Athenian courts jury members acted as judges.

using of nets and traps, against fishing, and against treating other humans or their property as prey (823d–824a).

The doctrine of the rule of law is also qualified in important ways. First, legislation is an ongoing process, at least until the legal code is fully drafted. The initial legislators can only provide a blueprint for their successors, who will have to fill out and modify it in some details (V.745e–746d, cf. 737c–d; VI.753b). The Nocturnal Council in particular must design its own curriculum as it discovers what its members need to know (XII.968b–e). Second, although wherever possible the laws are to be recorded on pieces of cypress wood and deposited in temples (V.741c–d, cf. X.891a), there is sometimes a need for unwritten laws. For example, in the case of pregnancy and childbearing there are many so-called "unwritten customs and "ancestral laws," which are "the bonds of every constitution, linking all the things established in writing, and laid down, with the things that will be set forth in the future" (VII.793b, cf. VI.773e). Third, rather than merely laying down commands combined with punishments for disobedience, the wise legislator seeks to "mix compulsion with persuasion," unlike past legislators who relied on sheer force and "tyrannical commands." A legislator should proceed like a doctor to free persons, who persuades the patient first before giving orders, and unlike a doctor to slaves, who merely examines the patient and issues commands (IV.720e). The free doctor is said to use arguments "that come close to philosophizing" by tracing the causes of diseases and discussing the nature of bodies (IX.857d). Similarly, the wise legislator uses a preamble (*prooimion*), a speech which precedes the law "so that he who receives the law uttered by the legislator might receive the command—that is, the law—in a frame of mind more favorably disposed and therefore apt to learn something" (IV.718a–724b). However, although the use of preambles presupposes that the citizens are amenable to persuasion in some sense, commentators disagree over whether this is supposed to be *rational* persuasion or merely rhetorical exhortation. For the preambles offered by the Athenian are of different sorts and open to different interpretations (e.g., IV.721b–e, IX.854b–c, 870e, 872e, 879c–880a, X.888a–907c, XI.916d–917b). In any case the doctor analogy reinforces the aforementioned theme of trickle-down rationality: the preludes exemplify the sort of persuasion an expert with greater understanding would use with a layperson with less understanding.[36]

---

[36]For the latter point see Malcolm Schofield, *Plato: Political Philosophy* (Oxford: Oxford University Press, 2006), 83–86. On the question whether the preambles employ rational persuasion, A. B. Hentschke (*Politik und Philosophie bei Plato und Aristoteles* (Frankfurt: Klostermann, 1971) and Christopher Bobonich ("Persuasion, Freedom, and Compulsion in Plato's *Laws*," *Classical Quarterly* 41 (1991), 365–88) argue in the affirmative. R. F. Stalley ("Persuasion in Plato's *Laws*," *History of Political Thought* 15 (1994), 157–77) objects that the preambles rely on rhetorical rather than rational arguments, a view generally shared by Laks (2000, 285–90) and Hitz (2009, 375–79). Bobonich offers a rebuttal for the "rational" interpretation in *Plato's Utopia Recast* (2002, 97–119). It will be evident from the following section that the present chapter assumes that the persuasion is in some sense rational.

Obedience to the Law

The final question to be considered is whether the rule of reason provides the citizens with a ground for them to obey the law. The *Laws* indicates that it does. The most famous dialogue in which Plato considers legal obligation is the *Crito*, which presents a widely discussed argument that Socrates has made a just agreement to obey the laws of Athens. The argument in the *Laws*, taking a very different tack, has attracted far less attention. Derivation 2 of the obligation to obey the law builds on Derivation 1 of the rule of law discussed in the previous section. It has the following general structure:

Derivation 2. The obligation to obey the law.

2.1. Each citizen should seek what is best for himself or herself.
2.2. What is best for oneself is leading a virtuous life, i.e., a life according to reason.
2.3. Like the best constitution, the best attainable constitution has as its primary aim the virtue of the whole city and as its secondary aim the virtue of the individual citizens.
2.4. The best attainable constitution achieves its aim through the rule of law.
2.5. Therefore, each citizen ought to comply with the rule of law.

Premises 2.1 and 2.2 cover ground common to Socratic dialogues such as the *Meno* and *Laches* as well as the *Republic*. They involve the familiar Platonic argument that an individual agent has a self-interested reason to be virtuous—that prudence and morality converge. This argument is set forth in the general preamble to the proposed constitution of Magnesia (V.732b–734e). Anticipating Jeremy Bentham two millennia hence,[37] the Athenian declares, "By nature, the human consists above all in pleasures and pains. To these every animal is, as it were, inextricably attached and bound in the most serious ways." A rational animal will, however, engage in a kind of self-legislation as he tries to determine which course of action will produce the greatest excess of pleasure over pain given his nature.[38] The Athenian goes on to argue that virtue will produce "more delight and less pain throughout the whole of one's life" (732e–734e). Hence a rational agent is advised to pursue a life that is prudent, temperate, courageous and healthy, rather than a life that is foolish, cowardly, licentious, and diseased.[39]

---

[37]Jeremy Bentham, "Nature has placed mankind under the governance of two sovereign masters, *pain* and *pleasure*." *Introduction to the Principles of Morals and Legislation* (1789), ch. I.i.

[38]This discussion recalls *Prot.* 355a–358c. Elsewhere, in the prototypical preamble to the marriage laws, the Athenian appeals to a more expansive sense of self-interest: "it is the nature of everyone to desire immortality in every way" (IV.721b–c).

[39]This implies the Socratic paradox—that nobody is vicious voluntarily. This presents a problem for the justification of punishment but it is not essential to the present chapter. On the paradox see IV.734b; IX.860c–862c, 880d–881a; X.905d–907b.

As Pangle remarks, however, the preamble's argument "leaves open the question whether a hedonistic calculation, guided by the 'law that one gives to oneself' (733e), dictates that one should obey the city's law."[40] What if the city's laws fail to promote the individual's happiness in some instances? Recall the Athenian's avowal: "I will legislate with a view to what is best for the entire city and family, and with a view to all this, will justly assign a lower rank to what belongs to each individual" (XI.923b). But why should the citizens follow the directions of the legislator if it is at the expense of their personal well-being? For example, Magnesia will have a system of compulsory public education and will not allow parents to teach their children privately, on the grounds that the children "belong more to the city than to those who generated them" (VII.804, cf. 807b). Does this not frustrate the parents' desire to bring up their children by their own lights?

Premise 2.3 seems intended to address this concern. Although the true aim of legislation should be the common good, "it is in the interest of both the common and the private that the common rather than the private, be established nobly" (IX.875a–b, cf. IV.715b, X.903d). If this means that the common good includes the interests of all of the citizens considered as individuals, then they will recognize that their personal well-being is bound up with that of all the other citizens and they will have a reason to obey the legislator's injunctions. This argument seems to depend on the optimistic assumption that there are no conflicts of interest, correctly understood, between individuals. For otherwise, if the "common good" did require the sacrifice of some individuals' interests, those who were to be sacrificed would have no reason to comply on the basis of Premise 2.1.

Premise 2.4 is equivalent to 1.6, the conclusion of the derivation of the rule of law, which was discussed in the previous section. The legislator will frame the laws which are in the citizens' interests properly understood: "Correct laws . . . make those who use them happy" (I.631b, cited above). This assumes the doctrine of *perfectionism*: that the aim of the laws, and the ultimate justification for their existence, is the inculcation and preservation of the citizens' virtuous happiness. This perfectionist doctrine is assumed even in the case of punishment, which should, according to the Athenian, have as one of its purposes the rehabilitation of the convicted criminal: "in general in whatever manner to bring about hatred of injustice and desire, or lack of hatred, for justice—it is this that is the task of the noblest laws" (862d-e).[41]

The Conclusion 2.5 is that each citizen should comply with the rule of law. The purpose of the preambles is to persuade the citizens to obey the laws by

[40]Pangle 1980, 457.

[41]The death penalty is reserved for those who are incurable, hence better off dead, and whose fate can serve as an example for others (IX.862d–863e).

bringing them to understand that "the hypothesis that underlies our laws aims at making the people as happy and as friendly to one another as possible" (V.743c). Insofar as they are guided by their own reason, the citizens will be "voluntary slaves of the law" (cf. III.700a, cited above). For they will obey the laws voluntarily if they recognize that only in this way can they achieve their proper aim: a free, virtuous, and happy life involving friendship with each other. If the citizens believe that the laws have been framed by a benevolent and intelligent legislator, they will be disposed to obey the laws even when these frustrate their immediate desires. For they will realize that they will fall prey to their own irrational desires and impair their own virtue (which is their most valued possession) if they take the law into their own hands. By way of example the Athenian mentions a legator who wishes to name as heir not his own children but someone else who has flattered him while he was sick or feeble with age (XI.923b).

Limits to the Rule of Law?

Assuming that the *Laws* offers an argument that citizens of Magnesia have an obligation to obey the law, what is the scope of this obligation? Does a citizen have an obligation to obey *every* law? Plato's answer seems clear if the law commands a just act or prohibits an unjust act. But does a citizen have an obligation to obey any given law independently of its content?[42] Must the citizen obey the law even if there is no preamble attached to it that gives specific reasons why the citizen must do so? This depends on whether laws are *defined* as regulations established by an intelligent legislator aiming at the virtuous life. If so, the Athenian would probably answer in the affirmative. For he has argued that ordinary citizens cannot rely on their own capacity to know what is in the common interest and how their own true private interests are bound up with the common good or to act on that knowledge if they are unrestrained by such laws.[43] If, however, the laws are defined as mere regulations established by any

[42]This discussion is indebted to conversation with Bas van der Vossen.

[43]For an opposing view see Hitz (2009), who notes that many particular laws lack preambles and concludes "that the preludes simply soften up citizens into an obedient frame of mind," on the grounds that "they are not capable of justifying the specific types of obedience that the laws command, but only obedience generally. Hence the form of order "achieved by passive obedience rather than active understanding . . . may well be all that the regime outlined in the *Laws* can obtain for a great many of its citizens" (378–80). Against this interpretation, it can be argued that it may well be rational to defer to authority in particular cases, e.g., a patient lacking medical knowledge who follows a specialist's recommendation that a particular regimen is best is not merely "passively obedient" if the patient has a rational basis for relying on the specialist. Nor is a citizen who has reason to judge that a legislator has the correct aim and political expertise. In such a case there can be a content-independent reason to obey a particular law.

legislator whosoever with any aim whatsoever, there would seem to be no content-independent moral obligation to obey them. The Athenian's etymological derivation of *nomos* from *nous* suggests that he would favor the former definition, although there is no explicit textual evidence for this.[44] But to avoid ambiguity let us rephrase the question: do the citizens have a content-independent moral reason to obey putative laws, i.e., regulations established by any legislator whosoever with any aim whatsoever? What if one finds the putative laws to be inimical to virtue? Does the citizen have an unqualified obligation to obey the law? Or are there cases in which it is permissible to disobey the law?

In an imaginary address to the Guardians of the Laws who are to become lawgivers themselves, he remarks that everyone, male or female, young or old, should strive for nothing else but to become a good person and possess the virtue of soul appropriate for a human being. The Athenian adds that:

> no one of any sort is to be seen giving precedence in honor to any of the other things that are impediments, not *even, finally, to the city*, if it appears necessary that the alternative to its destruction is either willingly tolerating the slavish yoke of being ruled by worse men or departing from the city in exile. All such things must be borne, and suffered, rather than allowing the regime to be changed into one whose nature is to make human beings worse.[45] (VI.770c–e.)

This provocative passage suggests that if the city were to fall into the wrong hands and the rulers to make laws for their own nefarious purposes, the Guardians of the Laws must contemplate alternatives such as exile or destroying the city. We might infer that in such an extreme case a private citizen such as Socrates would be justified in refusing to obey the rulers. But what if a particular law required a flagrantly unjust course of action, such as delivering up an innocent man for execution? And what if private citizens were barred from philosophizing?[46] If a particular law requires an individual to forsake virtue, is there any other course but disobedience or voluntary exile?

This obvious objection is not raised in the *Laws*, but the Athenian's reply is predictable. Private citizens who disobey the law on conscientious grounds place themselves, in effect, above the law in the sense that they make themselves

---

[44]The latter value-neutral definition is suggested when the Athenian mentions "incorrect" (*out' orthous nomous*) laws, which are vainly declared to be just by those engaged in faction (IV.715b). Saunders's translation is misleading: "we maintain that laws which are not established for the good of the whole state are bogus laws."

[45]The text is difficult but the general sense seems clear. The italicized words correspond to *teleutôn de kai poleôn* in Burnet's text. England reads *teleutân de kai poleôn* and translates "he must sacrifice even the state."

[46]These are examples in which Socrates says that he disobeyed or would disobey official commands in *Apol.* 32c–d and 29c–d.

the ultimate arbiter over whether the law is to be obeyed or not. In so doing they face the same two problems that confront the absolute ruler (cf. IX.874e–875d): how can one know for certain the right thing to do? And how can one overcome the all-too-human inclination of succumbing to one's own desires and passions in deciding whether to obey or not? Appreciating the general weakness of human nature, one should defer to the law rather than putting oneself above it. This reply is however open to worries: does one not sometimes have grounds for doubting the regime's rectitude? Can one really not tell a tyrant from a virtuous ruler? And, even if one can trust the legislator to be knowledgeable, competent, and scrupulous, does one never have a good reason to believe that a particular law is unjust? Are the reasons for supposing that the legislative process is reliable invariably stronger than one's grounds for objecting to a particular law? The Athenian's case for the rule of law and legal obedience seems at best restricted to cases where these questions have affirmative answers.

Plato's Legacy

Plato's idea of the rule of reason influenced many later thinkers and traditions.[47] It was of fundamental importance for Aristotle (384–322 BC), who declared that "intelligence (*nous*) rules over desire with political and kingly rule" and that "law is intelligence (*nous*) without desire" (*Politics* I.5.1254b5–6, III.16.1287a32).[48] During the Hellenistic era, however, the followers of Plato and Aristotle generally neglected political philosophy, and other schools struck out in new directions. The Cynics and Cyrenaics rejected traditional politics, and Diogenes of Sinope (c. 412–c. 324 BC) turned the Platonic analogy between city and cosmos on its head by declaring himself a citizen of the cosmos (*cosmopolitês*, Diogenes Laertius VI.2.63). Likewise, early Stoics such as Zeno of Citium (c. 334–261 BC) and Chrysippus of Soli (c. 280–c. 207 BC) criticized Plato in works of their own titled *Republic*, and defended a cosmopolitan alternative. In contrast with Plato's *Laws* they also rejected conventional taboos against incest, homosexuality, and cannibalism.[49] Yet Zeno's

[47]The following section is indebted to recent overviews by Eric Brown, "The Emergence of Natural Law and the Cosmopolis," in *A Companion to Ancient Greek Political Thought*, ed. Stephen Salkever (New York: Cambridge University Press, 2009), 331–63; and Bruno Centrone, "Platonism and Pythagoreanism in the Early Empire," in *The Cambridge History of Greek and Roman Political Thought*, eds. Christopher Rowe and Malcolm Schofield (Cambridge: Cambridge University Press, 2000), 559–84; and to the relevant chapters in *A History of the Philosophy of Law from the Ancient Greeks to the Scholastics*, eds. Fred D. Miller, Jr., and Carrie-Ann Biondi (Dordrecht: Springer, 2007).

[48]Aristotle was also influenced by Plato in his own oft-cited treatments of natural law and the rule of law in the *Rhetoric* and *Politics*.

[49]See Sextus Empiricus, *Adversos Mathematicos* 11.190–94; Plutarch, *On Stoic Self-Contradictions* 1044f–1055a; Diogenes Laertius VII.188. See n. 2 above for references to Plato's *Laws*.

prescription "live according to nature" was expounded by the later Stoics in terms reminiscent of Plato: that the proper end of human beings is to live in accordance with their own nature and that of the universe as a whole. The Stoics took a further step, however, in positing "the common law, which is right reason (*orthos logos*), that pervades all things." (Diogenes Laertius VII.87–8) There was also cross-fertilization, since Platonists like Antiochus of Ascalon (c. 130–c. 68 BC) explicated Plato in terms of Stoic ideas, for example, identifying the demiurge of the *Timaeus* with the cosmic *logos*. This eclectic amalgam of ideas was transmitted to Roman readers via Cicero (106–43 BC) in two dialogues, *De re publica* and *De legibus*, which were explicitly modeled on Plato's *Republic* and *Laws*. In *De legibus* Cicero defined law (*lex*) as "the highest reason (*ratio*), implanted in nature, which commands what ought to be done and forbids the opposite." (*Leg*. I.18)[50] He also argued that humans have law in common with the gods because they have reason in common with them and hence right reason (*recta ratio*), which is law (I.23). Through Cicero and the Roman Stoics such as Seneca (4 BC–65 AD), Epictetus (c. 50–135 AD), and Marcus Aurelius (121–180 AD), the ideas of the rule of reason and of law became increasingly influential and were appropriated by Roman jurists such as Gaius (c. 180 AD) and Ulpian (d. 228 AD), although these thinkers understood them in different ways.

Plato's legal thought also had an important, if largely indirect, influence on the later faith-based legal traditions. An early conduit was Philo of Alexandria (c. 20 BC–45 AD), a Hellenized Jew who praised Plato as "the sweetest of all writers" (*Every Good Man is Free* 13). Philo compared the cosmos to a city governed by law: "The unerring law is right reason (*orthos logos*); not an ordinance made by this or that mortal, a corruptible and perishable law, a lifeless law written on lifeless parchment or engraved on lifeless columns; but one imperishable, and stamped by immortal nature on the immortal mind." (Ibid. 46) Philo represented a confluence of Platonism and Greek Stoicism with Alexandrian Jewish thought, and his writings were studied in turn by early Christian thinkers, including Clement of Alexandria (c. 150–c. 215), Origen (c. 185–254), Ambrose (c. 340–397), and Eusebius (263–339).[51] Like Philo, the Jewish historian Flavius Josephus (37–95?) compared Moses to a Platonic legislator: "He believed that it was above all necessary for one who manages his own life nobly

[50]Translations of Cicero are from *De re publica* and *De legibus* trans. Clinton Walker Keyes (Cambridge, MA: Harvard University Press, 1928).

[51]The dates for these and subsequent figures are all AD. On reports that Philo conversed with early Christians and visited the church in Rome, see Eusebius, *Ecclesiastical History* II.17–18. On the influence of Plato's *Laws* on Philo's interpretation of the Torah, there is an insightful discussion by Julia Annas, "Virtue and Law in Plato," in *Plato's Laws: A Critical Guide*, ed. Christopher Bobonich (Cambridge: Cambridge University Press, 2010), 71–91.

and to legislate for others, first to study the nature of God and then having contemplated His works with his intelligence (*nous*) to imitate as far as possible that best model (*paradeigma*) of all and to try to follow it." (*Jewish Antiquities* Preface 4. 19). In addition, Cicero's ideas were transmitted by Christian writers such as Lactantius (c. 240–320) who quoted approvingly Cicero's definition of true law as "right reason in agreement with nature" of which God is the author, promulgator, and enforcing judge (*Institutes* VI.8 = *De re publica* III.22). Though the *Republic* and *Laws* were lost with the fall of the Roman Empire, they were cited in widely read works by Clement of Alexandria, Theodoret of Cyrrhus (393–466 CE), and John Stobaeus (early fifth century). The Platonic-Stoic idea of the rule of reason was also preserved in the writings of Augustine of Hippo (354–430), who remarked that "the eternal law is divine reason, or the will of God, which orders the preservation of the natural order and prohibits its transgression." (*Contra Faustem* XXII.27). Augustine construed divine reason, however, in Christian terms. Although he understood peace along the same lines as Plato, as consisting in "the tranquility of order," he also stated that "peace between mortal man and God is an ordered obedience, in faith, under an eternal law." Peace therefore consisted in an "ordered harmony," a concord rooted in God's law, contained in "two chief precepts: that is, love of God and love of neighbor" (*City of God* XIX.13–14). Moreover, departing from Plato, Augustine rejected the possibility of a rational order in human politics due to the corruption of human nature resulting from original sin.[52] Finally, Plato had a profound impact on medieval Islamic and Jewish political philosophy. His *Republic*, *Timaeus*, and *Laws* were translated into Arabic by the tenth century, and Al-Farabi (c. 970–95) wrote commentaries on the *Republic* and *Laws*. He equated the Islamic idea of Imam or religious authority with the Platonic ideas of philosopher and legislator who uses his intelligence to bring about virtue and happiness in the nations and cities. Plato's political works were discussed in turn by other major Islamic philosophers, including Averroes (Ibn Rushd, 1126–1198), who wrote a commentary on the *Republic*, as well as Moses Maimonides (1138–1204). In addition to secondary sources such as the aforementioned, manuscripts of the *Laws* finally appeared in the Latin West in the high Middle Ages.

Through these many avenues, the Platonic principle of the rule of reason became, ultimately, an important influence in modern philosophy. This was most evident in the case of two early modern movements. The first was the Platonic Academy of Florence, founded by Marsilio Ficino (1433–1499), a Renaissance humanist who translated some of Plato's dialogues into Latin and wrote commentaries on several of them, including the *Republic* and *Laws*. The second

[52]See R. A. Markus, "The Latin Fathers," in *The Cambridge History of Medieval Political Thought: c. 350–c. 1450*, ed. J. H. Burns (Cambridge: Cambridge University Press, 1988), 109, the source of the translation, on Augustine's shift from the Platonism of Ambrose to a Pauline perspective.

was the Cambridge Platonists, founded by Benjamin Whichcote (1609), who observed, "To go against Reason is to go against God; it is the self same thing, to do that which the Reason of the case doth require; and that which God Himself doth appoint: reason is the Divine Governor of Man's Life; it is the very Voice of God" (Aphorism 76). The Cambridge school included Henry More (1614–1687) and Ralph Cudworth (1617–1689), who were also attracted by the ideal of wisdom concerning a realm of eternal immutable objects and the thesis that divinely inspired human reason is the foundation for virtuous conduct. The Florentine and Cambridge movements evinced little interest in legal philosophy, however. Far more significant in this regard was Gottfried Wilhelm Leibniz (1646–1716), who aspired to establish a "universal jurisprudence" valid for all rational beings. In addition to his obvious debt to René Descartes (1596–1650), Leibniz expressed his longstanding admiration for "the moral philosophy of Plato, and even in a way with his metaphysics; for these two sciences accompany each other, like mathematics and physics." (Letter to N. Rémond) He maintained that the norms of conduct and the essence of the just depend not on arbitrary decisions (even those of God) but rather on "eternal truths, objects of divine intellect" (*Opinion on the Principles of Pufendorf.*) Leibniz rejected the claim of Hobbes and Locke that all men have by nature a claim to equality, appealing to the Platonic analogy of the ship of state: "If several men found themselves in a single ship on the open sea, it would not be in the least conformable either to reason or nature, that those who understand nothing of sea-going claim to be pilots; such that, following natural reason, government belongs to the wisest" (Letter to T. Burnett). In his *Codex Iuris Gentium*, Leibniz defined justice as "the charity of the wise man (*caritas sapientis*), that is, charity which follows the dictates of wisdom. . . . Charity is a universal benevolence, and benevolence the habit of loving or of willing the good." He understood charity as the Christian virtue described by St. Paul and St. Augustine. Hence, Leibniz agreed with "learned men . . . that the law of nature and of the nations should follow the teachings of Christianity." Leibniz represented the twilight of Platonic political philosophy. His synthesis of Platonic rationalism and Christian ethics was dismissed before long as obsolete by Enlightenment critics.[53]

---

[53]This interpretation of Leibniz follows Patrick Riley, who argues that Leibniz's "visible devotion to Plato and Platonism . . . runs like a red thread through his whole moral and political philosophy" (82). Riley views Leibniz as the last great legal philosopher to take this stance: "In many ways Leibnizian 'wise charity' is the last flowering (or last gasp) of a long and distinguished Graeco-Roman-Christian tradition which was to be definitively overturned by Hume, Rousseau, and Kant no more than a half-century after Leibniz' death." (91) See Patrick Riley, *The Philosophers' Philosophy of Law from the Seventeenth Century to Our Days* (Dordrecht: Springer, 2009), chapter 6. The quotations in the main text are from *Leibniz: Political Writings*, trans. Patrick Riley (Cambridge: Cambridge University Press, 1972), pp. 209, 45, 71, 192, 171. For fuller discussion see Patrick Riley, *Leibniz' Universal Jurisprudence: Justice as the Charity of the Wise* (Cambridge, Mass: Harvard University Press, 1996) and Donald Rutherford, *Leibniz and the Rational Order of Nature* (Cambridge: Cambridge University Press, 1995).

It is noteworthy that the rule of reason was affirmed also by Liebniz's philosophical adversary, John Locke (1632–1704), who declared that "the State of Nature has a Law of Nature to govern it" and that "Reason . . . is that Law," and who called reason man's "only star and compass" (*Second Treatise of Government* II. Ch. 2, sec. 6; *First Treatise*, ch. 6, sec. 58). Along with Locke, a series of influential political and legal thinkers, including Hugo Grotius (1583–1645), Thomas Hobbes (1588–1679), and Samuel Pufendorf (1632–1694), invoked the ideas of reason and natural law. By "reason," however, these early modern theorists had in mind nothing on the order of Plato's idea of an intelligence guided by eternal moral verities, because they accepted an empiricist epistemology, or a voluntarist theory of moral obligation, or both. In its new incarnation, the rule of reason continued to have traction during the Enlightenment under the influence of theorists like Montesquieu (1689–1755). It is, for example, a major theme in the American *Federalist*, which states that "it is the reason of the public alone that ought to control and regulate the government. The passions ought to be controlled and regulated by the government" (No. 49 by Madison).[54] Though detached from its roots in Platonic metaphysics and epistemology, the rule of reason continued to be a potent force in modern political thought.[55]

[54]See Fred D. Miller, Jr., "The Rule of Reason in Plato's *Statesman* and the American *Federalist*," *Social Philosophy & Policy* 24:2 (2007) 90–129.

[55]I am grateful to David Keyt, Anthony O'Hear, Pamela Phillips, Alexander Rosenberg, Nicholas Sars, and Bas van der Vossen for comments on earlier drafts. I also received helpful feedback from fellow authors at a seminar at Denison University and from Julia Annas, Rachan Kamtekar, and other attendees at a colloquium at the University of Arizona. I made final revisions while I was a visiting scholar at the Center for the Philosophy of Freedom at the University of Arizona. The editor Jonathan Jacobs provided valuable guidance and feedback throughout.

{ 2 }

Stoic Eudaimonism and the Natural Law Tradition[1]

Jacob Klein

Introduction

The identification of commonly accepted morality with nature is contrary to some of the earliest currents of Greek thought. The sophist Antiphon forcefully describes the conventions of law as bonds placed upon the natural order; the Athenians invoke a necessary law of nature to sanction the massacre at Melos; and Plato's Callicles offers, in the service of his immoralism, the image of a lion dominant and noble by nature, tamed and shackled by convention.[2] By the time of Cicero, however, one finds a notion of *lex naturalis* clearly applied to support a core of moral principles enjoining far-reaching obligations to others.[3] This law, says Cicero, is the product neither of human thought nor of civil legislation. It is diffused in the order of nature as a whole and identical to the purpose of Zeus. It is the source and spring of justice, commanding us to regard the welfare of others. In virtue of its prescriptions, Cicero maintains, the rape of Lucretia was wrong and the courage of Cocles right.[4]

That the Stoics were responsible for the account on which Cicero relies is commonly recognized, yet a careful assessment of the Stoic account faces distinctive

---

[1]I thank Noah Dauber, Sydney Penner, and Joe Yarbrough for helpful comments on earlier drafts of this chapter. I am indebted to Tad Brennan, Charles Brittain, Gail Fine, and Terence Irwin for discussion of some of the questions raised here and for comments on related material. They are not responsible for my errors.

[2]For the Athenian atrocity at Melos, see Thuc. 5.84–116 (esp. 5.105). For Antiphon's description of *nomoi* as bonds upon nature (*desmoi tês phuseôs*), see Antiph. fr. 44(a)iv.5. For Callicles's lion, see *Grg.* 483e5. Cf. also Dodds (1959), pp. 268–9.

[3]E.g., *Fin.* 3.62–68, *Off.* 1.50–57 and esp. *Off.* 3.21–32. Cicero frequently prefers *lex naturae* to *lex naturalis,* but he employs both constructions.

[4]See *Leg.* 1.19, 2.8, 2.10; *Rep.* 3.33. For nature as the *fons legum et iuris*, see *Leg.* 1.16, *Off.* 3.72. Cicero explicitly associates this account with Zeno of Citium at *Nat. d.* 1.36.

difficulties. Though some of the most striking statements of Stoic views about natural law appear in Cicero's philosophical treatises, Cicero's rhetorical formulations are frequently insensitive to questions about justificatory priority, or the scope and content of natural law, or the relation between the obligations it enjoins and the eudaimonist outlook of Stoic ethics as a whole. Later articulations of natural law theory are distinguished by the answers they supply to these questions, but Stoic views are difficult to determine with precision. Because knowledge of Stoicism passed into the medieval philosophical tradition primarily through the medium of Cicero, Cicero's own adaptations and omissions were passed on as well. Questions about the relation of Stoic theory to later views must be distinguished carefully from the question of how later thinkers received and understood the available sources.

These difficulties are reflected in the variety of assessments commentators have offered of Stoic contributions to ethics and to the natural law tradition in particular, assessments which might be loosely sorted into two categories. There are those, on the one hand, who find in Stoic theory the beginnings of a tradition of law-based theorizing, in contrast with classical eudaimonist views. Thus Alasdair MacIntyre maintains, for instance, that the Stoics abandon a teleological ethics for a law-based conception.[5] According to Gisela Striker, Stoicism is an "ancestor of modern deontological conceptions of virtue as obedience to the unchanging moral law."[6] Knud Haakonssen identifies Stoicism with the first of four central phases in the history of natural law, and Alan Donagan remarks that the Stoics "are to be credited with forming the first reasonably clear conception of morality."[7] In a similar vein, Mark Murphy finds the Stoics regarding the right as "prior to the good."[8]

These assessments all treat Stoic ethical theory as presciently modern in some respect and as an important departure from classical accounts. Accordingly, they may be contrasted with the judgments of those commentators who regard the foundations of Stoicism as broadly continuous with the eudaimonist framework of Platonic and Aristotelian ethics. Thus A. A. Long is concerned to emphasize (against MacIntyre) Stoicism's eudaimonist credentials; Terence

---

[5]MacIntyre (1981), p. 157. MacIntyre's view is discussed at length in Long (1983).

[6]Striker (1996), pp. 219–20.

[7]Haakonssen (2001), p. 1205; Donagan (1977), p. 4. Crowe (1977) remarks that the Stoics "are usually given the credit of having been the first to formulate the doctrine [of natural law]" (p. 17). Cf. Vogt (2008): "The early Stoics may justly be counted among the ancestors of natural law theory" (p. 3).

[8]Murphy (2008). Examples can be multiplied. Henry Sidgwick suggests that ancient Stoicism "from the prominence that it gives to the conception of Natural Law, forms a transitional link between ancient and modern ethics" (1907, p. 105). According to Julia Annas, the Stoics are the first to hold that "morality requires impartiality to all others from the moral point of view" (1993, p. 265). According to Max Forschner, "the Stoic school formulated crucial aspects of that which the Kantian tradition calls morality [die Stoa entscheidende Gesichtspunkte dessen ausformuliert, was die kantische Tradition Moralität nennt]" (1986, p. 327).

Irwin explicates Stoic ethics by way of an extended comparison with Aristotle; and Julia Annas argues at length that the eudaimonist basis of Stoicism excludes the possibility of any foundational appeal to the natural order at all.[9] Supposing these diverse assessments of Stoicism are consistent, how do they fit together, and how is the essential structure of Stoic ethics to be characterized?

The diversity of recent interpretations of Stoic ethics is due, in part, to the presence in Stoicism of a form of ethical naturalism that is largely absent in Plato and wholly absent in Aristotle. This is the Stoic claim that the best form of human life consists in living not merely in accordance with human nature but with the nature of the cosmos as a whole. The Stoic appeal to cosmic or common nature (*phusis koinê*) raises difficult questions about Stoic eudaimonism and about the justifying role of *eudaimonia* in Stoic theory. Commentators who view Stoic ethics as an anticipation of deontological or law-based accounts sometimes ignore the eudaimonist commitment of Stoic ethics, emphasizing the cosmic dimension of Stoic naturalism instead. Those who begin from the Stoics' commitment to eudaimonism, on the other hand, tend to neglect or minimize the role of cosmic nature.

I shall argue that the supposed tension between the eudaimonist and naturalist commitments of Stoic ethics rests on assumptions the Stoics themselves do not share, and that the Stoics defend a eudaimonist ethics that requires conformity to the rational order of nature as a condition of realizing the best form of life for human beings. Though Stoic ethics prefigures later views in important respects, some of the features of Stoicism which have been singled out as characteristically modern—its emphasis on conformity to law or its focus on the intentional features of virtuous action, for example—are not, in fact, a departure from the eudaimonist framework of earlier theories. They are rather a consequence of the Stoic commitment to rational eudaimonism conjoined to a substantive understanding of reason's requirements. The fullest expression of those requirements is found, according to the Stoics, in the teleological organization of nature as a whole. In what follows I first set out some of the main evidence for Stoic eudaimonism and consider its relation to Stoic appeals to nature. I then consider two questions of more specific relevance to the natural law tradition: first, whether Stoic theological views imply a voluntarist account of the principles to which rational agents are to adhere; second, whether the Stoics suppose that knowledge of moral truths can be derived from a knowledge of natural facts.[10]

---

[9]See, e.g., Irwin (1986, 1990); Long (1983). Cf. Long (1968, 1989). Though Annas focuses on Stoic appeals to cosmic nature, she also concludes, surprisingly, that the Stoics (and Greek ethicists generally) are not ethical naturalists. Annas's verdict rests on an idiosyncratic account of ethical naturalism. See Annas (1993), pp. 135–36.

[10]A view attributed to them by, e.g., John Finnis. See Finnis (1980), pp. 34–35.

Stoic Eudaimonism

Like most ancient ethical theorists, the Greek Stoics are eudaimonists in some sense of the term. The summaries of Stoic ethics preserved by Diogenes Laertius and Arius Didymus include explicit affirmations of eudaimonism, and eudaimonism of some form is assumed in Cicero's reports of Stoicism in the *De finibus*, *De officiis*, and *Tusculan Disputations*.[11] It is clear that Stoic scholarchs from Zeno until Antipater defended an analysis of the human *telos* or goal of life, and Chrysippus's concern with an account of the conditions under which *eudaimonia* may be achieved is well-attested.[12] The central interpretive question in approaching these reports is not whether early Stoicism includes a conception of the best life achievable for a human being, but whether this conception has the role, as it is plausibly understood to have in Aristotle's theory, of structuring Stoic ethical theory as a whole.

At this point various interpretive options arise. Though Stoic sources speak clearly of a human *telos* and highest good, they are apt to characterize it variously.[13] Although the end is frequently identified with *eudaimonia,* it is also characterized, perhaps even more frequently, as a life of conformity to nature, which is in turn said to be equivalent to virtue.[14] The Stoics regard these descriptions as extensionally equivalent: to live in accord with nature is, in their view, to be both virtuous and happy.[15] They are not intensionally equivalent, however, and the Stoic sources that survive do not say which of them is prior in order of justification. Is one to conform to nature because that is what virtue prescribes, or because it is what nature requires, or because a disposition that is virtuous and consonant with nature renders a human life happy and blessed?

There are good grounds for concluding that the Stoics intend their references to *eudaimonia* as the most fundamental characterization of the human *telos* and, indeed, that they regard an agent's own happiness as the only final end in virtue of which an aim or action may count as rational.[16] This thesis,

---

[11]E.g., *Fin.* 1.11, *Off.* 1.5–7, *Tusc.* 5.48.

[12]See DL 7.88; Plutarch, *Stoic. rep.* 1035c.

[13]For discussion of this point, see Striker (1986), pp. 185–90.

[14]Strictly speaking, the Stoics identify *eudaimonia* with the activities that flow from virtue, and in so doing they associate it with a range of normative predicates such as 'fine' (*kalon/honestum*) and 'good' (*agathon/bonum*). Here and throughout, I sometimes render *eudaimonia* as 'happiness,' mostly to avoid repetition of the Greek term.

[15]This extensional equivalence is generally attributed to the Stoics, but it is not wholly uncontroversial. Irwin holds that a Stoic may live virtuously yet fail to live according to nature, and Striker sometimes appears to intend a similar view. Cf. Striker (1986): "In Stoic theory natural things are of no value for the goal of life, but at most for a natural life . . . " (p. 191). I discuss Irwin's claim below.

[16]So described, rational eudaimonism is not a thesis about the description under which a rational agent will ordinarily act nor about the general character of her intentions; it is compatible with an objective account of human happiness as a life that includes concern for others. It is, however, a thesis about what could count as an ultimate normative reason for human agents, that is, about the character of the considerations an agent must ultimately invoke in order to defend her actions on rational grounds.

which I shall refer to as rational eudaimonism, is not explicit in any Stoic text, but there is good reason to suppose that it captures the Stoic position fairly. The best Stoic sources characterize the end as *eudaimonia* rather than virtue or conformity to nature in contexts in which the question of final or ultimate justification is clearly at issue. These texts explicitly hold, for example, that *eudaimonia* is that to which everything in life is appropriately referred but which is not itself referred to anything further.[17] They assert that *eudaimonia* is the final object of *orexis,* a species of rational motivation that belongs in its successful or veridical form (*boulêsis*) to the perfectly rational Stoic sage.[18] Most importantly, perhaps, they claim that every appropriate (*kathêkon*) action is done for the sake of *eudaimonia* and takes this as its standard or reference point.[19] Since in the Stoics' view an appropriate action (rendered by Cicero as *officium*) is one for which a rational defense (*eulogos apologia*) can be offered, these texts affirm that every rational action is one that is justified, at least in part, by its relation to the *telos* of human happiness.[20] In these reports the concept of *eudaimonia* seems intended to supply the most basic description under which action and motivation count as rational.

It seems clear then that *eudaimonia* enters into Stoic theory as at least one rational ground of practical action to which every ultimate, justifying explanation must refer. As a minimal condition of rationality, human action and motivation must aim further the goal of happiness and treat this end as a final aim.[21] By themselves, however, these texts do not clearly establish a commitment to rational eudaimonism as I have characterized it. In the first place, there is nothing in them to show conclusively that the relevant conception of happiness is that of the agent's own happiness in particular. It is consistent with these formulations to suppose (as at least one commentator has suggested) that in Stoic theory the conception of *eudaimonia* to which practical reason refers is an agent-neutral conception that includes the *eudaimonia* of others. Second, these references are not sufficient to show that one's own *eudaimonia* embraces all of the final objects at which a rational agent may aim. That is to say, the most reliable summaries of early Stoic views do not quite foreclose the possibility that although every rational action necessarily refers to the agent's happiness, there is some distinct final objective, such as conformity to nature, at which rational action may also be directed as such. Even if rational action must promote the agent's

---

[17]E.g., Stob. *Ecl.* 2.46 (= SVF 3.2).

[18]SVF 3.65. Cf. Stob. *Ecl.* 2.76 (=SVF 3.3), 2.98. As defined by the Stoics, *orexis* is a rational impulse (*hormê logikê*) directed at what is good *de dicto* in the case of fools, who (according to Epictetus) may misapply it, but exclusively at what is good *de re* in sages, who never do. Chrysippus restricts the rational appetition of the *logistikon* (i.e., the rational *hêgemonikon*) to the fine alone. See Kidd (1988, vol. 2), p. 211 (= fr. 160). Cf. also SVF 3.169, 3.441, 3.442, 3.438. For discussion, see Kidd (1988, vol. 3), pp. 569–70 and Inwood (1985), Appendix 2.

[19]Stob. *Ecl.* 2.46 (= SVF 3.2), 2.77 (= SVF 3.16).

[20]Stob. *Ecl.* 2.85.

[21]Though even this much is not clearly accepted by commentators, as I note below.

own good, this may not be the *only* feature in virtue of which it is rational on the Stoic account.[22]

Stoic Eudaimonism and the Scope of Rational Justification

These alternatives to rational eudaimonism are not clearly excluded by the formulations I have cited, but they can be fairly securely ruled out on other grounds. The suggestion that it is rational to promote the end of *eudaimonia* where this is conceived in agent-neutral terms is at least recognized by ancient philosophical sources.[23] Yet whether or not it is the correct view to take of other ancient theories, it does not appear to be the correct account of Stoicism. This point is not explicit in reports of early Stoic theory, but it is strongly implied by the dialectical framework assumed in later doxography and especially in Cicero. That Cicero takes the conception of happiness at issue in Stoic ethics to be the agent's own seems clear, for example, from his formulations of a challenge frequently leveled against the Stoic thesis that virtue is sufficient for happiness. Hellenistic defenders of a mixed account of the human good—one that includes both virtue and other goods in an analysis of happiness—regard the Stoics as outrageous for maintaining that the virtuous agent will retain her happiness even under torture. The happiness at issue in this criticism is quite clearly the agent's own, and so it is clear that the Stoics insist that a virtuous agent will retain her *own* happiness in even the worst external circumstances.[24] It is difficult to see why the Stoics defend this thesis in the way they do unless they also regard the realization of one's own happiness as the formal end of rational agency. That is to say, if the prospect of a virtuous but unpleasant death could be justified in other-regarding terms while remaining faithful to Stoic principles, the Stoic effort to justify it in agent-relative ones would make little sense. That the Stoics are prepared to defend the rationality of even a virtuous death by reference to the agent's own happiness strongly suggests that they intend to justify all rational action in agent-centered terms.

---

[22]There are at least three ways in which the scope of rational justification might be thought to come apart from the concept of an agent's *eudaimonia*. We might suppose (1) that although every rational action is one that promotes *eudaimonia*, the *eudaimonia* at issue is not the agent's own, (2) that one's own *eudaimonia* is not the only rational aim of action and hence that other rational aims may sometimes conflict with this aim, (3) that although an agent's own well-being is not the only rational aim she may have, other rational aims will *reinforce* rather than conflict with the aim of promoting her own happiness. Whiting (2002) proposes a version of (1) as an interpretation of Aristotle's eudaimonism. Kraut (1989, 1999) attributes (2) to Aristotle. Crisp (2003) attributes (3) to Socrates. I do not think any of these accounts of the role of *eudaimonia* in rational justification fits the Stoic view, but I have not had space to discuss (3) here.

[23]Augustine's summary of Marcus Varro's classification of possible accounts of the supreme good (*De civ. d.* 19.1) explicitly recognizes this conception of *eudaimonia*.

[24]See, e.g., *Fin.* 3.42. Cicero alludes to this Stoic doctrine frequently.

The second alternative to rational eudaimonism is less easy to dismiss. It also offers an attractive reading of Stoicism in some respects. If the Stoics regard conformity to nature or to natural law as a rational aim extensionally distinct from the aim of realizing one's own happiness, this doctrine might indeed appear to signal a shift away from the comprehensive eudaimonism of earlier theories.[25] It also suggests a more sympathetic way of understanding Stoic theory overall. Terence Irwin, for instance, relies on the claim that the Stoics do not treat happiness as the only final rational objective to show that the Stoic view of emotion is less extreme than has sometimes been thought. According to Irwin, the Stoic thesis that loss and tragedy do not affect an agent's welfare does not imply that a rational agent has no reason to regret such a loss, for on Irwin's account of Stoic theory the life of virtue and happiness and the life that accords with nature constitute independently rational aims.[26] If this understanding of Stoic theory is correct, the Stoics might be said to adopt a more familiar attitude towards those objects or outcomes they characterize as indifferent than they are ordinarily thought to hold, for in their view it will sometimes be rational to regret an outcome that fails to promote a life of conformity to nature even if this failure makes no difference to achieving the *telos* of *eudaimonia*.[27] Since it does not take *eudaimonia* to be the only final aim of rational agency, this account of Stoic theory is incompatible with rational eudaimonism as I have described it.

A number of considerations tell against this interpretation, however. One such consideration is merely an *ex silentio* appeal. No Stoic source, to my knowledge, suggests that actions may be justified with respect to anything other than what contributes to the end of happiness, and virtue alone does this in the Stoics view. A few texts, moreover, are explicit on this point. Cicero's summary of Stoics' ethics in *De finibus* 3 considers and rejects the suggestion that Stoic theory is implicitly committed to two final ends, virtue and a life that accords with nature, where these are conceived as independent objectives at which a

---

[25]This depends, of course, on how the eudaimonism of earlier theories is understood. I understand Aristotle to be committed to rational eudaimonism of the form I have described here, but this is not uncontroversial. According to Richard Kraut, for instance, Aristotle's view allows that considerations unconnected to one's own happiness may count as independent reasons for action, and that these reasons may sometimes conflict with what the agent's happiness requires. See Kraut (1989), Chapter 2; Kraut (1999).

[26]Independent, that is, in the strong sense according to which one of these rational objectives may be realized while the other is not. See Irwin (2007), p. 316: "Virtuous action, therefore, is not sufficient for achieving the life according to nature, which includes the natural advantages." Irwin is certainly correct to point out that virtue is not sufficient for attaining the natural advantages, preferred indifferents such as health and wealth. But it is the Stoics' critics, not the Stoics themselves, who maintain that the actual possession of these items is a necessary condition of the life according to nature.

[27]Cf. Irwin (1986), (1998a), (1998b).

rational agent might aim.[28] Seneca, considering the possibility that a mixed account of the end encompassing both virtue and pleasant circumstances might be superior to the Stoic view, says that the Stoic sage does nothing for the sake of pleasure (*causa voluptatis*).[29] Since the Stoics classify pleasure among those objects that accord with nature (preferred indifferents, in Stoic terminology), then on the assumption that the sage acts both for the sake of virtue and happiness and for the independently rational objective of conformity to nature, Seneca's statement appears to be false.[30] Similar statements in other texts strongly suggest that the Stoics regard a life lived in accordance with nature as constitutive of virtue and happiness, and not as an independently rational aim with which happiness might in principle conflict.[31]

There is a more fundamental reason, however, for supposing that the Stoics restrict the scope of rational justification to those aims that promote *eudaimonia*. This is based on the Stoic claim, attested in a range of sources, that justice cannot be preserved if objects that accord with nature (such as health and wealth) but are not essential to virtue and happiness are counted as genuine goods.[32] By this the Stoics mean that if rational weight is accorded to final objectives other than virtue it will not be rational to preserve the virtue of justice in every circumstance. Their argument seems to rest on the assumption that, given such an account, one cannot rule out the possibility that rational considerations distinct from virtue may sometimes outweigh the requirements of virtue so that an agent has overriding reason to act viciously.[33] Since the Stoics treat this outcome as a *reductio*, they restrict the scope of rational action to the virtue in which, according to them, *eudaimonia* consists. Whether or not this line of argument is defensible, it confirms that the Stoics' restriction of

---

[28]*Fin.* 3.22.

[29]Seneca, *Vit. beat.* 11.1. Cf. *Vit. beat.* 9.4.

[30]On pleasure as an indifferent, see DL 7.102, Cicero, *Fin.* 3.17.

[31]Seneca elsewhere writes that a virtuous agent "is never filled with regret because at the time nothing better could have been done than was done, no better decision could have been made than was made" (*Ben* 4.34, trans. Basore). Cf. also *Ben.* 4.21 and 4.33.

[32]Plutarch attributes a thesis of this form to Chrysippus (*Stoic. rep.* 1038d–e, 1040c–f). Cicero attributes it to the Stoics in several passages (e.g., *Fin.* 4.45). It is affirmed by Seneca (*Ep.* 76.22) and Marcus Aurelius (*Med.* 11.10).

[33]Were the Stoics prepared to grant the existence of rational aims beyond the scope of happiness, there would be far less significance in their claim that virtue is sufficient for happiness. For in that case considerations having to do with virtue would not exhaust the aims of rational agents, an implication Irwin accepts. The Stoics are prepared to argue, however, that such aims are not rational. See esp. Seneca *Ep.* 76.22: "If, however, you accept the view that there is anything good besides that which is honorable (*honestum*), all the virtues will suffer. For it will never be possible for any virtue to be won and held if there is anything outside itself which virtue must take into consideration. If there is any such thing, then it is at variance with reason (*quod si est, rationi repugnat*), from which the virtues spring, and with truth also, which cannot exist without reason" (trans. Gummere). Here the formal end of practical reason, as Seneca represents it, coincides with the Stoics' restriction of goodness and happiness to virtue alone. Cf. also Seneca, *Vit. beat.* 10.11.

happiness and goodness to virtue is not intended merely as a terminological point but as a substantive claim about the range of objectives rational agency may take as its end. In identifying happiness with virtue and the activities that flow from it, the Stoics mean to ensure the coincidence of virtue with what is rational in every case.

There are good grounds, therefore, for supposing that the Stoics restrict the scope of rational justification to their account of the human *telos* as consisting in virtue alone. Like Plato and Aristotle, they treat the concept of *eudaimonia* as the most basic justificatory concept and the life that satisfies it as the single object at which rational action, as such, will aim.[34] On this view, the considerations to which a rational agent will respond must serve her own happiness in the final analysis. Despite claims sometimes made for Stoicism as a presciently modern ethical theory, there is little reason to suppose that the Greek Stoics depart from the framework of eudaimonism either by casting their account of *eudaimonia* in agent-neutral terms or by positing some further rational objective beyond its scope. The formal aim of practical reason, as they conceive it, is to secure the good life for the agent, and a rational justification of motivation and action must ultimately be couched in agent-centered terms. Whether such an outlook can amount to an adequate moral theory is a further question.[35]

Stoic Naturalism

These considerations suggest that at least the conceptual foundations of Stoic ethics are broadly continuous with those of Platonic and Aristotelian ethics. To act on the reasons that apply to rational agents is to act in a way that is good for the agent and to do so, in the final analysis, because so acting is good for the agent. So understood, the acceptance of rational eudaimonism commits the Stoics to a formally egocentric or agent-relative account of rational justification. By itself, however, this framework places few constraints on a substantive analysis of human well-being or on the specific requirements of virtue. The way in which the Stoics fill in their account of the human good and the role they give to cosmic nature in fixing the content of rational obligation distinguish their theory from classical accounts and from rival Hellenistic views. Although

[34]For an older and more authoritative attribution of this view to the Stoics, see Sidgwick (1892): "In Platonism and Stoicism, and in Greek moral philosophy generally, but *one* regulative and governing faculty is recognized under the name of Reason—however the regulation of Reason may be understood; in the modern ethical view, when it has worked itself clear, there are found to be *two*—Universal Reason and Egoistic Reason, or Conscience and Self-love" (p. 197).

[35]Nagel argues, for instance, that a view according to which "the content of morality is derived from the necessary conditions for a good life . . . is wrong, because moral requirements have their source in the claims of other persons" (1989, pp. 195–97). Nagel attributes this view to Aristotle.

the Stoics assert the justificatory priority of human happiness, in identifying happiness with virtue and virtue with conformity to nature they are prepared to defend an account of well-being that is both objective and (even from the ancient point of view) highly revisionist.

This is an important point, for recent studies of Stoic ethics have taken divergent views of the Stoic claim that happiness consists in living according to nature, and questions about the import of eudaimonism have figured centrally in this debate. A number of commentators appeal to Stoic eudaimonism as grounds for minimizing the role of cosmic nature in particular in Stoic ethical theory. Julia Annas argues at length that since facts about the structure of the cosmos are extrinsic to any plausible account of human happiness, Stoic ethical theory must rest, like Aristotle's, on an account of specifically *human* nature instead.[36] Annas's argument largely depends on her assumption of a subjectivist constraint on any adequate eudaimonist ethics, namely, that in order to be of relevance to ethical theory, a given account of *eudaimonia* must be endorsable from the perspective of the agent whose welfare it purports to describe.[37] Since Annas finds that the aim of conforming to cosmic nature fails to satisfy this condition, she takes Stoic eudaimonism to exclude certain forms of ethical naturalism.

A second line of interpretation, running in the opposite direction, evidently takes the cosmic naturalism of Stoic ethics to exclude rational eudaimonism. According to John Finnis, the Stoic requirement to conform to cosmic nature "is taken [in Stoic theory] as rendering superfluous all further questions . . . about the point or good-for-man of conforming to it."[38] Michael Frede suggests that one reason one ought to conform to nature, according to the Stoics, "is precisely that this is what nature means us to do."[39] Nicholas White argues

[36]See Annas (1993), pp. 159–79. For Annas's assumption that there is a tension between eudaimonism and an appeal to cosmic nature, see esp. p. 161: "Ethical theory begins from reflection on the agent's final good and how this is to be made determinate in a way which will enable the agent to make sense of her life and correctly order her priorities. The appeal to cosmic nature, however, does the opposite of what is required; it pulls the agent away from the kind of attachment to her own concerns which is needed for useful reflection on her final end to be possible." Annas concludes that Stoic ethical theory does not depend on Stoic cosmology for either its content or its normative justification. She is followed in a number of studies by Christopher Gill. See esp. Gill (2004), pp. 101–25.

[37]Annas (1993), pp. 161–62: "Suppose I did come to have a definite conception of cosmic nature and its demands on me; this would still not be relevant to any of the concerns I need ethical theory for, until endorsed by reflection from the relevant point of view. But that point of view is the agent's point of view on his life as a whole and how best to order his priorities. The cosmic point of view, then, is useless for ethics unless endorsed as part of a theory that is eudaimonist in form."

[38]Finnis (1980), p. 377.

[39]Frede (1999). According to Frede, the Stoics hold that in the ideal case "we come to realize that appropriate action, if done for the reason that it accords with nature—i.e. for the reason that it is what nature means us to do—constitutes what is good, and recognizing this, it henceforth is our overriding aim to act in this way" (p. 81). Frede suggests that such a motive is "no longer self-regarding" on the Stoic account (p. 84).

that Stoic ethics cannot accurately be described as a "self-realizationist" theory such as Aristotle's, which "[fixes] upon certain features of a human being that are thought to constitute its somehow essential nature and urges that those features be developed."[40] Though these characterizations of Stoic theory may be consistent with some forms of eudaimonism, they appear to treat the requirement of conformity to cosmic nature as an independently rational obligation, one not derived, that is to say, from a rational requirement to realize the human good as such.

While these lines of interpretation disagree about the relevance of cosmic nature in Stoic ethics, they appear to agree in assuming that Stoic appeals to cosmic nature are in tension with a commitment to rational eudaimonism. This assumption is difficult to square with the role assigned to *eudaimonia* in the sources I have considered, however. There is no evidence that the Stoics themselves acknowledged any problematic opposition between the eudaimonist and naturalist commitments of their ethics or that they marginalized one to explain the other. On the one hand, Annas's account of Stoic eudaimonism appears to prove too much. To the extent that *eudaimonia* is understood in subjectivist terms, that is, as strongly conditioned by the beliefs and desires with which an agent begins, it may prove to be in tension not simply with appeals to the teleological order of the cosmos but, much more generally, with any appeal to objective, naturalistic foundations at all.[41] If the content of *eudaimonia* is strongly constrained by what agents themselves can be brought to believe or endorse, then given the truth of rational eudaimonism, the requirements of practical reason will also be constrained in this way. On such a view there is little antecedent reason to suppose either that an account of human nature (which Annas allows) will prove of particular relevance to ethics or that practical reason, so conceived, will be seen to support the other-regarding requirements of traditional morality. Yet as Annas herself acknowledges, Stoic ethics supports significant commitments to the welfare of others. Although the Stoic analysis of

[40]White (1979), p. 146. Cf. also Annas (1993), p. 171n43. White's assertion that Stoicism is not a "self-realizationist" theory is puzzling. Diogenes Laertius's report of Stoic theory characterizes the human good as "the natural perfection of a rational being *qua* rational," and Cicero's synoptic account of Stoic ethics in *De finibus* 3 gives a central place to the Stoic analysis of human nature and to its development in the ideal case. According to Seneca, "if every thing, when it has perfected (*perfecit*) its own good, is praiseworthy and has reached the end of its own nature, and man's own good is reason, if he has perfected reason, he is praiseworthy and has attained the end of his nature" (*Ep*. 76.9–10, trans. Long and Sedley). Cf. also Cicero, *Fin*. 3.33; Seneca, *Ep*. 41.79, 89.4; Cicero, *Leg*. 1.25, *Tusc*. 5.39; Marcus, *Med*. 6.44.

[41]That is, as naturalistic foundations are ordinarily understood. There is no antecedent reason to deny the label of naturalism to ethical theories, such as those of Hume or Hobbes, which begin from the psychological commitments of human agents. But since contemporary uses of the realist label do not usually extend to subjectivist theories of this sort, and since ethical naturalism is typically understood to entail a commitment to realism, subjectivist views are not often characterized as naturalist theories, at least in contemporary discussion. See, e.g., Railton (1996).

practical reason is formally self-interested, it should be distinguished carefully from accounts that make the content of the reasons that apply to an agent strongly dependent on her beliefs and motivations. Annas's claim that eudaimonism excludes cosmic naturalism rests on assumptions the Stoics themselves do not accept.[42]

On the other hand, although Stoic eudaimonism does not imply a subjective conception of well-being, it equally does not imply that the requirement to conform to cosmic nature applies independently of an obligation to realize the distinctive good for human beings.[43] Although facts about the cosmos do not introduce the most basic justification for living a rationally ordered life, the Stoics regard the cosmic order as an expression of substantive norms of rationality that determine what such a life consists in. This assumption is apparent, for instance, in the Stoic doctrine that the cosmos has the character of a city, citizenship in which imposes duties of mutual concern upon its members.[44] Though this claim is not confined to facts about human nature alone, it plays a substantive role in fixing the obligations that apply to human agents *qua* rational. Stoic naturalism is more extensive, in this respect, than its classical and Hellenistic counterparts.[45]

In broad outline, Stoic ethics might fairly be said to rest on a substantive and objective account of human well-being according to which happiness depends exclusively on the perfection of reason, the cognitive capacity that regulates belief and action in human agents. This perfection, in turn, centrally requires a grasp of the teleological structure of nature as a whole. The conception of practical reason on which this picture depends should be distinguished carefully from accounts according to which the content of reason's requirements is substantively determined by an agent's beliefs and motivations, but it should also be distinguished from agent-neutral theories that divorce the content of practical rationality from a formal conception of the agent's benefit. To questions

[42]For criticisms of Annas's account of cosmic nature in Stoic ethics, see Inwood (1995), Cooper (1995), Betegh (2003).

[43]A range of Stoic sources suggest this order of priority, e.g., Cleanthes, *Hymn to Zeus* (SVF 1.537 = LS 54I): "[T]he wretched . . . neither see nor hear god's universal law (*theou koinos nomos*), by obeying which they could lead a good life in partnership with intelligence" (trans. Long and Sedley); Stob., *Ecl.* 2.75: "And the virtue of the happy man and his good flow of life are just this: always doing everything on the basis of the concordance of each man's guardian spirit with the will of the administrator of the whole" (trans. Long and Sedley); Seneca *Ep.* 92.3: "What is a happy life? Peacefulness and constant tranquility . . . How are these things reached? If all of truth has been seen, if orderliness, moderation, and seemliness are preserved in actions . . ." (trans. Long and Sedley); Cicero, *Leg.* 1.56: "[T]o live on the basis of nature (*ex natura vivere*) is the highest good. This is a life of moderation based upon virtue, or following nature and living, as it were, according to her law" (trans. after Keyes).

[44]See, e.g., SVF 2.528 (= LS 67L); Cicero, *Leg.* 1.23–25, *Fin.* 3.64–67, *Off.* 3.21–24, *Nat. d.* 2.154; Epictetus, *Diss.* 2.10.3–7; Marcus, *Med.* 4.4; Seneca, *Ot.* 3–4. Cf. also Philo Judaeus, *Jos.* 29–31.

[45]See, e.g., DL 7.87; Plutarch, *Stoic. rep.* 1035c–d; Cicero, *Fin.* 2.37, 3.31, 3.73, *Off.* 1.153, 2.5, *Tusc.* 4.57, 5.7; Seneca, *Ep.* 88.33, 89.5. For discussion of some of these passages, see Kerford (1978).

of justificatory priority the Stoics accept the fundamental answers given by Platonic and Aristotelian ethics: a good human life is one that is structured by an appropriate understanding of human nature and by a corresponding account of what is beneficial to human beings as such. At the same time, the Stoics hold that the principles of reason, which determine the actions appropriate to virtue, are expressed in the order of the cosmos as a whole and grasped through an experience of that order. Though this position is prefigured, in some respects, in the *Timaeus* and the *Laws*, the Stoics are the first to develop it carefully and extensively.

I have focused on these antecedent features of Stoic ethics because they are important for fixing the sense in which the Stoics can be said to defend a law-based account. On the one hand, Stoic ethics clearly includes some of the core features associated with natural law theories. The Stoics are committed to the view that natural facts supply the basis for the ethical requirements that apply to human beings, and they believe that these requirements are wholly accessible to the faculty of reason.[46] On the other hand, if it is a criterion of a law-based ethics that it endorse principles that obligate independently of their relation to some further end or good, there is little reason to attribute such a view to the Stoics. The rational principles expressed in the cosmos as a whole apply to human beings, in the Stoics' view, in virtue of what is good for them as rational agents.[47] The justification for living according to cosmic nature rests on the Stoic conviction that knowledge of the rational pattern instantiated there is a sufficient condition of a virtuous disposition and, consequently, of human happiness.

Natural Law and the Will of Zeus

Two further questions are relevant to an attempt to relate this account to later theories of natural law. The first, which is metaphysical, concerns the relation implied by Stoic theory of normative facts to theological facts. Stoic sources explicitly identify natural law both with right reason (*orthos logos*/*recta ratio*) and with the will (*boulêsis*/*voluntas*) of Zeus.[48] As with their descriptions of the

---

[46]These commitments, as I understand them, are shared by Aristotle and Aquinas and are central to the natural law tradition as such. I have not tried to offer a more comprehensive characterization of the essential features of natural law theories, a question on which there appears to be little scholarly consensus. For recent relevant discussion, see, e.g., Murphy (2008); Irwin (2007), pp. 545–71; Irwin (2008), pp. 70–88; Irwin (forthcoming).

[47]Cf. Schofield (1991): "The thesis that social morality flows from adherence to the dictates of natural law [as the Stoics understand it] . . . is a thesis solely about what is enjoined upon man or any rational animal *qua* rational social animal" (103).

[48]See DL 7.88; Epictetus, *Diss.* 1.17.13–19, *En.* 26; SVF 3.180.

human *telos*, the Stoics clearly regard these descriptions as extensionally equivalent: the content of natural law is identical to the content of right reason, which is also the content of Zeus's rational will. Once again, these characterizations raise questions about justificatory priority. Though their adherence to rational eudaimonism implies that the obligation to conform to natural law rests on a prior conception of the human good, the Stoics might nonetheless regard the principles to which human nature must conform to secure this good as rational because Zeus wills them.

Such an interpretation, if correct, would align Stoic theory with voluntarist conceptions of natural law in an important respect. Ockham, for example, rejects the framework of rational eudaimonism, and he does not believe, as the Stoics do, that principles accessible to unaided reason exhaust the obligations that apply to human agents. Yet on some interpretations, Ockham treats the divine will as antecedent to even the most basic principles of *recta ratio*.[49] The content of right reason is fixed, on such an account, by the will (*voluntas*) of God, who is not Himself bound by them. It is worth asking whether the Stoics intend a similar order of priority with respect to the principles of *orthos logos*. John Cooper suggests, for instance, that according to Stoic theory, "the standards and norms of reason. . . are ultimately constituted by Zeus's or nature's own thinking."[50] Brad Inwood writes that the divine will "is an imperative expression of what god wants men to do and what he wants to happen in nature."[51] We might suppose that Stoic ethics combines a eudaimonist account of the obligation to live as reason directs with a voluntarist account of reason's requirements.

It may not be possible to settle this point conclusively with respect to early Stoic theory, but it is worth considering some of the evidence that bears on it. The issue may be sharpened somewhat by a consideration of Stoic cosmology. Though the Stoics are sometimes described as pantheists and materialists, both terms are misleading. God, understood as *logos* or *ratio,* is certainly *in*

49See, e.g., Irwin (2007): "Ockham does not simply hold, as Aquinas holds, that the divine will and correct reason necessarily agree; he also holds that correct reason prescribes a given action only because God wills it" (p. 715). Strongly voluntarist readings of Ockham have been challenged. According to a second interpretation, were God to countermand a basic requirement of right reason, this commandment would not remove the basic requirement but would instead generate a conflict within reason itself. See, e.g., Adams (1986, 1999).

50Cooper (2004), p. 231. But cf. p. 218: "While we do not find in our sources any special elaboration of such "rules" or "standards" of right reason, it is clear that the Stoics do suppose that rational nature presents itself to itself as answerable to such standards. . . . But, in principle, all of these are standards to which rational beings, as such, are committed simply by their nature as rational."

51Inwood (1985), p. 108. Neither Cooper nor Inwood explicitly commits the Stoics to any such doctrine, and no Stoic source raises the question in these terms. The Stoic identification of right reason with Zeus and the content of divine *boulêsis* invites a basic and important question about the structure of Stoic theory, however.

everything, on the Stoic account, but he is not to be *identified* with everything. The Stoics are corporealists in that they conceive of both *logos* and qualityless primary matter as bodies that are spatially extended and causally efficacious. But the articulate, highly organized matter that is everywhere the object of human perception arises only through the thorough interblending of these two principles: the one divine, active, and rational, the other inarticulate, passive, and non-rational. Zeus, who is sometimes characterized in personal terms, sometimes in impersonal ones, is intermingled with but not identical to the otherwise formless material on which he acts.[52] Given that Zeus is co-extensive but not identical to the cosmos as a whole, one might ask (and given the Platonic backdrop to their views, the Stoics no doubt did ask) whether Zeus himself fixes the standards of rationality that structure the natural order or whether, like the demiurge of the *Timaeus*, he organizes the world in accordance with independently fixed principles.[53]

Some of the features of natural law identified by Cicero may appear to suggest the former answer. Cicero identifies law with the divine mind (*mens dei, mens divina*) and characterizes it both as heavenly law (*lex caelestis*) and as the right reason of supreme Zeus (*ratio recta summi Iovis*). Divine reason is said to have the power to enact or ordain (*sancire*) law, and law is said to have come into existence simultaneously with the divine mind (*orta est simul cum mente divina*).[54] The *De republica* in particular describes Zeus as the "author" (*inventor*), "judge" (*disceptator*), and "legislator" (*lator*) of eternal and unchanging law.[55] These characterizations are consistent with the view that the natural order is rational and therefore binding on rational agents because it is the product of divine legislation. If they accurately reflect earlier Stoic views, then in spite of their commitment to rational eudaimonism, the Stoics may seem to accept a broadly legislative account of the principles by which a human life is rendered happy because rational.

Cicero, however, is our only source for the strongly legislative cast given to the doctrine of natural law in these passages. Though they clearly preserve much of what is essential to the Stoic conception, the characterizations of the *De republica* in particular go beyond anything affirmed in explicitly Stoic sources that survive. To the Greek Stoics, and to Chrysippus in particular, we may securely attribute the identification of law with right reason, the claim that law is prescriptive for agents whose nature is rational and political, and the

---

[52]Cooper (2009) provides a detailed account of these aspects of Stoic cosmology.

[53]The Stoics clearly reject the Platonic conception of incorporeal, intelligible paradigms, and there are other fundamental differences between the cosmology of the *Timaeus* and that of Stoicism. Here I mean only to raise a question of explanatory priority. For recent discussions of Stoic cosmology and its relation to the *Timaeus*, see Sedley (2002) and Gourinat (2009).

[54]For these characterizations, see *Leg.* 1.23, 2.8–11.

[55]*Rep.* 3.33.

assertion that law is diffused and implanted in the order of nature as a whole.[56] It is difficult, on the other hand, to find any clear precedent in early Stoicism for Cicero's descriptions of Zeus as the *inventor, disceptator,* and *lator* of natural law.[57] Though Chrysippus identifies reason and common law with Zeus, this identification may indicate nothing more than the extensional equivalence I have indicated. Nothing in the reports of early Stoic theory suggests that Zeus's will transcends the most basic principles of right reason or that his creative activity is prior to their fundamental content.[58] The legislative terminology applied in these passages may reflect an amalgam of Stoic and Platonist views, or it may simply be due to Cicero himself.[59]

There are independent indications, moreover, that the Stoics do not intend the voluntarist order of priority. Though they do not accept the immaterial paradigmatism of the *Timaeus,* Stoic accounts of Zeus's creative activity suggest that in ordering the cosmos, Zeus is himself responsive to independently determined standards of rational and aesthetic perfection.[60] This point emerges most clearly in Cicero's treatise on the nature of the gods, which, unlike material from the *De legibus* and *De republica,* is framed as an explicit report of Stoic theological views. Zeus's creative activity is there characterized, continuously with Greek sources, as an artisanal fire concerned to realize in the structure of the cosmos the most orderly arrangement possible and one directed towards three specific ends: it secures the permanence of the world, ensures that it lacks nothing, and causes it, finally, to manifest every sort of excellence and beauty.[61] Such an expression of artifice, Cicero says, requires foresight and counsel on the part of Zeus. This point is not sufficient to show that divine will does not establish or specify any of the principles of right reason, on the Stoic account, but it does suggest that in giving order to the cosmos, Zeus himself is

---

[56]See, e.g., DL 7.88; SVF 3.314 (= LS 67R). Cf. Schofield (1991), pp. 69–74; Dyck (2004), p. 109.

[57]Though Cicero's descriptions resemble Philo's references to a divine *nomothetês* or lawgiver (e.g., *De vita Mos.* 2.48, *Fug.* 66, 69), such descriptions are absent from clearly orthodox Stoic accounts. Texts that may be firmly associated with the early Stoics do not present Zeus as giving and therefore transcending the law but simply as identical to it (on which point see esp. Horsley [1978, pp. 52–54]). It should be emphasized, however, that law is said to be identical to perfected *human* reason as well. Though a few Stoicizing sources employ the epithet *nomothetês,* they apply it to the Stoic *sage* and to the perfected rationality in which human virtue consists (e.g., SVF 3.332, 3.619, 3.273, 3.301; cf. Plutarch, *Stoic. rep.* 1037f–1038a). This point suggests that right reason, in the Stoics' view, has the force of law wherever it appears.

[58]I.e., I do not mean to suggest that the content of right reason is in *no way* determined by Zeus's activity, in the Stoics' view.

[59]For discussion of Platonist antecedents and their possible influence on Cicero's account of natural law, see Koester (1970) and esp. Horsley (1978). Cf. also Dyck (2004), pp. 12–15, 50–51,103–5; Annas (1993), pp. 303–4. Watson (1971) emphasizes Cicero's possible role in shaping the doctrine of natural law as it appears in his treatises.

[60]On the aesthetic character of the Stoic conception of goodness, see Frede (1999), Bett (2010).

[61]*Nat. d.* 2.57–58. Cf. SVF 2.1027 (= LS 46A).

guided by independent norms.[62] If that is what the Stoics intend, their account of rationality cannot be voluntarist, as it were, all the way down.

Two additional Stoic doctrines, moreover, suggest a more comprehensive rejection of voluntarism. In the first place, the Stoic doctrine of world conflagration, according to which the train of events unfolding in the cosmos is a pattern destined to recur eternally, and down to the smallest detail, implies that Zeus's rational agency is guided by independent standards at a quite specific level. For one reason the same cosmic pattern is destined to recur, according to the Stoics, is that it already instantiates the most rational arrangement possible.[63] This is not the only argument by which the Stoics support the doctrine of world conflagration, but this particular rationale for the qualitative identity of successive world stages would not be available to them if they also supposed that reason's content is simply fixed and explained by the content of Zeus's will. If facts about the divine will explain the rationality of the cosmic arrangement, the Stoics should not explain the necessity of its recursion, *qua* rational, by reference to its intrinsic features.[64]

There is a more general reason, finally, to doubt that Stoicism implies a voluntarist account of right reason. This arises from the fact that the Stoics explicitly treat the structure of rational human agency in the ideal case as closely isomorphic to that of Zeus. This isomorphism is expressed, in general terms, in the Stoic claim that human reason is a fragment of the divine nature. It is much more explicit, however, in the Stoic doctrine that Zeus himself is subject to the same psychological phenomena as human agents, albeit on a cosmic scale. Cicero writes that the world-nature undergoes "all the voluntary motions (*motus voluntarii*), conations (*conatus*), and strivings (*adpetitiones*) which the Greeks call impulses (*hormai*), and follows these up with actions in the same way as we ourselves."[65] Since the practical deliberation of fully rational human agents is structurally analogous to that of Zeus, we can plausibly look to the Stoic analysis of human rationality to answer some of the questions that arise in the theological case.

---

[62]Cf. Menn (1995): "The knowledge Zeus needs in order to produce the world is knowledge of what is *kata phusin* [according to nature]. He is not like the God of Descartes, who arbitrarily decrees what the laws of nature will be: since Zeus's will is determined by his normative knowledge of what actions are *kathêkon* [appropriate], the norms must be independent of his will" (p. 27). Cf. Algra (2003): Zeus's "workings do entail a degree of imperfection and are bound by certain constraints" . . . "as a rational principle [Zeus] incorporates the laws of rationality" (p. 172).

[63]Cf. SVF 1.98 (= LS 46G). Long and Sedley (1987) write, "Since every previous world has been excellent . . . god can have no reason to modify any succeeding world" (p. 311). For further discussion of the Stoic doctrine of world conflagration, see Long (1985).

[64]Cf. e.g., *Nat. d.* 2.33–39.

[65]*Nat. d.* 2.58, trans. after Rackham. Cf. Algra (2003): "Behind [the Stoics' anthropomorphic conception of god] "lies the firm conviction that god's rationality—or, for that matter, the rationality of the cosmos—does not differ in kind from human rationality" (p. 168).

When we do so, however, it is clear that the Stoics wish to explain the rationality of choice and action by reference to facts that are fixed independently of an agent's psychology. Because motivational states are propositionally structured mental attitudes, on the Stoic account, their rationality is to be measured by their representational fit with the world. Indeed, the Stoics claim that the faculty of reason itself is constituted by conceptions (*ennoiai*) and preconceptions (*prolêpseis*) built up from pre-rational assents (*sugkatatheseis*) to true and reliable impressions. Though it certainly includes discursive and inferential functions, reason consists, first and foremost, in an accurate conceptual grip on the world and in knowledge of its independently constituted features.[66] Whether an agent is practically rational depends on whether, as a consequence of the conceptions she possesses, she assents only to those evaluative impressions that are reliably true. There is good reason to suppose that the Stoics extend at least the central features of this analysis to the divine case, and that Zeus's perfected reason is similarly thought to depend on assent to true impressions. In both its divine and human forms rationality is said to be a property instantiated by the leading part of the soul, the *hêgemonikon*, and in both cases it is characterized in terms of truth and knowledge.[67] In each case, too, the Stoics describe the faculty of reason as a craftsman or artificer structuring and ordering motivation through the psychological mechanisms of assent and impulse and, more fundamentally, through a knowledge of what is good.[68]

These elements of Stoic doctrine strongly suggest that the Greek Stoics do not conceive of the content of natural law as an artifact, as it were, of the divine will, but rather identify it with knowledge that Zeus himself possesses to a perfect degree, in accordance with which he has organized the cosmos, and which is likewise available, on a lesser scale, to human agents.[69] The imperative to conform to nature is fundamentally an imperative to acquire, to the fullest extent possible, a character that instantiates this knowledge and expresses it in action.[70] This suggests that the older Stoic position fits more closely with intellectualist rather than voluntarist approaches to the content of natural law, and it helps to explain Chrysippus's remark, borrowed from Pindar, that law is king of things both human and divine.[71]

---

[66]According to Chrysippus, "Reason is a collection of certain conceptions and preconceptions" (SVF 2.841 = LS 53V), trans. Long and Sedley. Cf. Cicero, *Tusc.* 4.65. For discussion of the Stoic account of reason, see Frede (1994); Schofield (1991), pp. 70–71; Cooper (2004), pp. 216–18.

[67]See esp. SVF 2.913 and the discussion in Kerford (1978), pp. 130–32.

[68]Given the state of the sources, it is impossible to say how the Stoics understand the knowledge on which Zeus's own rationality is supposed to depend, or how they might attempt to characterize it at the most fundamental level, if indeed they attempted to do so. The Stoics would perhaps say that it is knowledge of axiological principles that apply to any aesthetically perfect whole. See, e.g., *Nat. d.* 2.35. Cf. Bobzien (1998): the "specific element in providence seems to be an element of value or evaluation: god can only will what is best, hence what is good" (p. 47).

[69]Cf. Cooper (2004), pp. 222–23.

[70]See esp. Cicero, *Leg.* 1.18–19, 23.

[71]SVF 3.314 (=LS 67R).

No Stoic source, to my knowledge, affirms that natural law is rational and authoritative *because* Zeus wills it, and this interpretation is difficult to square with the account implicit in the texts that survive.

Knowledge of the Law

That the Stoics regard the facts that determine the content of virtue and happiness as part of the natural order is clear, and to this extent their theory is a naturalist account. It is also clear that they extend the scope of the knowledge in which virtue consists so that it includes an understanding of cosmos. This association of law with nature raises a further, epistemological question about the relation between knowledge of the natural order and knowledge of the rational law it is supposed to embody. Stoicism has come in for special criticism in this regard from John Finnis, who writes that the Stoic theory of natural law in particular involves "an illicit inference from 'is' to 'ought.'" On this score Finnis distinguishes the Stoic position sharply from that of Aristotle and Aquinas, for whom, in his view, the principles of practical reason are epistemically basic, self-evident and indemonstrable.[72] According to Finnis, since Aristotle and Aquinas begin from ethical principles that are known non-inferentially, inferences to ethical conclusions do not present a special problem in their case.[73] By contrast, the Stoic theory of natural law is open to two criticisms: (1) Unlike Aristotle and Aquinas, the Stoics commit themselves to inferences from *is* to *ought*, (2) in speaking of a law of nature, the Stoics "confuse 'is' laws and 'ought' laws."[74]

Much might be said about the questions these criticisms raise; my aim here is merely to outline what I take to be the Stoic approach. One thing to notice, in passing, is a tension between Finnis's charges. If the Stoics assign a normative status to the principles by which the cosmos is organized, then even if they are mistaken or confused on this score, it is not obvious that in inferring normative conclusions from claims about nature they are guilty of moving from *is* to *ought*. For the principles from which they begin are, by their own lights, normative principles. This point suggests a measure of caution in accepting both of Finnis's accusations. It also suggests, correctly, that the moral epistemology implicit in Stoic ethics is a complex affair. Finnis's own position (which, in his view, Aristotle and Aquinas share) combines a commitment to the autonomy of ethics—roughly, the claim that there are no reasonable inferences from nonethical truths to ethical ones—with an intuitionist account of moral knowledge,

---

[72]See esp. Finnis (1980), pp. 29–36 and Chapter 3.

[73]According to Finnis (1980), Aristotle and Aquinas "would readily grant that *ought* cannot be deduced from *is*" (p. 47).

[74]Finnis (1980), pp. 34–35, 35n39. Cf. pp. 374–78.

roughly, the view that some ethical truths may be known non-inferentially.[75] Both of these views remain controversial among contemporary naturalists, some of whom accept naturalism while rejecting one or the other of them.[76] I do not think it is obvious where the Stoics stand on either question.

I shall set aside the first question, whether the Stoics are committed to something like an intuitionist view of moral knowledge, both because it may seem to be the less pressing of the two and because addressing it would require a lengthy consideration of Stoic epistemology.[77] With regard to the second question, whether the Stoics involve themselves in inferences from *is* to *ought,* there is some initial plausibility in Finnis's claim. Stoic texts include a number of inferences about what is rational and therefore obligatory from claims about the way in which nature is organized. At least three examples of such inferences can be firmly associated with Chrysippus: a derivation (1) of the principle that it accords with nature's purpose to care for and preserve oneself, (2) of the principle that it accords with nature to care for one's offspring, and (3) of the principle that it accords with nature to care for other human beings as such. The Stoics may have intended a close connection between (2) and (3) so that these claims reduce, in effect, to a demonstration of self-regarding duties and other-regarding ones. In each case Chrysippus appears to have supported his conclusions not by appealing to a teleological analysis of human nature, but by a probabilistic inference to the types of behavior that nature as a whole intends for a creature in equipping it with faculties and motivation of a particular sort. In support of the duty to self-preservation, for instance, Chrysippus argues that nature would not make a creature that possessed an aversion to itself and would consequently undermine its own existence. That, the reasoning goes, is not something that a self-consistent artificer would do. Nor would it create an animal that possessed neither attraction nor aversion to anything at all. The remaining possibility is that it accords with nature for creatures to care for themselves, a mode of behavior consistent with the faculties they possess.[78]

It is clear that these arguments are ultimately intended to support conclusions about basic forms of behavior that are rational for human beings. It is also clear that they depend on an appeal to cosmic teleology and not merely, as

[75]Sturgeon (2003).

[76]See, e.g., Sturgeon (2003, 2006). Sturgeon himself rejects the second commitment. As Sturgeon (2003) notes, Foot (1958) arguably rejects the first.

[77]Answering it might also require more evidence than our sources supply. If Stoicism involves a rejection of intuitionism, then since the Stoics maintain that moral knowledge is possible, they will be committed to the view that moral knowledge is inferential. In view of the role the Stoics assign to inference and reasoning from analogy in the acquisition of moral conceptions (*ennoiai*), I do not think this possibility can be ruled out in advance of a careful consideration of the sources, which I have not attempted here.

[78]See, e.g., DL 7.85; Cicero, *Fin.* 3.62–68, *Off.* 1.11–12; Plutarch, *Stoic. rep.* 1038b.

in Aristotle, on an appeal to the goal-directed functions of individual organisms. It is difficult to see how they support Finnis's criticisms, however, for although they require a normative premise, namely, that nature's purposes are rational, this premise is explicit in any number of Stoic texts, and the Stoics are prepared to defend it on independent grounds.[79] The Stoics do not argue, in these passages, that it is rational to care for self and others because that is what nature intends, but because that is what rational nature intends. This claim may be false, certainly, and it was frequently so regarded in antiquity, but this does not show that the patterns of inference in which it figures are illicit. Stoic appeals to nature's design are not offered in isolation, as it were, but in conjunction with the claim that cosmic nature is itself a paradigmatic expression of rationality.

What is striking, moreover, about the principles that inferences of this form are supposed to support—that it is rational to care for oneself and for others—is their generality. Normative appeals to nature for which there is clear evidence in Stoic sources are hardly derivations of narrowly controversial moral views. The Stoics do not appear to be in the business of deriving narrowly specific social injunctions (e.g., about the best political order, or about human sexuality, or about the status of women, all topics of interest to Stoics early and late), directly from claims about nature.[80] Though they clearly do regard the natural order as the (metaphysical) basis for such injunctions, there is little evidence to suggest that the specific content of the virtues may be filled in, according to Stoic theory, by claims about what is natural. The clear appeals to nature associated with Chrysippus are not intended to support narrowly controversial moral injunctions but to supply broad spheres of obligation with naturalistic foundations. They are, moreover, teleological in character.

At the same time, Stoic ethics clearly does make room for debate about more finely grained principles.[81] Stoic sources defend such principles, however, not by appealing directly to claims about nature but by appealing to conceptions (*ennoiai*) and preconceptions (*prolêpseis*), which may well be evaluative in character, and by

---

[79]For Stoic arguments for this premise, see Cicero, *Nat. d.* 2.29–39. For further Stoic arguments, together with an unsympathetic review of them from an Academic perspective, see *Nat. d.* 3.20–28.

[80]See, e.g., Seneca, *Ep.* 94–95. Cf. Cicero, *Off.* 1.15–161; Ramelli (2009) collects the fragments of Hierocles's ethical treatises with an English translation and commentary. Accounts of Musonius Rufus's lectures are collected in Lutz (1947). Inwood and Gerson (2008) includes useful selections from Musonius, Epictetus, and Seneca (pp. 177–205). Though these Stoic sources certainly identify appropriate action with what accords with nature, they regularly appeal to normative conceptions (*ennoiai*) and preconceptions (*prolêpseis*), and they clearly rely on a teleological account of nature as a whole.

[81]A good deal of recent literature on Stoicism and natural law has focused on the status of rules in Stoic ethics. At issue is the question of whether the Stoics conceive of law as "a deontological system incorporating universal, exceptionless and substantive moral commands" as opposed to "a somewhat looser and more procedural understanding of moral 'law'" (Inwood, 1999, p. 96). Cf., e.g., Mitsis and DiFilippo (1994), Mitsis (1999), and Vander Waerdt (1994).

a dialectical refinement of these starting points.[82] Although the Stoics regard the content of these conceptions as derived from experience and as fixed and explained by the natural order, their methodological approach to specific moral claims does not move narrowly from the factual to the normative. Although nature, Seneca says, has "given us the seeds of knowledge" she "could not have taught us" our "initial conception of the good and honourable."[83] That conception is derived through the operation of analogy (*per analogian*), which draws from our observations of appropriate action in others a likeness or image (*species, imago*), on which the conception (*notitia*) of the good is based.[84] Similarly, according to Cicero, it is through perception of the order and harmony that governs conduct (*agendarum ordo et concordia*) that we acquire an understanding of the human good.[85]

There is no need to assume, then, that Stoic claims about the content of the good life take off from judgments about nature that are value-neutral. The Stoics clearly reserve a preeminent role for ethical and value-laden conceptions, and this methodology seems to underlie many of the fine-grained judgments preserved in Stoic discussions of specific normative principles. It would be a mistake to distinguish too narrowly between these more specific evaluative conceptions and what the Stoics intend in speaking of knowledge of cosmic or common nature, for the Stoics regard the conventionally recognized virtues, wherever they are found, as expressions of nature's rationality and, indeed, as part of the good with a view to which nature as a whole has been organized. Although an understanding of the good is acquired through an experience of the natural order, this order includes the expressions of human virtue on which this understanding is based. Stoic texts give us little reason to suppose that ethical knowledge, as the Stoics conceive it, may be acquired in the absence of normative starting points.

Conclusion

Though the Stoics remain strongly committed to the eudaimonist framework of classical views, their modification of the character and scope of ethical naturalism from within this framework distinguishes their theory in important respects. Stoic naturalism is, in the first place, more thoroughgoing than its

[82]See, e.g., Cicero, *Off.* 3.76; Epictetus, *Diss.* 1.22, 1.28.26–30, 2.11; DL 7.46–7.

[83]*Ep.* 120.4 (trans., Inwood).

[84]Cf. *Off.* 3.16.

[85]*Fin.* 3.21. Cf. 3.33. The order and harmony to which Cicero refers grounds the goodness of both divine and human virtue. The good, as Cleanthes puts it, is "well-ordered, just, holy, pious, self-controlled, useful, honorable, due, austere, candid, always helpful, fearless, undistressed, profitable, unpained, beneficial, contented, secure, friendly, precious, consistent, fair-famed, unpretentious, caring, gentle, keen, patient, faultless, everlasting" (SVF 1.557 = LS 60Q, trans. Long and Sedley).

classical antecedents. Plato and Aristotle challenge the antithesis of nature and convention that had become, by the fifth century, a standard sophistic trope, and they strongly defend the naturalistic basis of justice and the conventionally recognized virtues. Yet both also recognize the legitimacy of some requirements rooted in convention and artifice, where these are understood to contrast meaningfully with the claims of nature. By contrast, the Stoics attack the classical opposition between *nomos* and *phusis* from two directions. On the one hand, they hold that social forms and conventions may be regarded as rational only to the extent to which they accord with nature. Though they do not deny that social convention may sometimes fix or determine the content of ethical requirements, they do deny that such conventions, when they are rationally justified, may be meaningfully contrasted with nature.[86] At the same time, the Stoics characterize nature itself as a rational artisan, identifying both law and artifice, rightly understood, with what is natural in the deepest sense. On the resulting picture nature (*phusis*) is to be contrasted neither with law (*nomos*) nor artifice (*technê*), but is instead regarded as a paradigmatic expression of both.[87]

These claims mark a contrast with, or perhaps an extension of, classical views, but arguably they do not capture the most distinctive or influential features of Stoic ethics. Conjoined to the Stoic claim that virtue is sufficient for happiness, the Stoic commitment to rational eudaimonism implies a striking axiology of virtue and one that anticipates, at points profoundly, later developments in ethical thought. Since Stoic theory admits no final, rational aims distinct from virtue and happiness, the goodness of virtue is non-derivative, on the Stoic account, independent of outcomes external to the agent. The Stoics express this point in their claim that virtue is a "self-sufficing" principle, by which they mean that the value of a virtuous disposition is not derived from any further, distinct outcome (such as health or wealth) it may secure.[88] The activities that flow from a virtuous character are good in virtue of their origin rather than their outcome. Such a picture reverses the axiology of consequentialism and, indeed, of any broadly instrumental analysis of practical reason.[89]

This axiological point, moreover, has a motivational corollary. Since happiness consisting in virtue is the single end of rational desire, no desire for any objective that cannot be realized through one's own agency can be rational, in the

---

[86]Cf. Cicero, *Off.* 3.23; *Leg.* 2.10–11.

[87]When they wish to contrast nature with convention, the Stoics prefer *thesis* rather than *nomos*, thereby preserving their identification of nature and law. See DL 7.128, Stob. *Ecl.* 2.94 (SVF 3.611). Cf. Stob. *Flor.* 3.39.36., translated in Ramelli (2009), pp. 71–73.

[88]Mar. Ant., *Med.* 5.14; Cf. *Fin.* 3.24.

[89]This view would be difficult to defend apart from the Stoics' commitment to a cognitive (i.e., representational) account of motivation. An agent does not act, on the Stoic view, because she possesses a non-cognitive desire for an external object, but wholly on the basis of her assent to evaluative impressions with propositional content.

Stoics' view, and no outcome outside the scope of virtue can be the final focus of a rational agent's motivation. Although the justification for human motivation and action rests upon an appeal to the human *telos*, the Stoic analysis of virtue excludes from an account of the *telos* any additional good at which virtuous action may aim. Here, then, is a respect in which Stoic ethics is non-teleological. Virtuous action is not justified by any contribution to the human good that is distinct from itself, on the Stoic account, but simply by the internal aim of realizing in the actions and decisions of the agent the same principles of rational order that govern the cosmos as whole. This feature of Stoicism aligns the Stoic analysis of virtue with Kant's thesis about the unqualified value of the good will and, indeed, with Kant's analysis of moral motivation.

While Stoic theory did much to solidify the association of *nomos* and *phusis* in the centuries prior to Cicero, what is true of Greek Stoicism does not always emerge clearly or with emphasis in Cicero's treatises. The conceptions of law, divinity, reason, and nature are repeatedly fused in the *De legibus* and *De republica,* and Cicero's treatment of natural law does not carefully distinguish questions about the comparative priority of these conceptions or about the fundamental grounds of obligation in Stoic ethics. If the *eudaimonist* framework of earlier Stoicism is neglected, it becomes easier to regard the prescriptions of natural law not simply as principles to which one must adhere in order to live a life that is happy because rational, but as a source of obligation in their own right. This aspect of Cicero's treatment obscures our view of early Stoicism, but it helps to explain how the doctrine preserved in his accounts inspired later, diverse articulations of natural law theory.

{ PART II }

Medieval Jewish Philosophy

{ 3 }

Natural Law in Judaism

A RECONSIDERATION[1]

Tamar Rudavsky

"Therefore I say that the Law, although it is not natural, enters into what is natural."[2]

Introduction

In his polemical autobiographical work *Example of a Human Life*, written in Latin and published in 1687, the Jewish apostate and heretic Uriel da Costa (b. in Oporto 1583/4, d. in Amsterdam 1640) railed against what he took to be Jewish antagonism to natural law. A converso who contemplated a return to Judaism, da Costa was particularly drawn to Neo-Stoic philosophy and the emphasis of this Humanist movement upon human dignity as expressed through natural law. Describing what he takes to be the virtues of a natural law system, da Costa writes: "I contend nobly in the cause of truth, and assert the natural rights of mankind, whom it becomes [i.e., behooves] to live suitably to the dignity of their nature, free from the burden of superstitions and vain ceremonies." He then castigates the Jews for not recognizing the force of natural law, and for claiming that even a Jew may be denied salvation through the Seven Noahide Laws, which he identifies as a Jewish version of natural law: "by your own confession then, there is one other religion that I may trust in, though I am descended from the Jews [and thus not a "Noachide" but subject to Mosaic law] . . . O thou blind Pharisee, who unmindful of that primary Law which was from the beginning, and will be so to the end of things, only makest mention of other laws of

---

[1]I would like to thank Professor Jonathan Jacobs for sustained comments on earlier versions of this chapter, a draft of which was read at Denison University in 2010. My thanks as well to David Frankel, OSU graduate student, who helped to edit and strengthen several points in this chapter.

[2]Moses Maimonides, *The Guide of the Perplexed*, trans. Shlomo Pines, (Chicago: University of Chicago Press, 1963), p. 382 (II.40).

a latter date, all of which though condemnest except they own [i.e., Mosaic and rabbinic law]." Explaining the natural law, he points out that "Whatever is excellent in the law of Moses or any other institution, it is perfectly contained in the law of nature . . . Now there is nothing in these [laws of Moses] which is not dictated by the laws of nature, and does not entirely agree with that rule of right of reason."[3]

Goldish notes that da Costa's treatment of natural law represents a "brilliant study of an idea originating in pagan antiquity, Christianized during the Middle Ages, gingerly humanized in the Renaissance, and returned to its pagan origins at the hands of a seventeenth-century *converso* rationalist."[4] While we cannot in this chapter explore either the neo-Scholastic underpinnings or the Suarezian influences on da Costa's understanding of natural law, nevertheless da Costa's trenchant criticism, picked up and reflected by his near-contemporary Spinoza, should give us pause: why was natural law such an important topic to somebody like da Costa, who became increasingly repulsed by what he took to be the narrow parochialism of the rabbis? Was he right to suggest that Jewish sources rejected natural law?

My concern in this chapter is to focus our lens upon da Costa's predecessors in the medieval period; doing so will enable us to understand where the Jewish understanding of natural law fits into this extended narrative. One way of approaching this issue is to ask whether there exists a realm of morality independent of *halakha* (Jewish law, both written and oral). Given the ubiquity of *halakha* in practically every aspect of Jewish life, rabbis both modern and ancient have argued over whether *halakha* is all-inclusive, or whether there exists an independent moral standard to which even *halakha* (and the giver of *halakha*, namely God) is beholden.[5] For if *halakha* is the only system providing what we might call "ethical" behavior, then what sense can we make of any natural law theory that imputes the foundation of *nomos* on something other than God? While there may be room for natural law in a theology not ultimately dependent upon divine command, this is not applicable to Judaism, in which case da Costa's characterization of Judaism represents a valid critique.

---

[3]Carl Gebhardt, *Die Schriften des Uriel da Costa: mit Einleitung, Übertragung und Regesten* (Amsterdam: Menno Hertzberger, 1922), pp. 117–19. Cf. Uriel da Costa, *Examination of Pharisaic Traditions: supplemented by Semuel da Silva's Treatise on the Immortality of the Soul*, ed. and trans. H.P. Salomon and I.S.D. Sassoon (Leiden: Brill, 1993), p. 562; Uriel de Costa, *A Specimen of Human Life* (New York: Bergman, 1967), pp. 32–32; quoted in Matt Goldish "Perspectives on Uriel da Costa's Examination of a Life," *Studia Rosenthaliana* (forthcoming).

[4]Goldish, "Perspectives."

[5]This Euthyphro-type conundrum has found contemporary currency in the words of the noted (and controversial) Israeli philosopher Yeshaya Leibowitz, who claimed famously that there is no such thing as Jewish ethics, that there is no law, and that there is no room for any *nomos* beyond divine command. Asa Kasher and Jacob Levinger, *The Yeshayahu Leibowitz Book* [in Hebrew] (Tel Aviv: Tel Aviv University Press, 1977). Leibowitz's claims have obvious implications with respect to the status of natural law in Judaism.

In this paper, I explore whether or not we can locate a natural law theory in medieval Jewish philosophy. While I shall focus primarily upon the status of law in the works of Moses Maimonides (1135/8–1204 CE), attention to Maimonides's predecessors Saadiah Gaon (882–942 CE) and Abraham Ibn Ezra (1089–1164), as well as his successor Joseph Albo (1380–1444 CE), will enable us to situate Maimonides's discussions more fully. First, however, we must clarify the use of the term "natural law" in the context of Jewish philosophical theology by contrasting what Joseph David has termed the "incommensurability thesis" according to which elements in Maimonides's theory are incompatible with natural law, and the "compatibility thesis," which claims that it is plausible to accept them both.[6] I shall argue that while a full-fledged natural law theory in the modern sense is absent in the medieval Jewish tradition, nevertheless we can point to evidence of what I shall term "natural law sentiments" in this tradition. I argue that Maimonides's notion of *mefursamot* (generally accepted opinions), already adumbrated in Saadiah Gaon's work, is critical to his theory of this fledgling natural law.

Is There a Natural Law Tradition in Jewish Thought?

The very process of defining the term natural law is itself rife with problems. Adding to our difficulty is that prior to Joseph Albo, no Jewish philosophers use the actual term "natural law." Albo's work *Book of Principles* (*Sefer ha-'Ikkarim*) is the only medieval Jewish work devoted at least in part to an investigation of the foundation or roots of all kinds of law. While he was one of the very few (if not the only) Jewish philosophers to make use of the term "natural law," Albo's discussion, drawn primarily from Aquinas, is confused at best. Since Aquinas's theory is so well-known, I shall not discuss it in detail except to point out that Aquinas's notion of natural law does incorporate divine command. In his canonical discussion of natural law in the *Summa Theologiae*, Aquinas claims that natural law participates in the eternal law and as such reflects God's providential interaction with human beings: "we call such participation in the eternal law by rational creatures the natural law."[7] In addition to eternal and natural law, Aquinas recognizes both divine and human law: divine law represents the old and new covenants and circumscribes human action in general, while human law is essential for human

---

[6]See Joseph E. David, "Maimonides, Nature and Natural Law," *Journal of Law, Philosophy and Culture*. (forthcoming). David attributes the incommensurability thesis to Marvin Fox and the compatibility thesis to David Novak. See Marvin Fox, "Maimonides and Aquinas on Natural Law," in *Interpreting Maimonides: Studies in Methodology, Metaphysics, and Moral Philosophy* (Chicago: University of Chicago Press, 1990), pp. 124–51; David Novak, *Natural Law in Judaism* (Cambridge: Cambridge University Press, 1998). Novak expresses his thesis in ch. 4, "Maimonides's teleology of the law."

[7]Thomas Aquinas, *Summa Theologica*, trans. Fathers of the English Dominican Province, vol. 2 (Westminster, MD: Christian Classics, 1948), 997 (question 91.2).

survival in society. The precepts of natural law are analogous to those of scientific demonstration in that both sets of precepts are self-evident. The first precept of natural law, to do good and shun evil, is the basis for all subsequent precepts[8] and is the same for all human beings.[9]

Albo adapts portions of Aquinas's discussion and in the fifth chapter of the first part (*ma'amar*) of the *Book of Principles*, Albo turns to the topic of natural law. He starts this chapter by noting that humans are political by nature, and that it is almost necessary for them to be part of a city,[10] but in order to preserve justice and eliminate wrong-doing, humans need what he terms a "natural law." This law is natural in the sense that it is something that humans need as part of their nature. Humans living in a group need a certain modicum of order allowing them to maintain justice; "this order the wise men call natural law (*dat tiv'it*), meaning by natural that is necessary for man by his nature, whether the order emanates from a wise man or a prophet."[11] Albo notes in II.31 that natural law is not sufficient for political society and must therefore be supplemented by a *nomos* or conventional law that enables political life to unfold. The prescriptions of natural law are indispensable for achieving the preservation of the species. Thus by the end of Albo's chapter five, the reader realizes that natural law must be supplemented by conventional law, and chapter six explains that divine law rules all other laws.

In I.7 this notion of natural law is amplified. Albo asserts that there are three kinds of law (*dat*), natural, conventional, and divine, and distinguishes them on the basis of both their establishment and intention: "there are three kinds of law, natural, positive or conventional, and divine. Natural law is the same among all peoples, at all times, and in all places. Positive or conventional is a law ordered by a wise man or men to suit the place and the time and the nature of the persons who are to be controlled by it . . . Divine law is one that is ordered by God through a prophet, like Adam or Noah, or like the custom or law which Abraham taught men, . . . or one that is ordered by God through a messenger whom He sends and through whom He gives a law, like the law of Moses."[12] Albo suggests that natural law is universal in that it applies equally to all humans, times and places, the conventional law takes account of contingencies of place and time, and the divine law is ordered by God through a prophet or messenger (e.g., Adam, Noah, Moses, or Abraham). Albo's conventional law is thus analogous to Aquinas's human law. The reader is left with the impression that natural law serves as the foundation of the other kinds of law, each of which supplements and completes the natural law, but it is not clear from Albo's work what natural law is.

---

[8]Aquinas, *Summa*, 1009ff. (question 94.2).

[9]Aquinas, *Summa*, 1010ff. (question 94.4).

[10]See Joseph Albo, *Sefer Ha-'Ikkarim (Book of Principles)*, ed. and trans. Isaac Husik, 4 vols. (Philadelphia: The Jewish Publication Society of America, 1929), vol. 1, p. 72.

[11]Albo, *Book of Principles*, vol. 1, p. 27.

[12]Albo, *Book of Principles*, vol. 1, p. 78.

Apart from Albo's discussion, the term "natural law" does not appear in Jewish texts. Furthermore, numerous writers have pointed out that the term "nature" does not figure prominently in Jewish legal and philosophical texts. Fox notes that the Hebrew word for "nature" (*ṭeva'*) is not used in the Hebrew Bible or the Mishnah, the first written recording of the Oral Torah.[13] The biblical significance of the trilliteral root *t-b-'*, from which the Hebrew word derives, relates to "sinking" and "signet rings" by extension, as they were produced by the metal sinking into a mold. The word *ṭeva'* did not come to mean "nature" in Hebrew until the famous translator Judah ibn Tibbon (1120–1190) used it systematically as a translation for the Arabic words *ṭabi'ah* and *ṭab'*.[14] These words, which are virtually synonymous in Arabic, also relate to the ancient meaning of "sinking" and "signets," yet the definition changed in early Islamic literature to denote the primary elements of creation. The *mutakallimun*, with whom the Jews of the Geonic period were familiar, used these words to mean "nature" in the sense of a causal agency that brings about the processes of the world's phenomena, an idea which was the heart of much debate.[15] It is clear that Judah ibn Tibbon coined the Hebrew word *ṭeva'* according to the meaning of *ṭabi'ah/ṭab'* in the Islamo-Arabic milieu.

But that does not mean that "nature" as an idea is absent altogether before the Jewish exposure to the Arabic language. Rather, the doctrine of natural law is embedded in a number of related issues, including the nature of nature; the nature of reason itself; the relation between reason and revelation; the function of law; and the relation of law to human nature. Novak, for example, reminds us that the rabbis often refer to "orders of creation" (*sidrei berei'shit*) that are distinguished from singular historical experience (*nes*). The latter are never universal, whereas reasons based on common nature are "inevitably universal."[16] We can find examples of both, he argues, in *halakhah*.

---

[13]Fox, "Maimonides and Aquinas on Natural Law," p. 126. The word *teva'* appears in the Talmud with reference to a coin, wherein its meaning is similar to the biblical word for "ring" (*taba'at*) of the same root. See, for example, Meg. 14b. The Talmud is the earliest attestation of the Hebrew *teva'*. I owe the comments in the following paragraph to my student David Frankel, whose interest in Arabic etymologies led to this material.

[14]See, for example, Saadiah Gaon, *The Book of Beliefs and Opinions*, trans. Samuel Rosenblatt (New Haven, CT: Yale University Press, 1948), p. 41 (I.1). Saadiah disagrees with the notion that there can be multiple earths and multiple heavens because it is "impossible by nature" (Arabic *tab'*; Ibn Tibbon's Heb. *teva'*). Another example occurs in his translation of Judah Ha-Levi's *Kuzari*, wherein we read that the Khazar King admits that the miracles associated with Moses do not belong to the "natural world" (Arabic *tabi'i*; Ibn Tibbon's Heb. *tiv'i*). See Judah Halevi, *Kitab al-Khazari*, trans. Hartwig Hirschfeld (New York: E.P. Dutton, 1905), p. 47 (I.42). Again, I thank David Frankel for this point. For further discussion of the notion of "nature" in Jewish thought, see also Noah J. Efron, "Nature, Human Nature, and Jewish Nature in Early Modern Europe" in *Science in Context* 15(1) 29–49, (2002).

[15]See *Encyclopedia of Islam*, 2nd ed., s.v. Ṭabīa.

[16]David Novak, "Jewish Ethics and Natural Law," *The Journal of Jewish Thought and Philosophy* 5, no. 2 (1996): p. 208.

Compounding our difficulty even further is the recognition that the term "natural law" took on many different meanings in secular (non-Jewish) circles, ranging from Cicero's emphasis upon universality to Suarez's characterization of the infusion of divine light into the human mind. Catherine Wilson notes that the notion of a law of nature appears only rarely in ancient writings, in part because of the distinction in the ancient writings between *physis* and *nomos*, the realms of the natural and the realm of the normative; *nomoi* were viewed not as universal but rather as local and conventional.[17] We find in Plato's *Gorgias* the exact opposite of natural law, according to which the 'law of nature' is presented as the law of superior people whom the majority try to keep in check; Plato contrasts it with "artificial" or conventional law "which we invent and impose upon our fellows."[18] We find a more tempered view of natural law in *Republic* IV.444e in the analogy between health (the natural order in the body) and justice (the natural order of things in the state); and in V.501b where Plato refers to the formal idea of justice as "the just by nature" (*to physei dikaion*).

Several references to "natural law" appear in Aristotle. Aristotle discusses an unchanging, universal law in the *Rhetoric* in the context of giving advice to a lawyer or prosecutor. He distinguishes particular law from universal law, and then suggests that universal law is "the law of nature."[19] Aristotle makes similar comments in *Nicomachean Ethics* V.7 1134b18–1135a4, where he distinguishes natural justice from legal justice, and claims that natural justice is "that which everywhere has the same force and does not exist by people's thinking this or that . . . With us there is something that is just even by nature, yet all of it is changeable; but still some is by nature, some not by nature."

The Stoics introduce divine authority into their conceptions of natural law. Cicero's famous definition of nature in *On the Republic*, brings out its universality and timelessness, as well as the inseparability of reason and nature.[20] But in *The Laws* Cicero identifies the law with the mind of God, making the case for

---

[17]See Catherine Wilson, "From Limits to Laws: The Construction of the Nomological Image of Nature in Early Modern Philosophy," in *Natural Law and Laws of Nature in Early Modern Europe: Jurisprudence, Theology, Moral and Natural Philosophy*, eds. Lorraine Daston and Michael Stolleis (Farnham, UK: Ashgate Publishing Limited, 2008), pp. 13–28.

[18]Plato, *Gorgias*, 483e.

[19]"For there really is, as every one to some extent divines, a natural justice and injustice that is binding on all men . . ." (*Rhetorica* 1,13 1373b 6–17).

[20]See Marcus Tullius Cicero, "On the Commonwealth," in *The Treatises of M.T. Cicero: On the Nature of the Gods; On Divination; On Fate; On the Republic; On the Laws; and On Standing for the Consulship*, ed. and trans. Charles Duke Yonge (London: H.G. Bohn, 1853), p. 360 (III.22). He writes that "true law is right reason conformable to nature, universal, unchangeable, eternal, whose commands urge us to duty, and whose prohibitions restrain us from evil . . . This law cannot be contradicted by any other law, and is not liable either to derogation or abrogation . . . It needs no other expositor and interpreter than our own conscience. It is not one thing at Rome, and another at Athens, one thing today and another tomorrow, but in all times and nations this universal law must for ever reign, eternal and imperishable. It is the sovereign master and emperor of all beings. God himself is its author, its promulgator, its enforcer. And he who does not obey it flies from himself, and does violence to the very nature of man."

a benevolent Providence.[21] The Stoics posited laws of nature in an ethical sense and so laws of nature included obligations to abstain from theft, murder, deviant sexual practices, honoring one's parents, and so on.

While I take it as uncontroversial that ancient conceptions of natural law totally divorced from a providential divine lawgiver do not appear in Jewish texts, this does not mean that natural law theorizing is totally absent. Another way of making this point is to return to the Euthyphro conundrum with which we started, and ask whether any aspects of *halakha* are discoverable by reason alone, or whether they are completely dependent upon God's will. In an attempt to deny an ethic independent of God, Marvin Fox has argued that the vast majority of laws in the Written and Oral Torah are directed at the Israelites alone and further, that these laws were posited at a particular point in time in history and as such they are not universally applicable to all of humanity. Fox argues further that according to Maimonides, the paramount importance of revelation precludes these laws from being known independently of God's revelatory will.[22] More recently, Nadler reiterates the claim that in rabbinic Judaism there is generally no distinction between law and morality. Because there is no independent code of moral behavior distinct from divine law, Nadler claims that there is no natural law, by which he means a universally valid law discoverable by and justified through reason without appeal to God.[23]

In contradistinction to Fox and more recently Nadler, other scholars have offered evidence of, at the very least, a natural morality reflected in both *halakha* itself, as well as in Jewish texts. Thus Lichtenstein makes use of the classic rabbinic passage "If the Torah had not been given, we would have learnt modesty from the cat, [aversion to] robbery from the ant, chastity from the dove, and [conjugal] manners from the cock" to suggest that a cluster of logically ante-halakhic virtues exists and can be inferred from natural phenomena.[24] He carefully distinguishes between natural law (*lex naturalis*) and natural morality, and mentions numerous biblical passages supporting the thesis that the bulk of

---

[21]See Marcus Tullius Cicero, "On the Laws," in *The Treatises of M.T. Cicero: On the Nature of the Gods; On Divination; On Fate; On the Republic; On the Laws; and On Standing for the Consulship*, ed. and trans. Charles Duke Yonge (London: H.G. Bohn, 1853), p. 431 (II.4). He writes: "A certain eternal principle, which governs the entire universe, wisely commanding what is right and prohibiting what is wrong. Therefore they called that aboriginal and supreme law the mind of God, enjoining or forbidding each separate thing in accordance with reason."

[22]See Marvin Fox, "Maimonides's Views on the Relations of Law and Morality," in *Interpreting Maimonides: Studies in Methodology, Metaphysics, and Moral Philosophy* (Chicago: University of Chicago Press, 1990), pp. 199–228.

[23]Nadler suggests that Spinoza is the first to depart from Jewish tradition on this issue. See Steven Nadler, "Baruch Spinoza and the Naturalization of Judaism," in *The Cambridge Companion to Modern Jewish Philosophy*, eds. Michael L. Morgan and Peter Eli Gordon (Cambridge: Cambridge University Press, 2007), pp. 14–34.

[24]Aharon Lichtenstein, "Does Jewish Tradition Recognize an Ethic Independent of Halakha," in *Modern Jewish Ethics: Theory and Practice*, ed. Marvin Fox (Columbus: Ohio State University Press, 1975), 62. Cf. *Sifra*, Aharei-Mot; B. Yoma 67b. Note that Lichtensein quotes it as Eruvin 100b.

revealed Torah could have been naturally and logically discovered. Arguing that at most, the rabbis rejected natural law, not natural morality, he goes on to maintain that "the traditional acceptance of some form of natural morality seems to me beyond doubt."[25] According to Lichtenstein, the notion of *lifnim mishurat hadin* (going beyond the letter/sense of the law) represents in Jewish law the sphere of contextual morality. The contextualist is a nominalist in ethics, arguing that because individual, particular differences are so crucial that no meaningful directives can be formulated to cover them, the halakhic norm must ultimately become situational. Thus while law imposes fixed objective standards, *lifnim mishurat hadin* depends upon individual circumstances and "may vary with the agent."[26]

Perhaps the strongest champion of an ethic independent of *halakha* is David Novak, who has offered a number of arguments in support of natural law theory in Judaism in general, and in Maimonides in particular. His contention is based primarily on a reevaluation of Noahide Law, and the role played by the Noahide commandments in Jewish thought from rabbinic texts onward. Novak argues that the dichotomy between natural law and Torah is apparent rather than real, and that there is an intelligible basis in reason for moral requirements, which is what we call natural law. But what about *halakha*? Novak reminds us that the large bulk of *halakha* comes from human reason, and *not* from divine revelation. According to Novak, then, *halakha* involves natural law factors in its very initiation.

We have, then, many ways of construing the role of law in Jewish thought, ranging from an explicit denial of any law independent of *halakha* to the implicit postulation of natural law theory in Maimonides and other authors. Navigating these waters thus requires providing a much more nuanced articulation of what we mean by natural law. Mark Murphy's recent characterization of natural law emphasizes two criteria, both of which are found in Aquinas's characterization: first, that natural law represents one aspect of God's divine providence, thus recognizing God's role in natural law; and second, that natural law constitutes the principles of practical rationality by which human action is judged as reasonable or unreasonable.[27] Note that according to this characterization, natural law is intertwined with divine law; note further that natural law is universally binding and knowable by human beings. Following Murphy, I shall argue in this chapter that we can locate in our authors a fledgling, or qualified, notion of natural law that is universally binding, reflective of human nature, and accessible to human reasoning. I am not suggesting, pace Novak,

---

[25]Lichtenstein, "Does Jewish Tradition Recognize an Ethic Independent of Halakha?" p. 64.

[26]Lichtenstein, "Does Jewish Tradition Recognize an Ethic Independent of Halakha?" p. 79.

[27]See Mark Murphy, "The Natural Law Tradition in Ethics," in *Stanford Encyclopedia of Philosophy*, ed. Edward N. Zalta, Stanford University, 1997. Article published September 23, 2002. http://plato.stanford.edu/archives/fall2008/entries/natural-law-ethics/.

that our thinkers employed a notion of natural law theory that was totally independent of divine will, but rather, that they were working toward articulating an autonomous sphere of morality that was independent of God's command. Like that of Aquinas, this view is embedded in a theory of divine providential care and command. If I am right, then assessments of Judaic law such as we see in da Costa are misplaced at best, erroneous at worst.

Natural Law and Rationality of the Commandments in Saadiah Gaon

While Albo is the only Jewish philosopher to talk about "natural law" explicitly, other Jewish philosophers did broach the larger topic surrounding the universality of the commandments in the context of trying to ascertain reasons for the commandments. The exercise of trying to provide rational reasons for the commandments (*ta'amei ha-mitzvot*) dates back to rabbinic times, and continued throughout the medieval (into the modern) period. It is based on comments of earlier rabbinic sources, the most famous of which is the following: "And My ordinances you shall practice" (Leviticus 18:4): These are matters written in the Torah which even if they had not been written there, reason would have required that they be written. Some examples: laws prohibiting robbery, laws prohibiting incest, adultery, homosexuality and bestiality, laws prohibiting idolatry and blasphemy, and laws prohibiting shedding human blood (e.g., Sifra Aharei-Mot; B. Yoma 67b). Clearly the rabbis were suggesting that some commandments (in fact the very ones reflected in the Noahide Laws, more on which below) are "inherently" or "intuitively" grounded, and not totally dependent upon divine command.

This sense of an independent grounding for some of the commandments is articulated in a more systematic manner by the tenth-century Jewish philosopher Saadiah Gaon. In *The Book of Beliefs and Opinions [Kitab al-Amanat wa-al-I'tiqadat (Sefer ha-Emunot ve-ha De'ot)]*, a work much influenced by Islamic Kalam epistemology and cosmology, Saadiah distinguished between the rational commandments (*al-shara'i' al-'aqliyyah*; *mitzvoth sikhliyyot*), which in theory are discoverable by means of reason, and the traditional laws (*al-shara'i' al-sam'iyyah*; *mitzvoth shimm'iyot*), which comprise rituals and ceremonial laws (such as the dietary laws) that are not rooted in reason. Saadiah is the first Jewish philosopher to frame his discussion of ethical precepts in the context of rational apprehension. In the introduction to the work, Saadiah distinguishes four sources of reliable knowledge (*'ilm*): sensation (*'ilm al-shahid*; *yedi'at hanir'eh*), reason or nous (*'ilm al-'aql*; *mada' ha-sekhel*), logical inference (*'ilm ma dafa'at al-darura 'ilayhi*; *yedi'at mah sheha-hekhreh mevi elav*), and reliable tradition (*al-khabr al-sadiq*; *ha-hagadah ha-ne'emenet* or *ha-masoret ha-amitit*). Sense knowledge is based on empirical contingents and is posited as the basis for all other knowledge forms, which are rooted in this indubitable epistemic foundation. Reason represents the faculty of immediate, intuitive knowledge by means of which we apprehend self-evident axioms of reason. Reason, Saadiah tells us, emanates ultimately from God, resulting in an innatist theory according to which ideas are "implanted" in the mind—the word "implanted" connotes a source for knowledge that lies outside the realm of human consciousness. In chapter II.13, for example, Saadiah asks how is it possible to establish the concept of God in our minds if we have never seen God, and responds that "it is done in the same manner in which such notions arise in them as the approbation of the truth and the disapproval of lying, although these matters are not subject to the perception of any of our senses."[28] In a similar manner, we are able to "recognize" a violation of the law of non-contradiction, even though it is not based on the senses.

In contradistinction to reason, reliable tradition is not universal, but is common to "the community of monotheists." If however, reason, with the help of this outside source, enables humans to determine both the self-evident axioms and necessary principles of thought, what becomes of tradition? Saadiah relegates to tradition two roles: first, tradition enables us to determine the particulars necessary for observing the more general rational precepts; and second, tradition speeds up the rather tedious process of discovering these rational principles. Thus while reason allows one a limited amount of epistemic authority, tradition with the aid of revelation enables us to achieve salvation. As Jospe points out, what is known in revelation is rational, and in principle is identical to the truth arrived at by rational investigation. Revelation permits us to access truth we could arrive at rationally after a long process.[29]

Based on these epistemological distinctions, the foundations for moral obligation are delineated primarily in Book III, while details on how to achieve the good life are to be found in Book X. The classification of ethical precepts into rational and revelatory is straightforward:[30] rational commandments are those whose "approval" has been implanted in our minds.[31] In other words, humans have an intuitive grasp of the content of these commandments inasmuch as they determine right action. Saadiah further argues that the rational commandments are inherently related to the dictates of reason, and that they represent logical inferences from these dictates.[32] Revelatory commandments, which constitute the second general division of law, are not inherently dependent upon

---

[28]Saadiah Gaon, *The Book of Beliefs and Opinions*, trans. Samuel Rosenblatt (New Haven, CT: Yale University Press, 1948), p. 131 (II.13).

[29]Raphael Jospe, *Jewish Philosophy in the Middle Ages* (Boston: Academic Studies Press, 2009), p. 59.

[30]Let us suspend judgment for the moment on Altmann's suggestion that Saadia wrote this chapter at various intervals of his life, one of which reflects Kalam influence and the other Hellenistic influences. See Alexander Altmann, "Saadya's Conception of the Law," *Bulletin of the John Rylands Library* 28 (1944): pp. 3–24.

[31]See Saadiah, *Book of Beliefs and Opinions*, p. 140 (III.2).

[32]See Saadiah, *Book of Beliefs and Opinions*, p. 106 (II.5); p. 139 (III.1).

the above-mentioned rational dictates, but rather are imposed by God without regard to their inherent rationality. Thus the approbation of these laws implies no more than simple submissiveness to God. As we shall see, however, Saadiah discerns a social utility for nearly all these laws. Thus, Saadiah will want to argue that although these laws are not grounded in reason, nevertheless they may too be justified by rational argument. Saadiah offers many examples (sanctifying certain times rather than others; the dietary laws, etc.) to explicate the overall social utility of the traditional laws.

Working through Saadiah's examples, scholars have uniformly noted the tensions inherent in his presentation: on the one hand Saadiah offers us rational justification that is based on intuition, whereas on the other hand we have a faith-based system grounded in divine revelation.[33] Thus, for example, in Book III Saadiah evinces utilitarian arguments to substantiate the "innateness" of the rational commandments, but these arguments are clearly incompatible with the spirit of rationality he has adduced earlier. Saadiah wants to argue that the approval of certain acts is implanted in our mind/reason, but at the same time his examples all draw from utilitarian arguments. While I agree with critics who highlight the inherent tensions in Saadiah's discussion, I do think it is important to emphasize the overall spirit of Saadiah's attempt to uphold a distinction between the rational and revealed commandments based on the idea that the former have their own intrinsic rationality that, in his opinion, any rational person would recognize.[34] Seen in this light, Saadiah's system incorporates a theory of rational obligation into the rubric of revelatory commandments, thus affecting an attempted synthesis, or at least a reconciliation between reason and revelation. Although I would not describe this attempt as a strict "natural law theory," we can nevertheless acknowledge Saadiah's sustained efforts to articulate the underlying idea that at least some of the commandments are objective, based on human nature, and accessible to human reasoning.

Maimonides on the Reasonableness of the Commandments

Maimonides's analysis of the commandments reflects Saadiah's distinction between rational and ritualistic commandments, but in contradistinction to Saadiah, Maimonides claims that *all* the commandments are rational: both the laws (*mishpatim*) and the statutes (*huqqim*) have beneficial ends, the only difference being that the former are recognizable to all, whereas the latter possess

[33]Altmann has argued that Saadia's position represents a compromise between the Mu'tazilah, who claimed that the rational commandments were commanded because of their inherent goodness, and the Ash'ariyyah, who claimed that the traditional commandments are good because they were commanded. See Altmann, "Saadya's Conception of the Law," pp. 3–24.

[34]Cf. Daniel Rynhold, *An Introduction to Medieval Jewish Philosophy* (London: I. B. Taurus Publishers, 2009), p. 140.

ends that are only manifest to the wise. The laws correspond to Saadiah's rational commandments, while the statutes correspond (in general) to Saadiah's listing of ceremonial laws and rituals. For Maimonides, however, both laws and statutes have a basis in reason.

Aspects of a natural law sentiment can be found throughout Maimonides's work. Maimonides is clear that "governance of the Law is absolute and universal."[35] In *The Guide of the Perplexed* III. 25 Maimonides offers several proofs based on philosophical reasoning for the rationality of law. He argues that to attribute to God non-purposive and non-rational actions, namely laws that are the arbitrary result of God's will, would be blasphemous, for frivolous actions are the most demeaning. Furthermore, he argues that in order to command the respect of the nations of the world, Jewish law must be rational. In an interesting aside, Maimonides claims that were the law not rational, the peoples of the world would not look up to the Jews, and they would lose their standing among the moral peoples.

Turning specifically to the utility of commandments, Maimonides distinguishes between the generalities and the particulars of a commandment. While the generalities of the commandments were given for utilitarian reasons, the particular details may not have the same utilitarian value. While the overall purpose of the particulars is to purify the people,[36] Maimonides castigates those who try to find causes for every particular detail in the laws. Such individuals are stricken with "madness" and "are as far from truth as those who imagine that the generalities of a commandment are not designed with a view to some real utility."[37] In fact, Maimonides goes to great lengths to warn his reader that for some particulars no cause can be found. Why, for example, did the Law prescribe the sacrifice of a ram rather than a lamb? No reason can be given, but one or another particular had to be chosen.

Maimonides argues further that the commandments serve to support social and political beliefs. In an extended passage, Maimonides offers a historical deconstruction of the law.[38] In order to explain the importance of sacrifices, he traces the laws back to Moses's attempts to combat Sabianism. The Sabians were a polytheistic tribe steeped in magic and myth. In the context of refuting the idolatry of the Sabians who "explicitly asserted that the stars are the deity and that the sun is the greatest deity,"[39] Maimonides tells us that the first intention of the Law as a whole is to put an end to idolatry: "it is explicitly stated in the text of the Torah that everything that was regarded by them as worship of their gods and as a way of coming near to them, is hateful and odious to

---

[35]Maimonides, *Guide*, p. 534 (III.34).

[36]See Maimonides, *Guide*, p. 508 (III.26).

[37]Maimonides, *Guide*, p. 509 (III.26).

[38]See Maimonides, *Guide*, pp. 514–22 (III.29); pp. 525–31 (III.32); pp. 540–50 (III.37); pp. 575–92 (III.45–46).

[39]Maimonides, *Guide*, p. 514 (II.29).

God."[40] According to Maimonides's deconstructive analysis, Moses knew that weaning the Israelites would be an arduous task, and so in order to wean the Israelites away from idolatry and sacrifice rituals gradually, the commandments regarding sacrifice were relaxed so as to require sacrifices only to God, the idea being that eventually sacrifices would be abandoned altogether.

Maimonides thus distinguishes two intentions in the mind of God: the first intention is that humans reject idolatry, while God's second intention is the satisfaction of the commandments. Because human nature is inherently fallible, and humans cannot always act in their own best interest, God must occasionally resort to secondary intentions in order to achieve primary goals. Sabianism represents one form of idolatry, but Maimonides knew that because of their corporeal nature, human beings are always tempted by some form of idolatry or other. Even if there had been no Sabianism to combat, presumably God's second intention would have remained inviolable, and so the commandments would have served God's purposes. Let us grant Maimonides the claim that God needed to resort to second intentions in order to achieve God's aims. But ought these rationally graspable and intelligible reasons for the commandments be divulged to the public? Maimonides clearly states that "all laws have causes and were given with a view to some utility."[41] This utility is applicable to both welfare of the soul (achieved by acquisition of true beliefs) and welfare of the body (achieved by practical and moral virtues). Might not the very process of uncovering the reasons for the commandments lead to a sort of philosophical anti-nomianism among the masses, if they were to understand both the causes and goals of particular commandments? Could not this understanding lead to the seductive conclusion that these prescribed actions are dispensable? If the goal of human existence (namely intellectual perfection) can be achieved in a way that does not require performance of the commandments, does that not render the commandments otiose? Maimonides offers no response to this challenge. Perhaps the best he can do is suggest that the laws function in much the same way as does Aristotle's virtuous individual: just as the virtuous individual provides the model for proper human behavior, so too has God provided us a model for proper behavior in the form of commandments. We shall return to this vexing problem below, in the context of the nature of human beings.

The Noahide Commandments: Universalist or Particularist?

I have been preparing the ground for supporting my contention that aspects of a qualified or fledgling natural law theory can be found throughout Maimonides's work. My contention is strengthened further by Maimonides's

---

[40]Maimonides, *Guide*, p. 517 (III.29).

[41]Maimonides, *Guide*, p. 507 (III.26).

discussion of the Noahide Laws. The Noahide laws, discussed in Sanhedrin 56–60 and Melakhim 8:10; 10:12, represent the minimal moral duties enjoined by the Bible upon all human beings: prohibitions of idolatry, blasphemy, bloodshed, sexual sins, theft and eating from a live animal, as well as an injunction to establish a legal system. They are derived ultimately from divine command addressed to Adam (Genesis 2:16) and Noah (Genesis Rabbah 34; Sanhedrin 59b), and are generally regarded by the rabbis as universally applicable. Do these Noahide laws present a natural law underpinning to Jewish thought? In Yoma 67b we have the suggestion that "they would have been made mandatory even had they not been revealed," thus suggesting a universally applicable, natural component. Further, the fact that six of the laws were revealed to Adam suggests a universalistic thrust.[42]

According to Maimonides, Noahides must not only accept these seven laws, but must accept them as divinely revealed. In *Kings* 8.11, Maimonides has the following to say:

> A heathen who accepts the seven commandments and observes them scrupulously is a "righteous heathen" and will have a portion in the world to come, provided that he accepts them and performs them because the Holy One, blessed be He, commanded them in the Law and made known through Moses, our teacher, that the observance thereof had been enjoined upon the descendants of Noah even before the Law was given. But if his observance thereof is based upon a reasoned conclusion he is not deemed a resident alien, or one of the pious of the gentiles, but one of their wise men.[43]

In this text Maimonides appears to distinguish between those (gentile) individuals who accept and perform righteous actions because God commanded them, and those who perform those commandments on the basis of "a reasoned conclusion." But Maimonides's text on this point is ambiguous, and subsequent editions have incorporated different variations (differing in one letter only) of the last sentence: did Maimonides say "but (*ela*) one of their wise men," or did he say "nor (*ve-lo*) one of their wise men"? On the former, more inclusive reading, a person who does not recognize divine authority of the Noahide commandments is still considered a wise man, while on the latter more restrictive reading, it is not enough simply to recognize and to perform these seven Noahide commandments; a truly righteous gentile must perform them out of acknowledgement that they were divinely revealed. The second interpretation of this passage is less supportive of a natural law reading, suggesting possibly that ethics are not natural, but must be embedded in a theological framework. But

---

[42]Gen R. 16:6; 24:5.

[43]Moses Maimonides, "Kings and Wars," in *A Maimonides Reader*, ed. Isadore Twersky (New York: Behrman House, 1972), p. 221.

as Kellner has recently pointed out, the latter reading of Kings 8.11 is technically inconsistent with everything else Maimonides has said about intellectual perfection. The very fact that Maimonides recognizes that these laws *can* be ascertained independently of divine command lends credence to my thesis that this passage supports a natural law reading. As I shall discuss in the end of this paper, Maimonides has advocated repeatedly that one's portion in the world to come depends upon one's intellectual perfection, and so on my and Kellner's reading, any person (Jew or gentile) whose intellect is truly perfected will recognize the ultimate divinity of law, and so will be included in the world to come.[44] In other words, even one who does recognize the wisdom of Torah is not (*ve-lo*) necessarily wise.

Conventionalism, "*Mefursamot*," and Natural Law

One possible counterargument to my position arises from several passages in the *Guide* that appear to impute to Maimonides a conventionalist morality that precludes natural law: *Guide* I.2 having to do with knowledge of good and evil; *Guide* II:33 having to do with the Decalogue; and Maimonides's discussion of moral weakness in the *Eight Chapters*. All three passages make use of the notion *mefursamot* (Arabic *mashhurat*) or "generally accepted notions," and reflect Maimonides's distinction in his *Treatise on the Art of Logic*, between four kinds of premises upon which arguments are based: sense percepts (*ha-muhashim*); first intelligibles or axioms (*ha-muskalot*); generally agreed upon opinions (*ha-mefursamot*); and opinions received through tradition (*hamequbalot*). Of these four, only demonstrative arguments or syllogisms (*ha-heqqesh ha-mofti*) based on "first intelligibles" are productive of scientific knowledge; these must rest on premises that are true and available to everybody. Maimonides here defines a demonstrative syllogism as one whose premises are certain. "*Mefursamot*," a translation of the Greek *ta endoxa*, (those universal moral beliefs accepted by all), have a rational basis weaker than demonstration and yet stronger than tradition; they play an important role in Maimonides's conception of moral principles. Maimonides's distinction reflects Saadiah's earlier epistemological taxonomy, with the important difference that for Saadiah, tradition comprises both the commonality of opinion among monotheists as well as a basic level of argumentation, whereas Maimonides separates these two. Thus Maimonides's *mefursamot* lie between Saadiah's tradition and reason.

---

[44]Note that in 1991 Kellner wrote: "I have no intention of getting involved in the question of whether or not Maimonides adopted some theory or other of natural law. The question itself is in grave danger of being anachronistic." See Menachem Kellner, *Maimonides on Judaism and the Jewish People* (Albany, NY: SUNY Press, 1991), p. 76. He returns to the issue in Menachem Kellner, *Maimonides's Confrontation with Mysticism* (Oxford: The Littman Library of Jewish Civilization, 2006), pp. 247–64.

Based on these four types of reasoning, Maimonides distinguishes in *Eight Chapters* between two types of virtue: rational and moral. Rational virtues include wisdom and intelligence, which in turn comprise theoretical intellect, acquired intellect, and what he calls "brilliance and excellent comprehension" or intuition.[45] Moral virtues are found in the appetitive part of the soul, not the rational part, and include a number of characteristics: moderation, liberality, justice, gentleness, humility, contentment, and courage. Maimonides maintains a sharp distinction between intellect and imagination, arguing that this distinction allows a further parallel between true/false on the one hand, and good/evil on the other. It is by virtue of the imagination alone, he argues, that we fall into error.[46]

This separation between intellectual and moral virtues raises a concern about the epistemological status of ethical knowledge.[47] Maimonides uses the story of Adam and Eve to argue that good and evil, as opposed to truth and falsity, are not intellectual concepts but rather notions that arise as a result of the act of the imagination. Maimonides relegates knowledge of good and evil to the level of "popularly accepted notions": "Through the intellect one distinguishes between truth and falsehood, and that was found in [Adam] in its perfection and integrity. Fine and bad [good and evil], on the other hand, belong to the things generally accepted as known (*mefursamot*), not to those cognized by the intellect."[48] From a metaethical perspective, the terms "good" and "evil" have no definitive meaning and can be contrasted with the propositions of mathematics and physics, which we can come to know through the science of demonstration. Theoretically, an individual ruled entirely by intellect would not even entertain notions of good and evil (a point to which we return at the end of this paper).[49]

What do we make then of the fact that only after Adam and Eve ate from the tree of knowledge did they come to know (as opposed to see) that they were naked? Maimonides points out that even in his original pre-lapsarian state, Adam was given a "law" that was "imposed upon him on account of his intellect." However, in this most perfect state, Adam was not concerned with "generally accepted

---

45 Moses Maimonides, "Eight Chapters," in *Ethical Writings of Maimonides*, trans. Charles E. Butterworth and Raymond L. Weiss (New York: New York University Press, 1975), 65. See especially ch. 2.

46 See Maimonides, *Guide*, pp. 23–26 (I.2).

47 For discussion of this difficulty, see Isadore Twersky, *Introduction to the Code of Maimonides (Mishneh Torah)* (New Haven: Yale University Press, 1980), pp. 453–59; Menachem Kellner, *Maimonides on Human Perfection* (Atlanta, GA: Scholars Press, 1990); Fox, "Maimonides and Aquinas on Natural Law," pp. 93–151; Shlomo Pines, "Truth and Falsehood Versus Good and Evil," in *Studies in Maimonides*, ed. Isadore Twersky (Cambridge, MA: Harvard University Press, 1990), pp. 95–157; David Shatz, "Maimonides's Moral Theory," in *The Cambridge Companion to Maimonides*, ed. Kenneth Seeskin (Cambridge: Cambridge University Press, 2005), pp. 167–93.

48 See Maimonides, *Guide*, pp. 23–26 (I.2).

49 See Warren Zev Harvey, "A Portrait of Spinoza as a Maimonidean," *Journal of the History of Philosophy* 19 (1981): pp. 151–72.

things" and so such matters, even one "most manifestly bad, namely, uncovering the genitals, was not bad according to him, and he did not apprehend that it was bad."[50] Only after eating from the tree did Adam become "endowed with the faculty of apprehending generally accepted things," and only then was he able to recognize that some things are good and others bad.[51]

Clearly, the pre-lapsarian Adam had no need for practical reasoning, and was fully engaged in intellectual speculation. But this still does not explain the inherent 'badness' of exposing the genitals: How did Adam (and Eve) *know* that nakedness was wrong if there is no indication in the text that God told them that nakedness is wrong? Although Maimonides does not say so explicitly, Adam's recognition of the badness of this action suggests an innate or intuitive understanding independent of God's command. Consider that one of the examples given in the *Treatise on Logic* of the "generally agreed upon opinions (*ha-mefursamot*)" is that "uncovering the privy parts is ugly, or that compensating a benefactor generously is beautiful." Maimonides's point, rooted in his overall antipathy towards the corporeality of matter and the human body, is that any rational person should and would intuitively come to know that uncovering the genitals represents inappropriate behavior.[52] Maimonides is not telling us (pace Fox) that ethical precepts are conventional: he is simply reiterating the distinction made in the *Eight Chapters* between rational and moral virtue, and reminding us that while pre-lapsarian Adam had only the first, after the fall he acquired a moral faculty as well.[53]

A second passage has to do with Maimonides's comments about the Decalogue itself. The Decalogue appears twice in the Scriptures, in Exodus 20 and in Deuteronomy 5, and is interpreted differently throughout Jewish thought. For one thing, the first two statements of the Decalogue "I am the Lord your God" and "Have no other gods before me" are expressed in the first person, while in the other commandments, Moses is the speaker. This stylistic difference gave rise to the midrashic interpretation that while the entire people of Israel heard only the first two commandments directly from God, the subsequent

[50]To paraphrase Oliver Leaman, the question of how Adam ought to dress is simply not the sort of question to be asked by somebody at the pinnacle of his human intellectual powers, since it is not a question to which a definitive, determinate answer can be given. See Oliver Leaman, *Moses Maimonides* (London: Routledge Press, 1990), p. 82.

[51]Maimonides, *Guide*, p. 25 (I.2).

[52]For an extended discussion of Maimonides's antipathy toward matter, corporeality, and human bodies, see T. M. Rudavsky, *Maimonides* (Malden, MA: Wiley-Blackwell, 2010). This antipathy is particularly interesting inasmuch as Maimonides was a medical doctor and devoted his life toward curing bodily ills.

[53]For a similar reading of this passage, see Michael P. Levine, "The Role of Reason in the Ethics of Maimonides: or, Why Maimonides Could Have Had a Doctrine of Natural Law Even if He Did Not," *The Journal of Religious Ethics* 14, no. 2 (Fall 1986): p. 287. Levine points out that Adam was non-moral despite his intellectual abilities, and that the faculty of judging things to be good or bad was not endowed until after the Fall. See also Twersky, *A Maimonides Reader*, p. 458.

eight commandments were mediated by Moses.[54] Ibn Ezra for example, in his commentary to Exodus, suggested that the first version reflected the actual record of the revelation at Sinai, while the second version was Moses's paraphrase of the event forty years later.[55] According to Ibn Ezra, rational laws are those that God has implanted into the minds of all intelligent human beings. Other commandments, what Ibn Ezra calls "hidden commandments," do not contradict reason, although their meaning or purpose may not be obvious. All but one of the ten commandments (he exempts the commandment to honor the Sabbath) are universally comprehensible and rational: "every intelligent human being of every nation and of every tongue assents to them, for they are implanted in the human mind by reason."[56] The first commandment "I am the Lord thy God" functions as the basis for the subsequent nine and emphasizes the importance of coming to know God by learning the ways of God, presumably by studying nature.[57]

Maimonides's analysis in *Guide* II.33 follows in Ibn Ezra's tradition. Maimonides claims that the first two commandments reflect demonstrable truths capable of being understood and acquired by anybody with rational demonstration. Falling under the category of intelligible propositions or "*muskalot*" (Arabic *ma'qulat*), these first two commandments are accessible equally to all humans through reason, and do not depend upon prophetic revelation: "these two principles are not known through prophecy alone."[58] The other eight commandments "belong to the class of generally accepted opinions and those adopted in virtue of tradition, not to the class of the intellect."[59]

Fox maintains that "it is difficult to imagine a more categorical rejection of natural law theory than that contained in this passage," and claims that the last eight commandments reflect "merely conventions."[60] But Fox has missed Maimonides's point here, namely that these laws comprise the content of practical as opposed to demonstrative reason. These conventions or *mefursamot* are rooted in human nature itself, and thus are part of the natural order. Once again, Maimonides's point is that the last eight commandments are not arbitrary, but that these are the very actions that any rational person would expect a lawgiver to command or prohibit. Further, it is important to note that Maimonides states explicitly that the first two commandments are "first intelligibles" and can be fully understood through the intellect.

---

[54]See Jospe, *Jewish Philosophy*, p. 483.

[55]See Ibn Ezra's *Commentary to Exodus* 20:2 in Abraham Ibn Ezra, *Commentary on the Pentateuch: Exodus (Shemot)*, trans. H. Norman Strickman and Arthur M. Silver (New York: Menorah Publishing Company, Inc., 1996), pp. 393–446.

[56]Ibn Ezra, *Commentary to Exodus*, p. 408.

[57]See Ibn Ezra, *Commentary to Exodus*, p. 412.

[58]Maimonides, *Guide*, p. 364 (II.33).

[59]Maimonides, *Guide*, p. 364 (II.33).

[60]Fox, "Maimonides and Aquinas on Natural Law," p. 139.

Compare Maimonides's comments with Aquinas's claim that the moral commands found in the second tablet are part of natural law theory and not dispensable even in the case of miracles. Contrast, further, Aquinas's views with those of Scotus, who argues that they are not part of natural law theory directly. For Scotus only the first two commandments found in the first tablet pertain to the natural law because they are unchangeable and universally valid maxims. They refer to necessary propositions about the love of God and follow analytically from the concept of the essence of God.[61] Albo follows Aquinas's lead and argues that the laws of the second table of commandments (having to do with prohibitions against murder, theft, adultery, false witness, and covetousness) are all parts of natural law and are essential to human perfection in the polis.[62] Thus while our thinkers disagree over *which* of the commandments are universally accessible through reason, all agree that at least some of the commandments are either part of natural law (Aquinas, Scotus, and Albo), or first intelligibles (Maimonides), or rational laws implanted in the minds of all humans (Maimonides, Ibn Ezra).

Our final passage has to do with Maimonides's discussion of moral weakness. Both Al-Farabi and Maimonides reflect Aristotle's discussion of *akrasia* in *Nicomachean Ethics* 7.2, and attempt to explain why it is that often we choose knowingly to sin, or not follow the law.[63] Maimonides's discussion (which picks up on al-Farabi's lead in distinguishing different types of moral agents), occurs in the context of the following rabbinic query: who is superior—the innately righteous person who never desires to sin, or the one who achieves righteousness by prolonged discipline or self-control? In *Mishneh Torah* 7.4, Maimonides supports the rabbinic view (against Aristotle) that one who has struggled with and overcome the evil impulse is more perfect morally than one who has no such impulses.[64] But in the sixth chapter of his short ethical work *Eight Chapters*, Maimonides acknowledges the conflict between the religious and philosophical views, and describes the difference between the continent and the virtuous individual in terms of desires: while the virtuous agent performs those actions that his "desire and the state of his soul arouse him to do," both desiring and acting upon virtuous actions, the continent agent performs virtuous actions "while craving and strongly desiring to perform bad actions."[65] According

---

[61]For more detailed discussions of Aquinas and Scotus, see the articles by Lisska and Cross, respectively, in this volume.

[62]Albo, *Book of Principles*, vol. 3, p. 246.

[63]For al-Farabi's discussion and Maimonides's use of it, see Herbert A. Davidson, "Maimonides's Shemonah Peraqim and Alfarabi's Fusūl al-Madanī," *Proceedings of the American Academy for Jewish Research* 31 (1963): pp. 33–50.

[64]"The penitent should not imagine himself to be removed from the rank of the righteous on account of the iniquities and sins he has committed. Not so! He is beloved and cherished in the Creator's eyes, and is as if he had never sinned. Indeed, his reward is greater, for he savored sin yet desisted and conquered his evil impulse." (Maimonides "Book of Knoweldge" 7:4).

[65]Maimonides, "Eight Chapters," p. 78.

to Maimonides, the philosophers claimed that the virtuous individual is more perfect than the continent one, but the sages claimed that somebody who craves vice, and overcomes the desire in favor of virtue, is more perfect than someone "who does not crave them and suffers no pain in abstaining from them."[66] In this work he sides against the Sages and with the philosophers who maintained that the virtuous person who does not crave bad actions is superior to the continent individual.

In order to harmonize the two positions, Maimonides suggests that while the view of the philosophers refers primarily to *mefursamot*, namely those universal moral actions that all people recognize, the sages have in mind only traditional (or ceremonial) prohibitions:

> Both of them are true, and there is no conflict between them at all. For the bad things to which the philosophers referred when they said that someone who does not desire them is more virtuous than someone who does desire them and restrains himself—these are the things generally accepted (*ha-mefursamot*) by all the people as bad, such as murder, theft, robbery, fraud, harming an innocent man, repaying a benefactor with evil, degrading parents, and things like these . . . When the sages said that the continent man is more virtuous and his reward is greater, they had in mind the traditional laws."[67]

Since these traditional prohibitions are established only by divine legislation and not recognized universally, it is only the *mefursamot* that we would expect everybody to recognize and adhere to without struggle. Maimonides acknowledges that violating the ceremonial laws is "bad" only because they have been commanded, and not because of any intrinsic or universal value.[68]

Maimonides's discussion of moral weakness thus underscores the point made at the beginning of the *Guide* in I.2. We saw that Maimonides argues that good and evil, as opposed to true and false, are not intellectual concepts, but rather are notions that arise as a result of the act of the imagination.[69] In saying this, Maimonides is describing the use of the word in ordinary language, and not anything more objective than that. The question of what things conform to our intent turns out to be based on our physical differences qua human beings: "The cause [of the difference between individuals] is the difference of temperament."[70] While the subjectivity of moral terms can be contrasted with the propositions of mathematics and physics, which we can know through the science of

---

[66]Maimonides, "Eight Chapters," p. 79.

[67]Maimonides, "Eight Chapters," pp. 79–80.

[68]Note that other Jewish philosophers (e.g., Bahya ibn Paquda) opted for the opposite position. See Bahya ibn Paquda, *Duties of the Heart*, trans. Daniel Haberman, 2 vols. (New York: Feldheim, 1996).

[69]See also Maimonides, *Guide*, pp. 23–26 (I.2); p. 354 (II.30); pp. 363–63 (II.33); pp. 438–40 (III.10); pp. 441–48 (III.12); p. 453 (III.13).

[70]Maimonides, *Guide*, p. 381 (II.40).

demonstration, nevertheless our nature qua humans guarantees that we all recognize certain actions to be intrinsically choiceworthy and others not.

Conclusion: Nature, Law and Human Perfection

I have presented a view of Maimonides, rooted in his philosophical forebears Saadiah Gaon and Ibn Ezra, according to which humans have an intuitive sense of what is right and wrong; this intuitive sense is reflected in the commandments and supported by generally accepted opinions. Further, by a careful reasoning process, we can often uncover the inherent rationality of the laws. On this reading, Maimonides's emphasis on generally accepted opinions does not amount to conventionalism but rather is rooted in a carefully delineated philosophical anthropology. Part of Maimonides's understanding of the *mefursamot* has to do with understanding our nature as human beings. This understanding incorporates both moral and intellectual perfection, and it is reflective of our nature *qua* both corporeal and spiritual beings. Welfare of the soul and body reflect perfections of the body and the soul respectively. Bodily perfection is dependent upon achieving physical health and the best bodily state, both of which are dependent upon living in society. But perfection of the soul, although it does not pertain to moral qualities, nevertheless is dependent upon achievement of bodily perfection, for one cannot achieve intellectual perfection when "he is in pain or is very hungry or is thirsty or is hot or is very cold."[71] Welfare of the soul consists in the multitude's acquiring correct opinions, whereas welfare of the body comprises the improvement of ways of living one with another, by acquiring moral qualities that are useful for life in society.[72] Of the two types of welfare, the former, Maimonides argues, is nobler than the latter. As I have argued in this paper, halakhic law is reflective of the latter, while natural law falls into the domain of the former.

Once again, however, scholars have noted a tension in Maimonides's characterization of human perfection in terms of praxis or theoria, a tension that goes back to Aristotle's *Ethics*, and is reflective of Maimonides's attitude toward a natural law sentiment that transcends the Law. On the one hand, Maimonides is quite explicit that humans are fundamentally social creatures—"man is political by nature and that it is his nature to live in society."[73] Speaking of the ways in which we perfect ourselves, he tells us that the first perfection "consists in being healthy and in the other things needed for the governance of his body such as shelter, bathing, and so forth. This cannot be achieved in any way by

[71]Maimonides, *Guide*, p. 511 (III.27).

[72]Maimonides, *Guide*, p. 510 (III.27).

[73]Maimonides, *Guide*, p. 381 (II.40). For detailed discussion of the scholarly dispute, see Rudavsky *Maimonides*.

one isolated individual. For an individual can only attain all this through a political association it already being known that man is political by nature."[74] The *nomos* is thus intended to foster human flourishing in a social and political context. The task of the ruler is to provide for a well-oiled society, one in which both actions and moral habits are practiced in the same way.

On the other hand, Maimonides argues that the end of human existence is intellectual perfection, and that whatever directs us toward that ultimate goal is good. Maimonides's vision of human perfection in terms of intellectual cognition is expressed at the very end of the *Guide*.[75] In his famous parable of the palace, Maimonides suggests that only those scholars who engage in speculation (demonstrative science or philosophy) can gain entrance to the antechambers of the palace, and only knowledge of physics and metaphysics can guarantee entrance to the inner court and knowledge of the king. Note that the king is not synonymous with God, but represents "the intellect that overflows toward us and is the bond between us and Him, may He be exalted."[76] True perfection consists in union with this king, who functions as the gatekeeper as it were to God. The ultimate purpose of the commandments is to achieve union with God, as well as to inculcate us with both love and fear of God. Maimonides thus returns to the motif articulated in Aristotle's *De Anima* 3.5, arguing that intellectuality alone allows for ultimate communication between supreme divine thought and the human being. Intellectual perfection is the only way to reach God, but this union can only occur through the Active Intellect, which is exemplified by the king.

One who possesses moral virtues—the *hasid*—is clearly held in high esteem by the multitude. However, given Maimonides's rejection of the view of the "masses" in so many other contexts, we can only expect that Maimonides will not concur with the multitude on this point. In fact, Maimonides claims that the commandments do not compare with intellectual perfection: "all the actions prescribed by the Law—I refer to the various species of worship and also the moral habits that are useful to all people in their mutual dealings—that all this is not to be compared with this ultimate end, and does not equal it, being but preparations made for the sake of this end."[77] In this remarkable passage, Maimonides is suggesting that the purpose of the commandments has little to do with intellectual perfection, which is the true aim of human existence; the commandments only serve an instrumental purpose, enabling people to interact in a social situation. Once again, conventional norms accede to a higher, intuitive yet rational mode of comportment.

Moral perfection in Maimonides's scheme cannot be supreme, since the ultimate perfection must be achievable even by a solitary individual with no social

---

[74]Maimonides, *Guide*, p. 511 (III.27).
[75]See Maimonides, *Guide*, pp. 632–38 (III:54).
[76]Maimonides, *Guide*, p. 628 (III.52).
[77]Maimonides, *Guide*, p. 636 (III.54).

interaction, and Maimonides is adamant that the law does not apply to isolated individuals who live the life of contemplation: "to this ultimate perfection there do not belong either actions or moral qualities."[78] Because moral values are rooted in and reflect decision-making in particular situations, the highest moral knowledge must derive from intellectual knowledge.[79] Reflecting the Platonic dictum in the Euthyphro that the gods command pious acts because they are pious, Maimonides is suggesting that there exists a rational, autonomous nature of what is right: these actions have been commanded because they are intrinsically good and right (justly balanced), and can be ascertained independently of *halakha*. One who has achieved intellectual perfection, and surpassed corporeality, has transcended the need for the commandments. But this does not mean that such a person is amoral.[80] Unlike Adam, who had no conventional moral sense in his pre-lapsarian state, the truly perfect individual has incorporated the universally recognizable moral concerns into the intellectual.

Let us return, finally, to Uriel da Costa, with whose castigation of the rabbis we started this study. I maintain that da Costa was wrong-headed in his assessment of what he took to be the narrow parochialism of the rabbis. Maimonides, along with his medieval forebears, recognized a law of nature, one that agreed with the "rule of right of reason." Thus, on the reading I have presented, medieval Jewish philosophers, drawing upon ingredients found already in rabbinic sources, were moving toward a natural law theory according to which moral truths are universally binding, reflective of our human nature, and accessible to human reasoning.

---

[78]Maimonides, *Guide*, p. 511 (III.27).

[79]Maimonides's early work *Character Traits* 1:3 and 1:4 is saturated with normative language—the good and right way that ought to be followed. Reflecting Aristotle, Maimonides provides rational reasons to follow these norms, namely to be a completed person, and then follows up with *halakhic* reasons, telling us that "we have been commanded to follow these justly balanced ways." Maimonides, "Laws Concerning Character Traits," I:5.

[80]For an extended discussion of this point, see Shatz, "Maimonides's Moral Theory," pp. 167–93.

{ 4 }

The Reasons of the Commandments

RATIONAL TRADITION WITHOUT NATURAL LAW

Jonathan A. Jacobs

Natural law theorizing had no explicit presence in medieval Jewish thought, and ascertaining why that is so can illuminate both Jewish thought and natural law. The issue is not quite, 'why was there no natural law theorizing in medieval Jewish thought?' but, 'what were the main features of medieval Jewish thought and what do they suggest about why natural law theorizing did not figure in it?' Given the Greek inheritance that Jewish and Christian philosophy shared, and given important, shared features of Abrahamic monotheism, the question of why Jewish philosophy developed so differently from Christian philosophy is of wider significance than as an internal matter for Jewish thought.

My approach to the question, as it concerns natural law, focuses on how some important Jewish philosophers understood the issue of 'the reasons of the commandments' and the accompanying conception of tradition and its epistemic role. The issue of 'the reasons of the commandments' concerned the rational justifications of the commandments in Torah, traditionally thought to number six hundred and thirteen. Examining the view in question will highlight some of the main elements of the metaethics of an important rationalistic current of medieval Jewish thought. That, in turn, will help us see why natural law theorizing did not have a place in it. It will also show some of the respects in which features of medieval Jewish moral thought are relevant beyond its own tradition.

The relevant current of thought is one in which the rational justifications of ethical requirements are elaborated progressively through leading life in accord with tradition, understood in a specific way. The view maintains that reflection upon tradition is *part* of fulfilling its requirements, and that what I shall call the 'non-evident rationality' of ethical considerations is partly constitutive of the tradition. This current of thought combines a rationalist disposition with a kind of intellectual humility. For present purposes, the main point is to see how the view is distinct from practical wisdom approaches and from natural law approaches. To be sure, aspects of it appear apt for interpretation in terms of natural law, and some recent Jewish thinkers argue that there are significant natural law elements in medieval Jewish thought. (Professor Rudavsky's chapter in this volume makes a case for that view.) I am not especially anxious to distance this view of tradition from natural law. I am more concerned to show how and why it is especially illuminating to understand the view in its distinctive terms, and those do not, I believe, involve natural law elements.

Saadia and Maimonides are particularly important figures in the development of the view on which I am focusing. Both held that the commandments are rationally justified but that, for a great many of them, their justifications are not evident and we may not be able to ascertain them in their full detail. Still, we are to regard the commandments as flowing from God's wisdom and benevolence and, as such, none of them is a test of blind or thoughtless obedience. Moreover, fulfilling the commandments puts us in a position to be able to understand their justifications. Understanding and ethically virtuous activity interact in a spiral of mutual reinforcement.

Before proceeding to develop the account, we might ask why it should matter whether we categorize this or that approach to moral thought as a natural law approach? One reason is that if an approach is a version of natural law, then it contains resources for explicating how its requirements reflect universal, objective values. It can respond to the objection that it is confined in its scope to just one particular tradition, people, or culture. Historically, one of the more familiar criticisms of Jewish moral thought is that it lacks universal scope. The universality issue is connected with the rationality issue. The universality of natural law is grounded in rational considerations that hold in the same way for all human beings. We will need to see if the view to be discussed has resources with which to reply to the objection that its values are not objective or universal.

Some General Comments about Natural Law

Natural law theorizing exhibits considerable diversity. Scotist natural law differs from Thomist natural law in important respects, and both Thomist and Scotist natural law differ from ancient Stoic conceptions and many early modern approaches. The latter tended to assign a role to rational agreement or the agent's endorsement of principles in a way that was not part of the medieval view. This was connected with the fact that much early modern theorizing tended to take an agent's conception of his *interest* as centrally important. In some respects, the notion of a rational individual's end was replaced by the notion of a rational individual's interest. (This could be described as a transition from a central concern with the conception of the objectively right, to a concern with the conception of subjective rights.)

That contrast is a simplification but it is accurate in an important way. At least for Hobbes and Locke the agreement into which agents enter as part of leaving the state of nature and transitioning into the civil condition involves them recognizing that it is rational to give up some of their natural liberty for the advantages of being in the civil condition. In Grotius's conception as well, natural law involves principles supplying a normatively authoritative resolution of certain kinds of conflict and insecurity. The medievals were less inclined to appeal to natural law as a strategy for resolving fundamental *problems* such as disagreement, conflict, and insecurity. That is a different way of formulating the significance of the authority of natural law. In both cases, natural law's application is based upon it being rationally authoritative but each is a different mode of application of that authority.

There is no question that medieval natural law owed a great deal to ancient roots and sources, especially Greek and Hellenistic notions of the world as an intelligible order. Medieval Jewish philosophy appropriated a great deal of Neoplatonism and Aristotelianism and while there are also some likenesses between some Jewish moral psychology and Stoic moral psychology, there does not appear to have been direct influence. Also, the predominant philosophical influences on medieval Jewish thought came through Islam rather than the Latin world and there is not a clearly recognizable natural law tradition in Islam. Moreover, the Neoplatonism and Aristotelianism appropriated by Jewish thinkers was modified in significant ways. For instance, Maimonides employs much of Aristotle's ethical idiom but makes some very unAristotelian claims. This is true of Christian thought, too, but in different ways, to be discussed below. (One especially prominent topical area in which the faith-traditions departed from Aristotle has to do with repentance and the possibility of ethical re-orientation, even in a mature agent with seemingly settled dispositions.)

Despite the considerable diversity of conceptions of natural law, the core notion most relevant to the present discussion is roughly that *there are fundamental practical principles accessible to and applicable to all human beings, those principles enabling persons to reason rightly and to act such that good is realized.*

The characterization does not make reference to the derivation of practical principles from anthropological considerations. That is, it does not say that those practical principles are based upon facts about the human *telos*. The characterization is meant to apply as well to views maintaining that there are principles known to practical reason without being *derived* from facts about the *telos* of human nature. (Aquinas's theory of natural law has been interpreted in both ways.) In the second interpretation the goods recognized by reason are not comprehended *first* by theoretical reason, with practical principles then being inferred from what theoretical reason informs us about human good. Instead, practical reason recognizes certain goods directly and formulates appropriate principles of right action without the need for any (allegedly problematic) derivation from theoretical reason's 'input.' Still, this is a view in which objective, universal considerations of human good are known by reason.

Both the anthropological-teleological conception and the 'goods evident to practical reason' conception count as natural law approaches. They both maintain that there are universal principles for shaping the reasoned actions through which objective good can be actualized. This holds even for the non-anthropological approach because the goods evident to practical reason are goods for a nature such as ours. They may not be derived from facts about our nature but they are appropriate to it. Even when practical principles are not derived from facts about human nature the rightness of those principles reflects truths about goods for human beings.

The characterization above may seem too narrow. Does it capture and express Scotus's conception of natural law as constituting principles concerning duties to God? Scotus's conception of natural law does not include broadly Aristotelian considerations of human good in the way Aquinas's conception does. Scotus's principles of natural law are few in number and they concern matters indicated in the first table of the Decalogue, matters of the gratitude and obedience owed to God. The rest of what is ethically required is 'exceedingly in harmony' with that small number of rationally evident requirements but not derived from them. The characterization does apply to Scotus's conception because what we owe to God depends on facts about God but also on facts about us and about what is good for a human being, formulated in terms of rational requirements.

Much of the present discussion of natural law will focus on Thomistic natural law and on Maimonides's ethical thought. The emphasis on contrasting Aquinas and Maimonides is apt because both of them learned and borrowed a great deal from Aristotle, and there are instructive contrasts between (a) Maimonides and Aquinas on the one hand, and Aristotle on the other, and (b) between Maimonides and Aquinas. Contrasting Maimonides and Aquinas is an especially effective way to explicate the absence of natural law theorizing in medieval Jewish thought.

A Conception of Rational Tradition

For Jewish thinkers explication of 'the reasons of the commandments' was the chief way of explaining the rational justification of practical requirements. The vector of explanation was different from that of Christian thought and the focus on 'the reasons of the commandments' was not displaced in favor of natural law considerations. For Jewish thinkers Torah was the primary resource for the rational account of practical requirements despite the fact that Torah was revealed. Reason and revelation were thought to be complementary modes of access to one, overall body of rational truth. Also, while it was thought that some of the commandments apply to all of humankind and not just the Jewish people, it was held that seeking the reasons of the commandments was a special responsibility of Jews. Jewish thinkers held also that fulfilling the commandments involved attaining an enlarged and deepened understanding of the reasons for them and their purposes.

Torah was held to supply a fully adequate basis for reasoning regarding practical requirements. This is not to say that Torah was thought to supply a fixed, exhaustive code to be followed without the need for deliberation, judgment, and elaboration. In some respects a good deal of the sort of reasoning Aquinas called 'determination' was required to fulfill the commandments. (We will say more about this below.) In fact, the complex project of interpretation, elaboration, and commentary is itself regarded as part of Torah.

Moreover, it was held that the practical and the intellectual reinforce each other. A person is better able to attain understanding of the commandments if that person has ethical virtues (a line of argumentation similar to one in Aristotle). A person has ethical virtues in a more full-fledged, more perfect way if that person also possesses understanding. The mutual support of the practical and the intellectual is emphasized by Saadia, Bahya, Maimonides, and others even though they did not regard practical wisdom as a virtue in the way Aristotle did. Some of the reasons for not identifying a specific virtue of practical wisdom will be mentioned below.

In the Thomistic project divine governance informs principles of practical reason, habitual knowledge of which (*synderesis*) is possessed by human beings on account of their nature. In order to act well and in order to realize the *telos* proper to a human being, a person needs to exercise practical wisdom. "It should be said that the rational is the principal part of man, but something is rational in two ways, essentially or by way of participation and, just as reason itself is more principal that [sic] the powers participating in reason, so prudence is more principal than the other virtues."[1] Prudence is needed to guide and orient the virtues of character. Prudence, Aquinas remarks, is held by Aristotle to be "right reason with respect to things to be done." . . . "Therefore, prudence agrees with the moral virtues because of its matter, and on account of this is numbered among them, although with respect to its essence or subject it is an intellectual virtue."[2]

For Aquinas, practical wisdom is a virtue, the exercise of which involves the agent making correct determinations of natural law and acting upon those determinations. Natural law supplies general principles governing the exercise of practical wisdom. Maimonides endorsed virtue-centered perfectionism but did

---

[1]Thomas Aquinas, *Disputed Questions on the Cardinal Virtues*, ed. Ralph McInerny, South Bend, IN: St. Augustine Press, 1999, Art 1, Ad. 11, p. 112.

[2]Ibid., Art. 1, Ad. 3, p. 111.

so without recognizing practical wisdom as an intellectual virtue. Explanation of the fact also goes some distance to accounting for why he was not a natural law theorist. (However, I am not suggesting that practical wisdom and natural law imply each other). There is considerable overlap between practical wisdom (in the Aristotelian/Thomistic conception), natural law (in the Thomistic conception), and medieval Jewish rationalist ethics. But the latter is distinct from the former two in significant respects, in large part because of the nature and role of tradition.

That there should be a prominent role for tradition is not, in its own right, a basis for distinguishing Jewish moral thought from natural law and practical wisdom. Tradition can be important to the cultivation of habits of thought and action enabling agents to acquire dispositions to act in ways that reflect understanding of natural law. To become the sort of person who has good judgment about what kinds of considerations to take into account, and to take them into account in the right way, depends upon acquisition of the virtues, and education in virtues can be shaped and transmitted by tradition. But the role of tradition in medieval Jewish moral thought extends well beyond the cultivation of certain dispositions. In the Jewish view, tradition is the mode of access to the rationality of moral requirements.

It might be thought that tradition could be especially important to morality if there are *not* objective moral considerations. In that case, tradition could be a way of sustaining features of moral discourse and reasoning that are cognitivist-seeming even though the metaethics is not objectivist. A tradition could be a way of preserving certain perspectives, practices, strategies of justification, and so forth, which, in being public and enduring, have the appearance of being objectively underwritten though they, in fact, are not. That is not the interpretation of Jewish tradition we find in thinkers such as Saadia and Maimonides. For them, tradition is important not only for transmission but also for inquiry and understanding.

We can more clearly see the significance of tradition in this view if we contrast it with some influential modern ideas concerning morality. Much modern moral thought reflects the notion that an agent is not to regard considerations as genuinely obligating unless the grounds for them are rationally evident. This insistence may reflect the early modern concern with the transparency of epistemological considerations; the concern that what is rationally necessary should be fully evident to the cognitive subject. This insistence, in a variety of specific forms, tends to be highly critical of tradition. Kant's moral philosophy is paradigmatic in this regard and multiple versions of modern moral theory—some of them descendants of Kant's thought, some not—resonate with this modern insistence. It is remote from the medieval Jewish view even in the case of the more rationalistic current of the latter. While one is to seek understanding, it is not the authority of one's own reason that is the ultimate authority, and the rational justifications of many of the commandments are non-evident. It is a kind of non-evident cognitivism. MacIntyre writes, "Traditions fail the Cartesian test of beginning from unassailable evident truths."[3] Perhaps it is a basically Cartesian disposition to insist upon epistemic transparency (clear and distinct ideas) as the only measure fully honoring epistemic responsibility. In that regard, it is surely not an obviously mistaken or negligible view. We do not have the space to pursue that question here. We can, however, highlight the contrast between the modern insistence and the medieval Jewish view.

There is a quite different, additional modern current of thought, already mentioned briefly. Many modern versions of *relativism* could comfortably accommodate a significant role for tradition, regarding it as a way of supplying stable, shared norms in the absence of objectivity. From the cognitivist end of the spectrum the objection to tradition is that tradition-based morality falls short of what is needed for moral considerations to have genuine authority; tradition, it seems, is at odds with rationally evident justification. From the noncognitivist end of the spectrum tradition may appear to be a generic category capturing a variety of distinct moralities, each set of moral considerations domesticated to the norms and values different communities or societies happen to accept. Thus, an influential conception of modern cognitivism contrasts sharply with this medieval Jewish view of tradition, and an influential conception of modern noncognitivism contrasts sharply with this medieval Jewish view of tradition.

We should acknowledge that there are respects in which 'tradition' and 'traditional' may be vague or at least ambiguous. For example, we could say that there is a tradition of critical innovation in Western science yet this is just the type of intellectual disposition that might seem to be at odds with an institution or practice being traditional or traditionalist. In philosophy we speak of 'the rationalist tradition' and the 'empiricist tradition,' each of which exhibits a good deal of internal criticism, development, and innovation. Modern societies are sometimes contrasted with traditional societies and there are clear differences between a highly traditional society and a modern one. Still, in a modern society there may be significant traditional elements. For example, there are some strongly traditional aspects of legal systems in some modern societies. I am not talking about the wigs worn by some judges. A tradition of respecting individual liberties, for example, can be both strongly conservative in some ways but it may also develop and be responsive to changing conditions.

Rather than trying to resolve the vagueness and ambiguity of 'tradition' or 'traditional' I will identify what I take to be some main features of tradition as it was understood by thinkers such as Saadia and Maimonides and then make

[3]Alasdair MacIntyre, *Whose Justice? Which Rationality?* Notre Dame: University of Notre Dame Press, 1988, p. 361.

some suggestions about moral epistemology on the basis of those features. Saadia made the following remarks concerning tradition.

1. "That is [to say, we believe in] the validity of authentic tradition, by reason of the fact that it is based upon the knowledge of the senses as well as that of reason, . . .[4] (p. 18)
2. "we remark that this type of knowledge (I mean that which is furnished by authentic tradition and the books of prophetic revelation), corroborates for us the validity of the first three sources of knowledge." [direct observation, intuition of the intellect, knowledge inferred by logical necessity][5] (p. 18)
3. "Furthermore [authentic tradition] verifies for us the validity of the intuition of reason. It enjoins us, namely, to speak the truth and not to lie."[6] (pp. 18–19)
4. "Besides that it confirms for us the validity of knowledge inferred by logical necessity, [that is to say] that whatever leads to the rejection of the perception of the senses or rational intuition is false."[7] (p. 19)
5. "Next [tradition] informs us that all sciences are [ultimately] based on what we grasp with our aforementioned senses, from which they are deduced and derived."[8] (p. 19)
6. "were it not for the fact that man felt satisfied in their hearts that there is such a thing in the world as authentic tradition, no person would be able to cherish legitimate expectations on the basis of the reports he receives about the success of a certain commercial transaction, or the usefulness of a specified art—and, after all, the realization of man's potentialities and the satisfaction of his needs depend upon enterprise."[9] (p. 156)
7. "Again, were it not for the assumption that there exists in the world [such a thing as] authentic tradition, men would accept neither the command nor the interdict of their ruler, except when they saw him with their own eyes and heard his words with their own ears . . . But if things were like that, it would mean the end of law and order, and the death of many human beings."[10] (p. 156)
8. Also, were it not for the existence in the world of such a thing as authentic tradition, no man would be able to identify the property of his father or his inheritance from his grandfather. Nay, he would not

[4]Saadia Gaon, *The Book of Beliefs and Opinions*, trans. Samuel Rosenblatt, New Haven, Yale University Press, 1976, p. 18.

[5]Ibid., p. 18.

[6]Ibid., pp. 18–19.

[7]Ibid., p. 19.

[8]Ibid., p. 19.

[9]Ibid., p. 156.

[10]Ibid., p. 156.

even be certain of being the son of his mother, let alone of his being the son of his father. The result would then be that the affairs of men would always be subject to doubt, to the point where human beings would believe only what they perceive with their senses at the time of perception."[11] (p. 156)

9. "Now the Scriptures, too, assert that authentic tradition is as trustworthy as things perceived with our own eyes."[12] (p. 157)
10. "a report is subject to falsification in two directions from which direct observation is immune. It may be due either to false impression or else to deliberate misrepresentation. That is why Scripture says: and consider diligently."[13] (p. 157)
11. "the Bible is not the sole basis of our religion, for in addition to it we have two other bases. One of these is anterior to it; namely, the fountain of reason. The second is posterior to it; namely, the source of tradition."[14]

Some of the main elements of Maimonides's view of tradition are expressed in the following passages.

> In some cases a commandment communicates a correct belief, which is the one and only thing aimed at—as, for instance, the belief in the unity and eternity of the deity and in His not being a body. In other cases the belief is necessary for the abolition of reciprocal wrongdoing or for the acquisition of a noble moral quality—as, for instance, the belief that He, may He be exalted, has a violent anger against those who do injustice, according to what is said: *And My wrath shall wax hot, and I will kill, and so on*, and as the belief that He, may He be exalted, responds instantaneously to the prayer of someone wronged or deceived: *And it shall come to pass, when he crieth unto Me, that I will hear; for I am gracious.*[15]

And:

> His wisdom, may He be exalted, and His gracious ruse, which is manifest in regard to all His creatures, did not require that He give us a Law prescribing the rejection, abandonment, and abolition of all these kinds of worship. For one could not then conceive the acceptance of [such a Law], considering the nature of man, which always likes that to which it is accustomed.[16]

---

[11]Ibid., p. 156.

[12]Ibid., p. 157.

[13]Ibid., p. 157.

[14]Ibid., p. 174.

[15]Moses Maimonides, *The Guide of the Perplexed*, trans. Shlomo Pines, Chicago: The University of Chicago Press, 1963, III, Ch. 29, pp. 513–14.

[16]Ibid., III, Ch. 32, p. 526.

Also:

> . . . every commandment from among these six hundred and thirteen commandments exists either with a view to communicating a correct opinion, or to putting an end to an unhealthy opinion, or to communicating a rule of justice, or to warding off an injustice, or to endowing men with a noble moral quality, or to warning them against an evil moral quality. Thus all [the commandments] are bound up with three things: opinions, moral qualities, and political civic actions.[17]

The second passage expresses the important point that in giving Torah, God would not ask and expect of human beings that they should begin to act in ways requiring radical disruption of accustomed practice. Their actions can take on a new meaning but the forms of practice need to be familiar in important respects so that what is required is recognizably doable. (See also Saadia, p. 397: "he does not, however, make it a regular practice to change the law of nature that has been fixed by Him.") The third quotation expresses Maimonides's view that there is a reason for each commandment and that the understanding of each of them has a place in the realization of human perfection.

Given the ways in which ethical virtue and intellectual virtue reinforce each other, tradition is not dispensable even if we have attained understanding. It is still necessary as a manner in which rightly ordered habit is supported and understanding is enlarged. A good habit needs discipline and the discipline of practice can facilitate and reinforce understanding. In discussing Maimonides and the question of whether the *Guide* and the *Mishneh Torah* present not only different but divergent views Twersky writes:

> However, law, as we shall see, is also propaedeutic and a prophylactic for true belief, i.e., laws protect and promulgate true opinions, solidify and concretize abstract notions. "You know from what I have said that opinions do not last unless they are accompanied by actions that strengthen them, make them generally known, and perpetuate them among the multitude."[18]

Maimonides argued that study and practice are essential and they can support each other in a virtuous spiral. That way, the integrity of practice is transmitted and comprehension of its rightness is enlarged. This conception of tradition and perfection depends upon commitment to a kind of rationalism in which acceptance of the rationally non-evident is crucial. The view combines realist aspiration and a rationalist disposition but without rationalist conceit about the power of human understanding.

---

[17]Ibid., III, Ch. 54, p. 524.

[18]Isadore Twersky, *Introduction to the Code of Maimonides*, New Haven: Yale University Press, 1980, p. 363.

The giving of the Law is, so to speak, a referential anchor for the chain of tradition. In that respect the anchor of tradition is a body of truth but it takes the historical life of the people to steadily deepen and extend the comprehension of that truth and how all of its parts are integrated and how they apply. For example, it may take several generations to come to a clear understanding of how a certain practice facilitates the development of a disposition that encourages a particular virtue. Without the generations of practice that understanding would not be achieved.

The study of Torah leads to knowledge of the commandments and knowledge of God through deepened understanding of the created order. Maimonides emphasized that all of the commandments have as their purposes either correct belief, the good of the community, or excellences of character. The more we study the world and Torah the more clearly does this come into view and the more fully we are able to appreciate divine wisdom. At the most abstract level we see that the purpose of the Law is to abolish idolatry. The Law eliminates all its traces and orients us to true good through understanding of "the existence and oneness of the deity."[19] "For Maimonides this cultivation of the intellect is unthinkable apart from the study of Torah, or to be more specific, it is only possible when one reflects on the reasons for divine commandments as well as obeying them."[20]

Michael Levine writes:

> In saying that the law is not natural Maimonides does not mean that it is not rational or objective. Certainly divine commandments are objective, and for Maimonides they are accessible to reason as well, in the sense already stated. We can discover what the reasons for the laws are. Moral rules and human law are also objective insofar as a moral rule or law must fulfill a function if it is to be counted as a moral rule or law at all. Merely the fact that Law has been revealed does not imply that it cannot be known through reason as well and extended in the establishment and embellishment of the moral-legal code."[21]

Saadia had written:

> Thus He has enjoined us to accept these matters as binding and observe them. He has furthermore informed us, however, that, if we would engage in speculation and diligent research, inquiry would produce for us in each instance the complete truth, tallying with His announcements to us by the speech of His prophets.[22]

---

[19]Maimonides, *Guide*, III, Ch. 32, p. 527.

[20]Michael P. Levine, "The Role of Reason in the Ethics of Maimonides," *The Journal of Religious Ethics*, Vol. 14, No. 2, Fall 1986, p. 282.

[21]Ibid., p. 285.

[22]Saadia, *The Book of Beliefs and Opinions*, p. 28.

And Bahya ibn Pakuda wrote, "Wisdom is the life of their [human beings'] soul, the light of their mind, their way to the favor of God (glory and praise be unto Him), and their guardian from His anger in this world and the next . . ."[23] Tradition and the study of tradition is a part of our finite, imperfect way of imitating God, and a way for us to come closer to God. Saadia, Bahya, and Maimonides indicate the way in which medieval Jewish thought held that there is a complex interpenetration of theoretical and practical understanding. Theoretical understanding enables us to comprehend the grounds of ethical requirements, and ethical excellence is an enactment, an effective realization of understanding the good.

This is an interpretation of tradition as something much more intellectually informed than those notions of tradition intended to express practice or perspective closed to reflection, criticism, and critical reflection. The notion of tradition in which it means roughly, 'the preservation of ancient ways, unresponsive to or disposed against critical examination or critical integration with other commitments, beliefs, and practices' clearly is not the relevant notion. The medieval Jewish conception of tradition was not such that its antiquity in its own right was authoritative. Instead, the wisdom of its source was the ground of its authority. Tradition supplies, so to speak, 'rigid designation' to a body of requirements and practices not yet fully comprehended. Sustained reference is necessary for that comprehension to be increased. Antiquity alone is not the relevant basis of its orthodoxy.

In this view we should say that we need tradition because of the way in which it is anchored in fundamental truths crucial to our perfection and because of the way fulfilling the requirements of tradition enables us to understand those truths. Maimonides wrote:

> The Law as a whole aims at two things: the welfare of the soul and the welfare of the body. As for the welfare of the soul, it consists in the multitude's acquiring correct opinions corresponding to their respective capacity. Therefore some of them [namely, the opinions] are set forth explicitly and some of them are set forth in parables. For it is not within the nature of the common multitude that its capacity should suffice for apprehending that subject matter as it is.[24]

But tradition is not parable, allegory, or image 'all the way down.' It is informed with truth and for those with intellectual capacity, study of the tradition leads to fuller understanding. Moreover, it is not a dispensable mode of access to truth. We need tradition in order to come to the truth about many

---

[23]Bahya ibn Pakuda, *The Book of Direction to the Duties of the Heart*, trans. Menahem Mansoor, Oxford: Littman Library of Jewish Civilization, 2000, p. 85.

[24]Maimonides, *Guide*, III, Ch. 27, p. 510.

fundamental matters. This is neither Cartesian nor Hegelian rationalism. Nor is it significant in a merely instrumental respect, as a ladder to be dispensed with once it has been scaled.

The Moral Epistemology of Tradition

The Maimonidean project of giving an account of 'the reasons of the commandments' was different from the Thomistic project of integrating Aristotelian practical wisdom with natural law. For both thinkers there is a centrally important role for reason in ethical judgment and decision. But their explications of how reason operates involve different conceptions. Thomistic natural law showed how divine governance is reflected in principles of practical reason. Compared to non-rational creatures

> the rational creature is subject to divine providence in a more excellent manner, insofar as he comes to be a participant in providence, providing for himself and others. Hence in him the eternal reason is participated in in such a way that he has a natural inclination to the fitting act and end. Such a participation in eternal law in the rational creature is called natural law.[25]

Maimonides was emphatic that there are reasons for all of the commandments and he was no less convinced of the rationality of ethical requirements than Aquinas. (See *Guide*, III, 31, p. 524).

"It is, however, the doctrine of all of us—both of the multitude and of the elite—that all the Laws have a cause, though we ignore the causes for some of them and we do not know the manner in which they conform to wisdom."[26]

While ethical requirements are rationally justified, neither Saadia nor Maimonides recognized a virtue of practical wisdom. Moreover, neither of them was committed to natural law. Nor is there a counterpart to *synderesis* in the Jewish tradition even though reasonableness has a role similar to that assigned to it by Aquinas. He held that "synderesis is called the law of our intellect insofar as it is a habit containing the precepts of natural law, which are the first principles of human acts."[27] And, "reason naturally grasps as goods all those things to which man has a natural inclination, and consequently as to be pursued in action, and the contrary of these are grasped as evils to be avoided. Therefore, there is an order of the precepts of the law of nature that follows the order of the natural inclinations."[28] If we ask, what would be missing from

---

[25]Thomas Aquinas, *Summa Theologiae*, Q. 91, Art. 2, Response, in *Thomas Aquinas: Selected Writings*, ed. Ralph McInerny New York: Penguin Books, 1998, p. 620.

[26]Maimonides, *Guide*, III, Ch. 26, p. 507.

[27]Aquinas, *ST*, Q. 94, Art. 1, Ad. 2.

[28]Ibid., Art. 2, p. 645.

ethical thought if natural law were absent from it, Aquinas would answer that *synderesis* and principles of practical reason would not be known as a matter of habitual knowledge. A consequence would be the absence of rationally objective and universal ethical conceptions.

One of the most longstanding criticisms of Jewish moral thought is that it appears to be parochial, domesticated to one people. However, there are resources in the concept of tradition with which to reply to that criticism. The tradition is not a substitute for reason; it is not what is relied upon in the absence of objective of universal values. Instead, it was understood to be a mode of access to such values. The manner of access reflects the fact that people typically acquire their ethical commitments, their modes of ethical awareness, and their motivational tendencies in the concrete contexts of the various departments of life within a social and political community. Medieval Jewish thinkers were keenly aware of the ways in which virtue needs to be encouraged and learned and the centrally important role tradition can have in those processes.

I am not suggesting that either Aristotle or Aquinas was not also mindful of this aspect of moral education. Maimonides clearly learned from Aristotle on this score. But it is especially pronounced in Jewish thought and it is elaborated in a manner showing how it is possible to attain objective valuative conceptions through the specificity of a particular community's way of life without reliance on universal principles claimed to be known apart from that way of life.

Aristotle put a great deal of weight on habituation but his ethical thought does not have a role for tradition in the way it figures in medieval Jewish moral thought. Aristotle's moral epistemology does not have a place for the progressively articulated comprehension of an anchoring body of truth, and it does not have a comparable role for the historically unfolding life of the nation, though the social and political aspects of human life are thickly interrelated with ethics in his thought. There is considerable overlap between the thinking and judgment that would be part of Aristotelian practical wisdom and the thinking and judgment that would be part of Maimonidean ethical thought. But the latter is guided by tradition in more substantive and significant ways than is the case for Aristotle's ethics. There is much that unaided human reason could ascertain, in Maimonides's view, but Torah is a discipline of perfection offered by God in covenantal relation with human beings. It supplies guidance and underwrites confidence in the rightness of certain practices.

One reason Aristotle thought it so important to have laws is that we cannot count on virtue being common. He wrote

> for the many naturally obey fear, not shame; they avoid what is base because of the penalties, not because it is disgraceful. For since they live by their feelings, they pursue their proper pleasures and the sources of

> them, and avoid the opposed pains, and have not even a notion of what is fine and [hence] truly pleasant, since they have had no taste of it.[29]

And:

> It is difficult, however, for someone to be trained correctly for virtue from his youth if he has not been brought up under correct law; for the many, especially the young, do not find it pleasant to live in a temperate and resistant way. That is why laws must prescribe their upbringing and practices; for they will not find these things painful when they get used to them.[30]

While Aristotle clearly held that a human being wishes for happiness and that we each shape our lives with a view to attaining it, he was less explicit than Aquinas on the issue of whether we each are inclined to seek those things that are genuine human goods. Aquinas did not think that effective, wise seeking of the good is guaranteed by our nature but he did maintain that we do have inclinations toward various basic human goods. Principles of natural law are primary and secondary principles for guiding action in ways that reflect those inclinations. There is a natural basis for our activity to be informed by sound principles of practical reason.

Aquinas writes, "for the will is naturally inclined to the ultimate end, and where it is a matter of action the end has the note of a natural principle. Therefore, the inclination of will is an active principle with respect to every disposition acquired by the affective part through exercise."[31] There is, in Aquinas's view, not only an inclination to the good but there are also principles to guide practical reasoning—principles of which we have non-acquired habitual knowledge.

However, this does not ensure virtue or even that knowledge of natural law will not be obscured. Aquinas considered whether the principles of natural law could be blotted out. He held that the first principles of natural law could not be blotted out though vicious habits could so corrupt an individual that the person does not act on a sound grasp of those first principles. Secondary principles could be blotted out.

> . . . to natural law first pertains certain most common principles, known to all, and certain secondary precepts, more proper, which are, as it were, conclusions close to the principles. With respect to those common principles, natural law in general can in no way be erased from the hearts of men, but it can be in the particular thing to be done, insofar as reason is prevented from applying the common principles to the particular things

---

[29]Aristotle, *Nicomachean Ethics*, Second Edition, trans. T. Irwin, Indianapolis: Hackett Publishing Company, 1999, 1179b 11–15.

[30]Ibid., 1179b 32–35.

[31]Thomas Aquinas, *Disputed Questions on the Virtues in General*, Art. 8, "Do We Have Any Natural Virtues?" Response, p. 49.

> to be done because of concupiscence or some other passion . . . With respect to the other, secondary principles, natural law can be erased from the hearts of men, either because of bad persuasion, in the way in which errors occur in speculative matters with respect to necessary conclusions, or because of depraved customs and corrupt habits, as with those who do not think theft or even sins against nature to be sin . . .[32]

We can imagine a community long established in wrong practices and values, to the extent that members do not recognize their values as wrong because it is second nature to them to endorse and act on those values. Still, it is part of Aquinas's view that this would involve a corruption of habitual knowledge possessed by *synderesis*. That is not a component of Aristotle's view. Thus, there does seem to be a sense in which basic principles of practical reason—the sorts of principles the elaboration of which would be central elements of practical wisdom—are naturally accessible to agents in the Thomistic conception in a more determinate manner than in the Aristotelian conception. This is a respect in which Thomistic natural law involves some revision of Aristotle's moral epistemology. Even though Aristotle, Maimonides, and Aquinas agree on many matters, and there is considerable overlap in their moral anthropologies, there are some important differences in their metaethics and—though we are not taking it up here—in their conceptions of specific virtues.

Maimonides classified all of the commandments into fourteen classes and he argued that commandments serve three basic ends. Those are (i) inculcating true opinions, (ii) cultivating ethical virtues, and (iii) promoting social well-being. Overall, "the Law always tends to assimilate itself to nature, perfecting the natural matters in a certain respect. For nature is not endowed with thought and understanding, whereas the Law is the determining ruling and the governance of the deity, who grants the intellect to all its possessors."[33] Torah offers guidance to human beings so that in their activities they might attain the distinctive perfections proper to them. At a highly abstract level perhaps this is not so unlike Aquinas saying that, "natural law is nothing other than the participation in eternal law on the part of the rational creature"[34] and saying that all virtuous actions can be said to reflect natural law. "Hence since the rational soul is the proper form of man, there is a natural inclination in man to act according to reason. And this is to act according to virtue. On this basis, all acts of virtue are of natural law, for everyone's own reason dictates this, that he should act virtuously."[35] Still, that likeness of the two views is *very* abstract and it leaves out important differences of moral epistemology.

---

[32]Aquinas, *ST*, Q. 94, Art. 6, pp. 651–52.
[33]Maimonides, *Guide*, III, Ch. 43, p. 571.
[34]Aquinas, *ST*, Q. 91, Art. 2, p. 620.
[35]Ibid., Q. 94, Art. 3, p. 646.

I mentioned above that it might be said that the role for judgment and elaboration of many commandments in the application of them to particular situations is comparable to what Aquinas calls 'determinations' of reason in moral judgment guided by natural law. Aquinas employs an undefined notion of reasonableness, which is perhaps similar in some ways to Maimonides's notion of the rationality that leads to (correct) 'generally accepted' ethical views. For Aquinas, many specific ethical determinations of natural law are not strictly logical derivations *from* natural law. In his discussion of the way in which Thomistic natural law needs specification by practical rationality James Ross writes:

> Those conclusions that are deducible from the absolutely first principle, through the employment of per se truths about man and without any other contingent truths, are the *primary principles* of natural law; those general principles deducible from the primary principles by means of additional contingent but not per se premises are *secondary principles* of natural law. For instance, from the primary principle that life in human communities ought to be promoted one can, with various true *contingent* premises, deduce such secondary principles as that things entrusted to one ought to be returned, that family life ought to be stable, and so forth."[36]
>
> Aquinas wrote, "But it must be noted that something may be derived from the natural law in two ways; first, as a conclusion from principles; secondly, by way of determination of certain common notions. The first way is like that by which, in the sciences, demonstrated conclusions are drawn from the principles; while the second is likened to that whereby, in the arts, common forms are determined to some particular. Thus, the craftsman needs to determine the common form of a house to the shape of this or that particular house."[37] In addition to derivation from common principles of natural law by way of conclusions there is also derivation by way of determination; e.g., "the law of nature has it that the evil-doer should be punished, but that he be punished in this or that way is a determination of the law of nature."[38]

The way in which tradition is a basis for further articulation and explication of the commandments has some likeness to the role assigned to *determination* by Aquinas in his account of natural law. Whether the basis is the commandments or natural law, much reasoning fashions a conception of what is

---

[36]James Ross, "Justice is Reasonableness: Aquinas on Human Law and Morality," *The Monist*, Vol. 58, No. 1, 1974, pp. 86–103; p. 94.

[37]Aquinas, *ST*, Q. 95, Art. 2, in *Introduction to St. Thomas Aquinas*, ed., Anton C. Pegis, New York: Modern Library, 1948, p. 649.

[38]Ibid, p. 650.

required rather than just tracking the way in which the requirement is entailed. (It's *not* entailed, any more than the architect's design is entailed by the end of designing a house for a family of six, to be made of wood, in a locale subject to extremes of temperature in the different seasons.) Also, for Maimonides much of such reasoning is preserved by tradition. Given the role of the search for understanding in tradition, it is a 'living' tradition, not simply passed down. It shapes and guides activity that involves development and not just preservation. In important respects, it informs and guides current activity and it is much more than just a record of earlier thought, if by 'earlier' we mean 'now closed.'

Scotus's account of the relation between principles of natural law and specific requirements differs markedly from Aquinas's, as does his conception of the role of command and sanction in natural law. In Scotus's theory, the only principles of natural law are those laws of the Decalogue concerning human duties of gratitude and obedience owed to God. All other ethical requirements are, he said, "exceedingly in harmony" with natural law but are not derived from it. They cohere with natural law but there is not a way to show that they are implied by it. Maimonides, Aquinas, and Scotus all regarded ethical requirements as rationally explicable but even in the case of the natural law theorists, those requirements are not known by deductive reasoning from principles of natural law.

In Maimonides's view neither demonstration nor self-evidence is an appropriate measure of the rational justifications of ethical requirements. Nonetheless, ". . . given Maimonides's view of the law as rational, and given what he says about human law and the virtues associated with the Golden Mean, a denial that man can discover, through reason, certain moral principles that are objective and necessary for improvement and perfection seems purely ad hoc."[39]

> To say that morals are not true or false for Maimonides means that they are not to be apprehended by the intellect, but rather through some other, unspecified, capacity of the rational faculty capable of "apprehending things as good and evil." To say that moral rules are neither true nor false has implications concerning the method of acquiring moral knowledge, but moral assertions themselves should not be interpreted as noncognitive assertions. If an action is not in accordance with the mean, *imitatio dei*, a divine command, or a utilitarian rule then it is true that the action is bad.[40]

In regard to non-Jews, those who had no access to revealed truth, Levine writes:

> It is likely that Maimonides thought such individuals could distinguish right from wrong, at least in a great many instances, through reason and

[39]Michael P. Levine, p. 282.

[40]Ibid., p. 288.

experience alone. Minimally these individuals would have access to the moral truths that are necessary for social wellbeing.[41]

Maimonides employed the idiom of what is 'generally accepted.' (It is used by other medieval philosophers, as well, e.g., Alfarabi. Examples of its use can be found at *Guide*, III, 29, p. 517, III, 30, p. 523, III, 32, 526; "Eight Chapters," Ch. 6, p. 79; "Treatise on the Art of Logic," Ch. 8, p. 158.) In one sense, that which is 'generally accepted' is what an ethically well-ordered person would reasonably judge or conclude to be the case on the basis of thought but without the rigorous justification of demonstration. In one of the senses of 'generally accepted' it is more or less equivalent to 'correct.' In a second sense there are beliefs and practices that are 'generally accepted' in that only the weight of custom and habit supports them. For instance, Maimonides says of the practice of sacrifice that it was, 'generally accepted' and "customary in the whole world and the universal service upon which we were brought up."[42] There are some practices and beliefs that are 'generally accepted' in that they have persisted, are customary, whether or not they are also well-supported by reasons. Torah preserved many 'generally accepted' practices—sacrifice is an example—though changing the point and meaning so that they concerned only the worship of God. The preservation of accustomed practice, but with a change in its meaning was, Maimonides thought, an example of God's "wily graciousness."

Practical rationality unaided by tradition would arrive at several components of sound ethical understanding but it would be far less complete than the understanding and virtue attainable through fidelity to tradition. The enlargement of comprehension does not rationalize an abandonment of tradition, as though it can now be displaced. There is another aspect of tradition that helps explain why Jewish philosophers, and Maimonides in particular, argued that the growth of rational comprehension does not obviate the role for tradition. This aspect has to do with the relation between the practical dimension of Torah, in the sense of law, i.e., *halakha*, and the theoretical dimension of it.

Twersky writes, "Halaḵah is, of course, metamorphosed by Maimonides so that it emerges several pages later as including not only positive law but also all other sciences as well. No comprehensive description of the components of Torah will be allowed to omit hokmah"[43] ('Hokmah' can be translated as 'wisdom'). "His sole concern is to establish *hokmah* as an original part of the Oral Law, from which it follows that the study of the latter in its encyclopedic totality—that is, Gemara—includes philosophy."[44] "In other words, the *fiqh*, the Oral Law, contains philosophic truths preserved descriptively or apodictically

---

[41]Ibid., p. 289.

[42]Maimonides, *Guide*, III, Ch. 32, p. 526.

[43]Twersky, *Introduction to the Code of Maimonides*, pp. 495–96.

[44]Ibid., p. 497.

as articles of tradition instead of being elaborated demonstratively as syllogistic premises and conclusions.

These key elements of tradition may ultimately be rationalized, just as the judicial part of Torah *sebbe-al peh* is subject to amplification."[45]

> Of course, the scale of values established by the halakha, with its ideal of study, would not require radical transfiguration to accommodate the philosophic ideal of the *vita contemplativa*. At least formally, no drastic transvaluation was involved. If, in addition, we recall that philosophy was considered to be a major integral component of Torah, the Maimonidean ideal could be presented as firmly entrenched in the Jewish tradition.[46]
>
> The legitimacy of philosophy in religion was not the issue; rather the legitimacy of religion without philosophy was the issue. Maimonides thus saw himself as restoring, perhaps consummating, a philosophic tradition not only of metaphysics but of jurisprudence. The outer-directed motive, which was sharp and influential, was naturally sustained by inner forces. As we have noted, religious rationalism was not merely a response to external pressures, not only an enterprise of apologetics and polemics; it was also a fulfillment of the inner need for understanding and rationalizing.[47]

Maimonides believed that the combination of reason and Torah was sufficient to supply the guidance required for human beings to realize the perfections proper to them. In addition, this highlights the graciousness of God in giving Torah. There is much that human beings could ascertain just through the use of reason but they could not ascertain practical matters as comprehensively and determinately as they are able to through tradition. In Maimonides's view the relation between ethical requirements and the understanding of the created order is intelligible inasmuch as many of the reasons for the commandments are based upon facts about human nature and the created order.

Objectivity without Natural Law

Given that the current of Jewish thought I have described maintained that its tradition was a mode of access to objective, universal ethical values, it is understandable that interpreters and commentators find in it elements of natural law theorizing. The very idiom 'natural law,' is, in some regards, plausible shorthand for ethical views that aspire to objectivity, especially when that objectivity

---

[45]Ibid., p. 500.
[46]Ibid., p. 501.
[47]Ibid., p. 502.

is grounded in considerations of human nature. If Maimonides's philosophical anthropology had that general character, why oppose the notion that it included natural law elements?

Consider Lenn Goodman's explication of the natural law features of Jewish moral thought. He writes (in an unpublished essay)

> All legitimate laws, I believe, are grounded in natural law and thus in an appreciation of human nature and our place in the cosmos. All natural laws, when they frame genuine obligations, rest on the deserts of beings, and notably, on the rights and dignities of persons. Needs anchor deserts, and deserts are legitimated, I have argued, when claims are equilibrated and coordinated. The essence of any being is its dynamic, the claims it makes. And the heart of ethics is the treatment of all beings as what they are.[48]

David Novak has argued in several places that Jewish moral thought should be interpreted in terms of natural law, and Goodman comments:

> Biblical and rabbinic law, as David Novak has shown extensively, is grounded in natural law. But the Torah has its own unique way of articulating that law—in the commandments that frame the halakhic constitution, in the narrative that contextualizes, thematizes, and elaborates those imperatives in dicta of the prophets and scriptures, and the dialectic of the rabbis.[49]

And:

> It is to Maimonides that we owe the brilliant analytic work that finds the purposes of all these laws under three rubrics: civil, moral, and spiritual. The scheme recasts Plato's division of our appetitive, disciplined, and rational interests. No individual or society flourishes without all three.[50]

I have discussed Novak's argument in some detail elsewhere, acknowledging some of the intellectual motives for finding natural law in Judaism but presenting reasons why I believe there are grounds for not interpreting medieval Jewish philosophy in natural law terms.[51] Here, I just comment briefly on Goodman's

---

[48]Lenn Goodman, "Judaism and Natural Law," unpublished manuscript, p. 6. Its use here is by permission of the author.

[49]Ibid., p. 6.

[50]Ibid., p. 6.

[51]See my *Law, Reason, and Morality in Medieval Jewish Ethics*, Oxford: Oxford University Press, 2010. I discuss Judaism and natural law in chapters six and seven, and in chapter seven I consider Novak's argument for finding natural law in Jewish thought. In brief, I argue that his view depends upon some conceptions distinctive of modern philosophy, and that those conceptions are not well-suited to medieval Jewish thought. However, my point is not simply that medieval philosophy and modern philosophy differ in some important ways. I argue that some of the commitments of medieval Jewish philosophers have philosophical plausibility in ways that include alternatives to a natural law conception of a rational ethics.

perspective and his appeal to Novak's interpretation. Goodman is arguing that cogent ethical claims possess their cogency through resting on natural law considerations. He is not arguing for a specific conception of the proper form of natural law theory but, in a more general way, claiming that the plausibility and resonance of sound ethical claims rest on broadly anthropological considerations of the sort that show the anchoring of ethics in human nature and the most fundamental features of human lives. There are normative aspects of human nature shaping ethical requirements and limits. Neglect of those aspects or failure to recognize their normative significance will inevitably issue in stunted, inadequate ethical conceptions.

If we interpret natural law in that very broad sense, in the sense that an ethics is an ethics of natural law through finding the reasons for ethical requirements in an anthropology that is also cognizant of our "place in the cosmos" then I suppose it is fair to regard Saadia and Maimonides's ethics of rational tradition as a form of natural law. However, if we recognize the distinct features of an ethics of rational tradition, and the importance of those distinct features to Jewish thinkers, then I believe we can see that there are reasons not to assimilate the view to either practical wisdom or natural law, though it shares quite a lot with each.

A defender of the natural law interpretation might also point to the rational character of Maimonides's 'generally accepted' matters and the likenesses between those and Thomistic determinations of natural law and Scotus's notion of ethical requirements as "exceedingly in harmony" with natural law. It is true that Maimonides insisted that all commandments had rational justifications, and one might point to that as reinforcing the likeness to natural law. Here, again, there is an important difference. Like Saadia, he also insisted that revelation reflected divine wisdom and benevolence in supplying a great deal of specificity human beings would not have arrived at on their own, and it offered guidance for repentance, forgiving, and a wide range of complex, important aspects of ethical life. Torah addressed the full range of human life, including its many departments, and also human weaknesses, propensities, and susceptibilities. Torah 'speaks in the language of man.' A defender of a natural law interpretation could point out that the natural law elements are found in the ethical requirements; there is no claim that all of Torah is natural law.

Nonetheless, I think it is important that Jewish thinkers held that even in regard to those matters most fully ascertainable as matter of rational ethics it is important to see them within the context of the tradition overall, including its other elements. That may seem to be precisely the reason for objecting that the Jewish view is particularist in a way that ill comports with the universality of values. It insists on placing even the most fundamental ethical matters within the context of tradition and that domesticates them to the context of one people and its unique history.

However, we should note that the Jewish thinkers were keenly attuned to the way in which ways of life, in all of their complexity, shape and are also shaped by overall perspectives on the world and conceptions of human nature. They saw that ethical ideals and aspirations are not stand-alone matters, compartmentalized in a well-defined, distinct department of life, viz., *the ethical.* They were keenly attuned to relations between the intellectual and the practical and also the individual and the communal. Those were thematic concerns of their conception of tradition. I emphasize this by way of pointing out that these were subtle, insightful moral psychologists, attentive to the interactions between different aspects of life and strongly interested in how those can be perfectively integrated. On this point, Goodman writes

> The Torah articulates as law and moral admonition the ideas of justice and mercy that it traces to Abraham's discovery of God's ways, just as the Talmud and later rabbinic tradition elaborate a fuller legal and moral code from the principles embedded in the Torah. All these norms form an integrated system: Physical well-being is a prerequisite of the higher reaches of the moral and spiritual quest. But physical well-being is not adequately understood without moral principle to channel it—nor without spiritual insight to guide it.[52]

With this background in mind we might see in bolder relief the significance of tradition for those thinkers. For them, a specific, concrete form of life was necessary to perfect a human being, given a person's rational capacities but also the other propensities, susceptibilities, and tendencies of human nature. The natural law-like elements of their understanding were not separated out from the rest of that anthropology. That in its own right is an approach to ethical thought meriting consideration. They argued that in ethical life human beings best attain rationally objective, universal values and ideals through participation in particular ways of life. This conception of the significance of tradition might be a way of explicating *objective* ethical rationality. They held that tradition is essential as a steady anchoring needed to carry on elaborating and explicating ethical requirements. Granted, the anchor they had in mind was a revelation to a particular people. Still, the view was that the employment of reason (which is itself commanded by the revelation) is essential to leading the life anchored in tradition. Through the exercise of reason the rational justification of what is commanded is brought into view. In that respect, the anchor of the tradition itself comes to be seen as the wisdom informing it.

Natural law, whether interpreted as Aquinas understood it or as Scotus understood it, supplies principles of practical reason to human beings either as habitual knowledge furnished by our nature (Aquinas) or as rationally evident principles (Scotus). Jewish thinkers agreed with Christian thinkers on many ethical principles and agreed that they are known to reason, though Jewish

---

[52]Goodman, p. 15.

thinkers did not regard fundamental principles as having the status of natural law. It might seem odd to suggest that tradition had a place in the moral epistemology of Jewish thinkers similar to the place of natural law for Christian thinkers—apparently odd because the naturalness of natural law might appear to contrast sharply with tradition. Yet, as I have tried to show, the Jewish thinkers articulated a conception of rational tradition or, we might say, tradition suited to rational agents, though those agents are not the sole authors of the tradition.

With regard to approaches to ethical theory and ethical life, perhaps in addition to conceptions of practical wisdom and natural law, there is a third thing, a conception of rational tradition, which has distinct features, sufficiently distinct to perhaps supply the contours of a moral epistemology meriting explication and elaboration in its own terms. In the view of some important medieval Jewish thinkers the examination of its ethical content indicates that it *resonates with*, and is historically, a *key source* of what are widely regarded as universal requirements, values, and ideals.

{ PART III }

Medieval Christian Philosophy

{ 5 }

Thomas Aquinas on The Natural Law Written on Our Hearts

Eileen C. Sweeney

The divisions over how to interpret Thomas Aquinas's account of natural law cut deep, and range broadly up to and including whether it is grounded in nature and whether it is law, as opposed to prudential guideline or capacity for moral insight. A good number of these debates are proxy battles in a larger war over modernity and Aquinas's relationship to it. For Alasdair MacIntyre, Aquinas and natural law are a bulwark against modernity and in radical opposition to classical liberalism, with its emphasis on individual rights, agnosticism about the good, and creation of the administrative state. John Milbank, in *Theology and Social Theory*, crafted his own "radical Augustinianism" in opposition to an Aquinas he saw as essentially opening the floodgates to modernity by granting separate status to nature and the state as the secular as opposed to the spiritual realm.[1] Leo Strauss, certainly no fan of modernity, prefers Aristotle to Aquinas on the grounds that Aquinas's account of the good is based on the exceptionless rules that are the precepts of natural law, and that it is based not just in theism (the God who bestows the natural law) but on Christian revelation, from which the precepts are derived.[2]

There is the same kind of divide between those who are more positively disposed toward modernity, with Martha Nussbaum finding in Aquinas too little room for diverse and incompatible goods and too much top-down control over individual human pursuit of the good.[3] For Nussbaum, Aquinas is both

[1]John Milbank, *Theology and Social Theory: Beyond Secular Reason* (Malden, MA: Blackwell, [2006], c1990), 412. Milbank has renamed his movement "radical orthodoxy" and taken Aquinas into the fold of those resisting the secularizing forces of modernity, though the second edition from which I cite has retained the critical comments about Aquinas also present in the first edition, published in 1990.

[2]Leo Strauss, *Natural Right and History*, (Chicago: University of Chicago Press, 1950), 163–64. Cited in Pamela M. Hall, *Narrative and Natural Law: An Interpretation of Thomistic Ethics* (Notre Dame, IN: University of Notre Dame Press, 1994), 3–4.

[3]Martha Craven Nussbaum, *Aristotle's de Motu Animalium* (Princeton, NJ: Princeton University Press, 1978), 168–69.

anti-modern and anti-Aristotelian, placing the human good and the conflict between human goods under the single, transcendent good—God. Anthony Lisska's retrieval of Thomistic natural law theory sees it as supporting the modern notion of human rights, and not essentially dependent on the notion of God as ground of natural law. The political theorist E. A. Goerner, who wants to put Aquinas to work in the practical and real business of politics and law, objects to those whose interpretations of Aquinas "smell too much of the incense of the altar or the smoke of the lamp."[4] Though they might not put it in these terms, the so-called "neo-classical" theorists of natural law in Aquinas, John Finnis and Germaine Grisez, also attempt to articulate a Thomistic theory that abstracts from the theological and specifically Christian character of Aquinas's thought, as well as an Aristotelian account of nature (even while reaching conclusions supportive of the Catholic Church's moral teaching).

From within theology as well, Aquinas's natural law doctrine has been viewed radically differently. For Reinhold Niebuhr, Thomistic accounts of natural law downplay the effects of sin in the claim that 'natural justice' remains intact and is sufficient to ground our moral and political judgments; further, he complains, natural law theorists are content to operate in the narrow realm of justice rather than justice transformed by love.[5] Natural law is, in other words, too worldly a standard for morality and politics and too blind to the effects of sin and history, not just on action but on our theory and self-justification. Stanley Hauerwas agrees, warning that "too often natural law assumptions function as an ideology for sustaining some Christians' presuppositions that their societies—particularly societies of Western Democracies—are intrinsic to God's purposes."[6] Eugene Rogers, also a theologian, enters from the other extreme, bringing natural law in Aquinas back to its roots in Paul's Letter to the Romans. Aquinas's notion of natural law cannot, he argues, be severed from the theological story of its ineffectuality, that despite (or perhaps even because of) their knowledge of God and the natural law, as St. Paul writes, the Gentiles were given up to shameful practices.[7]

---

[4]E. A. Goerner, "Response to Hall," *Political Theory* 18, 4 (1990): 654. Goerner is responding to the critique by Pamela Hall of his views in her "Goerner on Thomistic Natural Law," *Political Theory* 18, 4 (1990): 638–49.

[5]Reinhold Niebuhr, "Christian Faith and Natural Law," in *Love and Justice: Selections from the Shorter Writings of Reinhold Niebuhr*, ed. D. B. Robertson (Philadelphia: Westminster Press, [1992], c1957), 46–54. Also excerpted in *St. Thomas Aquinas On Politics and Ethics. A New Translation, Backgrounds, Interpretations*, trans. and ed. Paul E. Sigmund (New York: W. W. Norton, 1988), 222–25.

[6]Stanley Hauerwas, *The Peaceable Kingdom: A Primer in Christian Ethics* (Notre Dame, IN: University of Notre Dame Press, 1983), 59. Cited in Jean Porter, *Nature as Reason: A Thomistic Theory of Natural Law* (Grand Rapids, MI: W. B. Eerdmans, 2005), 332.

[7]Eugene F. Rogers, Jr., "The Narrative of Natural Law in Aquinas's Commentary on Romans 1," *Theological Studies* 59 (1998): 254–76. In his commentary, Aquinas argues that the Gentiles recognized God as the super-eminent good but failed to worship God once recognized and, instead of gratitude to God, "ascrib[ed] their good things to their own ingenuity and virtue." See Rogers, 268 and Thomas Aquinas, *Super Epistolam ad Romanos Lectura*, in *Super Epistolas S. Pauli Lectura* (Taurini: Marietti, 1953), 1:21, #127. Hereafter cited as "In Rom." with the chapter and verse commented on, and the numbered division from the Marietti edition.

For Rogers, as opposed to Niebuhr, Aquinas recognizes the limitations of our ability to recognize and apply moral principles, asserting the necessity of grace for any good action. On such a view the value of natural law on its own as a means for knowing and doing the good is insufficient.

Rogers is a minority voice in connecting Aquinas's account back to Romans.[8] Patrick Farrell's 50+ year old study of Aquinas's sources is still the broadest ranging account, going back to Homer and forward through Plato, Aristotle, the Stoics, legal sources, and so on. Farrell spends only a few of his 58 pages on Christian sources and no mention is made of scripture.[9] Jean Porter's *Natural and Divine Law: Reclaiming the Tradition for Christian Ethics* takes considerable care to note the scriptural warrants for natural law that were important for scholastic accounts, arguing that for the scholastics natural law was, indeed, a "scriptural" rather than philosophical concept; she concludes, however, that for the scholastics nature, reason, and scripture were taken to be harmonious sources for the same moral principles rather than in some kind of tension.[10]

In what follows, I will look at how these diverse views of natural law are derived from Aquinas's writings. Instead of concluding, as most have, that opposing accounts of Aquinas's natural law are a result of misinterpretation by one side or the other, I would like to suggest that it is Aquinas himself who is responsible for this divergence of interpretations, that they flow out of tensions, ambivalences, and the methodological assumptions of his writing. I will look at four areas of tension. First, I examine the idea of 'nature' in natural law, in light of the multiple states of nature in the Christian story of paradise, fall, and redemption. Second, I will consider the way in which what it is to be rational stands in tension with what it is to have a nature in the sense described in Aristotle's *Physics*. Third, I will consider the relationship between the largely non-theological focus of the questions of the so-called "treatise on law" and the strongly theological context of these questions within the *Summa theologiae*. Fourth, I will look at the ways in which Aquinas's answers to particular questions on natural and human law reveal similar tensions. I will conclude with some thoughts about what Aquinas might be trying to achieve in constructing an account so carefully and precariously perched on a point between the extremes that have been attributed to him.

---

[8]Cf. B. Montagnes, "Autonomie et dignité de l'homme" *Angelicum* 51 (1974): 186–211. Montagnes argues that Aquinas's account of natural law is based in Romans but argues that what Aquinas finds warrant for in Paul's notion of the natural law is the dignity and autonomy of human nature rather than the Augustinian emphasis on the universality of sin. I discuss these divergent interpretations of Aquinas's views of Romans below.

[9]Patrick Farrell, O.P., "Sources of St. Thomas' Concept of Natural Law," *The Thomist* 20 (1957): 237–94. Christian sources are discussed on pages 275–83; the article includes several appendices of texts from ancient sources.

[10]Jean Porter, *Natural and Divine Law: Reclaiming the Tradition for Christian Ethics* (Ottawa: Novalis; Grand Rapids, MI: Eerdmans, 1999). See also Jean Porter, "Natural Law as a Scriptural Concept: Theological Reflections on a Medieval Theme," *Theology Today* 59, 2 (2002): 226–41.

Nature That Never Was

It is one of the great (perhaps *the* great) truism that for Aquinas "grace completes and does not destroy nature." Moreover, nature, Aquinas asserts in his discussion of original sin, is "neither subtracted from nor given by sin."[11] Whatever truly belonged to nature in the Garden would have remained after sin, Aquinas maintains.[12] But there is difficulty over what is meant by nature in Aquinas and thus for the nature in "natural law." For though nature is constant even in states of sin and grace, Aquinas also holds that its moral expression and ability are different in these different circumstances.

Aquinas himself often gives the impression that the state of Adam before sin was the state of pure nature. For example, while considering whether man can do or will any good without grace, Aquinas begins with the distinction, "human nature may be considered in two ways: first, in its integrity, as it was in our first parent before sin, secondly, as it is corrupted in us after the sin of our first parent."[13] Yet when discussing Adam's state directly, he is very explicit that Adam is not natural man. In Adam, he explains, "the primitive subjection by which reason was subject to God [and hence the lower powers to reason and the body to the soul] was not a merely natural gift, but a supernatural gift of grace."[14] Not only were the passions entirely subject to reason in Adam but Adam lacked any passions having to do with evil, such as fear or sorrow, and had only the habit but not the act of virtues connected to any imperfection not present in the primitive state, such as penance or mercy or shame.[15] Moreover, he possesses temperance and fortitude only as regards positive goods rather than evil; thus fortitude in Adam moderates daring and hope but not fear and sorrow, and temperance moderates only joy not sorrow.[16]

Aquinas navigates a host of other fascinating questions on the state of innocence—such as whether Adam ate, whether he begot children by coition,

---

[11] Thomas Aquinas, *Summa theologiae*, Part I, q. 98, 2. Hereafter referred to by "ST" along with the part number, question, and article number (along with objection or response number where appropriate), e.g., "I ST 98, 2." I have adjusted the Blackfriars translation into English (New York: Benzinger, 1947–8) on the basis of the Leonine edition, made digitally available by Roberto Buso, http://www.corpusthomisticum.org/iopera.html. Aquinas makes this claim in the context of discussing whether there would be generation through coition in the state of nature. I will discuss these and other issues for life before the fall below, but I note here that when discussing whether *sin* "diminishes the good of nature," Aquinas argues that while the natural powers of the soul are unchanged by sin, "the natural inclination to virtue" *is diminished* though not extinguished by sin. I–II ST, 85, 1.

[12] I ST 95, 1. Aquinas is extremely subtle on this, calling original sin "the sin of nature," because of its transmission to all those sharing Adam's nature but describing its effects not as the loss of nature but the loss of the supernatural gift of original justice without which "the diverse powers of the soul are pulled in different directions." I–II ST 81, 1; 82, 2, ad 2.

[13] I–II ST 109, 2.

[14] I ST 95. 1.

[15] I ST 95, 3.

[16] I ST 95, 3, ad 2.

and whether females of the species would have been born. To these questions Aquinas answers yes; moreover, he rejects the claims that children in the state of nature would have immediate and perfect use of reason and their bodies. All these responses assert continuity between the state of humankind before and after the fall. But besides the different configurations of virtue before and after the fall just noted, Aquinas asserts other important differences between pre- and post-lapsarian human life. Before the fall, Adam possessed immortality that was not natural but a supernatural gift;[17] in paradise there was no subjugation of one man to another and animals were subject to human beings but not in any way used by them, except for purposes of gaining knowledge.[18]

I focus on such details to make it clear just how different the state of Adam is from what we think of, thanks to modern philosophers, as the "state of nature." Adam's choices and virtues are, moreover, quite far from the life of virtue as described by Aristotle. Aristotle's life of virtue involves the acquisition of virtue in a world in which loss is possible: death and vulnerability are its hallmarks, and the achievement of virtue is measured against the possibility of being overwhelmed by those losses, as well as by concupiscence and moral weakness.[19]

Nature is not for Aquinas found in its essential, pure state in Adam but nor is it in the moral life of either the vicious or virtuous. In the wicked, Aquinas notes, "the natural inclination to virtue is corrupted by vicious habits, and, moreover, the natural knowledge of good is darkened by passions and habits of sin." Contrariwise in the good, "beyond the natural knowledge of good, there is added knowledge of faith and wisdom, and beyond the natural inclination to good, there is added the interior motive of grace and virtue."[20] As Aquinas notes, nature is not inclined "at first" to all virtuous acts but men are led to them by reason.[21] Thus the purely natural knowledge of right and wrong that is the natural law is, before we even think about opening Aquinas's *Commentary on Romans*, harder to find in human life as actually lived than most natural law theorists have implied. Though Aquinas emphasizes that the natural law can never be completely obliterated from the heart, he also claims that that remaining knowledge is of the most general principles, not of particular actions.[22] Natural law, the "naturally known principles of both knowledge and action," are, he writes, "*nurseries* (*seminalia*) of the intellectual and moral

---

[17]I ST 97, 1. This is, nonetheless, a difficult position for Aquinas to hold and he later argues that death is both natural and unnatural or penal, natural for the body and unnatural or penal for the soul. II–II ST 164, 1, ad 1.

[18]I ST 96, 1, ad 3; see also I ST 96, 2 & 4.

[19]Aquinas is clearly aware of this, asking whether the actions of Adam were less meritorious than ours because they would have been without difficulty and struggle. I ST 95, 4.

[20]I–II ST 93, 6.

[21]I–II ST 94, 3.

[22]I ST 94, 6. Cf. I ST 94, 4.

virtues."[23] Those principles are, to shift the metaphor slightly, no more than seeds, and those seeds are always grown into something better or worse than neutral nature. The moral state and moral knowledge is dynamic rather than fixed, growing out of and beyond those natural seeds into virtue and grace or decaying under the weight of vice and sin.

Nonetheless, in a host of other passages, passages better known and more often quoted by natural law theorists, Aquinas seems to assert without qualification a natural state, natural virtue, and natural end for the human being as if they do or can exist independently. Early in the second part of the *Summa theologiae* Aquinas describes the human being as having two ends, one natural, one supernatural, a distinction he averts to frequently in the discussion of happiness, virtue, law, and grace.[24] He calls the happiness proportionate to human nature "imperfect happiness" and asserts that it "can be had in this life, acquired by human being by natural powers in the same way as virtue, in whose operation it consists."[25] He follows through on this claim, using the distinction between natural (or imperfect) and supernatural (or perfect) happiness, and maintaining the achievability of the former in the discussion of the virtues: "Human beatitude or happiness is two-fold . . . one is proportionate to human nature, which man can obtain by the principles of his nature."[26] Perhaps the most direct, indicative statement of this possibility as actualized is this one: "it is possible by means of human works to acquire moral virtues, in so far as they produce good works that are directed to an end not exceeding the natural human power; and thus acquired, they can be without charity, just as they were in many of the Gentiles."[27] Again in discussing the necessity for grace, Aquinas divides the natural from the supernatural end: "In the state of the integrity of nature, as regards the sufficiency of the operative power, human being could by his natural powers will and do the good proportionate to his nature, such as the

[23]I–II ST 63, 1. The question is whether virtue is in us by nature. Aquinas adds, moreover, that what is in us by nature are these undeveloped aptitudes, but they are not in us perfectly. The imperfection in this case is not our imperfection as moral or finite beings; it is rather that as natural they are determined to one thing but that their perfection "does not depend on one particular mode of action, but on various modes, in respect of various matters which constitute the sphere of action of the virtues, and according to various circumstances." I will return to the issue of the indetermination of reason as opposed to nature below.

[24]The first time the distinction is used in the opening questions on happiness is I–II ST, 3, 2, ad 4 and it is invoked many times after that: I–II ST, 3, aa. 3, 5, 6, 7; 4, aa. 5, 6, 7, 8; 5, aa. 3, 4, 5. Much could be said (and much of it has been said) about how Aquinas moves between the notion of imperfect happiness *as an anticipation of or participation in* perfect happiness (in the beatific vision) and the notion of natural *as opposed to* supernatural happiness. The former implies a single end to which there are lesser approximations, while the latter seems to posit two separate and independent ends. The ambiguity is exploited by those claiming that there is and is achievable a natural happiness and hence natural virtue and natural moral knowledge (in the principles of natural law) vs. those who argue that there is no such natural or secular end that can be abstracted from Aquinas's larger theology.

[25]I–II ST 5, 5.

[26]I–II ST 62, 1.

[27]I–II ST 65, 2.

good of acquired virtue."[28] In asserting the need for another law besides eternal law, of which natural law is a participation by human reason, Aquinas notes "if human being were ordained only to an end proportionate to his natural power, human being would have no need for any further direction on the part of reason beyond the natural law and human law derived from it."[29] This language returns to the conditional but, nonetheless, asserts the separability of the natural from the supernatural. In such passages, Aquinas seems to invite readers to do what modern commentators like Lisska and Goerner have done: simply abstract nature from supernature, with or without precision.

According to Eugene Rogers, Aquinas's *Commentary on Romans* tells a very different story from the one implied by the comments just cited. In the Romans commentary Aquinas insists that natural knowledge can no longer "lead beings to the good" because human beings after the fall are captured by sin; what natural law reveals is sin rather than virtue and self-determination.[30] Rogers draws our attention to an important passage in which Aquinas wonders what Paul can mean by his claim that the Gentiles "naturally did those things that were of the law"; for, he continues, such a claim "seems to furnish a defense for the Pelagians, who taught that human beings were able to observe all the precepts of the law by their own nature." Aquinas responds that by "naturally" Paul must mean either "nature reformed by grace" or "the natural law . . . which is the light of natural reason." In the latter case, he adds, grace is still needed for moving the affect to action.[31] The story told in Romans is of natural knowledge leading toward ignorance and degradation, not the contrary. "In short," Rogers concludes, "in the Romans commentary, Aquinas followed Paul to make knowledge depend upon justice. Under conditions of injustice, human knowledge fails so badly that Aquinas called it ignorance."[32] As we saw above, in the *Summa*, by contrast, Aquinas seems to say that the Gentiles did have natural knowledge of the good and did achieve natural virtue. Moreover, he separates knowledge from justice in the *Summa*, arguing that those possessed of nature without grace, even after the fall, know the truth though they cannot do it.[33] Rogers brings these two sets of passages into alignment by assimilating the *Summa* to the Romans commentary such that the positive and independent account of nature in the *Summa* must be understood as nature reformed or moved by grace. Rogers concludes that Aquinas only "abstract[s] from the context of grace for temporary purposes of analysis."[34]

---

[28]I–II ST 109, 2.

[29]I–II ST 91, 4.

[30]In Rom. 1:18, #112; 3:20, #297.

[31]In Rom. 2:14, #215–6. Cited in Rogers, 261.

[32]Rogers, "Narrative of Natural Law," 272.

[33]I–II ST 109, 1.

[34]Rogers, "Narrative of Natural Law," 261–2, n. 36; 265.

The near paradox here is that nature in the form to which Aquinas so often appeals: integral or whole nature, that is, nature without sin or grace (the nature which grounds Aquinas's entire morality and anthropology, which he insists is neither forfeited nor acquired by sin) never existed in the past and does not, for Aquinas, exist in the present, or in the future. For Charles Curran, that nature as such is "an abstraction that has never existed in history" is a reason to rethink and perhaps look elsewhere for a foundation of morality.[35] For philosophical commentators like Goerner, Lisska, Finnis, and Grisez, the abstraction of nature from grace they perform begins in Aquinas himself and in his apparent assertions, contra Romans, that nature and natural law *can* function independently and successfully without grace, before and to some degree after the fall. Aquinas's Romans commentary can be reconciled with the account of nature and natural law in the *Summa* but only by using the claims of one as strong interpretive principle for the other, in effect reducing one to the other.

Nature and Reason

There is also another kind of tension in Aquinas's account of nature. Martin Rhonheimer draws a clear distinction between natural law as located in reason, which itself generates the notion of human nature, versus natural law as read off the natural or cosmic order of things, to which reason then conforms. Rhonheimer argues strongly that Aquinas's view is the former, but there are passages which sound like the latter. Aquinas derives the precepts of natural law not just from the general idea of having a nature directed (as all natures are) toward an end, but from what human beings share with plant and animal natures.[36] As is well known, Aquinas grounds his arguments against homosexuality on the notion of the nature human beings share with

[35]Charles Curran, *The Catholic Moral Tradition Today: A Synthesis* (Washington, D.C.: Georgetown University Press, 1999), 40–42. Cited in Porter, *Nature as Reason*, 379–80, n. 64. Curran's objections to standard accounts of Thomistic natural law are to the dichotomy of nature and supernature and the resulting separation between life in this world and the next, as well as to the emphasis on nature and reason as the sources for Christian morality to the detriment of scripture, lessening both the reality of sin and the promise of resurrection. Porter admits that nature is an abstraction for Aquinas but this admission neither undermines nor changes her version of natural law theory in any appreciable way. Porter concludes her book with an account of the work the distinction between nature and grace does for Aquinas, without which theology has difficulties making grace even partially intelligible. It's quite clear that "nature" does a lot of work for Aquinas and that doing theology or philosophy without it presents huge, perhaps insuperable, difficulties, but that does not make it unproblematic as a category. See Porter, *Nature as Reason*, 385.

[36]Martin Rhonheimer, "The Cognitive Structure of the Natural Law and the Truth of Subjectivity," *The Thomist* 67 (2003): 1–44.

animals.[37] Yet just as often Aquinas argues that having rationality frees human beings from the instinctual path followed by non-rational animals. While the appetite of animals is determined to one thing by their natures, the intellect considers, judges, and chooses freely from among all things it knows and may consider as good.[38]

Like the question of distinct natural and supernatural ends, the issue of whether the morality of nature owes more to the determination of nature or to the freedom brought by reason is much vexed in Aquinas. Aquinas insists that human beings, like any nature, have a natural end that determines their good, but he also insists that rationality removes the determination of that end by instinct. Reason opens up as possible choices of the good all that the intellect can consider. Having a rational nature, in other words, means having a nature *not* determined by inclination or any particular ends; rather it is moved necessarily only by the universal and perfect good. The nature of rationality is, to put it somewhat provocatively, to lack the determination of nature for Aquinas. Jean Porter, who ultimately rejects Rhonheimer's view and tries to ground natural law in a human nature we can discover empirically, nonetheless realizes the pitfalls of this view. For appeals to what animals do and what human beings as animals do as normative for human beings are extremely problematic, resting as they do on empirical studies either of evolutionary biology, primatology, and/or anthropology.[39] And Porter, like many contemporary theorists, rejects the version of 'natural law' in which nature determines the end not just of the whole but of the parts of organisms (e.g., sexual organs have the function of reproduction). Such an interpretation can make of Aquinas a kind of Aristotelian socio-biologist.

---

[37]I–II ST 94, 3, ad 2. Aquinas distinguishes between two ways something can be against nature—anything against reason is against nature and, in this sense, all vices are against nature, or something can be against "the nature common to man and other animals, according to which only certain sins are against nature, so that against the commingling of male and female, which is the natural to all animals, is the intercourse of men, which is called a vice against nature in a special way." This reply captures the tension between the notion that what is against nature for human beings is what is against reason, and nature law as against nature as found in the natural or cosmic order displayed in the world and which humans need to discern and to which they should conform. Rhonheimer lays out this distinction well and locates the latter view in the Stoics and Cicero. See Rhonheimer, "Cognitive Structure of Natural Law."

[38]See for example I ST 82, 2, ad 1–3; 83, 1; cf. QDV 22, 6; 24, 1. See Eileen C. Sweeney, "From Determined Motion to Undetermined Will and Nature to Supernature in Aquinas," *Philosophical Topics*, 20, 2 (Fall 1992):192–96. What I show is that Aquinas's argument for free choice is grounded in the analogy of free choice to natural motion such that in the *Summa theologiae* he builds up to the notion of free choice from nature rather than by contrasting directly the determination of nature to the indetermination of choice in a rational being. The parallel passages in *De veritate* tend to oppose nature and freedom rather than seeing freedom as the nature of a rational being. However, even in the *Summa*, though couched in terms of continuity between nature and freedom, it is clear that what it means to have a rational nature is to be undetermined except in the face of the universal and perfect good from which, Aquinas argues, we can still avert our gaze.

[39]Porter, *Nature as Reason*, 105–6.

At the other extreme, with the emphasis on the freedom that comes with rationality, Aquinas begins to sound notes more at home in existentialism. This issue of nature vs. reason is connected to the debate about whether or not there is for Aquinas a "pure nature" for human beings whose end can be discerned and achieved apart from grace. Henri De Lubac strongly rejected the notion of pure nature in Aquinas as a modern importation. He did so not just because in his view the supernatural end is the one and only end for human beings but also because reason, freedom, and history, he argued, place human beings outside the constraints of nature, and free them from having a determinate natural end.[40] On De Lubac's view, it is not the analogy between human nature and those of animals and plants that provides content to the moral law; rather it is reason itself and its freedom from natural instinct that gives morality its character. Rational beings are not satisfied with a single or finite good because they are able to consider all things under the aspect of good and desire a universal and perfect good. Thus we arrive at another paradox, that human nature, because it is rational, exceeds its nature, desiring more than the good merely proportionate to its nature.

The "Treatise on Law": Context and Autonomy

What theologians and more historically minded commentators on Aquinas never tire of pointing out (and what philosophers and systematicians never tire of ignoring) is that the questions discussing law are not a "treatise on law" at all but a part of the much larger summa of *theology*.[41] The questions abstracted from the *Summa* as the "treatise on law" are bookended by topics that by Aquinas's own definition fall completely and only under *sacra doctrina*, not philosophy; the questions on law are preceded by a discussion of sin and followed by Aquinas's account of the "Old Law," the prescriptions and prohibitions for human action in the Hebrew bible, and the "New Law," the same from the

---

[40]See Porter, *Nature as Reason*, 104. De Lubac, *Mystery of the Supernatural*, 131–53.

[41]Eugene Rogers, as we saw above, insists on the context of Paul's letter to Romans as the context for the discussion of natural law. Rogers, "Natural Law, Aquinas and Romans 1," 254–8. In a very different way Romanus Cessario also insists on the theological character of natural law, arguing that there is a "properly theological appreciation of natural law only within the context of the Trinitarian ordering of human existence in conformity with the rhythms established within the eternal law." Romanus Cessario, O. P., "Why Aquinas Locates Natural Law within the *Sacra Doctrina*," in *St. Thomas Aquinas and the Natural Law Tradition: Contemporary Perspectives*, John Goyette, Mark S. Latkovic, and Richard S. Myers, eds., (Washington, D.C.: The Catholic University of America Press, 2004), 92. Pamela Hall and Jean Porter, one a philosopher and the other a theologian, make the most sustained attempts to both read the "treatise on law" in some sense on its own and place it in its context in the *Summa*. In *Narrative and the Natural Law*, Hall reads the questions on the Old and New Law as adumbrating human moral development from, against, and beyond natural law in Aquinas. In *Nature as Reason* Porter attempts to see nature and natural law as part of Aquinas's theology which, she argues, needs nature and natural happiness as a separate category, not just, as I mentioned above, to provide a backdrop for grace but also to assert the goodness of creation.

Christian New Testament. Part I–II ends with a long series of questions on grace. In the second part of part II, the questions on the natural virtues and vices are similarly sandwiched between the theological virtues of faith, hope, and love and the graces of prophecy, tongues, and miracles.

Nonetheless, we find that Aquinas keeps his focus mainly on political rather than theological matters within the questions on law. In the first question on law, after answering the objection from Romans that perhaps the 'law' operative in human life is the law of sin or inclination rather than reason, Aquinas defines the 'essence of law' in terms most clearly applicable to human or civil law, laying the groundwork for the criteria for just human law. It is of the essence of law to seek the common good, and since the common good belongs to the whole people, it is of the essence of law that the people make law, either directly or indirectly through a representative "who has the care of the whole people."[42] These two elements Aquinas expands on in his account of unjust laws.[43] A law is just when it is ordered to the common good and "imposed according to equality of proportion." Moreover, the law is just when it is within the power of the lawgiver to make it.[44] The additional element of the "essence of law" not explicitly revisited in the account of just human law is promulgation.[45] Promulgation belongs only in an extended sense to natural law but applies, of course, most directly to human laws, such that those to whom it will be applied be notified.[46]

After having constructed the frame of the discussion of law, within eternal law and in relation to divine law, Aquinas's focus in the discussion of natural and human law within that frame is on how human political life should work; it is the issue around which the account of law begins, asking about the essence of law, and at which it ends, discussing the standards for just laws, the limits of law, and the ways and mechanisms by which human law can be changed.

On the limits of human law and government, Aquinas attempts to craft a balanced compromise between ancient, theocratic, and modern notions of the role and limits of government. Thus Aquinas argues that human laws do not forbid all but only the most grievous vices from which the majority can refrain, "chiefly those that are to the hurt of others, without the prohibition of which human society could not be maintained."[47] Similarly, Aquinas argues, human law doesn't prescribe all virtues but only those that pertain to the common

[42]I–II ST 90, 2–3.

[43]I–II ST 96, 4.

[44]I–II ST 94, 4.

[45]I–II ST 90, 4.

[46]In fact, that laws must be promulgated is the basis of one of Harry Jaffa's criticisms of natural law as *law* in Aquinas: laws have to be promulgated by the legitimate legislator. Thus, to accept natural law *as law* requires belief in God as legislator. Harry Jaffa, *Thomism and Aristotelianism* (Chicago: University of Chicago Press, 1950), 167–70. Cited in Hall, 3–4.

[47]I–II ST 96, 2.

good. It isn't just a matter of doing what is minimal or possible, however, for Aquinas maintains that when it comes to law, restraint actually promotes virtue, by leading to it gradually and without creating such a large burden on "the imperfect" that they will "break out in greater evils."[48] Thus, Aquinas supports the ancient Greek view that the role of government and law is to make human beings good, thereby rejecting the modern notion, which has roots in Augustine, that government is only about preventing violence and cannot or should not aim at more.[49] Yet, as we have seen, Aquinas at the same time calls for pragmatic limits on what government can and should do to prohibit vice and command virtue, thereby rejecting the notion that the coercive power of government is to be used to bring the population to full virtue, as it is in theocracies.[50]

There are, of course, delicate nuances and tremendous difficulties that have been and continue to be debated about what exactly Aquinas's political theory might mean for the governing of the earthly city, and I don't pretend to even name them, no less solve them here. What I wish to point out is only that Aquinas himself seems to set his sights on the earthly city in concrete ways and is moved by political rather than theological concerns. For in what Aquinas does (and not just what he leaves out) in these questions, his perspective is pragmatic and predominantly secular. To use Goerner's memorable phrase, there is very little of the "incense of the altar or the smoke of the lamp" in these questions.

An argument can be made that the first part of part II of the *Summa theologiae*, given its subjects of the natural law, Old Law, New Law, and grace, is really driven by theological concerns, that it takes up one of the crucial topics found in Paul's letter to the Romans in the relationship between these as paths to righteousness. However, what is most striking about this portion of the *Summa* is that for the duration of the so-called "treatise on law," Aquinas softens and postpones the completion of the Pauline story about what happens to human nature guided by natural law alone. Paul's Letter to the Romans is a potent presence in these questions, as Rogers and Montagnes note, but Aquinas uses Romans for the claim there *is* a natural law, saving for much later what Paul Harvey used to call "the rest of the story": the *failure* of natural law. For Paul argues in Romans that natural knowledge of the good did not make the Gentiles more but rather less moral; claiming to be wise, they became fools and God "gave them up to degrading passions." (Rom 1: 22-26) Aquinas quotes Paul's assertion (Rom 2: 14) that "the Gentiles, who have not the law, do by nature those things that are of the law," in the *sed contra* of the article devoted

---

[48] I–II ST 96, 2., ad 2.

[49] I–II ST 92, 1; 95, 1.

[50] Alasdair MacIntyre describes Aquinas as disagreeing with both later "puritans" and "liberals." "Like those puritans and unlike those liberals [Aquinas] understands the law as an instrument for our moral education. But, like those liberals and unlike those puritans, he is against making law by itself an attempt to repress all vice." Alasdair MacIntyre, "Natural Law as Subversive: The Case of Aquinas," *Journal of Medieval and Early Modern Studies* 26.1 (1996): 66.

to affirming the existence of natural law.[51] His only comment on it is to quote the *Glossa ordinaria*, which explains that the natural law is that "whereby each one knows, and is conscious of, what is good and what is evil."[52] Only in a later question, in an objection, does Aquinas quote the continuation of the gloss: "the law of justice, which sin had blotted out, is graven on the heart of man when he is restored by grace." In this context, Aquinas does not take up the issue of whether grace is *inter alia* a restoration of natural law, but he rejects the implication that the natural law *could be* blotted out in the first place.[53]

When Aquinas is arguing for the need for a divine law in addition to natural and human law, he gives four reasons for it, but none of them assert, except very obliquely, the Romans narrative of natural law leading to sin. He cites, first, the supernatural end of human beings, for which end a new law is required; second, the uncertainty of human judgment, such that we need divine law to know exactly what to do and refrain from doing; third, the inability of human law to judge of interior acts, and, fourth, the inability of human law to forbid or punish all evil deeds (because it would go against the common good).[54] That human judgments fail in matters contingent and particular, the argument of these four that comes closest to asserting Paul's narrative, is a considerably more anodyne statement on human weakness than Paul's account of the human condition captured in his lament, "I do not do the good that I want but the evil I do not want is what I do." (Rom. 7: 19)

Aquinas does bring up the "law in the fomes of sin" more than once in these questions. The phrase goes back to Peter Lombard and John Damascene to describe the consequences of original sin; in response to the passage from Romans just cited (7: 19), Aquinas describes the "fomes" as "the continual corruption of the sensuality."[55] Aquinas glosses the "law in the fomes of sin," with a similar sentiment from Romans: "I see another law in my members, fighting against the law in my mind" (Rom. 7: 23). When we look beyond the archaic language of "fomes," we see that an important question is being asked: whether what is natural to human beings is sin and vice, whether human beings are naturally inclined toward good or evil. Natural law accounts of morality must maintain that our natural inclinations are toward rather than away from the good.

---

[51]The same verse, Rom 2:14, is quoted a number of times, all without reference to the failure of natural law. See I–II ST 90, 3, obj 1; 91, 2, sed contra; 96, 5, ad 1; 100, 1, sed contra; 106, 1, obj 2 again 106, 1, obj 2. On Aquinas's use of this passage see Montagnes, "Autonomie et dignité," 186–211.

[52]I–II ST 91, 2, sed contra.

[53]I–II ST 94, 6, obj 1 and cor. The Gloss says both that sin cannot completely remove the image of God from the soul and that the law of justice is "deleted" or "blotted out" by sin. *Glossa ordinaria*, ed. Migne, *Patrologiae Cursus Completus*, (1852): v. 114, 475–76. Translated in Porter, *Nature as Reason*, 4.

[54]I–II ST 91, 4.

[55]I–II ST 74, 3. Cf., III ST 27, 4, Peter Lombard, *Sententiarum Quatuor Libri*, Book II, distinction 30, chap. 8–9, http://franciscan-archive.org/lombardus/opera/ls2-30.html; John Damascene, *De Fide Orthodoxa*, Book IV, 22 (*Patrologia Graeca*, vol. 94, 1200).

Aquinas addresses the possibility that the law that rules human nature is in the "fomes" rather than reason, that, in other words, what is natural to human beings is the propensity to sin rather than virtue, with the cool of the clinician rather than the fervor of the preacher. He is careful not to allow any human propensity to sin to overwhelm the claim he wants to maintain against objections: that human beings have connatural knowledge of the basic principles of morality, a knowledge that is universal and indelible. The opposite movement, the "inclination of sensuality," Aquinas explains, is natural law for the other animals, while in human beings it is "a deviation" from the law of reason, the law that is natural to human beings, even though it can, of course, happen that the sensual inclination to sin can become in some sense 'natural' to a human being "the more he withdraws from reason."[56]

In the Letter to the Romans, Paul does not use the notion of natural law to argue for natural human goodness nor, of course, to ground an ethics. Rather, it is used to chastise both Jew and Gentile for their wickedness. Gentiles have the knowledge but fail to live according to it, rejecting its source, and Jews are reminded that they are not exclusive possessors of the law, that the Gentiles have it as natural while they have it as revealed law; thus, all have the law but, more importantly all fail to keep the law, so they are, "without excuse" and in need of grace. Rom. 1-2. Aquinas comes to the overwhelming of natural law by sin in the *Summa* that is the moral of Paul's account in Romans, but it occurs quite late, after the discussion of natural and human law, and the Old Law and the New, in the first question on grace. It is worth noting that some of the clearest and most direct accounts of what nature is and can do on its own are made in this first question on grace. As Aquinas considers whether without grace one can know truth, do good, love God, fulfill the law, merit eternal life, or prepare oneself for grace, he rather carefully and gradually turns from an emphasis on nature to one on grace. He argues, first, that in order to know truths proportionate to human nature, a human being does not need a "new light added to its natural light." Only in article 2, on willing good, does he answer in terms of the distinction between nature "in its integrity" versus "as corrupted in us" after the first sin.[57] In terms of willing the good, it is only in the "integrity of nature" that "human being by his natural powers could will and do the good proportionate to his nature, such as the good of acquired virtue." Fallen human nature can, he

---

[56]I–II ST 91, 6. The "fomes of sin" arises again in an objection to the notion that every law is derived from eternal law. I–II ST 93, 3, obj 1. Aquinas replies that *qua* punishment for sin, it is part of eternal law, but *qua* proneness to sin, it is not. Ibid., ad 1. Worry about the same issue opens the questions on law; to the question of whether law is something to do with reason, the first objection quotes Paul on "another law in my members." Rom. 7: 23. I–II 90, 1, obj 1.

[57]I–II ST 109, 2. As Jean-Pierre Torrell points out, "integrity of nature" here can only mean nature before the fall but abstracting from original justice, which Adam had but which is not natural but a gift beyond nature. See Jean-Pierre Torrell, "Nature et grâce chez Thomas d'Aquin," *Revue Thomiste* 101 (2001): 167–202.

adds, "by virtue of its natural powers, accomplish some particular good, such as building houses, planting vineyards, and the like. . . ."[58] It's not clear whether Aquinas's examples are meant to exclude moral acts since he lists none, and when he turns to moral acts specifically, his answer is mixed. In the state of integral nature, a human being could, as regards the "substance" of the act, act justly, though he cannot act from the right motive of charity. When Aquinas turns to whether without grace one can avoid sin, the answer is a nest of distinctions, parsing the issue even more finely. In the state of nature, Adam could avoid both mortal and venial sin (though needing God "to uphold him in good," which may only mean support him in existence). With healing grace, which heals the mind but not the appetite, one can avoid all mortal sin and each but not all venial sin. Without justifying grace, one can avoid each mortal sin though not every one and not for long.[59] These are very fine distinctions, with every step toward natural goodness counterbalanced by one step back toward the inability to do good. He moves away from both extremes –nature remains fully good and nature has become perversely evil, yet never completely rejects either.

Only when Aquinas considers whether those who already have grace need additional grace or can act themselves do we get the full Pauline account of the need for grace. In this reply there are four scripture passages, two from Romans, one from Wisdom and a citation of "lead us not into temptation" from the "Our Father." "For," Aquinas argues, human nature "though healed by grace as to the mind, yet remains corrupted and infected in the flesh by which it serves the law of sin." Even in the intellect, which is what is healed by grace, "there remains the darkness of ignorance." Here, at last, is the Pauline/Augustinian language of the anguish and darkness of sin; grace is needed for "directing and protecting" both body and mind, reason and passion.[60] Paradoxically, Aquinas moves to assert the weakness of nature only after he has already carefully mapped out what nature can do without grace and only in the context of arguing for what nature *even with grace* still needs in additional grace in order to do good.

There are, as I have noted, passages in which the larger theological context is signaled within the questions on natural and human law, just as in more overtly theological topics, more (to our ways of thinking) philosophical concerns are addressed. It is a question of overall tone, of which melody, if you will, is allowed to dominate. In the questions on law, Aquinas does not altogether mute themes voicing the realities of sin, redemption, and grace, though he does lower their volume, dealing with them just enough to keep them from being silenced but not enough to allow them to sound in dissonance with his main fugue subject. Even the scripture passages are less plentiful in these questions, outnumbered by

---

[58]I–II ST 109, 2.

[59]I–II ST 109, 8.

[60]I–II ST 109, 9.Rom. 7: 25; Rom. 8: 26; Wisd. 9: 14.

Isidore, Gratian, and Aristotle.[61] Both his arguments and his deployment of authorities, then, make it easy for those trying to find or craft a philosophical or secular account of natural law to cut natural law loose from the biblical narrative of paradise, fall, and redemption in which it is placed.

Liberal vs. Conservative, Phronesis vs. Law

Aquinas's attempt to craft the ever so delicate balance isn't restricted to that between nature as essence and nature as history, or nature as inclined toward good and toward evil. His responses to particular political questions tend to mirror the strategy of 'on the one hand, on the other hand' we have already seen. On this score, I find it hard to give much credence to those, either among defenders or detractors of Aquinas, who make his account of natural law a deductive ethical system that is rigid and rule-governed.[62] Aquinas crafts a way between extremes on many issues, and so too on this one, he maintains exceptionless principles yet at such a general level that the real work of thought and action is in interpretation and application where there is room for flexibility and a guiding role for phronesis.[63] We already saw his path between ancient and modern notions of the role and limits of government. Similarly on this issue Aquinas embraces the foundation of moral and political life on rules, but he gives prudential reasons (borrowed from Aristotle) for preferring a social order based on laws as opposed to the particular judgments of the wise judge: one needs to find fewer lawmakers to make general rules than judges for each case, that judgments about individual cases have to be made quickly while the construction of laws can proceed more thoughtfully, and because judges judge of the present rather than the future, like lawmakers, they are more influenced by their feelings; thus it is better that as much as possible be crafted as general rules and principles to follow.[64]

The same combination of prudence and principle also shows up on the question of whether to obey an unjust law and whether and how laws can be changed. Aquinas asserts firmly and boldly that unjust laws are not binding in conscience, as we saw, but then argues that, in order to avoid "scandal or disturbance," they

[61] By my informal count of authorities,in questions 94–97 on natural and human law, Isidore is cited 20 times, Aristotle, 18, and Gratian and the Decretals, 17; Augustine is cited 11 times and Paul, 7; other scripture passages are cited 14 times. In the earlier questions on law in general, eternal and divine law, Augustine is cited 30 times, Paul, 18, but 7 for Isidore, 12 for Aristotle, 4 for Gratian and the Decretals, and 16 for other books of scripture.

[62] For an early and clear argument to this effect, see James F. Ross, "Justice is Reasonableness: Aquinas on Human Law and Morality," *Monist* 58 (1974): 86–103.

[63] See for example, I–II ST 94, 5; 95, 2. For a thoughtful look at this issue see John Boler, "Aquinas on Exceptions in Natural Law," in *Aquinas's Moral Theory: Essays in Honor of Norman Kretzmann*, ed. Scott MacDonald and Eleonore Stump (Ithaca, NY: Cornell University Press, 1999), 161–92.

[64] I–II ST 95, 1, ad 2.

should be obeyed, unless they are against the law of God.[65] Similarly, he affirms that human laws can be changed, based on changes in understanding or changes in the condition of the people, but he adds that changing laws is itself damaging to the common good, undermining custom and, hence, the observance of law. Thus, unless the common good is served in a way that overcomes the negative effects of change itself, Aquinas is for maintaining the status quo.[66] Aquinas takes essentially the same position on whether individuals can make exceptions to laws.[67] Similarly, Aquinas splits the difference of whether the sovereign is subject to the law (it is not, he argues, according to its coercive power but is according to its directive power).[68] Aquinas argues strongly in favor of custom as having the force of law since, he writes, "the consensus of the whole people expressed by custom is more important for a particular observance than the authority of the sovereign, who does not have the power to make laws except insofar as in his person he governs for the people"; thus, custom "has the force of law, abolishes law, and is the interpreter of law."[69] But this strong and high-minded support for what MacIntyre calls "plain persons" and communal practices is qualified in two significant ways.[70] First, natural and divine law can only be changed by divine authority, not human action for Aquinas; thus custom must yield to authority, and law and reason trump custom; second, the ability of the people to make law by their customs pertains only to those who are self-governing; if not, they are limited in their customs by what the lawmaker allows.[71] There is never any argument that people should in principle be

---

[65]I–II ST 96, 4. Aquinas adds that laws that inflict unjust suffering exceed the power God gives to lawgivers so such laws can be disobeyed, as long as one can do so "without scandal or inflicting a greater harm" (ad 3).

[66]I–II ST 97, 1–2. Even though suiting laws to the condition of the population has a certain modern and flexible ring to it, Aquinas's example, taken from Augustine, is of a people changed by having lost their "moderation and responsibility" such that they lose the right to govern themselves. See Augustine, *De liberoarbitrio* I, 6.

[67]I–II ST 96, 6.

[68]I–II ST 96, 5, ad 3. Since no one can coerce themselves and since no one can pass judgment on the sovereign, the sovereign is not subject to the coercion of the law. But the sovereign is subject to the law in the sense that it should follow and apply to itself the laws it makes for others, Aquinas argues.

[69]I–II ST 97, 3, cor. and ad 3.

[70]See MacIntyre, "Natural Law as Subversive," 70. MacIntyre argues that Aquinas, in rejecting the view that human law should repress all vice, would have rejected Louis IX's restrictions on gambling, swearing, prostitution, usury, and so forth. In this Aquinas is opposing Louis IX's arrogation of the application of law from "plain persons" to an "exclusive professionalized authority." I find this less persuasive than MacIntyre's related claim that Aquinas rejected in both Louis IX and Frederick II and the Constitutions of Melfi investing "imperial authority with a sacred and numinous quality . . . designed to place actions performed and judgments uttered in the name of that authority quite beyond appeal and quite beyond question." (p. 72). MacIntyre does persuade me that Aquinas's strong support of custom as having the force of law is a stance against royal power and for local control. My only larger point in response to MacIntyre is that for every point Aquinas makes for custom and the people, he makes others supporting the authority of rulers and, above all, priests.

[71]I–II ST 98, 4.

self-governed; it depends on their "moderation and seriousness" as well as custom and tradition, Aquinas maintains.

It is quite difficult to place Aquinas on the political spectrum of liberal vs. conservative, pragmatist or idealist, traditionalist or revolutionary. We could, I suppose, locate him in terms of our contemporary notions of these poles as traditionalist, but within his own political context, things are murkier. What he gives to the revolutionary reformer with one hand, he takes away with the other. Laws can be changed but not often. Unjust laws don't bind in conscience but should often be obeyed anyway. Custom is law and instructs the lawmaker chosen by the people but must bend to the will of the lawmaker when he or she is not so chosen. Laws are without exception, in general but not in particular cases, in principle but not in specification and application. The sovereign is obliged to obey the law but is not subject to punishment or coercion for disregarding the law. Laws that harm people *can* under certain conditions be disobeyed, but laws contrary to divine law *must* be disobeyed. And so on. These are the positions of a determined moderate whose conclusions about more specific political arrangements are a mirror of his very complex notion of human nature as both capable of moral action but not perfect moral action and as both corrupted by sin but not wholly incapable of resisting evil. His positions give, it seems to me, ample evidence to both those who assert and those who deny that one can find precursors in Aquinas of modern political notions like rights, and modern values, like self-governance and even separation of church and state.

Conclusion

It has been quite rightly pointed out that there is only one question devoted to natural law in the entire *Summa theologiae* and there are many ways in which far too much has been hung on this single thread, weighing it down with far more than it can bear. However, from another point of view, we can say that no concept is more important to Aquinas's analysis of morality than nature. As Anthony Lisska puts it, "natural law is not a method for making laws. It is the ontological foundation in human nature which explains the possibility of a moral theory and of lawmaking in the first place."[72] Nature is, one could argue, *the* conceptual tool of the *Summa*.[73] We would find, for example, if we went on in the text, that it is natural law that Aquinas uses to frame his analysis of the Old and New Law.[74] Natural law is the pivot on which he turns from eternal to human law, from the theological

[72]Anthony Lisska, *Aquinas's Theory of Natural Law: An Analytical Reconstruction* (Oxford: Clarendon Press, 1996), 80.

[73]This is not to say that grace is not more important but that, as Porter points out, Aquinas needs the notion of nature off of which to build his notion of grace and supernature.

[74]See Hall, *Narrative of Natural Law*, 45–92.

frame of this discussion to the painting of the body politic within it. But the account of nature is complex and nuanced, sometimes, I fear, to the point of obscurity.

Nature is never lost for Aquinas (this is the melody he plays quite boldly) but it is also never quite found in the sense that perfect and pure nature (without grace or sin) has never existed nor will ever exist (this is the harmony he uses to qualify and nuance the melody). Nature for Aquinas is a bit like source "Q" in New Testament studies. Scholars have good reason to think there was a common source used by the three synoptic gospels because of what is common to Matthew, and Luke, but the existence of "Q" is inferred, not directly experienced outside the synoptic gospels, and within the gospels it is mixed with other elements. If there is no human nature untouched by either the corruption of sin or grace, then the principles of natural law, like source "Q," have to be inferred, not in the sense that we will deduce them from other principles (clearly not, since Aquinas thinks of them as first principles), but in the same sense we have to come to our understanding of other principles: from experience guided by reason. What makes this process more problematic and more difficult is that moral insight, which either is or is the source of natural law, is encumbered, Aquinas reminds us at certain points, even as he, at other points, asserts its integrity. Like those judges Aquinas does not trust because they judge things "towards which they are affected by love, hatred, or some kind of cupidity, so that their judgment is perverted," human moral insight is neither perfect nor immediate. While Aquinas is clearly no skeptic about moral knowledge, neither is he supremely confident that the goodness of nature always will clearly shine through. He is, if you will, neither Rousseau, for whom nature's instincts are infallible, nor Calvin, for whom natural instinct is perverse. Nor is he Aristotle or Cicero. As a Christian, the heights to which nature can aspire and, with grace, achieve, and the depths to which it can fall are greater than for these two philosophers whose ideal is political and philosophical life.

The next tension we explored in this essay, between the directedness of nature and the free ranging capacity of reason is, in a way, that between nature as fulfilled within the world and on its model versus nature as straining beyond its limits toward the infinite. If reason changes in kind and not just degree what it means to have a nature, any attempt to apply or specify the general goods for human beings named in the precepts is, even for the functions humans share with other natures, more complex than simply adducing evidence of what is law-like in non-human natures. Human beings enact the capacities they share with other natures as rational beings, and rational beings may consider an infinite number of ways of fulfilling them and must, in order to fulfill their natures, enter into them as deliberatively and rationally as possible. As Aquinas says quite directly, for human beings to fulfill those capacities as animals do is *against* human nature rather than fulfillment of it.

This is not to say that reaching objectively good conclusions is impossible or that everything that can be considered should be done, but it does mean that there is no simple way of deducing which deviations from animal behavior are contrary to or in accord with human fulfillment because of the way in which natural law for a rational being is affected by free choice in regard to the means and having the supreme infinite good (rather than the mere finite good of a finite nature) as its end.

Aquinas's attempt to give an account of nature and natural law is a tree in the larger forest of the *Summa*, whose model is Jesus Christ and whose end is beatitude. Arguably throughout his writings but certainly in the *Summa*, Aquinas's method and the content of his answers take the position that it is possible to find common ground amongst all his authorities and interlocutors, whether secular or sacred, Christian or not, on any given topic without having a common theory; his aim is to maximize that common ground. That is what allows him to take in so much from these different sources and moves him to concede the truth of so much of what they have to say, shaping it slightly and placing it ever so gently next to the previously carved piece. This, we could say, is the height of practical reason, its true aim. Aquinas's account of natural law is crafted in this way and natural law itself becomes one of the tools Aquinas uses to craft common ground between philosophers and scripture and between Old and New Testaments. Aquinas perhaps makes the most use of the notion of natural law in his analysis of the Old Law to make sense of its precepts. It is a tremendously complex and delicate balancing act. Aquinas seems to think he can keep both particular trees—different authorities and contrary concerns—and larger forest—his own unified vision—in sight at all times.

While there is much to admire in the delicacy and nuance of this composition, its complexities make it easy to ignore whichever is counter-subject to the melody at any given moment. Admonitions to read the *Summa theologiae* as a whole, such that all those melodies are heard in their places within a single symphonic composition notwithstanding, the task is just about impossible. Besides the vastness of the text and its attempt to be a *summa* taking up all topics, the division of subjects, questions, and articles makes the joints very easy to cut. Moreover, Aquinas needs these divisions; he needs to break down the subjects and problems to deal with them one at a time, but, even more, he exploits these divisions to balance one part against another, to emphasize sin and grace in one section and natural goodness and fulfillment in another, to lean in one context on nature and its fixed ends, in another on the open-endedness of reason.

As we have seen, many of the pieces Aquinas finds a place for in his account of natural law pull against others, though the tensions are muffled because spread over such a vast surface. This approach also invites the many divergent readings, nearly all of which can find some support in the text.[75] Moreover, that he is able to take in both reason and nature, heaven and earth, this life and the next seems to give to generation after generation the impression that what he has constructed is the *summa* of all truth rather than something both more flexible and more fleeting. In this too, Aquinas perhaps bears some responsibility, for while he has built complexity into his account of nature that qualifies any inerrancy that might be claimed for it, he seems to assume for the most part unproblematic access to natural law and its conclusions. The reason, perhaps, that Aquinas feels he can in some sense not worry about the uncertainty of moral *reasoning* is because, as we have seen, he seems to think the problem is not intellectual, not a matter of *not knowing* but only of *not doing* the good we necessarily know. This seems naïve about the degree to which reasonable arguments can be put forward for that which is self-interested, about the degree to which human beings are capable not just of moral weakness but moral blindness and self-deception, deploying moral claims to support immoral purposes.

Even the breadth of his vision, the many resources at his disposal, including, importantly, the standard of natural and divine law against which to measure human law, along with the disposition toward careful and moderate answers, does not guarantee wise and just conclusions. Aquinas supported the Church in its persecution of heresy, enlisting secular power for purposes of coercion.[76] He argued that slavery was not part of nature yet argued that it was an allowable arrangement in human society.[77] He gives way, we think today, to theocratic tendencies in relationship to heresy and concedes too much to custom in regard to slavery. Further, I would argue, though I know many Thomists would disagree, he put too much weight on biological nature and not enough on rationality and its transformation of non-rational functions, defining too narrowly the nature and capacities of women and restricting too much the role and meaning of sexual expression and activity.[78]

---

[75]Thus, I take it that it is not just, as Mark Jordan implies, the ideology of those who turn to Aquinas that explains the different things they find there, but that those things are actually there but standing in a complex and subtle relationship to many other things. See Mark D. Jordan, *The Invention of Sodomy in Christian Theology* (Chicago: University of Chicago Press, 1997), 157.

[76]II–II ST 10, 8.

[77]II–II ST 57, ad 2. Cf. III ST Suppl., 52. Aquinas's support of slavery is not complete, but my point is that his condemnation is not complete either, and that his qualified support is based more on utility and custom.

[78]The issues surrounding Aquinas's positions on sexual morality are complicated and long debated, and I do no more than signal one way they might be complicated here. Cf. Jordan, *Inventing Sodomy*, 136–158. See also only as a beginning the selected texts debating some issues in sexual ethics in *St. Thomas Aquinas on Politics and Ethics*, ed. Paul E. Sigmund, 229–48, and Porter, *Natural and Divine Law*, 187–244.

MacIntyre is confident that Aquinas, using natural law, can distinguish between "local prejudice" and "local custom."[79] I am not so sure about Aquinas or, indeed, anyone on that score. Both Reinhold Niebuhr and Bernard Williams express similar concerns about appeals to nature and natural law. Aristotle's defense of slavery as "natural" for Williams is an example of trying to "contrive a settled opinion [on] how far the existence of a worthwhile life for some people involves the imposition of suffering on others." As Williams remarks trenchantly, "that phenomenon has not so much been eliminated from modern life as shifted to different places."[80] We can be and surely are in some ways simply unable to see where it has shifted for us. For Niebuhr, "we had better realize how tentative" any natural law we elaborate is. "Otherwise," he continues, "we shall merely sanction some traditional relation between myself and my fellow man as a 'just' relation. . . . for it will be discovered invariably that my definition of justice guarantees certain advantages to myself to which I have no absolute right, but with which I have been invested by the accidents of history and the contingencies of nature."[81] Neither moral cloudiness nor clarity is the exclusive property of natural law theorists, and even as we cling to the notion that there is a moral standard beyond positive law and custom in natural law to which we can have some access, we have to be wary of enshrining what is merely the prejudice of our time and place as timeless nature. For Niebuhr, the reason for that wariness is the human tendency toward selfishness and sin. Williams's quite similar warning about the limits of natural law is not grounded in that Christian anthropology, though, following Aquinas, I am moved to stand on this important common ground even if—or maybe even because—it was mapped by those who don't share a common theory.

---

[79]This distinction is MacIntyre's. MacIntyre, "Natural Law as Subversive," 80–81. MacIntyre cites a number of Aquinas's particular political determinations. He argues that when Aquinas grounds his answer in natural law, his positions are "as much at odds with local prejudice—as contrasted with local custom—as it is with centralizing power." Thus for MacIntyre natural law *does* yield wise decisions that were contrary to popular prejudices of the time. His examples are Aquinas's positions that unbelievers should not be compelled to convert (as opposed to heretics), that the rule of unbelievers over believers can be legitimate, and that Jewish children should not be removed from their parents' authority for conversion. See II–II ST 10, aa. 8, 10, 12. Some qualifications are in order, however. Aquinas uses natural law to argue against forced conversion of children because "a child is by nature part of its father" and, as long as without reason, "does not differ from an irrational animal." (a. 12) And though Aquinas asserts that the divine law does not do away with the human law, "which is the law of natural reason" under which already existing authority of unbelievers over believers can continue, he adds that the Church *can* do away with the dominion of unbelievers over believers when it sees fit. (a. 10) And while Aquinas argues that because belief is a matter of will, non-Christians should not be compelled to believe; nonetheless, he continues, "they should be compelled by the faithful, if there is the opportunity, so that they do not hinder the faith. . . . " On this ground, he continues, Christians are justified in going to war against unbelievers. (a. 8). Thus, I cannot agree with MacIntyre that Aquinas goes wrong only when he fails to remain "faithful to his own conception of natural law."

[80]Bernard Williams, *Shame and Necessity* (Berkeley, CA: University of California Press, 2nd ed. 2008), 125.

[81]Niebuhr, "Christian Faith and Natural Law," 54. What Niebuhr gives the name "natural law" is grounded in a different view of human nature than Aquinas's, as "a realm of infinite possibilities of good and evil because of the character of human freedom."

{ 6 }

Right Reason in Natural Law Moral Theory

THOMAS AQUINAS AND WILLIAM OF OCKHAM

Anthony J. Lisska

This essay is an inquiry into medieval metaethical theory. Even though much serious scholarly work by philosophers in the analytic tradition has been undertaken on medieval matters, nonetheless a substantial amount of rigorous conceptual analysis still demands undertaking. This chapter is a modest attempt at pushing this project forward. The particular emphasis is on rendering a straightforward yet significant analysis of the concepts of Right Reason—*Recta ratio*—used in the moral philosophy of two giants of medieval philosophy, Thomas Aquinas and William of Ockham.

Contemporary Discussions on *Recta Ratio* in Ockham

This root of the major differences on right reason in Aquinas and Ockham is indicated rather perspicuously in Saul Bellow's novel, *More Die of Heartbreak*: "An apparent ethical logic drew him on. But by and by it became evident that the metaphysics that had long supported the ethical order had crumbled away."[1] Like the narrator of Bellow's novel, Ockham argues that the ontological order underpinning natural law theory has crumbled away. Aquinas, to the contrary, argues for both an ontological realism of structured natural kinds and an epistemological realism by which this realist structure might be known.

Given this "crumbling away" of ontological structures, the foil for this essay is the recent discussion on the metaethics of Ockham drawing attention to the role "*Recta ratio*" plays in his writings. In his groundbreaking work on natural rights theory, Brian Tierney writes:

---

[1]Saul Bellow, *More Die of Heartbreak* (New York: Morrow, 1987), p. 187.

> All medieval and early modern thinkers who considered these questions realized that both reason and will were necessary for the conduct of human affairs; but if we have to divide them into rationalists and voluntarists according to their emphases, Ockham clearly belongs in the rationalist camp.[2]

In her analysis concerning the role of reason in Ockham's moral and political writings, Janet Coleman provides a similar account:

> Ockham's emphasis on rationally guided choice is central to what has come to be called his voluntarism. . . . Right reason is an integral requirement of virtue and hence agents must intend to aim at what is most objectively rational.[3]

Addressing fundamental metaethical issues concerning the foundation of moral judgments in Ockham, these arguments, I suggest, temper radically Ockham's use of right reason and dismiss the unqualified voluntarism. Accordingly, recent medieval scholarship proposes that Ockham was not the radical voluntarist that several mid-twentieth century historians of philosophy like Copleston,[4] Bourke,[5] and Maurer,[6] among others, once suggested. The thrust of this recent work moves Ockham closer to rationalist natural law theory adopted by a philosopher like Aquinas. But, is such a closer alignment justified? In order to resolve this *aporia* in the history of late medieval philosophy, one must articulate an adequate account of *Recta ratio* in the writings of Aquinas and Ockham.

Aquinas on Natural Law

Thomas Aquinas played a pivotal role in the history and development of Western moral and political theory. During his productive but truncated life, Aquinas wrote extensively on moral matters, and as a corollary, on matters

---

[2]Brian Tierney, *The Idea of Natural Right: Studies in Natural Right, Natural Law and Church Law: 1150–1625* (Atlanta, GA: Scholars Press, 1997), p. 199. Tierney's substantive work is exciting in many regards, because it argues persuasively that one thread in the origin of the concept of individual natural rights is found in the writings of William of Ockham, thus much earlier than traditional history of rights theory had accepted.

[3]Janet Coleman. *A History of Political Thought: Vol. Two: From the Middle Ages to the Renaissance* (Oxford: Blackwell, 2000), p. 190.

[4]Frederick Copleston. *A History of Medieval Philosophy* (New York: Harper and Row, Publishers, 1974), p. 253.

[5]Vernon Bourke, *History of Ethics* (Garden City, NY: Doubleday and Company, 1968), pp. 104–95.

[6]Armand A. Maurer, *Medieval Philosophy* (New York: Random House Publishing Company, 1962), pp. 285–86.

of political and legal philosophy. His exposition in the *Summa Theologiae* on issues of law is often referred to as the classical canon of natural law theory. Anthony Kenny noted if one considers only the commonly acknowledged authentic works, Aquinas's *omnia opera* amount to over eight and one half million words; if one includes the texts of doubtful authenticity, the number of words jumps to eleven and one half million. To be more precise, Kenny notes that using a computer format, "we are now in a position to say that in the less than fifty years of his life he produced 8,686,572 words."[7] In contrast, Aristotle's textual record is about a million words and Descartes's texts hover somewhere in the neighborhood of half a million. Thomas died in 1274 at the early age of forty-eight, probably a victim of what contemporary medical science would call a stroke or a nervous breakdown. Simon Tugwell suggests that today we would probably call Thomas a "workaholic."[8]

Aquinas's treatment of the nature and scope of natural law in the *Summa Theologiae* follows an orderly progression considering the four kinds of law: eternal law (*lex aeterna*), natural law (*lex naturalis*), human or positive law (*lex humana*), and divine law (*lex divina*). Each of these concepts becomes part of the medieval and early modern "coin of the realm" in discussing natural law theory.

Moral and Political Texts of Aquinas

Aquinas never wrote a specific, "stand-alone," treatise devoted solely to a consideration of natural law; nonetheless the collection of Questions in the *Summa Theologiae* are often referred to as Aquinas's "Treatise on Law." John Finnis uses this title: "Most persons who study jurisprudence or political philosophy are invited at some stage to read Thomas Aquinas's Treatise on Law."[9] Paul Sigmund also: "(N)ext to the Five Ways of proving the existence of God (I, Q. 2), the Treatise on Law (I-II, Q. 90–97) is probably the best-known part of the *Summa Theologiae*."[10] While Ockham is often seen as more active with political writings than Aquinas, nonetheless, in addition to the analysis of law in the *Summa Theologiae*, Aquinas authored several treatises on political philosophy, one of which is his unfinished *Commentary on Aristotle's Politics*. Additionally, he wrote reflective comments on political leadership to the King

---

7Anthony Kenny, *Aquinas on Mind* (London: Routledge, 1993), pp. 10–11.

8Simon Tugwell, "Aquinas: Introduction, in Tugwell, *Albert and Thomas: Selected Writings* (New York: the Paulist Press, 1988), p. 261. This introduction to Aquinas's work may be the best overall account published in the last quarter of the twentieth century.

9John Finnis, *Natural Law and Natural Rights* (Oxford: The Clarendon Press, 1980), p. 378.

10Paul Sigmund, "Law and Politics," in The *Cambridge Companion to Aquinas*, edited by Norman Kretzmann and Eleonore Stump (Cambridge: Cambridge University Press, 1993), p. 222.

of Cypress, *De Regimine Principum*, frequently translated as *On Kingship*,[11] and a short selection on political theory to the Duchess of Brabant.[12] Sigmund writes that Aquinas's ". . . integrated and logically coherent theory of natural law . . . continues to be an important source of legal, political and moral norms"; and Aquinas's ". . . accomplishments have become part of the intellectual patrimony of the west, and have inspired political and legal philosophers . . . down to the present day."[13] On moral theory *per se*, Philippa Foot endorsed Aquinas's moral insights when she wrote: ". . . the *Summa Theologiae* is one of the best sources we have for moral philosophy."[14] Early on in this extended conceptual analysis, Aquinas defines law in the following general way:

> Law of its very nature is an ordinance of reason for the common good, which is made by the person who has care of the community, and this rule is promulgated (*Summa Theologiae*, I-II, Q. 90, a. 4).
>
> (*Et sic ex quatuor praedictis potest colligi definitio legis, quae nihil est aliud quam quaedam rationis ordinatio ad bonum commune, ab eo qui curam communitatis habet, promulgata.*)

Aquinas uses this definition of law for each of the four types of law that he discusses: eternal law, natural law, positive or human law, and divine law. To understand Aquinas's account of law and his differences with Ockham, one must pay careful attention to the distinctions among these four kinds of law. One must avoid the conceptual muddle found frequently conflating eternal law with divine law. Moreover, one must avoid equating natural law with divine law, even though these two categories of moral law are often considered as coextensive. The first three divisions of law—eternal, natural, and human or positive—while interrelated are distinct conceptually; furthermore, these three divisions are the result of philosophical and not theological analysis. Divine law, on the other hand, is a proper topic for theological investigation.

---

[11]There is serious scholarly debate over the structure and content of this *opusculum* of St. Thomas. Early manuscript collections conflate two texts; the first was Aquinas's *De Regno: Ad Regem Cypri* and the other *De Reginime Principum*, often attributed to Aquinas's confrere, Tolomeo of Lucca. The textual debate is beyond the limits of this enquiry. The interested reader should consult I. T. Eschmann's introduction to *On Kingship* (Toronto: The University of Toronto Press, 1949; 1982).

[12]Parts of this letter are found in Vernon Bourke's *The Pocket Aquinas* (New York: Washington Square Press, 1960), pp. 248–51.

[13]Sigmund, p. 217.

[14]Philippa Foot, *Virtues and Vices and Other Essays in Moral Philosophy* (Oxford: Blackwell, 1978), p. 2.

The Rediscovery of the Role of Nature

Medieval historians now suggest that in the mid-twelfth century a revived sense of the study of nature took place. The English historian, Richard Southern, notes that in that century, along with this renewal of an interest in the natural world, a systematic order was introduced into the matters of learning inherited from an earlier time.[15] Moreover, Charles Homer Haskins, in his earlier monumental *The Renaissance of the Twelfth Century*,[16] writes that one of the principal benchmarks of this era was a resurgence of interest in the natural world. The result of these inquiries into nature was the development of natural philosophy as an important philosophical discipline. With the growth of the universities in the early thirteenth century, comprehensive work in the philosophy of nature became embedded in the university curriculum.

This emerging interest in the natural world prompted philosophical and theological writers to appropriate these insights resulting in establishing a better understanding of nature and developing a rationale for the intelligibility of the natural world and suggesting the intrinsic goodness of the realm of nature. As Jean Porter argues, this study of nature conjoined with the texts of revelation, under the auspices of reason, worked in tandem during the beginning stages of medieval natural law theory.[17] Studying in Cologne with Albert the Great, young Thomas was part of this new age for the study of nature. Understanding this new interest in the natural world suggests that natural law theory as developed in the Aristotelian mode followed rather nicely from these studies in the philosophy of nature. For Aquinas, furthermore, this new understanding of the natural world required interpreting nature through the Aristotelian categories of matter and form, which Aquinas explained in his *Commentary on Aristotle's Physics*. In order to explain the causal structures of nature, Aquinas argues for the existence of natural kinds, another name for a metaphysical theory of essence. Appropriating Aristotelian categories, substantial form determines the content of a natural kind, which is reducible to the set of essential causal dispositional properties. In the *De Anima*, Aristotle wrote that the soul, which is the substantial form of a living organism, is "the first act of a body with the potency of life" (415b5–10).

---

[15]R. W. Southern, *Scholastic Humanism and the Unification of Europe*, Vol. One (Oxford: Blackwell, 1995), pp. 4–5.

[16]Charles Homer Haskins, *The Renaissance of the Twelfth Century* (Cambridge, MA: Harvard University Press, 1927), pp. 303–40 *passim*.

[17]Jean Porter, *Natural and Divine Law* (Grand Rapids, MI: Eerdmans, 1999), Chapters I and II, *passim*; Porter's analysis of the formative stages of natural law theory provides a useful guide to this subject.

The Natural Law

In order for Aquinas's account of natural law to hang together consistently, the concept of human nature as a natural kind must be viewed as a necessary condition. What Aquinas needs to account for his theory of natural law, accordingly, is a metaphysics of natural kinds. Human nature is defined perspicuously as a "set of dispositional properties" which becomes the ontological ground on which the moral theory of natural law is rooted. "Disposition" is the translated term for "*inclinatio*" in Thomas's texts. In Question 94, Article Two of the *Prima Secundae*, Aquinas delineates his famous explication of the three generic sortal categories of essential properties that determine the content for human nature; these properties are grounded in the substantial form which is always enmattered in the human person of a natural kind.[18] In a schematic fashion, human nature might be rendered in the following manner:

a. The set of *living* dispositions (What humans share with plants).
b. The set of *sensitive* dispositions (What humans share with animals).
c. The set of *rational* dispositions. (What makes humans unique in the material world).

Aquinas's analysis of the content of human nature is rooted in Aristotle's *Nicomachean Ethics*, the *Metaphysics*, and the *De Anima*. The concept of a sophisticated teleology grounded in a theory of the human person based on dispositional properties is central to an explication of Aquinas's position,

---

[18]Question 94, Article Two of the *Prima Secundae*; the text follows:

In so far as good has the intelligibility of end and evil has the intelligibility of contrary to end, it follows that reason grasps naturally as goods (accordingly, as things to be pursued by work, and their opposites as evils and thus things to be avoided) all the objects which follow from the natural inclinations central to the concept of human nature.

First, there is in human beings an inclination based upon the aspect of human nature which is shared with all living things; this is that everything according to its own nature tends to preserve its own being. In accord with this inclination or natural tendency, those things (actions, events, processes) by which human life is preserved and by which threats to human life are met fall under the natural law. Second, there are in human beings inclinations towards more restricted goods which are based upon the fact that human nature has common properties with other animals. In accord with this inclination, those things are said to be in agreement with the natural law (which nature teaches all animals) among which are the sexual union of male and female, the care of children, and so forth. Third, there is in human beings an inclination to those goods based upon the rational properties of human nature. These goods are uniquely related to human beings. For example, human beings have a natural inclination to know the true propositions about God and concerning those necessities required for living in a human society. In accord with this inclination arise elements of the natural law. For example, human beings should avoid ignorance and should not offend those persons among whom they must live in social units, and so on. (I-II, Q. 94, a. 2). Translation from Lisska, *Aquinas's Theory of Natural Law: An Analytic Reconstruction* (Oxford: The Clarendon Press, 1996), 2001, Appendix II.

which is rooted in his natural kind ontology. What is interesting textually and substantively is that Thomas composed the *Commentary on Aristotle's On the Soul* at the time he was writing the sections in the first part of the *Summa Theologiae* on the nature of the human person; the same holds for his writing the *Commentary on the Nicomachean Ethics* and the sections of the *Summa Theologiae* dealing with moral and legal theory. These structural connections certainly suggest Aquinas's naturalism has deep roots in the Aristotelian texts.

A living disposition is the capacity or active potency possessed by all living beings enabling them to continue in a life-form existence. Had human beings evolved or been created differently, a different schema of dispositional essential properties might hold. This living disposition is akin to what H. L. A. Hart in *The Concept of Law* referred to as the natural necessity of "survival."[19] Likewise, one of the rational dispositions Aquinas considered essential is the capacity that humans manifest in knowing, which would be innate curiosity rooted in the first lines of Aristotle's *Metaphysics*: "All human persons, by nature, desire to know" (980a21). Aquinas suggests that this rational disposition develops only when a human person knows true propositions. This essential trait of "rational curiosity" is similar analogously to Lon Fuller's human characteristic of "communication" found in *The Morality of Law*.[20] In his *Aquinas*, Finnis describes this structure of the human person in the following way:

> The order Aquinas here has in mind is a metaphysical stratification: (1) what we have in common with all substances, (2) what, more specifically, we have in common with other animals, and (3) what is peculiar to us as human beings.[21]

These dispositional properties determine the content of the natural kind of human nature. Columba Ryan wrote that these three general aspects of the human person are ". . . the good of individual survival, biological good, and the good of human communication."[22] Martin Golding referred to the living dispositions as the "basic requirements of human life," the sensitive dispositions as the basic requirements for the "furtherance of the human species," and the rational dispositions as the basic requirements for the "promotion of (a human person's) good as a rational and social being."[23] Martha Nussbaum once suggested eight properties that she claims, "we can nonetheless identify

---

[19]H. L. A. Hart, *The Concept of Law* (Oxford: The Clarendon Press, 1961), p. 190.

[20]Lon Fuller, *The Morality of Law* (New Haven, CT: Yale University Press, 1964), p. 185; here Fuller refers explicitly to Aquinas's *Summa Theologiae*.

[21]Finnis, *Aquinas* (Oxford, 1998), p. 81.

[22]Columba Ryan, "The Traditional Concept of Natural Law," in Iltud Evans (ed.), *Light on the Natural Law* (Baltimore: Helicon Press, 1965), p. 28.

[23]Martin Golding, "Aquinas and Some Contemporary Natural Law Theories." *Proceedings of the American Catholic Philosophical Association* (1974), pp. 242–33.

(as) certain features of our common humanity, closely related to Aristotle's (and Aquinas's) original list." Nussbaum's eight characteristics are mortality, the body, pleasure and pain, cognitive capability, practical reason, early infant development, affiliation or a sense of fellowship with other human beings, and humor.[24] In her later work, *Frontiers of Justice*, among others, Nussbaum develops what she has referred to as her "Capabilities Approach," which indicates the developmental characteristics of human persons on which moral and legal theory is built.[25] The point to be emphasized is that Aquinas attempted to elucidate in a general fashion those essential properties central to the concept of a human person on which a moral theory could be built. Thus moral theory is a second order inquiry.

Divine Law

In his analysis of law, Aquinas argued that divine law and eternal law are neither identical nor coextensive. In principle, divine law reduces to God's commandments which are the prescriptive propositions contained in the scriptures, which Medievals referred to as "revelation." Accordingly, religious faith fundamentally is propositional and not a commitment; this latter sense of faith has dominated the western religious world since the Reformation. This emphasis brings about the useful distinction between "believing that" and "believing in."

An adequate system of morality based upon Aristotle's philosophical anthropology is a difficult bit of metaphysics, philosophy of mind, and philosophy of biology. Accordingly, Aquinas argues that the Ten Commandments are God's mode of assisting cognitively limited moral agents in understanding the content of the moral law, which are the moral maxims necessary for human flourishing. Given the conceptual complexity of natural law, it resembles determining a consistent proof for God's existence, which is another difficult bit of metaphysics. Hence, revelation in terms of the divine law as well as regarding God's very existence reduces to a moral necessity on God's part. From this analysis, it follows that Aquinas differs substantively from those earlier and later medieval philosophers who suggested that the structure of divine law and natural law are co-extensive. An example would be the canonist Huguccio, who wrote the following: "Likewise, in a fourth sense, the divine law, that is, what is contained in the law of Moses and the evangelical law, is said to be a natural law."[26] Aquinas rejects this position.

---

[24]Martha Nussbaum, "Non-Relative Virtues," in Martha Nussbaum and Amartya Sen (eds.), *The Quality of Life* (Oxford: Oxford University Press, 1993), pp. 263–64.

[25]Nussbaum, *Frontiers of Justice* (Cambridge, MA: The Belknap Press of Harvard University Press, 2007), Chapter 5, *passim*.

[26]Found in Porter, p. 133.

From this it follows that for Aquinas, it is impossible for the precepts of divine law—or any form of theological definism—to be in opposition to moral prescriptions based on natural law. There is a category distinction between the structure and function of natural law and divine law. In his metaethics grounding moral maxims, Aquinas is not an advocate of divine prescriptivism. Since human nature is a copy of the divine exemplar in the Divine Mind, the moral maxims of natural law follow from this essence of human nature. If God were to command a moral maxim in opposition to the content of the human essence, in the mind of Aquinas, this would render God an inconsistent rational being. Put differently, what Aquinas holds in opposition to Ockham, is that God as a rational being cannot command human beings to undertake actions that are in opposition to the precepts of the natural moral law. Ockham, of course, will hold just the opposite. A fundamental meta-philosophical principle is Ockham's acceptance of the priority of voluntarism that runs through the Franciscan tradition of doing philosophical analysis; this voluntarist dimension is in direct opposition to the role of reason and the intellectualist tradition fostered by Aquinas. Here Scotus—and Ockham in a more radical fashion—part company with Aquinas's meta-philosophy. As a result, when considering moral theory in general, Aquinas would claim that God commands a certain action to be undertaken because it is good—i.e., because it is in accord with the content of human nature as determined in the divine archetype. For Ockham, to the contrary, God determines an action to be good by the very prescriptive act of commanding it. This is the cash value of a divine command metaethics, which is reducible to a form of Theological Definism. Eleonore Stump and Norman Kretzmann have argued in the following manner:

> And when Aquinas's naturalism is combined with his account of God as absolutely simple, it effects a connection between morality and theology that offers an attractive alternative to divine-command morality, construing morality not merely as a dictate of God's will but as an expression of his (God's) nature.[27]

Aquinas on *Recta Ratio*

The classical theory of natural law developed by Aquinas includes several uses of the concept of right reason.[28]

---

[27]Eleonore Stump and Norman Kretzmann, "Being and Goodness," in Scott MacDonald, Editor, *Being and Goodness: The Concept of the Good in Metaphysics and Philosophical Theology* (Ithaca, NY: Cornell University Press, 1991), p. 98.

[28]In their accounts of natural law theory, Bourke (op. cit., p. 99) and Patrick Lee refer to "right reason" as a sufficient explanatory principle for moral theory in the Aquinas texts. See Patrick Lee: "Is Thomas's Natural Law Theory Naturalist?," *American Catholic Philosophical Quarterly*, LXXI. # 4 (1997), p. 577.

In the preface to his *Commentary on Aristotle's Nicomachean Ethics*, Aquinas enumerates four distinct ways in which order is related to reason:

a. When reason *does not create but simply contemplates* (i.e., understands) the order of a thing (*res*). This is the principal use and is the "speculative reason" of Aristotelian philosophy of mind. I will call this *Recta ratio*-I.
b. When reason puts an order into *an action to be undertaken*. This is the moral dimension of "practical reason," which is a necessary condition for moral decision-making. I will call this *Recta ratio*-IIa.
c. When reason puts an order into *an artifact to be constructed*. This is the productive dimension of "practical reason." This is for Aquinas a practical "art." I will call this *Recta Ratio*-IIb.
d. When reason orders *words and concepts*. This would be logic as second intentional. This use does not pertain directly to the analysis put forward in this essay. Nonetheless, I will refer to this instance as *Recta ratio*-III.[29]

Ockham's sense of *Recta ratio*, which will be called *Recta ratio*-IV, will differ structurally from any of these four positions articulated by Aquinas. What is important for Aquinas in this analysis is *Recta ratio*-I. Aquinas's theory of ethical naturalism—his natural law theory—depends, first of all, on understanding the content of human nature, which is a function of speculative reason. Without understanding human nature, moral actions cannot be articulated or justified. When Aquinas treats *Recta ratio* in the sphere of human actions, this is *Recta ratio*-IIa, which is the undertaking of an action that is "objectively" right. This sense of "objectively right" will differ dramatically in Ockham's account of moral judgments. A necessary condition for this role of practical reason in Aquinas, however, is an understanding of the content of human nature, which is the "*res*" understood in the speculative realm by *Recta ratio*-I: this is what Alasdair MacIntyre calls Aristotle's "metaphysical biology."[30] Thus *Recta ratio*-II is a second order process depending on *Recta ratio*-I. As Stump and Kretzmann once noted, correctly in my judgment: "Aquinas's ethics is embedded in his metaphysics. . . ."[31] John Haldane referred to Aquinas's moral theory as "objectivist naturalism," a position that he in principle accepts.[32] This

[29] *Sententia libri ethicorum, prefatio*. The most recent English translation is by Charles I. Litzinger (Henry Regnery, 1966) and republished by Dumb Ox Books, 1993. Litzinger's translation is, however, not based on the critical Leonine edition. The order of the four senses has been altered in this translation.

[30] Alasdair MacIntyre, *Dependent Rational Animals: Why Human Beings Need the Virtues* (Chicago: Open Court Press, 1999), p. x.

[31] Stump and Kretzmann, p. 99.

[32] John Haldane, "Natural Law and Ethical Pluralism," in J. Haldane (ed.) *Faithful Reason* (London: Routledge, 2004), p. 136.

present analysis is in accord with Stump and Kretzmann and along the lines proposed by Haldane.

In Aquinas's moral theory, *Recta ratio* in its principal use refers to a veridical understanding of the essential properties of the human essence on which the moral theory is rooted. In the *Secunda Secundae* of the *Summa Theologiae*, Aquinas considers the concepts of right reason and nature: "It is to be said that just as (a) the order of right reason is from human nature, so also (b) the order of nature is from God himself."[33] In other words, Proposition (a) refers to the use of what I have called "*Recta ratio*-I, which is the mind's knowing the structure of reality from an externalist perspective. Proposition (b) refers to the structure of reality, which Aquinas would call "ontological truth"; this is rooted ultimately in the divine archetypes in the divine mind. This passage, in effect, suggests that Aquinas is both a metaphysical realist and an epistemological realist. Aquinas distinguishes between the use of right reason and the object to which right reason is directed. Reason is "right" when it understands—epistemological realism—the order of nature—metaphysical realism—that justifies Aquinas's externalism in his philosophy of mind. This use of right reason—*Recta ratio*-I—is the mental act of understanding by means of which a human intentional agent knows the set of essential, dispositional properties that determines a specific natural kind or, in Aquinas's medieval language, a *quidditas*. These essences in the external world are "copies" of the archetypes in the divine mind. The archetype is understood as the object, as it were, of an act of *divine understanding*. This is what Aquinas means by "the order of nature is from God himself." It is important to note that this is not an act of *divine willing* but of *divine understanding*. A reason is right in this primary sense when the human conceptual apparatus that structures what Aquinas calls the *intellectus agens* (agent intellect) and the *intellectus possibilis* (possible intellect) determines an array of concepts that "know" intentionally the sortal structure (read "form") of the things in the external world. This essential structure is determined by the archetype in the Divine Mind. Aquinas adopts a version of a correspondence theory of truth. Truth is an "adequation" ("*adequatio*") or correspondence of idea and thing. In the *Summa Theologiae*, Aquinas discusses the concept of truth in the following way: "Truth is defined by the conformity (*adequatio*) of mind and thing. Thus, to know this conformity is to know truth" (*Summa Theologiae*, Ia. 16. a. 4). Aquinas holds for what might be called (a) "formal truth," which is a correct "*adequatio*" between a human mind and the thing in the world, and (b) "ontological truth," which is truth in things. A thing is "true" because the "*adequatio*" holds between it and the divine archetype after which it is patterned. In Aquinas's theory of law, the eternal law, reducible to the Divine

[33] *Summa Theologiae*, II-II, Q. 154, art. 12, ad 1.

Ideas in the Divine Mind, is neither identical with nor coextensive with the divine law. The latter is reducible to the divine commandments. Eternal law is a philosophical concept separated conceptually from revelation. That Ockham will blur this conceptual separation will become apparent later in this essay.

The substantial form that provides the structure of an individual primary substance is the foundation for Aquinas's ontological realism and the basis for his epistemological realism. This, in turn, justifies the claim that Aquinas is an externalist and not an internalist in terms of his realist philosophy of mind. Aquinas does not adopt what Henry Veatch once called "The Transcendental Turn," which is characteristic of internalist theories of mind common to early modern and much contemporary philosophy of mind. Furthermore, Aquinas is not a foundationalist in his epistemology but rather a reliabilist rooted in his externalism.[34]

Aquinas's metaphysical realism is reducible to an ontological theory of natural kinds rooted in his theory of substantial forms. It is this theory of natural kinds about which Michael Ayers once commented that Kripke's view "is not at all unlike Aristotelian doctrine."[35] The essence or natural kind is composed of a set of synthetic necessary dispositional properties—read formal cause (*forma substantialis*)—that is directed towards a specific end—read final cause. The end to be attained is a good. In *De Veritate*, Aquinas writes: "All things found to have the criterion of an end at the same time meet the criterion of a good."[36] The end—or good—is the final cause indicating that the dispositional properties comprising the formal cause have reached fulfillment or completion, which is Aristotle's *eudaimonia* and Aquinas's *felicitas*—or what several contemporary Aristotelian philosophers call "flourishing." This is what the French Dominican Aquinas scholar, R-A Gauthier, refers to as the "Metaphysics of Finality."[37] In their essay, "Being and Goodness," Stump and Kretzmann once suggested that "in contemporary discussions, the unusual ethical naturalism that underlies all of (Aquinas's) moral philosophy has been neglected; consequently . . . its basis in his metaphysics (is) not as well known. . . . "[38] Stump and Kretzmann go on to write that "Aquinas's naturalism is a kind of moral realism that deserves serious reconsideration. It supplies for his virtue-centered morality the sort of metaethical foundation that recent virtue-centered morality has been criticized for lacking."[39]

---

[34]Stump, *Aquinas* (London: Routledge, 2005), pp. 231 ff.

[35]Michael Ayers, "Locke Versus Aristotle on Natural Kinds," *The Journal of Philosophy*, Vol. 78, #5 (May, 1981), p. 248.

[36]"*Omni id quod invenitur habere rationem finis, habet et rationem boni*" (*Quaestiones Disputatae De Veritate*: 21, I).

[37]Cf. *Sententia libri ethicorum, prefatio, Omnia Opera* 47 (Rome: Leonine Edition, 1969); Henry Veatch refers to Gauthier's analysis often in his later works and acknowledges his debt to Gauthier; *Swimming Against the Current in Contemporary Philosophy* (Washington, DC: Catholic University of America Press, 1990), p. 116.

[38]Stump and Kretzmann, p. 98.

[39]Ibid.

Scotus on the First and Second Tablets

To better understand Ockham's position, one needs to consider an issue distinguishing Scotus from Aquinas that hinges on the status of the first and second tablets of the Decalogue. The so-called second tablet consists of commandments four through ten. Aquinas holds that the moral commands found in the second tablet are part of natural law moral theory and are not dispensed with even in the case when miracles occur. Scotus, on the other hand, asserts that the second tablet is not part of natural law moral theory directly. In other words, according to Scotus, the second tablet consists of morally practical principles that are made binding or morally obligatory only through the will of God, which is reducible to a Divine Command. Hence, this distinction on the status of the two tablets demonstrates more clearly Scotus's voluntarism. For Scotus, only the first two commandments found in the first tablet pertain to the natural law because they are unchangeable and universally valid maxims. These refer to necessary propositions about the love of God and follow analytically from the concept of the essence of God as an infinite, all-good being. The maxims in the second tablet, on the other hand, derive their moral force reductively from the Divine Will; accordingly, these are moral maxims for which God in certain circumstances may make exceptions. This follows from the fact that the divine law is dependent on the act of divine willing, and this divine willing of an imperative is *a priori* justified in the very act of God's willing. If a commandment depends on God's willing, God might will whatever he so wishes. This is reducible to Divine legal positivism. For Aquinas, rationalist that he is, the divine willing depends on the divine understanding. God's willing is determined by this divine understanding, which is ultimately the set of divine archetypes expressed propositionally in the divine mind; Aquinas is not a non-cognitivist.[40] The natural law itself, however, is exceptionless. That Scotus's inviolable rendition of moral maxims based on the will begins to sound like Kant is not too far afield.

In his *Natural Law, Religion, & Rights*, Henrik Syse suggests that the challenge Scotus and Ockham faced was combining a theory of voluntarism with moral objectivity.[41] Syse argues that Scotus and Ockham adopted two voluntarist principles:

a. In moral theory (metaethics), voluntarism and moral objectivity can be articulated and defended coherently and consistently;

---

[40]Of course, in this context "set" is used analogously, since God, for Aquinas, is a simple metaphysical entity with no parts.

[41]Henrik Syse, *Natural Law, Religion, & Right* (South Bend, IN, St. Augustine's Press, 2007), Chapter 2. Syse's discussion of this set of issues is one of the more thorough accounts of the conceptual subtleties found in medieval natural law and rights theory.

b. In opposition to Aquinas's moral theory (metaethics), Divine Voluntarism is a "safer and more stable basis for moral norms than any Platonic or Aristotelian intellectualism (or moral realism)."[42]

The result of these directions fostered by Scotus and Ockham placed emphasis on human freedom as central in philosophical anthropology and moral theory.

Ockham on *Recta Ratio*

It appears that for Ockham the possibility of deriving a moral theory divorced from theological propositions is beyond the pale of philosophical possibility. Ockham's appropriation of right reason is in the context of divine prescriptivism. Hence, Ockham's philosophical justification for a moral prescription—what renders an action "objectively rational"—is that God wills the action to be undertaken or avoided. In a recent essay, Thomas Osborne argues that the foundation of the correctness of a moral judgment for Ockham is ultimately that it is a divine command.[43]

This thrust of Ockham's—and Scotus's—meta-philosophy exalts the role of Divine Freedom. Aquinas, on the other hand, rejects this paradigm of the philosophical enterprise "exalting the divine freedom and omnipotence." A form of voluntarism takes hold in Ockham, where, for instance, human dignity is rooted in the ability of a human person to be a free willing agent. The justification that "Act x is right" is dependent foundationally on the fact that God wills this to be the case. For Aquinas, on the other hand, "Act x is right" because it is in accord with human nature as constituted by the divine understanding in the archetype of human nature. For Aquinas, once God has created human nature, certain moral prescriptions follow. God cannot command that an action be "right" and contrary to human nature at the same time. Aquinas is not a Theological Definist.

In Ockham, it appears, voluntarism takes hold vigorously. In the *Reportatio*[44] Ockham writes: "By the very fact that God wills something, it is right for it to be done. . . ." As a nominalist, Ockham denies the possibility of essential properties existing outside the mind. Ockham is justly famous for his theory of signs and for a theory of supposition, which ultimately supports the claim that universal terms are reducible to logical or syncategorematic terms. This is

---

[42]Ibid., p. 44.

[43]Thomas M. Osborne, "Ockham as a Divine—Command Theorist," *Religious Studies*, Vol. 41, 2005, pp. 1–22. Professor Osborne's account of the many issues involved in this metaethical thicket is, in the judgment of this author, on the right track.

[44]*Reportatio*, IV, Q. 9: E-F. The *Reportatio* is a written record by persons attending the lectures that Ockham gave on the last three books of the *Sentences* of Peter Lombard.

second intentional, which would be *Recta ratio*-III noted above from the passage taken from Aquinas's *Commentary on the Ethics*. Ockham rejects the first "order of reason," *Recta ratio*-I, that Aquinas affirmed in the passage from his Aristotelian *Commentary*. This order in Aquinas is first intentional and categorematic. My reading of the materials suggests that on the issue of natural kinds Aquinas and Ockham part company radically. Seeing the structural difference between *Recta ratio*-I and *Recta ratio*-III indicates the profound division between Aquinas and Ockham on natural law theory and from whence the foundation is found.

Following Scotus, Ockham does not accept the position put forward by Aquinas that God's commandments must be in accord with human nature as established in the divine idea of that essence. In the *Reportatio*, Ockham writes: "Obligation does not fall on God, since God is not under any obligation to do anything."[45] Extending his voluntarism, Ockham notes, in opposition even to Scotus, that God could command a human person to hate him. The present moral order is dependent ultimately on the will of God. Hence, God could have, had he so chosen, promulgated a different set of commandments in what Scotus called the second tablet even though human persons remain the same kind of ontological beings. In his *Commentary on the Sentences* when considering *Recta ratio*, Ockham writes: "By the very fact that the divine will commands this, right reason says that it is to be willed (by human agents)."[46] In this same commentary, Ockham writes: "Every will is right through its conformity with right reason."[47] Of course, what is required is a conceptual analysis of "right reason" in passages like these found in Ockham's writings.

In the first passage from the *Commentary* noted above, Ockham argues that *Recta ratio* is determined when the human intellect understands what God *wills*. This would differ from Aquinas, where the intellect is *recta* in the first sense when it knows a *quidditas*, or through his externalist theory of natural law, human nature. Hence, Ockham's right reason exhibits structural differences from Aquinas. The case will be developed that Ockham's right reason does not render his voluntarism impotent but radically different from that put forward by Aquinas.[48]

---

[45] *Reportatio*, III, Q. 5: H.

[46] *In I Sent*. D. 41, Q. 1: K. The Latin text is: *"Eo ipso quod voluntas divina hoc vult, recta ratio dictat quod est volundum."*

[47] Ibid.

[48] See Marilyn McCord Adams, "Ockham on Will, Nature, and Morality," in *The Cambridge Companion to Ockham*, Ed. Paul Vincent Spade (Cambridge: Cambridge University Press, 1999), pp. 245–72. This analysis may be the best overall account of both recent work and more traditional analyses in Ockham on the relation between nature and moral theory. In the end, Adams indicates how the role of the will is central to Ockham's analysis of moral and political theory.

What Separates Aquinas from Ockham

What follows is an attempt to sort out several conceptual muddles comprising this hornet's nest in Ockham's metaethics.

a. The role of *Recta ratio*.
b. The role of the will.
c. The role of human nature or human essence.
d. The role of final cause in a human essence.

Recent discussions of Ockham's metaethics, I suggest, conflate these issues. In his limited use of right reason, Ockham posits the will as an unlimited power that leads to what, I suggest, Marilyn Adams called a "liberty of indifference."[49] Aquinas, on the other hand, argues in the opposite way. Ockham's nominalist analysis of human nature apparently unfettered by any Divine archetype eliminates a role for final cause in his philosophical anthropology. For Aquinas, in considering a knowledge of human nature, *Recta ratio*-I is only "right" when, in understanding the dispositional properties that constitute the human essence, it understands the way the world is. Ockham's use of right reason is less demanding, which one would expect from a nominalist metaphysician who downplays the role of essence, natural kind, and final cause. Ockham's use of right reason is what I will call *Recta ratio*-IV. This conceptual use of *Recta ratio-IV* is, I submit, at least analogous if not co-extensive with what some twentieth-century moral and legal philosophers called "a good reasons" theory of moral justification. In Anglo-American metaethical discussions, a "good-reasons theory" suggests establishing objectivity in moral judgments by a close examination of the modes of reasoning and rational discourse undertaken in support of these moral claims. Largely associated with Stephen Toulmin's *An Examination of the Place of Reason in Ethics*[50] and the moral justification of rights theory proposed in the writings of Ronald Dworkin, a good reasons theory argued against non-cognitivism, relativism, and moral skepticism. In principle, a good reasons theory argues that no ontological justification is required for moral claims and that the articulation of the reasons themselves for accepting such a claim is sufficient. A "good reason" for undertaking an action in Ockham's moral theory is, accordingly, that God wills that the action is to be undertaken. It appears that in his metaethics, this use of a good reasons approach explains Ockham's reconciliation of both voluntarism and objectivity. Providing good reasons for moral justification may be necessary for Aquinas, but it is never sufficient.

---

[49] Adams, op. cit., p. 262.

[50] Stephen Toulmin, *An Examination of the Place of Reason in Ethics* (Cambridge: Cambridge University Press, 1950).

Ockham never doubts that the will is prominent. He rejects Aquinas's position because he considers that Aquinas limits the will and subjects the act of willing to the requirements of the intellect. Aquinas, of course, adopts this position. In the *Summa Theologiae*, Aquinas writes the following about the superiority of the intellect over the will: "Reason precedes the will, and reason ordains the will; in other words, the will tends to its object only according to the order of reason since the intellect (*Recta ratio*-I) presents the object to the will" (*Summa Theologiae*, I-II, A. 18, art. 1). In Aquinas's moral theory, both the practical reason and the will depend on an awareness of the good. Aquinas's first principle of practical reason is "Good is to be done and sought, and evil avoided."[51] This awareness is understanding what the final cause is, and this awareness depends necessarily on knowing human nature. The final cause is rooted in the substantial form of the human natural kind. Without a dispositional account of human nature, Aquinas's ethical naturalism falls apart conceptually. The will is a rational appetite that undertakes actions under the guise of what is good; this cognitive content depends on both speculative and practical reason. Ockham denies that limits can be placed upon the will.[52] Aquinas does put cognitive limits on the will—both the human will and the divine will. Therefore, the human agent functions differently for Ockham than for Aquinas. These are two radically different theories of human action.

We need to recall Coleman's interpretation of Ockham's position on incorporating that which is rational into an historically interpreted voluntarist moral theory; Coleman wrote: "Right reason is an integral requirement of virtue and hence agents must intend to aim at what is most objectively rational."[53] "What is most objectively rational," I suggest, is similar structurally to the concept of rational consistency proposed by the good reasons philosophers like Toulmin, Dworkin, and R.M. Hare. It is a good reason for a moral agent to undertake actions that are in accord with the will of God; it is rational to accept what God has willed. This is not the right reason of essentialist natural law. The 'good reasons' philosophers require a clear articulation of principles and a consistency of application but not any reference to natural kind properties external to the mind. This choosing to act in harmony with the divine will is an example of *Recta ratio*-IV. It appears to be almost a prudential kind of judgment—like Pascal's wager, it is worth my while to act in accord with the Divine will.

---

[51]*Summa Theologiae*, I-II, 94, art. 2: "*Bonum est faciendum et prosequendum, et malum vitandum.*"
[52]This appears to be the point emphasized by Adams. Op. cit.
[53]Coleman, Ibid.

Ockham as a "Good Reasons" Philosopher

What is one to make of this? At the end of the day, Ockham has driven a wedge between *Recta ratio* and human nature. Since he is not, as I read the texts, a natural kind realist, the realm of freely chosen actions to be undertaken is what determines his philosophy of action. Ockham and Aquinas are categorically different regarding action theory. Since will is paramount in Ockham, this voluntarist superiority plays itself out in his metaethics. It is a good reason to act as God has willed; thus the morally relevant characteristic of a human action is that God has so willed it. For Aquinas, on the other hand, the morally relevant characteristic of the moral action is if it corresponds to the development of the human person. In Aquinas's metaethics, natural law is not equivalent with divine law; for Ockham, the opposite appears to hold. Aquinas maintains a category distinction between eternal law and divine law. This category distinction is foreign conceptually to Ockham.

While Ockham is not guilty of some mid-twentieth-century charges of blatant relativism because of his voluntarism, nonetheless in discussing Ockham's rationality, his voluntarist dimension places him at best in the category of a good reasons moral philosopher. When Tierney argues that Ockham is a rationalist, one must distinguish at least two kinds of rationalists:

a. The *realist/essentialist rationalists* who require an ontological foundation for the justification of moral claims—*Recta ratio*-I.
b. The *good reasons rationalists* who argue for a clear articulation of and a consistency in determination and application of moral principles and arguments—*Recta ratio*-IV.

Ockham is at best in the latter category. Reason as understanding has but a limited role to play in his account. Henry Veatch once offered an extended discussion of the limitations of a good reasons theory within the context of a robust natural law theory.[54] Veatch argued that any good reasons theory failed to answer what he often referred to as the "*Euthyphro* Principle," which is the foundational principle of ethical naturalism. Veatch argued that without an ontological foundation for the good in the human person, a prescriptivist position necessarily follows. Ockham's analysis succumbs to Veatch's criticisms. Ockham's account, it appears, falls into a category similar to Ronald Dworkin's good reasons rights thesis. Interestingly enough, in discussing Ockham and *Recta ratio*, Tierney refers to Dworkin.[55] Whatever Dworkin's "rationalism" is,

[54]Veatch, *Human Rights: Fact or Fancy?* (Baton Rouge, LA: Louisiana State University Press, 1985). Veatch discusses this issue in several other works.

[55]Tierney, op. cit., p. 193.

it is not the essentialist theory put forward by Aquinas. Dworkin—and Tierney's Ockham—hold for what one might call a "thin theory of the human good." In the words of Dworkin, philosophers steeped in the principles of rationality espoused by the Enlightenment cannot accept any realist theory for the human good. According to Dworkin, for example, a primary principle of a liberal democracy is that "the government must be neutral on what might be called the question of the good life."[56] Such theories determining an ontological good are based, so Dworkin argues, on metaphysical systems that are always problematic. Ockham would appear to adopt the same ontological skepticism and its subsequent use of good reasons for justification. Philosophers like Ockham and Dworkin, in accepting a "thin theory of the human good," are moved easily into a good reasons moral theory; they are agnostic at best regarding the possibility of articulating a theory of human nature, which natural law philosophers like Aquinas endorse based on their metaphysical theory of natural kinds. Ockham and Dworkin are, it would appear, soul mates on this issue. Both separate the "right" from the "good." Dworkin once stated the following position on his liberalism: ". . . the basic liberal idea (is) that justice must be independent of any idea of human excellence or of the good life. . . ."[57] In adopting a "thick theory of the human good" rooted in the natural kind of the human person, Aquinas denies this conceptual separation between the right and the good. A thick theory of the human good implies some set of ontological properties in the human person upon which the moral qualities are grounded. Aquinas's three-fold dispositional account of human nature and Nussbaum's "capabilities" provide a thick theory; the thin theory of the human good illustrated in a good reasons approach argues that the rational process itself in terms of consistency is sufficient for moral arguments. In a significant sense, it appears that the seeds of Enlightenment moral theories exemplified in Dworkin are found in Ockham. In commenting on Rawls's (and Dworkin's) formalist—or "good reasons"—theory of moral justification, Nussbaum once noted: "Aristotle's view of *phronesis* cannot avail itself of this strategy . . . (of) value neutral abilities such as imagination, empathy, factual knowledge."[58] Hence, Nussbaum argues that the person of practical reason utilizes more reasoning abilities than "an enumeration of intellectual abilities. . . ."[59] Nussbaum seeks more in her account of human rights theory than Rawls's procedural formalism. This follows from her capabilities approach to rights theory.

---

[56]Ronald Dworkin, "Liberalism," in *A Matter of Principle* (Cambridge, MA: Harvard University Press, 1985), p. 191.

[57]Dworkin, "Interview," in Bryan Magee, *Men of Ideas* (New York: Viking Press, 1978), p. 259.

[58]Nussbaum, *The Fragility of Goodness* (Cambridge: Cambridge University Press, 1986), p. 311.

[59]Ibid.

For Ockham, it is God who, in his willing, decides what actions are right or wrong; God freely decides! A moral agent then decides on a right action because the action corresponds to the divine will, *not* on the realist ground of a human nature foundation for moral properties. Furthermore, this moral rightness is known, it would seem, only through divine revelation as manifested in the Scriptures. Natural law moral theory for Ockham is reducible to the set of divine commands. The influence of Ockham's voluntarism on Reformation theologians appears to be persuasive. In the twentieth century, moreover, Protestant theologians like Karl Barth and Reinhold Niebuhr questioned the very possibility of a realist formulation for natural law moral theory. It appears that the shadow of Kierkegaard hovers over not only Barth and Niebuhr but Ockham as well.

In concluding this analysis of right reason in Aquinas and Ockham, it appears that Ockham fails to get beyond the thrust of Veatch's objection. Ockham provides at best a weak sense of *Recta ratio*, which diminishes Tierney's and Coleman's claims about the rationalist elements freshly found in Ockham's moral theory. With *Recta ratio*-IV, Ockham's rationalism is limited, like Dworkin, to a thin theory of the human good. For Ockham, it is a "good reason" to follow what God has willed or commanded. Following the command is sufficient, and this is not reducible to the structure of the human act itself. For Aquinas, the human act, if morally right, is grounded in the final cause of the human essence; this is what Gauthier meant by the "metaphysics of finality." In the end, Ockham's account of *Recta ratio*-IV is rooted in a form of Theological Definism, and a Theological Definism with a vengeance.

The author expresses his gratitude to his good friend, Jonathan Jacobs, for the invitation to write this chapter for this volume. Professors Jacobs, Douglas Rasmussen, and I jointly participated in a symposium on issues raised in this volume at the annual meetings of the Northeastern Political Science Association held in Boston in November 2010 and an earlier seminar held at Denison University in June 2010. Earlier versions of this essay were read at the St. John's University Philosophy Colloquium and the Denison University Philosophy Colloquium, and served as the basis for the annual Suarez Lecture given at Fordham University.

{ 7 }

Natural Law, Moral Constructivism, and Duns Scotus's Metaethics

THE CENTRALITY OF AESTHETIC EXPLANATION

Richard Cross

Scotus's metaethics has long been the subject of considerable controversy, focused in particular on the following question: does Scotus, or does he not, accept some kind of divine command theory, such that the moral value of an action is dependent simply on the divine will? All sides in the dispute (rightly) agree that, according to Scotus, moral norms governing human behavior towards God—represented by the first two (or perhaps three) commands of the Decalogue—belong to natural law, such that the goodness and obligatoriness of such actions follow automatically from the nature of the terms involved. But at stake is the status of moral norms contained in the second table of the Decalogue. The debate is caused by certain things that Scotus says quite clearly: first, that such norms are not part of natural law, but are somehow merely "consonant" with it; and, secondly, that God can dispense from any of these norms, such that the norm no longer obtains.

One side of the debate—defended by Allan B. Wolter and, more recently, by Mary Beth Ingham—finds in Scotus, at heart, a traditional teleological Aristotelianism. Wolter interprets the consonance claim to amount to a claim about human teleology: human nature is such that there are ways in which any instance of it should behave and be treated. On teleology—the notion of an ethic directed to the goal of human life, or human perfection—Wolter suggests the following:

> What right reason tells us . . . is what perfects man's human nature naturally, and this should suffice for the development of a rational ethics by those who claim man's moral behavior is not essentially dependent upon a divine command.[1]

---

[1]Allan B. Wolter, *Duns Scotus on the Will and Morality* [= *WM*] (Washington, DC: Catholic University of America, 1986), 29.

And, supposing that the second table of the Decalogue is somehow intrinsically related to this teleology, this reading in turn means that God's power to dispense from the second table of the Decalogue is somehow determined by features of human nature. As Wolter puts it,

> Scotus maintains . . . that while the second table represents what is "valde consonans" with natural law, certain aspects of the second table of the decalogue can be dispensed with according to right reason, when their observation would do more harm than good. But God could obviously not dispense from all its precepts at once, for this would be equivalent to creating man in one way and obligating him in an entirely different fashion, something contrary to what he "owes to human nature in virtue of his generosity."[2]

The crucial point here is that Wolter's reading presupposes that following the second table of the Decalogue, at least *ut in pluribus* (as for Aquinas)[3] is somehow intrinsically linked with the teleological attainment of the vision of God. At the other extreme of interpretation is the view of Thomas Williams, who maintains that the claim about consonance is to be understood simply in terms of God's will: what makes norms of the second table consonant with natural law is simply that God wills them, and, since God can will entirely different moral norms from those that he in fact wills, it follows that moral norms (other than those governing behavior towards God) can be known only by revelation. For Williams, God exhibits right reason simply in choosing ends before choosing means: thus making right reason a part of action theory, not moral psychology.[4]

A third interpretation is located between these two—though not quite midway, since it is clearly closer to Williams's than to Wolter's. Hannes Möhle agrees with Williams that Scotus's ethics abandons the kind of teleological approach accepted by Wolter, and he agrees too that God can make any and

---

[2]Wolter, *Duns Scotus on the Will*, 24. I discuss the quotations from Scotus below.

[3]See Aquinas, *Summa theologiae* [= *ST*] 1-2.94.4 c.

[4]See Thomas Williams, "How Scotus Separates Morality from Happiness," *American Catholic Philosophical Quarterly*, 69 (1995), 425–45; "Reason, Morality, and Voluntarism in Duns Scotus: A Pseudo-Problem Dissolved," *The Modern Schoolman*, 74 (1997), 73–94; "The Unmitigated Scotus," *Archiv für Geschichte der Philosophie*, 80 (1998), 162–81; "A Most Methodical Lover? On Scotus's Arbitrary Creator," *Journal of the History of Philosophy*, 38 (2000), 169–202. Williams provides a brief summary of his thinking on the matter in "From Metaethics to Action Theory," in Thomas Williams (ed.), *The Cambridge Companion to Duns Scotus* (Cambridge: Cambridge University Press, 2003), 332–51. Mary Beth Ingham has replied to Williams along lines consistent with Wolter's understanding in her "Duns Scotus, Morality, and Happiness: A Reply to Thomas Williams," *American Catholic Philosophical Quarterly*, 74 (2000), 173–95, and "Letting Scotus Speak for Himself," *Medieval Philosophy and Theology*, 10 (2001), 173–216. More recently, Allan B. Wolter too offered a reply to Williams in his "The Unshredded Scotus: A Response to Thomas Williams," *American Catholic Philosophical Quarterly*, 77 (2003), 315–56. Williams has an article on his website replying to some of this recent literature: http://shell.cas.usf.edu/~thomasw/The%20Divine%20Nature%20and%20Scotus%27s%20Libertarianism.pdf.

every norm of the second table other than it is.[5] But he understands the consonance claim to refer to the way in which general commands are made applicable to specific cases. For example, suppose such-and-such is a general objective (my term, not Möhle's), then the achievement of the objective may involve acting in this or that specific way: and thus, if the general objective amounts to something expressed as a moral norm, so too will be the specific activity. But nothing about human nature entails (other than in genuine cases of norms belonging to natural law) that the general objective might not be quite different from what it is, and amount to something expressed as a quite different moral norm. Given this conceptual relation between general and particular (a connection that Möhle describes as "neither purely intuitive nor deductive"),[6] it is possible to ascertain rationally the ways in which one should behave. God's actions are constrained by the principle of non-contradiction, and this entails that God's actions must be (morally) consistent within any given ordering:

> The validity of the principles of commutative justice and the weighing of goods . . . are not themselves called into question in [Scotus's] discussion of the possibility of dispensation. Instead, those principles are used in order to make clear the coherent structure of a whole ordering that is subject to dispensation.[7]

Möhle's discussion does justice to the rational accessibility of moral norms in a way that Williams has trouble dealing with, but which is clearly present in Scotus's texts.

In what follows, I attempt to give an account of Scotus's metaethics, focusing on what Scotus himself seems to regard as the most important feature of the system, namely, the different attitudes God takes to various moral norms, and the ways in which God is motivated to take these attitudes.[8] Scotus (unusually)

---

[5]See Hannes Möhle, *Ethik als scientia practica nach Johannes Duns Scotus: Eine philosophische Grundlegung*, Beiträge zur Geschichte der Philosophie und Theologie des Mittelalters, N.F., 44 (Münster: Aschendorff, 1995), summarized conveniently in Möhle, "Scotus's Theory of Natural Law," in Williams, ed., *Cambridge Companion*, 312–31.

[6]Möhle, "Scotus's Theory," 319.

[7]Möhle, "Scotus's Theory," 323. A position intermediate between Williams's and Wolter's is also defended in Terence Irwin, *The Development of Ethics: A Historical and Critical Study. Volume I: From Socrates to the Reformation* (Oxford: Oxford University Press, 2007), 687–700, though Irwin does not present his account in terms of the Williams-Wolter debate. I offer some comments on Irwin's discussion below.

[8]I have long thought that the question of the restrictions—or lack thereof—on God's will are the key to Scotus's ethics, and I have laid out some of these intuitions in past work (see my "Duns Scotus on Goodness, Justice, and What God Can Do," *Journal of Theological Studies*, 48 (1997), 48–76, and *Duns Scotus*, Great Medieval Thinkers (New York and Oxford: Oxford University Press, 1999), 89–95). The view I defend here, I hope, supersedes those accounts, but nevertheless starts from the same basic intuition. In particular, I now believe that the goodness, as well as the obligatoriness, of the entire second table of the Decalogue depends on God's free approval of the norms therein contained.

makes Aquinas his target,[9] so I begin by describing aspects of Aquinas's complex view, with an eye on bringing out the ways in which Scotus's contrasts with it. (I do not claim that my account of Aquinas fully integrates everything that he has to say about practical rationality—far from it. I focus merely on Aquinas's understanding of divine justice, and try to draw out certain consequences from it. This approach best allows us to see what Scotus believed he was reacting to in Aquinas. It may well be that what Aquinas has to say about divine justice does not comport well with other claims that Aquinas makes about human practical rationality. But that is a different story.) Compared with Aquinas's discussions, Scotus's treatment is brief and not very fully worked out. So where Scotus does not make his own philosophical motivations clear, I try to offer plausible speculations as to why Scotus might defend the views he does.

Aquinas

On Aquinas's teleological understanding of the created realm, certain kinds of activity and certain kinds of objects constitute natural goals for substances of given kinds. This view of reality drives Aquinas's account of moral normativity. Aquinas holds that the teleological requirements that ground normativity run, as it were, in two directions, relative to the agent and to the object (I use 'object' not in any technical sense here, but merely to pick out the thing affected by the action). The first is that the object of a given action is such that the action directed to it is somehow required for an agent to achieve a certain natural goal. The second is that the agent's action is somehow required for the object's teleological perfection too. Normativity, in other words, is explained by the fact that an action is good for the agent and good for the object, and the binding nature of moral norms is based on these requirements.[10] Aquinas makes the point most clearly in his discussion of divine justice:

> People are owed what is theirs. And something is said to belong to someone if it is ordered to him. . . . The term 'debt' implies a certain order of requirement or necessity of the thing to which it is ordered. And there is a two-fold order to be considered in things: one, by which something created is ordered to another created thing, as parts are ordered to a whole, and accidents to substances, and each thing to its goal; and another order by which all created things are ordered to God. . . . He, however, is not a debtor, because he is not ordered to other things; rather, they are ordered to him.[11]

---

[9]He lays out what he takes to be Aquinas's view at *Ordinatio* [= *Ord.*] 3.37.un., nn. 8–12 (ed. C. Balić and others (Vatican City: Vatican Polyglot Press, 1950–), X, 274–76).

[10]I leave on one side whether or not arguments from teleology to obligation are guilty of the naturalistic fallacy. If they are, then both Aquinas and Scotus are guilty, though Scotus less so since he grounds fewer obligations on teleology, as we shall see.

[11]Aquinas, *ST* 1.21.1 ad 3.

The opening two sentences here make it clear that part of the explanation for the binding nature of moral norms lies in the teleological requirements of the object (here, specifically, of intelligent agents, but I assume that the point can be generalized): what is required is that the object has what is "its": and this is, most crucially, its teleological perfection. Moral duties require too that there is a sense in which the agent is "ordered" to the object: that is to say, that the agent has its activity, relative to the object, as some sort of teleological goal. Aquinas makes this clear a little earlier in the quotation too: each thing is ordered "to its goal." And elsewhere Aquinas talks of the binding force of moral norms in terms of the agent's achievement of its teleological purpose:

> Binding has a place in those cases of necessity in which necessity is imposed by something else. There is a two-fold necessity which can be imposed by another agent: one [the necessity] of coercion; . . . the other conditioned necessity. . . . The first necessity, i.e. of coercion, has no place in the motions of the will. . . . The second necessity can be imposed on the will: namely, that it is necessary to choose this if this good ought to be pursued, or if this evil ought to be avoided.[12]

Despite the language ("conditioned necessity"), it would be a mistake, I think, to count this merely as a weak view of what it is for moral norms to be binding—i.e., to amount to nothing more than the assertion of a conditional kind of necessity: that such-and-such an action is necessary for the achievement of such-and-such a goal. Aquinas accepts a strong principle of practical rationality according to which it is not possible to will against an occurrent judgment that such-and-such is a good (I ignore questions of *akrasia* here). Aquinas expresses this most forcefully in the context of a discussion of the impossibility of not desiring God if granted direct acquaintance with God. In the limit case that we experience the vision of God, we simply cannot will against it: our willing it is naturally necessary:

> Natural necessity is not incompatible with the will. Furthermore, it is necessary that, just as the intellect of necessity inheres in first principles, so the will of necessity inheres in the ultimate goal, which is beatitude.[13]

So the fact that we necessarily desire the ultimate goal entails that we have an obligation to pursue it: and this obligation is the result of some kind of *categorical* necessity.

The general, idea, then, is that acts are obligatory simply to the extent that they foster the achievement of the final goals of the agent and/or object. Aquinas does not have an *additional* notion of obligation, over and above this. This might suggest that what it is to be binding is simply the necessity of acting *in accordance*

[12]Aquinas, *De veritate* 17.3 c.
[13]Aquinas, *ST* 1.82.1 c.

with moral norms, without there being the extra component, as it were, of having to *follow* the norm. What I mean here is that an agent might act in accordance with a moral norm even though that norm does not represent a strictly moral obligation for the agent, one that the agent is somehow subject to. In his account of God's justice Aquinas suggests that at least in the divine case there is indeed some kind of difference between these two ways of being related to a norm, and I mention it here because it forms a striking contrast with Scotus's account of divine justice (and a relevant one, given that Scotus's target, as I note below, is Aquinas's view). Thus, Aquinas maintains that God owes certain duties to himself:

> God's justice regards what befits him, inasmuch as he renders to himself what is owed to him.[14]

So—presumably—moral norms relating to the ways in which God is treated bind even God in some sense stronger than merely requiring God to act in accordance with the norm—although, of course, the ground for the norm is simply God's own teleological perfection as the final goal of all existence, including his own.[15] But God is not so bound in his dealings with creatures. Rather, Aquinas holds, God acts in ways which accord with what would be the duties of a moral agent were it the case that God was a moral agent (i.e., an agent subject to these kinds of moral obligations), and that he does so necessarily. Thus, "God is not a debtor" to creatures—his obligations do not relate to the teleological perfections of creatures—but, nevertheless,

> It is owed to any created thing that it has what is ordered to it: as [it is ordered] to a human being that he has two hands, and that other animals serve him. And in this way too God exercises justice, when he gives to each what is owed to him according to the notion of its nature and condition. . . . And although God gives what is owed to something, he, however, is not a debtor.[16]

In line with this, Aquinas thinks of the justice exhibited in God's actions towards creatures as merely an *analogue* of distributive justice:

> [There is a species of justice] that consists in distributing: and it is called distributive justice, by which a ruler or steward gives to each in accordance with its desert. Therefore just as the order appropriate to a family or any governed multitude reveals this sort of justice in the ruler, so the

---

[14]Aquinas, *ST* 1.21.1 ad 3.

[15]Note that Aquinas assumes that God necessarily follows his duties. Scotus makes a similar assumption, as we shall see below: from which we can infer that neither of these thinkers holds that *freedom* is a presupposition of duty. I take it that this is a striking divergence from modern understandings of duty, and one that might easily lead to misunderstanding. But having noted it, I do not comment on it further.

[16]Aquinas, *ST* 1.21.1 ad 3.

> order of the universe, which appears both in natural things and in voluntary ones reveals the justice of God.[17]

The idea, of course, is that the universe does indeed correspond to the requirements of distributive justice, and so do God's actions relative to creatures, even though these requirements are not morally binding on God. (Commutative justice governs exchanges between equals, and, since nothing is God's equal, commutative justice cannot govern God's dealings with creatures.)[18]

Aquinas is explicit that whatever God does is *necessarily* in accordance with the teleological dispositions of creatures—God acts in accordance with the relevant norms (but not such that his acting in accordance with the relevant rules amounts to following the rules):

> It is not appropriate to the maximal goodness of God that he does not lead to perfection the things that he has produced. The highest perfection of anything is in the pursuit of its goal. So it pertains to divine goodness that, just as he produced things in being, so he leads them to their goal.[19]

So the requirements of distributive justice are not morally binding on God; but they do seem to be binding in some other way.[20] Aquinas makes much the same point when addressing an objection to the effect that God's complete freedom entails that his will cannot be bound by considerations of justice:

> Since the cognized good is the object of the will, it is impossible for God to will other than the reason of his wisdom approves: which is a sort of law of justice, according to which his will is right and just. Whence, whatever he does according to his will he does justly, just as what we do according to law we do justly. But we [do so] in accordance with the law of some higher being, whereas God is a law for himself.[21]

The idea, again, is that in such cases God acts in accordance with moral norms, but not such that he treats these norms as rules to be followed. Aquinas's terminology is different from ours: his sense of "in accordance with," in the quotation, clearly means *following*, being bound by.

Now, all of this entails that Aquinas makes a strong distinction between his account of divine justice, on the one hand, and that of natural law, on the other. The only duties that God has are to himself. But the first principle of natural

---

[17]Aquinas, *ST* 1.21.1 c.

[18]Aquinas, *ST* 1.21.1 c.

[19]Aquinas, *ST* 1.103.1 c.

[20]The observant reader will have noted that I ascribe to Aquinas more or less exactly the position defended in Thomas V. Morris, "Duty and Divine Goodness," *American Philosophical Quarterly*, 21 (1984), 261–68.

[21]Aquinas, *ST* 1.21.1 ad 2.

law is wider than merely an expression of duties to God: it is a function of the natural dispositions of creatures:

> The first principle in practical reason is one that is grounded on the nature of the good, which is that the good is what all desire. Therefore this is the first precept of law, that the good is to be done and pursued, and the bad avoided.[22]

(As above, this secures that the binding nature of moral norms relates specifically to the necessity of our desiring our goal.) This is not the principle that God follows in his activity (even though he necessarily acts in accordance with it). As we shall see, Scotus disagrees strongly with this: he holds that the obligations imposed by natural law cannot extend further than the scope of divine justice, since natural law is supposed to include norms that are globally binding.

One result of God's acting in accordance with a rule (that does not bind him, and that he does not follow) is that humans who are bound by the rule (expressed in the second table of the Decalogue) necessarily *follow* the rule if they are to achieve their goal. And the reason for this is that following the commands of the second table of the Decalogue is necessary for the achievement of the ultimate goal of human existence. And in this context, Aquinas highlights two kinds of goals, corresponding to the two tables of the Decalogue:

> It is necessary in the divine law that there are firstly included precepts ordering a human being to God; and then other precepts ordering a human being to others, neighbours, living together under God.[23]

(Aquinas makes it clear that divine law, restricted to its expression in the Decalogue, is included in natural law.)[24]

So Aquinas holds that for a principle of natural law other than the first to be such it must be entailed by the first principle ("they can be known immediately from the first common principles").[25] Given this, the content of the various moral norms is, according to Aquinas, determined simply by considering the kinds of behavior that things standardly engage in, and using this analysis as the basis for an account of what the natural goals of things might be.[26] So the precepts of both tables of the Decalogue, normative for human activity, represent inferences from the same first principles of practical reasoning: not that the second table precepts can be inferred from the first, but that both can be

---

[22] Aquinas, *ST* 1-2.94.2 c.

[23] Aquinas, *ST* 1-2.100.5 c; see too *ST* 1-2.90.2 c.

[24] See Aquinas, *ST* 1-2.100.1 c. Divine law encompasses too divine *positive* law (see, e.g., *ST* 1-2.91.5).

[25] Aquinas, *ST* 1-2.100.3 c.

[26] Aquinas presents the first stages of such an analysis at *ST* 1-2.94.2 c. The details need not concern us here.

inferred from the first moral principle that the good is to be done—coupled, I assume, with teleological claims (howsoever derived) about what constitutes the good for human beings.[27] But God's reasons for affirming the two tables are nevertheless different: the first table represents expressions of divine duty, whereas the second, despite following from the same necessary principle, is commanded by God in virtue of his necessarily following what would be duties were he an agent that had duties in respect to his creatures.

Aquinas holds, then, first, that the moral norms of both tables of the Decalogue gain their content and their binding nature from considerations of teleology; secondly, that these moral norms are all derived inferentially from the same first principle of practical reasoning (i.e., that the good is to be done and evil avoided); and thirdly, that, while God has no obligations to creatures, he certainly acts in accordance with what would be moral obligations were he a moral agent—and this is what it is for God to be just in his dealings with creatures. Scotus dissents from all three of these claims, and this dissent results in his adopting a very different kind of metaethic. On the first of these, Scotus denies that any precepts of the second table can be derived from teleological analyses; on the second, while he agrees that any principle of natural law other than the first must be entailed by the first principle, he has a different account of what the first principle is; and on the third he holds that God acts contingently—he has motivations for affirming the precepts of the second table, but they are neither expressions of duties nor expressions of non-moral claims that would be duties if God had such. Indeed, as we shall see, Scotus's account of divine justice focuses on the question of God's just motivations. Aquinas's God does what he should, or what accords with what would be an obligation were God a moral agent, just because he should, or because it accords with what would be an obligation were God a moral agent. Scotus's God does what he should, but this is because he is *motivated* to do it: his justice (necessarily) inclines him to act in accordance with his obligations and normative judgments.

Duns Scotus

One of the most striking differences between the metaethical theories of Aquinas and Scotus is that Scotus holds that the first principle of natural law is not that good should be done, but that God should be loved. And—like Aquinas—he holds that any precept in natural law must be such that it is entailed by the first principle. Now, like Aquinas, Scotus holds that this entailment is grounded

---

[27]See, e.g., Aquinas, *ST* 1-2.90.2 c; *ST* 1-2.93.1 c; *ST* 1-2.100.5 c; *ST* 1-2.100.9 c; *ST* 2-2.59.4 sed contra and c. At *ST* 1.82.2 c Aquinas notes that there are certain particular goods that have "a necessary connection to beatitude," though he does not specify what these are.

in a teleological claim about the ultimate good of human nature as fulfilled in the beatific vision. But Scotus does not hold that the precepts of the second table of the Decalogue have any intrinsic connection with human teleology, and, as we shall see, the combination of these two claims (that the first principle of natural law is that God is to be loved, and that any precept of natural law must be such that it is entailed by the first principle) leads to a very different account of the explanation for the normativity of the second table of the Decalogue. Scotus's remarks are surprisingly sketchy, but I begin with his two main statements of the first principle of natural law:

> "If God exists, he is to be loved as God alone" is a necessary consequence.[28]
>
> Legal [justice] could be posited in God if there were some other law prior to the determination of his will, with which law and legislator, as other (as it were), his will would rightly agree. And there is indeed this law, "God is to be loved", if however it should be called a law and not a practical principle of law.[29]

Legal justice is the expression of binding moral norms.[30] The idea is that God has an obligation to love himself. This basic precept is morally binding on God, and thus represents a general moral norm, simply on the basis of what is owed to God as the necessary good.[31] As far as I can see, the reason for this shift from Aquinas's view is simply that the norms of natural law are supposed to be exceptionless and universally binding. Thus the first of the two passages just quoted comes from the very beginning of Scotus's discussion of natural law, and seems clearly to imply that God's activity is included under the scope of the norms of natural law; and the second passage arguably maintains that legal justice is present in God.[32] And the only norm that can bind God is this one, or norms entailed by it.

The second quotation here makes it clear that this obligation is a first principle of practical reasoning. The first seems to suggest that it is an immediate

---

[28]Scotus, *Ord.* 3.37.un., n. 20 (Vatican, X, 280). In this paragraph, Scotus suggests that this principle is one from which other practical principles of natural law follow, and the context makes it clear that he regards any unique principle from which other principles can be inferred as a practical principle "known from its terms" (*Ord.* 3.37.un., n. 16 (Vatican, X, 279): from which it can be gathered that the principle that "God is to be loved as God alone" is a (the) first principle of natural law.

[29]Scotus, *Ord.* 4.46.1, n. 3 (12 vols, ed. L. Wadding (Lyon, 1639), X, 238); I follow the lightly revised text in *WM*, 240.

[30]Scotus, *Ord.* 4.46.1, n. 2 (Wadding, X, 238).

[31]As Scotus puts it, even God's will is naturally inclined to will his own goodness: *Ord.* 4.46.1, n. 7 (Wadding, X, 252).

[32]Scotus's explicit opinion is that it is not possible to distinguish different kinds of justice in God, since God's justice is wholly unified: see *Ord.* 4.46.1, n. 7 (Wadding, X, 252). But, as he puts it in the same passage, he does not want to "disprove" the distinction between legal and other kinds of justice in God, since he clearly holds that something relevantly analogous to legal justice exists in God.

entailment of a theorem of theoretical reasoning, namely that there is a God. I am not sure whether this is Scotus's exact view or not. In particular, it is not clear to me whether or not Scotus would want to ground this entailment in some kind of teleology, such that the explanation for the normativity of this principle of practical reasoning is the fact that God is the ultimate goal of desire.[33] (Think of Aquinas's explanation of normativity: the good is desirable, and therefore should be desired.) The alternative, perhaps suggested by the first passage just quoted, grounds the normativity on God's nature independently of teleological considerations.[34]

Scotus also seems to assume that mere talk of normative reasons is not sufficient to explain God's good activity. Rather, he persistently claims that God's motivations (or, as Scotus puts it, *inclinations*) are wholly good, and the fact that the first principle of practical reasoning is automatically justified entails that it automatically motivates God:

> Since justice, properly speaking, is rectitude of a habituated will, and consequently inclines as it were naturally to another, or to oneself as to another, as it were, and [since] the divine will has no rectitude inclining it determinately to anything other than to its goodness as other, as it were . . . it follows that it has no justice other than for paying to his goodness what suits (*condecet*) it.[35]

The divine case here contrasts with creatures. As Peter King has shown, Scotus holds that the only natural motivations that rational creatures have is for their own advantage; following moral norms is in some cases a matter of willing *against* any natural internal inclination that might be in play, and doing the right thing simply because it is right.[36] (I return to this below.)

Scotus clearly holds that God does more than merely act in accordance with this first principle of practical reason: he follows it, as a *rule*. Scotus makes the point most clearly discussing a case in which God does merely act in accordance with a rule, rather than following it. Scotus holds that the procession of

---

[33] On this, see, e.g., Scotus, *Ord.* 1.2.1.1–2, n. 60 (Vatican, II, 165–66).

[34] As we shall see, Scotus also holds that following such a duty is good for creatures: that is to say, it is necessary for them to achieve their teleological goal. But this has no role in explaining its binding nature: this is perhaps because Scotus rejects the necessity of loving God even in the case of the beatific vision (see Scotus, *Ord.* 4.49.6, n, 11 (Wadding, X, 455)). There is no *necessity* in cases such as this, so there is no obvious explanation of bindingness either.

[35] Scotus, *Ord.* 4.46.1, n. 7 (Wadding, X, 252); I follow the text in *WM*, 246.

[36] See Peter King, "Scotus' Rejection of Anselm: The Two Wills Theory," in Ludger Honnefelder and others (ed.), *Johannes Duns Scotus 1308-2008: Investigations into his Philosophy*, Archa Verbi, Subsidia, 5 (Münster: Aschendorff; St Bonaventure, NY: Franciscan Institute Publications, 2010), 359–78. As I noted above, it is striking that Aquinas never speaks in terms that suggest that considerations of justice *motivate* God's activity (i.e., in the medieval jargon, "incline" God to act in certain ways). Aquinas's God does his duty simply because he should.

the Holy Spirit represents a case of God's acting in accordance with a duty that he has to himself (i.e., loving himself), but not following that duty. The basic Trinitarian idea here is that a perfect (i.e., infinite) will necessarily desires the divine essence, and its act of desire is supposed to be identified as a divine person—the Holy Spirit. But unlike the case of God's moral self-love, this act of desire can be sufficiently explained merely by appeal to the infinity of the divine will, irrespective of its rectitude:

> The divine essence is the first object of [his] will, and is to be willed of itself. Therefore that will is necessarily in a right act of willing that object which is rightly to be willed of itself.[37] . . . But it does not seem that the will's being right is to be assumed along with its being infinite, as two equal but different [premises in the argument for the necessity of the production of the Holy Spirit], because then the infinite will is not a sufficient power for communicating the [divine] nature, even when the object is present: rather, an infinite right will [is the sufficient power for communicating the divine nature]. Again, if this rectitude is conformity to right reason, it follows that reason is the principle of the production of the Holy Spirit, at least as a rule, just as it is the rule of an act of willing.[38]

The idea is that God does not produce the Holy Spirit as the result of an obligation to do so: he does it automatically, irrespective of his obligations.

Scotus makes much the same point, though less clearly, when discussing Anselm's definition of 'justice' as "rectitude of will observed for its own sake"[39] Scotus comments as follows:

> [God] has rectitude of will, indeed [he has] an unturnable (*inobliquabilem*) will, because it is the first rule, and "observed for its own sake"—not such that "observed" implies some reception (*susceptionem*) or passion in relation to the person observing it [viz. the will's justice], but "observed for its own sake", that is, always spontaneously disposed [to observe it].[40]

Scotus's point is that the divine will necessarily[41] and spontaneously observes its own norms (the moral rules that govern it), and follows (observes) these rules for their own sake.

So God's duties to himself are moral norms that he is automatically motivated to follow. There are no other norms like this. First of all, to belong to natural law, a moral norm must either be a first principle or be entailed by such

---

[37]Scotus, *Ord.* 1.10.un., n. 48 (Vatican, IV, 359).

[38]Scotus, *Ord.* 1.10.un., *text. int.* (Vatican, IV, 360, ll. 7–12).

[39]Anselm, *De veritate*. 12 (*Opera omnia*, 6 vols, ed. F. S. Schmitt (Edinburgh: Nelson, 1946–61), I, 194, l. 26).

[40]Scotus, *Ord.* 4.46.1, n. 2 (Wadding, X, 238).

[41]See also Scotus, *Ord.* 4.46.1, n. 7 (Wadding, X, 252), quoted above.

a principle. And, as Scotus notes, the precepts of the second table of the Decalogue do not satisfy this condition:

> In one way, something can be said to belong to the law of nature . . . as first practical principles known from their terms, or as conclusions necessarily following from them: and these [conclusions] are said to belong to the law of nature most strictly. . . . And it is not like this speaking in general of all the precepts of the second table, because the natures of the things that are there prescribed or prohibited are not simply necessary, or simply necessary conclusions. For in the things that are there prescribed there is no necessary goodness relative to the ultimate goal; neither in the things prohibited is there any malice that would necessarily turn someone away from the ultimate goal. For even if this good was not prescribed, the ultimate goal could be reached and loved; and if that evil was not prohibited, the acquisition of the final goal would be consistent with it.[42]

Basically, a moral norm would be entailed by the first principle of natural law if following the norm were a necessary condition for a creature's attainment of the final goal. But, Scotus claims, no precept of the second table of the Decalogue is such a necessary condition. Scotus puts the point most bluntly when considering an objection to the effect that someone's loving God requires that person to will that all other human beings love God too, on the grounds that the highest love is not jealous.[43] Scotus offers three alternative responses. First, it might be that the first principle of natural law, grounding the first table of the Decalogue, is not "love God", but "do not hate God": and this principle does not clearly entail that there are any norms governing behavior between human beings.[44] Secondly, supposing that the first principle is "love God," this principle does not obviously entail that we are obliged to will our neighbor to love God: consider, for example, the case of someone damned, whom God does not will to love God.[45] Thirdly, supposing (for the sake of argument, I think) that an obligation to love other human beings were part of the natural law, still this obligation would not entail any of the principles of the second table:

> It is possible for me to will that my neighbour love God, and nevertheless will that he not have corporeal life, or not will it [viz. that he has corporeal life]; or that his conjugal fidelity be preserved; and thus for the rest.[46]

---

[42]Scotus, *Ord.* 3.37.un., nn. 17–18 (Vatican, X, 279–80).
[43]Scotus, *Ord.* 3.37.un., n. 31 (Vatican, X, 285–6).
[44]Scotus, *Ord.* 3.37.un., n. 32 (Vatican, X, 286).
[45]Scotus, *Ord.* 3.37.un., n. 34 (Vatican, X, 287).
[46]Scotus, *Ord.* 3.37.un., n. 36 (Vatican, X, 288).

The modalities here are broadly logical: I can will that such-and-such a person love God, but this does not require that I will his or her following any of the precepts of the second table of the Decalogue—or *vice versa*—and this suggests that my willings of this various things, or God's willings of these things, are independent, and thus that the things themselves are independent.[47]

To see more clearly why Scotus believes this, we need to look in more detail at his account of what makes the second table binding. The claims cannot express universal norms, or norms that God necessarily wills, for reasons outlined already. So, basically, Scotus takes a constructivist line here: what makes the claims about moral duties outlined there true is simply God's attitude to those claims. It is not that God does not have reasons for favoring these claims: but that these reasons are not moral ones. Instead, Scotus appeals to *aesthetic* reasons, and these are the reasons that God has for favoring certain moral claims. God sees that the norms of the second table are, first, "in harmony"with the first principle of practical reasoning, and, secondly, somehow "fit" with the nature of the beings governed by the norms. On the first of these, Scotus comments as follows:

> In another way things are said to belong to the law of nature because they are very much in harmony (*multum consona*) with that law, even though they do not necessarily follow from the first practical principles which are known from their terms, and necessarily known to every intellect. And it is certain that all the precepts of the second table belong to the law of nature in this way, because their rectitude is greatly in harmony with the first practical principles, necessarily known.[48]

Scotus goes on to give an example:

> Given a practical principle of positive law that there should be peaceable living in a community or state, it does not necessarily follow from this that each person should have distinction of possession, or possessions distinct from someone else's possessions. For there could be peace in a community or society even if all things were common to them—and this is not a necessary consequence even if we grant that those who live or live together are weak. Nevertheless, that possessions are distinct in the case of human weakness is very much in harmony with peaceable living. For

[47]Scotus sometimes talks of God as willing in the most ordered or rational way. But by and large these discussions have to do merely with the sequence in which God wills things: the means before the end, for example. I explore some of this in my "Christocentrism and Theological Methodology in Duns Scotus," in Martín Carbajo Núñez (ed.), *Giovanni Duns Scoto: Studie e ricerche nel VII Centenario della sua morte, in onore di P. César Saco Alarcôn*, 2 vols (Rome: Antonianum, 2008), II, 109–31, basically following the insights of Thomas Williams, "A Most Methodical Lover?".

[48]Scotus, *Ord.* 3.37.un., nn. 25–66 (Vatican, X, 283).

> the weak care more about goods that are proper to them than [about] common goods, and more greatly will those common goods to be their own property than [they will them] to be shared with the community and the guardians of the community: and thus there would be strife and disorder [if there were no private property].[49]

The idea is that if the goal is peaceable living, this is most readily achieved with private property, at least in the state of weak (i.e., fallen) human nature—it is harmonious with the achievement of the goal of peaceable living that private property is the means. Now, the argument here seems to suggest that the aesthetic constraints here might be quite strong. But they fall short of the sort of logical constraints suggested by Aquinas's entailment claims—and this, I think, is all that Scotus needs to relax the relations between general deontological *principles* (i.e., that God should be loved) and further ethical norms.

Analogously to the case of private property and the objective of peaceable living, the precepts of the second table of the Decalogue are in harmony with the duty to love God. And they somehow fit with the natures of the creatures governed by the norms, too:

> In a second way, justice is said to be in a creature from the correspondence of one created thing to another (just as it is just on the part of the creature that fire is hot, and water cold, and that fire goes up and water goes down, and such-like), on the grounds that this created nature requires that as something corresponding to it.[50]

Admittedly, the language of harmony is lacking here. But elsewhere Scotus claims that we can make judgments about the appropriateness of certain moral acts—their appropriateness (*convenientia*) or lack thereof (*disconvenientia*) with creaturely natures—and (as we shall see in a moment) he takes 'appropriateness' and 'harmony' ('consonantia') to be equivalent:

> The [moral] goodness of a thing . . . which is accidental or supervenient on entity, is the integrity of its appropriateness; or its integral appropriateness to something else to which it should fit (*convenire*), or of something else to it. And these two kinds of appropriateness are generally connected.[51]

(Note here Scotus's tepid acceptance of Aquinas's two-fold reciprocal requirement: goodness (though not, in every case, obligation, according Scotus) requires both that the rational object is perfected, and that the agent is.) Equally, the talk of requirements should not be thought to commit Scotus to

[49]Scotus, *Ord.* 3.37.un., n. 27 (Vatican, X, 283–84).
[50]Scotus, *Ord.* 4.46.1, n. 8 (Wadding, X, 252).
[51]Scotus, *Quodlibet* 18, n. 3 (Wadding, XII, 475).

the view that God could not bring about the opposites of the states of affairs that express the natural fit of different kinds of natures. I will return to this in a moment.

On this view, God has reasons, but not moral ones, for endorsing certain moral claims. It might be thought that these aesthetic considerations are too weak to do the relevant grounding. But Scotus believes that they are much more robust than we might imagine, albeit falling short of the merely logical constraints that Aquinas holds to be relevant in these ethical cases. (Not that Scotus's God is not subject to logical constraints, but that these constraints are not relevant to the relation between first principles and other ethical norms, since these other norms are consistent with the first principle but not entailed by it.) For example, as part of his defense of the logical coherence of the concept "infinite being," Scotus appeals to such aesthetic considerations:

> The sense powers, which are less cognitive than the intellect, immediately perceive inappropriateness (*disconvenientiam*) in their object: this is clear in the case of hearing relative to an inappropriate object. Therefore if *infinite* were incompatible with *being*, the intellect would immediately perceive this inappropriateness and incompatibility, and then it could not have infinite being as its object.[52]

A parallel discussion makes the aesthetic component more explicit:

> The intellect, whose object is being, finds no incompatibility understanding something infinite: rather, it seems perfectly intelligible. But it is remarkable if a contradiction in relation to the first object is made evident to no intellect, when discord (*discordia*) in sound so easily offends the hearing.[53]

Aesthetic judgments are akin to detecting contradictions—again suggesting that the constraints they place are quite strong—though of course fall short

[52]Scotus, *Reportatio* 1–A.2.1.1–3, n. 72 (2 vols, ed. Allan B. Wolter and Oleg Bychkov (St. Bonaventure, NY: Franciscan Institute, 2004–8), I, 137).

[53]Scotus, *Ord.* 1.2.1.1–2, n. 136 (Vatican, II, 208). I am grateful to Oleg Bychkov's groundbreaking work on Scotus's aesthetics, and for (in conversation) drawing my attention to these two passages, the significance of which I would not have spotted but for his work and help. See, e.g., his "*Decor ex praesentia mali*: Aesthetic Explanation of Evil in the Thirteenth-Century Franciscan Thought," in *Recherches de Théologie et Philosophie médiévales*, 68 (2001), 245–69; "What does Beauty have to do with the Trinity? From Augustine to Duns Scotus," *Franciscan Studies*, 66 (2008), 197–212; "'Aesthetic' Epistemology: Parallels between the Perception of Musical Harmony and the Cognition of Truth in Duns Scotus," in Honnefelder and others (ed.), *John Duns Scotus 1308–2008*, 345–56. Irwin's account of Scotus's ethics also makes much of the notion of consonance in this context, though he does not make so explicit the seriously aesthetic connotations of the concept as Scotus understands it. For some emphasis on the aesthetic in this context, see too Mary Beth Ingham, "Duns Scotus' Moral Reasoning and the Artistic Paradigm," in Leonardo Sileo (ed.), *Via Scoti: Methodologica ad mentem Joannis Duns Scoti*, 2 vols (Rome: Antonianum, 1995), II, 825–37. For more on Scotus's aesthetics, see also Gérard Sondag, "The Conditional Definition of Beauty by Scotus," *Medioevo* 30 (2005), 191–206.

of the logical requirements in contradiction. "Discord," here, I take it, is the opposite of "harmony," and thus, just as "discord" and "inappropriateness" are equivalent, so too are "harmony" ("consonantia") and "appropriateness"("con venientia"). The kind of thing Scotus has in mind in these passages is the kind of aesthetic reaction that (say) mathematicians sometimes have to an elegant proof, or physicists to the order of the universe. It is not the sight—the sensory appearance—of the universe, for example, that provokes just that reaction. As Scotus thinks, both the senses and the intellect are capable of distinctive aesthetic perceptions: and it is this kind of perception that grounds God's endorsement of certain moral claims. Note that these reasons are not in fact *judgments* (despite my suggestion to the contrary above): Scotus claims, rather, that we immediately *perceive* the aesthetic properties of things, and (I take it) the intellect intuitively grasps them without the need for a judgment. The argument is that this kind of perception is a cognitive function: if the senses have it in relation to their objects, then the intellect—more perfectly cognitive than the senses—has it in relation to its object too.

So God perceives the aesthetic qualities of certain moral norms, and on the basis of this perception endorses these norms. Scotus takes it for granted that God's necessary goodness means that his endorsing the relevant norms is in accordance with his motivations. Just as in the case of the first table of the Decalogue, God's motivations correspond to the reasons that he has for endorsing certain norms (and not others). Talking of God's activity in relation to creatures, and of his endorsing certain moral norms on the basis of their harmony with God's genuine duties (i.e., to himself), Scotus comments as follows:

> The single justice [in God], which inclines him deterministically merely to his first act [i.e., self-love], modifies his secondary acts, although none of them necessarily, such that it could not modify them in the opposite direction. Neither does justice precede the [divine] will, by inclining it naturally to some secondary act. Rather, the will determines itself to any secondary object, and from this the act is modified by that first justice, because it is harmonious with the will to which it is conformed, as if the first justice were the rectitude inclining [the will].[54]

The idea is that whatever God wills is in accordance with his (good) motivations. Scotus seems simply to regard this as an assumption that does not need justification. The claim that justice does not "precede" the will is simply a way of expressing the fact that God is not bound by the relevant moral norms; neither is he bound to prefer any given norm over its opposite. There are many possible harmonious scenarios, incompatible with each other and governed by

[54]Scotus, *Ord.* 4.46.1, n. 8 (Wadding, X, 252).

different and conflicting moral norms. Scotus gives an example: God's permitting bigamy in the time of the Patriarchs:

> God could either have clarified or (in some case) revoked his law about the [marriage] exchange, and done so reasonably in the case in which a greater good would come from revoking the law than observing it. In this case, when there was a necessity for multiplying the human race, either simply speaking or on account of divine worship (since there were few who worshipped God), there was a necessity that those who worshipped God should procreate as much as they could, because faith and divine worship continued to exist in their succession: therefore in that case [God] reasonably dispensed so that one man might share his body with the bodies of many women, increasing the number who worship God, which could not have been achieved without this.[55]

Notoriously, Scotus holds that God could permit or even command murder, with no difference in the situation other than his command.[56] Presumably, Scotus holds that there would be an aesthetic appeal in either case (murder or not murder).[57] He has in mind, of course, the command to Abraham to sacrifice

---

[55]Scotus, *Ord.* 4.33.1, n. 4 (Wadding, IX, 705); I use the text in *WM*, 290–2. It is not clear to me that this would make a difference other than in the case that there were fewer women than men: but Scotus does not seem to consider this.

[56]Scotus, *Ord.* 3.37.un., n. 13 (Vatican, X, 276–7).

[57]Thus, in the passages just quoted, Scotus claims that God has reasons for his commands and dispensations—i.e., aesthetic ones. This leads Irwin to an objection: "How can it be up to God to choose the secondary principles, if some courses of action are especially consonant with nature and the higher principles? Scotus concedes that even though the correct secondary principles do not follow necessarily from the higher principles, rational inquiry can discover their special consonance with the higher principles. In that case God should have practical knowledge of the secondary principles, contrary to Scotus' view": Irwin, *Development of Ethics*, 694. Analogously, the converse argument can be raised against dispensations: "If we can discover by practical means that a general rule is consonant with the law of nature, we should also be able to discover by practical reason the exceptions to the general rule that are consonant with the primary aim of the rule. . . . If Scotus were to say this, he could not claim that God exercises freedom in dispensing us from the natural law; he would have to claim that God's superior practical knowledge sees appropriate grounds for recognizing exceptions to general rules": Irwin, *Development of Ethics*, 694 (at 694, n. 49, Irwin ascribes this latter strategy to Wolter's "right reason" approach to Scotus's ethics). My response: God has options in cases that each alternative choice can be perceived to be aesthetically pleasing; in other cases, he has no choice. But nothing about the choice requires that the two or more alternatives are equally pleasing (though of course they could be), and Scotus presumably could allow too that God might choose the less pleasing. What Scotus is explicit about is that there is no secondary precept that is such that it is *always* more pleasing than its opposite, or than its dispensation. Whether or not he also seems to believe that some secondary precepts are such that their opposites are sometimes not at all pleasing (and thus cannot be commanded by God I do not know; if he did, it would tend to moderate his voluntarism (for a version of this observation, see Irwin, *Development of Ethics*, 695)). But that seems fine: I think Scotus is more concerned with providing a non-empty account of the grounding of the secondary principles than he is with preserving radical voluntarism, and in any case it might be that no secondary precepts are such that their opposites are sometimes not at all pleasing. (I return to Scotus's voluntarism below.)

Isaac: where, perhaps, the aesthetic appeal lies in the simple obedience and service owed to God.

Now, the account thus raises an acute difficulty. Scotus holds that principles of natural law, and theorems entailed by them (given certain further claims about the ways in which created moral agents behave *ut in pluribus*, Aquinas-style), are universally and automatically binding. One way of showing that human beings have a duty to obey God would be by claiming that this duty follows from the duty to love God. But as far as I can see Scotus does not make such a claim, and so this way of accounting for the normativity of divine commands is not open to him. Aquinas proposes a different solution:

> Anyone who obeys is moved by the authority of the one whom he obeys, just as natural things are moved by their movers. But just as God is the first mover of all things that are moved naturally, so too he is the first mover of all wills. . . . And for this reason, all natural things are subject by natural necessity to divine motion, so also by a certain necessity of justice all wills are bound (*tenentur*) to obey divine authority.[58]

But Scotus does not appeal to this kind of teleological argument either. Scotus agrees that God is both universal legislator[59] and judge,[60] and he agrees that God's commands *bind* us:

> Positive law justly requires . . . authority in the legislator, . . . because 'law' (*lex*) comes from 'binding' (*ligando*), and not every judgment of a prudent person binds the community, or [binds] anyone if the person is head of nothing.[61]

But what explains the fact that God's commands have this kind of binding character? Scotus does not make his answer explicit. But he usually notes the *coercive* power of law-givers in this kind of context. For example, he notes that Sarah—Abraham's superior for these purposes—"quasi-coerced" Abraham into having sex with Hagar.[62] Scotus usually spells out this coercive force in terms of the threat of punishment. For example, defending his abhorrent belief that a ruler can justly promulgate laws constraining Jewish people to be baptized, Scotus notes that laws can "coerce with threats and terror" (*cogerentur minis et terroribus*).[63] And God is "a just judge, avenging sin":[64] God's laws bind in virtue of the threat of punishment. This account of Scotus's view of the

---

[58]Aquinas, *ST* 2-2.104.4 c.
[59]See, e.g., Scotus, *Ord.* 1.44.un., nn. 5–6 (Vatican, VI, 364–65).
[60]See, e.g., Scotus, *Ord.* 4.17.un., n. 7 (Wadding, IX, 298).
[61]Scotus, *Ord.* 4.15.2, n. 6 (Wadding, IX, 156).
[62]Scotus, *Ord.* 4.33.1, n. 5 (Wadding, IX, 705).
[63]Scotus, *Ord.* 4.4.4.2–3, n. 170 (Vatican, XI, 276).
[64]Scotus, *Ord.* 4.17.un., n. (Wadding, IX, 298).

binding character of legal norms is admittedly speculative. But if it is right, Scotus moves decidedly in the direction of grounding the binding nature of such norms in terms of *sanctions*. The cost of not obeying a law is not the failure to achieve teleological perfection, but suffering a sanction. And this is what explains the binding force of the norm.

Now, on the face of it, Scotus's view is puzzling in a further way too. Why not simply accept an account like Aquinas's, where God necessarily acts in accordance with principles that would be moral duties were he a moral agent? Underlying Scotus's shift away from such an account is his strong commitment to divine freedom, a commitment that Aquinas clearly does not share.[65] Scotus holds, if I am right, that there are two kinds of constraint on divine external activity: the principle of non-contradiction, and aesthetic perception. But this second sort of constraint, he maintains, is such that God can will against any given precept in the second table of the Decalogue, with the mere proviso that he can perceive some aesthetic appeal in so doing: and, of course, the assumption is that God can find such appeal in given cases. And in any case, they cannot count as *normative* for God, since for Scotus the only genuinely universal norm is expressed in the content of the deontological requirement to love God. Suppose there were norms guiding God's behavior to his creatures, antecedent to God's attitude towards the various norms. God's freedom is such that these norms would not provide a reason for God to act in accordance with the norms, or motivate him to do so. And this would be contrary to God's goodness:

> It does not seem probable that God could not act beyond the second [justice], because he can do, and thus will, whatever does not include a contradiction. But he cannot will something that he cannot rightly will, because his will is the first rule. Therefore, he can rightly will whatever does not include a contradiction, and thus, since this second justice determines to something whose opposite does not include a contradiction, God can will, and rightly will, and act, beyond this second justice.[66]

If God were governed by such norms, he would have necessary reasons for acting in certain ways, and these reasons (on Scotus's account) would amount to *causes* of God's activity. The fact that God is wholly good, and free in his activities *ad extra*, entails that the norms of the second table are dependent upon his approval. Scotus has an argument in favor of God's being free in relation to his activities *ad extra*:

> Something is caused contingently; therefore the first cause causes contingently. . . . The consequence is proved: any second cause causes insofar as

---

[65]Scotus is the first thinker, as far as I know, to develop a strong libertarian account of freedom, one that he applies to God too. On the libertarian account, see, e.g., *In metaph.* 9.15, nn. 31–32 (OP, IV, 683–4).

[66]Scotus, *Ord.* 4.46.1, n. 6 (Wadding, X, 241); I follow the text in *WM*, 244.

> it is moved by the first cause. Therefore, if the first cause moves necessarily, every [cause] is moved necessarily, and everything is caused necessarily.[67]

The argument—not very clearly expressed—is that we can infer the contingency of *all* divine activity *ad extra* on the basis of the fact that some creaturely activity is clearly contingent—i.e., free action. In the case at hand, obligation *ad extra* would amount to some kind of necessity in God's action *ad extra* (given that his obligations motivate him such that he is not free relative to them). (I am not concerned here with the cogency of this argument—I am simply trying to explain the intellectual motivations for Scotus's metaethical position.) The same would obtain if Scotus were to accept Aquinas's view that God necessarily acts in accordance with norms that would represent duties for a moral agent in God's relevant circumstances: God's freedom would be restricted. So, as I pointed out above, the first principle is not that good should be done (since this would restrict God's freedom), but that God should be loved.

Now, this is sufficient to show that the first principle endorsed by Aquinas cannot in fact be the first principle of practical reasoning. And Scotus sees no need to accept the view that God necessarily acts in accordance with what would be norms were he a moral agent, because Scotus believes that he can preserve both divine goodness and freedom by proposing an alternative account of divine goodness. On the face of it, the view might seem to provide an overly attenuated account of divine goodness. At worst, it might just be trivially true that God only approves the aesthetically appealing, since the content of the aesthetically appealing might be determined simply by the choices that God makes. But I think this analysis would be a mistake. Nothing in Scotus's texts suggests that he believes there to be no constraints on what God can will. Rather, God's willing is contingent in the sense that he could will a different order from the one that he *de facto* wills, and within any ordering there are no norms (other than those of natural law) that are such that God necessarily acts in accordance with them. God is free to vary the norms (in accordance, as I suggested above, with his aesthetic perceptions about the suitability of given ends and given means)—and God is free in principle to vary *any* norm not entailed by the first table of the Decalogue. Hannes Möhle makes the following helpful comment:

> This argumentative structure thus gives Scotus complete freedom to show the legitimacy of a plurality of orderings, but each of these must be shown to be rational in its own right.[68]

---

[67]Scotus, *De primo principio* 4, n. 5 (ed. Allan B. Wolter (Chicago: Franciscan Herald Press, 1982), 83 (¶ 4.15)).

[68]Möhle, "Scotus's Theory," 320.

Möhle is right to suggest that God's varying norms would result in a different order, but the point is tangential to my argument here. What is significant is that the fact that God can vary any norm entails that he is neither bound by the norms, nor such that he necessarily acts in accordance with such norms. God cannot command just anything, since the aesthetic requirement places limitations on what he can do. (Scotus does not give any clear examples of such limitations: though I suppose that he could not command murder if he perceived no aesthetic appeal in the state of affairs commanded.) In any case, the point is that any given norm is contingent, and might be varied as time and circumstance require. If the norms were moral norms belonging to natural law, or if God necessarily acted in accordance with such norms, they would be *invariable*, not allowing any exception. And this is what Scotus wants to avoid, and what he believes his aesthetic account can avoid.

But it seems to me that we can say more than this. One of the most striking features of Scotus's account, certainly if we contrast it with Aquinas's, is its focus on questions of divine *motivation*: in Scotus's language, on questions of the different ways in which justice *inclines* God's will. This is entirely absent from Aquinas, who seems to believe that normative reasons alone are sufficient to explain God's following, or acting in accordance with, moral rules. Scotus does not make his reasons for this explicit. As we saw above, he talks of God's will as "habituated" by justice (although not in such as way as to be "receptive" of a habit of justice: this habit is not an accident but a necessary feature of God). So we can get some understanding of the importance of motivation in Scotus's discussion if we look at his account of virtuous habits. Roughly, Scotus holds that moral goodness springs simply from the conformity of an act with right reason, and explicitly rejects the view that motivation (e.g., the presence of a moral virtue) could have any bearing on the moral status of an act.[69] But he believes that the only explanation for someone's *regularly* acting in a certain way is that they are inclined or motivated so to do: wherever there is habitual behavior of a certain kind, there is an inclination towards such behavior,[70] and wherever there is "habitual conformity to right reason" there is a virtuous habit or inclination.[71] So I think Scotus would claim that, since God's acts satisfy this condition, they must be motivated acts: and his necessarily good motivation is what God's goodness amounts to. God, rather than being

[69]Scotus, *Ord.* 1.17.1.1–2, n. 62 (Vatican, V, 164).

[70]Strictly, Scotus claims that the presence of a habit of a given kind entails that an agent can do certain corresponding sorts of acts "with pleasure, easily, expeditiously, and readily (*prompte*)": *Ord.* 1.17.1.1–2, n. 7 (Vatican, V, 142).

[71]Scotus, *Ord.* 1.17.1.1–2, n. 65 (Vatican, V, 167). Right reason requires the intellectual virtue of prudence (see Scotus, *Ord.* 1.17.1.1–2, n. 66 (Vatican, V, 168–69): but this guides cognitive judgment, and is not anything like a desire or motivation.

an agent who does what is right simply because he ought, is one who is necessarily maximally virtuous. And this view of divine goodness allows Scotus to offer a metaethics that is consistent both with divine freedom and with divine goodness.

Scotus's account of natural law represents an attempt to spell out a natural law metaethic that takes as its basis something other than teleological motivations. This is not, I think, because of a lessening of interest in, or commitment to, teleology in Scotus. Rather, Scotus sees aesthetic considerations to provide a way of grounding natural law without compromising divine freedom—a novel way, in other words, between the horns of the Euthyphro dilemma. What is perhaps striking is the way in which Scotus's view gets developed in a thinker such as Ockham. Ockham takes on the voluntaristic elements of Scotus's view, but without any grounding either in teleology or aesthetics: and this leads to a decided shift in favor of a straightforward divine command metaethic, something that Scotus believes he has the tools to avoid.

Turning again to the scholarship with which I began, I would suggest that both Wolter and Möhle are, in different ways, too restrictive on the nature of the aesthetic perception that grounds God's approval of the norms in the second table of the Decalogue. Presumably this approval might be based on a perception of the harmony of means with ends (Wolter) or of general with specific cases (Möhle)—though I do not think that (as Wolter seems to suppose) any such divine judgment about harmony necessitates God's approval of a certain norm in certain circumstances. Williams, it seems to me, is not sufficiently restrictive, but in any case seems not to consider the importance of aesthetic perception underlying Scotus's metaethics (on all of this, see the discussion in n. 57 above). And none of these commentators focuses much on the significance of God's motivations in all of this. To this extent, I hope to have made a small advance in the complex and difficult area that is Scotus's metaethics.[72]

[72] I acknowledged above my deep debt to Oleg Bychkov in framing this discussion. Thanks too to Jean Porter, and the other contributors to this volume for helpful comments, many of which guided my approach to the issues. But I perhaps owe most to Gerald J. Massey, whose detailed comments on the penultimate version of this paper forced me to deal with a set of objections that, I believe, would have proved fatal to the earlier version. Faults, of course, fatal or otherwise, remain mine and mine alone.

{ PART IV }

Spinoza and the Transition to Modern Thought

{ 8 }

Spinoza and Natural Law

Jon Miller

There is ongoing dispute among Spinoza scholars regarding how his ethics relate to natural law ethics. On the one side, some find strong affinities between the two. Errol Harris argues that because Spinoza takes "God's eternal law, the nature of nature in the world at large, and the law of reason" to be identical, he is "in quite close agreement with Aquinas, at all events in effect, although St. Thomas uses different language and does not work out the connexion between God's essence, the extended world in space and time, and the rational intellect with quite the same rigour and systematic coherence."[1] Those who agree with Harris include Huntington Cairns,[2] Matthew Kisner[3] and, less easily, Aaron Garrett.[4]

On the other side, many deny any meaningful similarity. Two decades ago, Edwin Curley tried to show that far from being fellow travelers, Spinoza seeks to mount a strong argument against natural law. His "rejection of the natural law tradition," Curley writes, "is thoroughgoing and radical."[5] More recently, Justin Steinberg has argued that "by adopting the view that nature is univocal

---

[1]Errol E. Harris, "Spinoza's Treatment of Natural Law," in *Spinoza's Political and Theological Thought*, ed. C. de Deugd (Amsterdam/Oxford/New York: North-Holland Publishing Company, 1984), p. 66.

[2]"Spinoza's Theory of Law," *Columbia Law Review*, vol. 48:7 (1948), pp. 1032–48. See especially pp. 1042–43.

[3]There is a long discussion of natural law in Kisner's new book on Spinoza's ethics (*Spinoza on Human Freedom* (Cambridge: Cambridge University Press, 2011); see esp. Chapter 6. At one point he says, "Spinoza's practical laws look a great deal like natural laws, as they were conceived by the tradition running from the Stoics, through Aquinas, Suarez, Grotius and Hobbes" (pp. 116–17).

[4]"Spinoza as Natural Lawyer," *Cardozo Law Review*, vol. 25.2 (2003–4), pp. 627–41. Garrett pithily concludes, "one can reasonably consider Spinoza a natural lawyer, just one so consistently naturalizing as to gut much of what we associate with the tradition" (p. 641).

[5]"The State of Nature and Its Law in Hobbes and Spinoza," *Philosophical Topics*, vol. 19:1 (1991), pp. 97–117.

and that man is governed by the same laws as everything else in nature, Spinoza rejects the whole natural law tradition."[6]

Now, Spinoza scholars are a quarrelsome lot. This may be another example of how we have trouble agreeing amongst ourselves. Perhaps it would be helpful to look outside our small world, to see what others have said about Spinoza and natural law. There is only one problem with this suggestion. While I have not searched all of the standard commentaries on natural law, I have examined a large number.[7] Without exception, they either entirely omit Spinoza for their discussion or mention him only in passing. So unfortunately, there is little chance that light will be shed on Spinoza's relation to natural law ethics by those who have thought the most about natural law.

So we have an impasse—some say that Spinoza's ethics belong to the natural law tradition, others don't—but should we care? After all, not all impasses deserve attempted resolution. In the present case, however, I think we should care. I say this because the attempt at resolving it will bring up interesting possibilities for understanding both Spinoza and the nature of natural law ethics itself.

This is how I intend to proceed. In the first section, I note the vagueness of the term "natural law." Given this vagueness, I propose a certain method for relating Spinoza's moral philosophy to that of the natural law tradition. After this method is set forth, I commence to execute it. The upshot will be that Spinoza both follows and parts company with natural law theory in various respects.

What Is Natural Law?

There is a problem that secondary literature on natural law ethics must inevitably confront. Mark Murphy puts his finger on it in a helpful introductory article:

> Some writers use the term with such a broad meaning that any moral theory that is a version of moral realism—that is, any moral theory that holds that some positive moral claims are literally true . . .—counts as a

[6]"Spinoza's Political Philosophy," *The Stanford Encyclopedia of Philosophy (Spring 2009 Edition)*, Edward N. Zalta (ed.), http://plato.stanford.edu/archives/spr2009/entries/spinoza-political/.

[7]Here are the main sources I consulted: Knud Haakonssen, "Divine/natural law theories in ethics," in *The Cambridge History of Seventeenth-Century Philosophy*, vols. 1–2, eds. Daniel Garber and Michael Ayers (Cambridge: Cambridge University Press, 1998), pp. 1317–57. Knud Haakonssen, *Natural Law and Moral Philosophy* (Cambridge: Cambridge University Press, 1996). J. B. Schneewind, *The Invention of Autonomy* (Cambridge: Cambridge University Press, 1998). Stephen Darwall, "The Foundations of Morality," in *The Cambridge Companion to Early Modern Philosophy*, ed. Donald Rutherford (Cambridge: Cambridge University Press, 2006), pp. 221–49. Richard Tuck, *Natural Rights Theories* (Cambridge: Cambridge University Press, 1979).

> natural law view. Some use it so narrowly that no moral theory that is not grounded in a very specific form of Aristotelian teleology could count as a natural law view.[8]

The natural law tradition in ethics has a rich history. Of the major schools of moral thought around today, such as Kantianism, Utilitarianism, and Virtue Ethics, it is the oldest and most continuous. Given the richness of the tradition and the vast number of thinkers who have contributed to it, there can be no surprise that the bounds of natural law have been pushed in many different directions. As the boundaries are pushed in different directions, the difficulty of defining "natural law" becomes acute. At least some of the priorities and challenges confronting a natural law theorist in the thirteenth century will differ from his heir in the twenty-first. When commentators are assigned the task of providing global accounts of natural law ethics, accounts which are supposed to encompass everyone from the Stoics to Aquinas to contemporary philosophers such as Murphy himself, they will almost inevitably choose to fasten on different aspects of the tradition.

With such being the case, one obvious way to compare Spinoza with his natural law counterparts is ruled out. The way I have in mind would first involve a definition of "natural law ethics" *simpliciter* and then an attempt at mapping it onto Spinoza's ethics. No matter which definition one provides, there will be too many important exceptions that the definition would fail to capture. Or at least, so much effort would be required to capture all the exceptions that little progress could be made in understanding how Spinoza relates to natural law ethics. Rather than wade into such murky waters, I will instead try to navigate around them entirely. Nowhere shall I advance a definition of what I mean by "natural law ethics." Accordingly, I will not attempt a global comparison between natural law ethics and Spinoza's ethics. Instead, I will focus on discrete aspects of natural law ethics, determine whether there are counterparts in Spinoza's moral system, and (if there are) show how they compare.

The Normativity of Natural Laws

In the piece from which I have just quoted, Murphy considers different solutions to the problem of determining what constitutes natural law ethics. One possibility, he argues, is to take as our "starting point the central role that the moral theorizing of Thomas Aquinas plays in the natural law tradition. If any moral theory is a theory of natural law, it is Aquinas's."[9]

---

[8] "The Natural Law Tradition in Ethics," *The Stanford Encyclopedia of Philosophy (Fall 2011 Edition)*, Edward N. Zalta (ed.), http://plato.stanford.edu/entries/natural-law-ethics/.

[9] Murphy (2011).

Murphy is right about Aquinas. Yet others are credited with being almost as central to the natural law tradition. High on this list would be the Stoics. Scholars have recently questioned whether Stoics are entitled to their place in the canon of natural law theorists.[10] But historically, there is no doubt that this was the consensus view. As one modern commentator has put it, "There are subtler points for investigation in the philosophy of the Stoics than their statements on natural law, but no doctrine attributed to them has been more influential."[11] This gives me an opening. If the Stoics are accepted as legitimate representatives of natural law ethics, then I can discuss how aspects of their moral theory compare to Spinoza's.

1. According to one ancient source, the Stoics defined natural law as "right reason commanding what must be done and prohibiting what must not be done."[12] According to another, Stoics also provided definitions of the two sorts of edicts issued by natural law: those actions that the law commands are "right actions" while those that are forbidden are "wrongdoing."[13] When the agent performs a right action—one for which she can give a good reason—she is acting in accord with nature (both hers and Nature as a whole).[14] It is by performing right actions that the agent becomes virtuous and it is by being virtuous that she is happy. Because it is up to the agent whether or not to perform right actions,[15] it turns out that whether or not they are happy is entirely within their control.[16] All of this shows that when the law tells an agent what she ought to do, the "ought" here is not merely prudential but it also has normative force.

This leads me to the first group of questions I want to investigate. The Stoics hold that the law of nature tells us what we ought to do. When the Stoics make this claim, they take the "ought" to be a moral "ought." Can we find anything similar in Spinoza? Does Spinoza think there are natural laws dictating which actions we ought to perform? And if he does, is the "ought" prescriptive or merely descriptive?[17]

---

[10]For a summary of the debate, together with full references to all the protagonists, see Jon Miller, "Stoics, Grotius and Spinoza on moral deliberation," *Hellenistic and Early Modern Philosophy*, ed. Jon Miller and Brad Inwood (Cambridge: Cambridge University Press, 2003), esp. pp. 117–20. See also the essay by Jacob Klein in this volume.

[11]Gerard Watson, "The Natural Law and Stoicism," in *Problems in Stoicism*, ed. A.A. Long (London: Athlone Press, 1971), p. 216.

[12]Alexander of Aphrodisias, *De fato* 35. Cf. Cicero, *De fato* I.18.

[13]Cicero, *De officiis*, III.23.

[14]See, e.g., Diogenes Laertius (henceforth: D.L.), *Lives of the Philosophers* VII.108 (trans. R.D. Hicks (Cambridge, MA: Harvard University Press).

[15]See, e.g., Alexander of Aphrodisias, *De fato* 62G.

[16]See, e.g., Cicero, *De fato* 42–43.

[17]Whether Spinoza's "ought" is prescriptive or merely descriptive has been much discussed in the secondary literature. Some references will be provided in the pages below. One recent nuanced analysis can be found in Donald Rutherford, "Spinoza's Conception of Law: Metaphysics and Ethics," in *Spinoza's Theological-Political Treatise: A Critical Guide*, eds. Yitzhak Y. Melamed and Michael A. Rosenthal (Cambridge: Cambridge University Press, 2010). See especially Section 2. Because Rutherford's proposals are so different from mine, I will not take up his paper in what follows.

We can get started with this argument from his *Theological-Political Treatise* (henceforth: *TTP*), Chapter XVI, paragraphs 3–7:

Argument One:

1. "[I]t is the supreme law of Nature that each thing endeavours to persist in its present being, as far as in it lies, taking account of no other thing but itself."
   Justification: *conatus* argument.[18]
2. "Whatever an individual does by the laws of its own nature, it does with sovereign right."
   Justification (from paragraph 2):
   A. "Nature has the sovereign right to do all that she can do."
   B. "Nature as a whole" is nothing more than "the power of all individual things taken together."
   C. So it follows that "each individual thing has the sovereign right to do all that it can do . . ."
3. From (2), "it follows that each individual has the sovereign right to do this, that is (as I have said), to exist and to act as it is naturally determined."
4. Some people live under the sole control of appetite; some people live under the control of reason.
   Justification: observation of human action.
5. From (4), it follows that people are under the control of different forces, that there is not one force which determines all people.
6. Instead of saying one force determines all people, we must say that all people are determined by their actual natures. More precisely, "the natural right of every man is determined not by sound reason, but by his desire and his power" (from 1, 4, and 5).
7. From (6), "it follows that Nature's right and her established order, under which all men are born and for the most part live, forbids only those things that no one desires and no one can do . . ."[19]

Notice the prominent role accorded laws of nature and the sovereignty of nature. In premise one, Spinoza tells us of the supreme law of nature. This law is immediately shown to have practical consequences, for it requires all individuals to pursue those actions that are necessary for the persistence of their present being. The ultimate source of this requirement is Nature itself. So

[18]Spinoza's *conatus* doctrine holds, *very* roughly, that all things always seek their own self-preservation. It has been much discussed in the secondary literature. I will not go into it here. For a clear if opinionated guide to the issues, see Michael Della Rocca, *Spinoza* (New York: Routledge, 2008), esp. Chapter 4, section 1.

[19]Translations of the *TTP* are by Samuel Shirley in *Spinoza: Complete Works*, ed. Michael Morgan (Indianapolis: Hackett Publishing, 2002). The argument of *TTP* XVI should be compared with the similar argument of *Tractatus Politicus* (henceforth: *TP*) II.3.

what makes individuals pursue their own interest, and to regard such pursuit as right, is Nature. Thus the whole argument—the opening premise, all the inferences, the conclusion itself—is structured in terms of laws and natural right.

Notice also the language used by Spinoza. He explicitly speaks of the "supreme law of Nature" in the first premise. He speaks of "the natural right of every man" in the third. In the conclusion, he talks about "Nature's right and her established order."

All of this is surely consonant with Natural Law ethics, at least of the Stoics. Compare these excerpts from Diogenes Laertius:

> An animal's first impulse, say the Stoics, is to self-preservation . . . for it was not likely that Nature should estrange the living thing from itself . . . Nature's rule is to follow the direction of impulse. But when reason . . . has been bestowed on the beings we call rational, for them life according to reason rightly becomes the natural life . . . This is why Zeno was the first . . . to designate the end "life in agreement with nature" . . ., which is the same as a virtuous life, virtue being the goal towards which nature guides us . . . And this is why the end may be defined as life in accordance with nature, or, in other words, in accordance with our own human nature as well as that of the universe, a life in which we refrain from every action forbidden by the law common to all things . . .[20]

There is a "law common to all things."[21] This law is self-preservation. It has practical consequences, for it enjoins the agent to "repel all that is injurious and give free access to all that is serviceable or akin to it" (D.L. VII.85). This law is legitimized by Nature itself, for it was "not likely that Nature should estrange the living being from itself." So individuals ought, rightly, to pursue their own interest simply because of Nature's rule.

On the basis of Argument One (and other passages to follow), we can safely answer the first of the questions stated in the second paragraph of this sub-section. While he may use other concepts in some of the places where he discusses moral issues, it is nonetheless true that Spinoza also makes frequent recourse to natural laws in his moral writings. He evidently thought nature was structured by principles or laws that together generate the terms we ought to follow if we are to act morally.

By themselves, however, the formal role of natural laws and the appearance of natural law language tell us nothing about how to answer the third question. Curley claims that Spinoza uses the trappings of natural law (such as its formal structure and vernacular) only to subvert and destroy it by stripping it of all prescriptivity. According to Curley, when the laws say what we ought to do, they are simply stating what we will and must do.[22]

---

[20] D.L. VII.85–87.

[21] An ambiguity here is whether "all things" includes both sentient and non-sentient beings.

[22] Curley (1991), p. 97.

I will begin to address this objection in the next sub-section. Beforehand, I want to take up another feature of Argument One. It has been suggested that the conclusion shows just how far Spinoza is from traditional natural law accounts.[23] With step seven, Spinoza allows an enormously wide range of permissible actions. Agents are forbidden *only* to do those things that they do not desire and cannot do. All else is fair game. This certainly makes Spinoza's ethics more radical than most of his contemporaries. Even Hobbes shied away from such views. For example, he seems to regard execution of prisoners of war as "dishonourable" and he argued that contracts in the state of nature be upheld, even if entered into under duress.[24] Spinoza never explicitly considered the treatment of prisoners of war or contracts in a state of nature. On the basis of his actual writings, however, we can speculate that he would disagree with Hobbes. If it is an object of desire and within the agent's ability, then the agent could treat prisoners of war as he liked (including executing them), just as he is free to disregard contracts, whether in or out of a state of nature.

That Spinoza's argument was so radical does not bother me. He was nothing if not a brave and original thinker. Just as he did in metaphysics (where he is often said to have been a better Cartesian than Descartes himself), so too he might have acted in ethics (where he may be a better natural law theorist—better in the sense of more consistent—than Hobbes). It may be that the prominence of natural law language does not deductively entail the attribution of a natural law ethic to Spinoza. At the same time, it is also the case that the distance which Spinoza's conclusion opens up between him and theorists of the natural law tradition regarding which actions are permissible does not, by itself, prove he is not cut from the same cloth as they. We need to investigate other parts of the argument to decide what it implies for Spinoza's views on natural law.

2. At this juncture, my opponents may be prepared to concede that the natural law dictates which actions we ought to perform. Simultaneously, however, they will want to argue that this is not the key question. If the natural law dictates actions that we ought to perform, but it does so non-normatively, then it does not matter that the law of nature is involved. Spinoza's ethical theory will prove to be fundamentally different from that of the Stoics (and other natural law theorists), because his "ought" is not at all moral. When Spinoza's natural law tells an agent what she ought to do, it is simply stating what she must and will do.

To bolster their case, my opponents might return to Argument One. The supreme law of Nature set out in premise one, they might argue, is a scientific or non-normative law. Moreover, since the other premises and the conclusion itself ultimately derive premise one, they must also be scientific or non-normative. So

[23]See, e.g., Curley (1991), p. 100.

[24]See *The Elements of Law* I.xix.2 and I.xv.13, respectively. For discussion, see Curley (1991), pp. 98–9.

when Spinoza issues the injunction against pursuing objectives one does not desire and cannot obtain (as he does in the conclusion), he is merely stating a fact and not issuing a norm. So, my opponents would conclude, Argument One either actively harms the case for taking Spinoza to have a moral "ought" or, at minimum, provides no support for it.

In reply to this objection, I want to draw attention to a different context where Spinoza speaks of the notion which he calls "the supreme law of nature" in *TTP* XVI. In the Scholium after IVP18 in the *Ethics*, Spinoza introduces some propositions that he calls "the dictates of reason."[25] In the last paragraph of this Scholium, Spinoza writes,

> These are the dictates of reason which I promised to present briefly here before I began to demonstrate them in a more cumbersome order. I have done this to win, if possible, the attention of those who believe that this principle—that everyone is bound to seek his own advantage—is the foundation, not of virtue and morality, but of immorality. After I have shown briefly that the contrary is true, I shall proceed to demonstrate in the same way I have followed up to this point.

Notice what Spinoza says about the "principle" that "everyone is bound to seek his own advantage," which I take to be substantially the same as the "supreme law of Nature" found in premise one of Argument one. In IVP18Sch, Spinoza says that this principle is the foundation of "virtue and morality." This surely complicates our understanding of the moral status of the principle/supreme law of Nature. Perhaps it is set out as a mere scientific law in the *TTP* but elsewhere Spinoza thinks of it differently. This raises the possibility that this law can be both descriptive and prescriptive.[26]

3. We could continue to analyze Argument One but it would be more fruitful to introduce more material for our consideration. So here is a second argument from *TTP* XVI:

Argument Two:

1. "[I]t is a universal law of human nature that nobody rejects what he judges to be good except through hope of a greater good or fear of greater loss; and that no one endures any evil except to avoid a greater evil or to gain a greater good."

Justification: "This law is so deeply inscribed in human nature that it should be counted among the eternal truths universally known."

---

[25]Unless otherwise mentioned, all translations of the *Ethics* are by Edwin Curley in *The Complete Works of Spinoza*, vol. I (Princeton: Princeton University Press, 1985). Also, I shall use the standard abbreviations when citing passages from the *Ethics*.

[26]Thanks to Michael LeBuffe for pointing out the relevance of this passage to my argument.

2. From (1), "it necessarily follows that nobody is going to promise in all good faith to give up his unrestricted right, and in general nobody is going to keep any promises whatsoever, except through fear of a greater evil or hope of a greater good."

Side-argument (at G III: 192):[27]

a. "[S]uppose that in all good faith I have promised somebody that I will not taste food or any other nourishment for twenty days."
b. Now suppose "that I later realized that I had made a foolish promise which could be kept only with considerable hurt to myself."
c. "[B]y natural right I am bound to choose [*eligere teneor*] the lesser of two evils."
d. So "I have the sovereign right to break faith and go back on my pledged word."
   - Clarification: "Now this, I say, is justified by natural right, whether it was true and infallible reasoning or whether it was fallible belief that made me realize I was wrong to have made the promise."

3. From (2), we may "conclude that the validity of an agreement rests on its utility, without which the agreement automatically becomes null and void."

Note in particular the side-argument. In step (c) of that argument, Spinoza says that I am "bound" to choose the lesser of two evils. "Bound" could mean either of two things: necessitated or morally obliged. If it is the latter, then Spinoza is making a normative claim. There is something I ought to do, on pain of breaking the natural law; I would be wrong not to go back on my "pledged word."

The Latin here somewhat supports taking "bound" to mean "obliged." The verb that Spinoza uses is *teneor*. When used in connection with laws, as Spinoza does here, Lewis & Short (the standard Latin reference dictionary) provide these definitions for it: "to bind, hold, obligate, be binding on, control, *etc.*" Given that Spinoza is combining *teneor* with *eligere*, the most plausible

[27]The Latin: "Vel ponatur me absque fraude alicui promisisse me spatio viginti dierum non gustaturum cibum neque ullum alimentum, et postea vidisse me stulte promisisse, nec sine damno maximo promisso stare posse; quandoquidem ex jure naturali de duobus malis minus eligere teneor, possum ergo summo jure fidem talis pacti rumpere, et dictum indictum ut sit facere. Atque hoc inquam jure naturali licere, sive vera et certa ratione videam, sive ex opinione videre videar me male promisisse; sive enim id vere sive falso videam, maximum timebo malum, quodque adeo ex naturae instituto omni modo vitare conabor."

sense of the word is bound or obliged. Granted, bound could have either of the two meanings mentioned in the previous paragraph but since the other most plausible sense of the word is obliged, Spinoza probably means "bound" in the sense of "obliged" when he writes *teneor*.

One final word, this time on step (3). It might be held that the whole argument must be non-normative because of the emphasis it places on utility in the conclusion. I do not, however, see the force of this objection. Utility is not a concept devoid of normative connotations. After all, if something is useful, then it is presumably good (cf. *Ethics* IVD1). Given that utility is not *prima facie* non-normative, then unless some evidence is provided that it *is* non-normative in the present context, to say otherwise is merely to make the question-begging assertion that Spinoza must have wanted it to be non-normative.

4. So far I have been wrestling with the question of whether natural laws *tout court* issue obligations that can be taken as moral. I have been arguing that there is reason to take *all* natural laws as normative. This is the hard case, for Spinoza actually distinguishes among different types of laws. If we follow his distinction, it becomes even clearer that at least *some* laws are normative and issue moral obligations.

The distinctions are stated most clearly in *TTP* IV. Spinoza starts his analysis with a generic definition: "The word law, taken in its absolute sense, means that according to which each individual thing . . . act [*sic*] in one and the same fixed and determinate manner, this manner depending either on Nature's necessity or on human will" (*TTP* IV, paragraph one). So a law, generically speaking, is that which compels all things to which it applies to act in certain ways. What enables us to distinguish among different types of laws is that not all laws have the same source of necessitation. The force of some laws, Spinoza tells us here, depends on "Nature's necessity" while that of other laws derives from "human will."

Spinoza continues his treatment of the concept of law in the paragraphs that follow, making important additions to what he said in the opening lines of *TTP* IV:

> [S]ince law is simply a rule of conduct which men lay down for themselves or for others to some end, it can be divided into human and divine law. By human law I mean a prescribed rule of conduct whose sole aim is to safeguard life and the commonwealth; by divine law I mean that which is concerned only with the supreme good, that is, the true knowledge and love of God. (*TTP* IV, paragraph six)

Here we are provided with a different description of what a law is. Whereas before it was that which makes things "act in one and the same fixed and determinate manner," now a law is "a rule of conduct which men lay down . . . to some end." Also, we are introduced to a new type of law, divine law. It is distinguished from human law on the basis of the different ends which each serve:

human law exists to "safeguard life and the commonwealth" while divine law "is concerned only with the supreme good."[28]

Since the concept of a human or civil law is not relevant to natural law ethics—natural law ethics is only concerned with laws that are natural, not those crafted by human beings—I will bracket Spinoza's remarks on it. And since I have already taken up the concept of a law of nature broadly described in the preceding sub-sections, I will not speak to it any further here. Instead, I want to focus solely on the idea of a divine law.

Let me first observe that the divine law is not a mere artifice or construction of human activity. It concerns a set of measures that humans must observe if they are to obtain their *summum bonum*. These measures are fixed not by humans but they exist naturally, having been "deduced . . . from human nature as such" (*TTP* IV, paragraph eleven). Next, consider the import of Spinoza's statement that a divine law is (paraphrasing him) "a rule of conduct laid down to some end." By stating that they are rules of conduct, he is asserting their intrinsically practical nature. Since the end is the supreme good, it follows that divine laws are the rules we must follow in order to be happy.

Now we are in a position to return to the main subject of this sub-section. This subject is whether Spinoza has natural laws which issue truly moral obligations. We now know that divine laws are natural in the sense that they exist independent of any human action. Moreover, they issue obligations since they reveal the true path to happiness. Finally, because the end that they serve is normative, the laws themselves must be normative and so must their obligations. So at least with respect to divine laws, the "ought" that arises in connection with them is truly prescriptive.[29]

5. To draw this section to a close, I shall change tactics. Rather than stick so closely to the texts, I want to step back from them temporarily. Concomitantly, I shall offer a different solution to the problem before me. As I have noted several times, Spinoza's writings contain a great deal of prescriptivist language.[30] Yet there are also many passages which deny the reality of moral entities (good,

---

[28]The concept of divine law is certainly not new with Spinoza. Aquinas and Scotus, among others, wrote about it. There are, however, two differences between early conceptions of divine law and Spinoza's. First, earlier thinkers took divine law to be *revealed* law. The very notion of *revealed* law implies that there are some other laws which are *not* revealed. Spinoza would ridicule this notion, because for him all law (and all facts about the universe) are in principle discoverable. The second difference centers on the purpose of divine law. For Aquinas and Scotus, divine law is significant because it points out the way that humans may attain an end higher than—transcending—their natural end. Not so for Spinoza, who denied that there is anything transcendent. Instead, divine law helps us to attain our highest good, which is manifestly natural. Thanks to Jonathan Jacobs for prompting me to clarify how divine law in Spinoza differs from divine law in earlier thinkers.

[29]I gladly acknowledge my indebtedness to Matt Kisner's discussion of divine laws in Kisner (2011), pp. 114-ff.

[30]A much fuller list of normative claims is given in Michael LeBuffe, *From Bondage to Freedom: Spinoza on Human Excellence* (Oxford: Oxford University Press, 2010), pp. 177–79.

evil, justice, and the like).[31] Perhaps the solution to the tension is to regard Spinoza's system as both prescriptive and descriptive. To use a modern term, perhaps his moral system is quasi-realist: it accepts the reality of moral discourse while rejecting an ontology endowed with moral properties.

The term "quasi-realist" was (so far as I am aware) coined by Simon Blackburn.[32] It may be helpful to understand Spinoza by contrasting Blackburn with him. Blackburn is both a moral non-cognitivist and a moral projectivist. By the former, I mean that Blackburn is someone who denies that moral judgments have truth-values and affirms that moral judgments are mental states but not beliefs. That is to say, moral judgments are fundamentally attitudinal, reflecting sensibility and desire rather than beliefs about what kinds of entities there are or what is factually the case. By the latter, Blackburn holds a causal account of moral experience, according to which an actual event in the world leads the person who perceives that event to have an evaluative reaction to it. Then, she projects her evaluation onto the event, with the result being a new creation in the world. To use a classic example,[33] Sue sees some kids burning a cat and thinks "That is wrong." The causal elements are her perceptions; these lead her to form beliefs and hence a disapproving emotion. Finally, she projects this emotion onto the world, leading to a new creation.[34]

Now, Blackburn wants to maintain his moral non-cognitivism and moral projectivism without sacrificing ordinary moral phenomena. Thus, unlike Mackie, who rejects ordinary moral discourse as uniformly mistaken,[35] Blackburn wants to retain it. Blackburn writes,

> How can a projective theory accompany the view that no mistake is made in talking as we do? We would only make a mistake in saying that things ought to be done, or have to be so, if *these judgements have a false content*. But if their content arises as the projectivist + quasi-realist story maintains, they do not. No error occurs in moralizing . . . even if philosophers have mistaken the kind of content these judgements have. Error exists only if there is a real *mismatch* between the truth about the nature of the claims, and their content, or what we make them do in our theories of things.[36]

Blackburn thinks it is acceptable for people to say that "Lying is wrong." Writers such as Mackie who dismiss this kind of talk as entirely erroneous fail

---

[31]See, e.g., *TdIE* §12, *Cogitata Metaphysics* I.6, *Ep.* 19, etc.

[32]See, e.g., Simon Blackburn, *Essays in Quasi-Realism* (Oxford: Oxford University Press, 1993).

[33]The example comes from Gilbert Harman, *The Nature of Morality* (New York: Oxford University Press, 1977), Chapter 1.

[34]The words "new creation" are borrowed from a passage in Hume (*An Enquiry Concerning the Principles of Morals*, Appendix 1, 21). He is often credited with being the first projectivist. If I'm right, Spinoza deserves part of the credit.

[35]See J. L. Mackie, *Ethics: Inventing Right and Wrong* (Harmondsworth: Penguin, 1977).

[36]Blackburn (1993), p. 56 (emphases in the original).

to grasp the extent of our commitments to the states of affairs or ideas expressed in such propositions. As Blackburn says, "these propositions [are] constructions that stand at a needed point in our cognitive lives—they are objects to be discussed, rejected, or improved upon when the habits, dispositions, or attitudes need discussion, rejection, or improvement."[37] At the same time as it allows the necessity of moral discourse, quasi-realism remains *quasi-* and not *full-blown* realism. It does so by refusing to say "that correctness in modal or moral judgement is simply representing the modal or moral facts as they are." Blackburn suggests various ways in which the quasi-realist avoids full-blown realism. For example, he tries to show that the sentence "Lying is wrong" can possess a truth predicate even though there is no "fact" of the matter supporting it; once this is shown, other features of realism quickly follow.[38]

Let us return to Spinoza. There is (imperfect) evidence of his (1) non-cognitivism, (2) projectivism, and (3) desire to hold onto realism without necessarily being a realist. This passage illustrates (2):

> Every man judges what is good according to his own way of thinking . . . Thus the ignorant man who has conferred a favour on someone will value it according to his own way of thinking, and if he sees that the recipient values it less, he will feel pain.
> (*Ethics* IVP70Dem.)

Here we find a causal account of moral experience: because of one's actions, one assigns a value to an action; alternatively, because one perceives another not appreciating what one does, one will feel pain. This is projectivism but with a twist. For rather than projecting the evaluation out onto the world, one projects it into oneself. I feel pain because someone else does not value the favor I have done him.

Even better evidence in support of the attribution of (2) to Spinoza lies in his account of the emotions given in *Ethics* III. The mind is affected by things outside itself. If the external object is beneficial to the mind, the mind experiences a positive emotion (joy or a species thereof) and it regards the object positively. If object is harmful, the mind experiences a negative emotion (pain or species thereof) and it regards the object negatively.[39]

Turning to (1), Spinoza's non-cognitivism, take this passage from IVPref: "As for the terms 'good' and 'bad', they likewise indicate nothing positive considered in themselves, and are nothing but modes of thinking, or notions which we form from comparing things with one another." Granted, we do not find here all the hallmarks of non-cognitivism, for while Spinoza does deny that moral judgments have truth-values, he seems to take moral judgments to be

---

[37]Blackburn (1993), p. 55.

[38]See, e.g., Blackburn (1993), pp. 19-ff.

[39]For more on Spinoza's projectivism, see LeBuffe (2010), pp. 154–59.

beliefs and not desires. Weighing against this, however, are other passages where moral judgments are presented as desires or other sorts of pro-attitudes. Most famously, there is IIIP39Sch: "we desire nothing because we judge it to be good, but on the contrary, we call it good because we desire it . . . So each one, from his own affect, judges, or [*sive*] evaluates, what is good and what is bad, what is better and what is worse, and finally, what is best and what is worst." Since the content of our judgments always bears the traces of their origins, then because our judgments about goodness come from our desires, so too our judgments about goodness are really just expressions of our desires. On balance, then, I think Spinoza does affirm both non-cognitivist theses: he denies that moral judgments have truth-values and he affirms that they are ultimately just mental expressions of our desires.[40]

Coming at last to (3), let me advance two sorts of considerations which show that Spinoza seeks to enjoy the trappings of realism without necessarily being a realist. Take this passage from *TTP* Three, paragraph six:

> All worthy objects of desire can be classified under one of these general headings:
>
> 1. To know things through their primary causes.
> 2. To subjugate the passions; i.e., to acquire the habit of virtue.
> 3. To live in security and good health.
>
> The means that directly serve for the attainment of the first and second objectives . . . lie within the bounds of human nature itself, so that their acquisition chiefly depends on human power alone; i.e. solely on the laws of human nature . . . But the means that serve for the attainment of security and well-being lie principally in external circumstances.

There is a set of worthy objects of desire; this is a fact. There is also a set of certain means for attaining those goods; this is also a fact. Perhaps these goods and the concomitant means to them would be different if we were different. These goods and the means to them are contingent on our present natures. This might entail that they are not real in the sense of being goods and means of moral value in all possible worlds. Nevertheless, in our world, they do have moral value, which allows us to sanction them as morally worthy.

Mention of possible worlds raises a whole new set of issues. There is much debate among scholars over the relationship between the actual and the possible in Spinoza's metaphysics, but that discussion is beyond the scope of this chapter.[41] Suffice to say that Spinoza posits a very close relationship between

---

[40] For more on Spinoza's non-cognitivism, see William K. Frankena, "Spinoza's New Morality: Notes on Book IV," in *Spinoza: Essays in Interpretation*, ed. Maurice Mandelbaum and E. Freeman (LaSalle, IL: Open Court, 1975), at, e.g., pp. 93–94.

[41] For a recent overview, see Samuel Newlands, "The Harmony of Spinoza and Leibniz," *Philosophy and Phenomenological Research*, vol. LXXXI, no. 1 (July 2010), pp. 64–104.

the two, so that he likely endorses at least the claim that the actual world is the only possible world *that could possibly exist*. If this is the case, then the point made in the preceding paragraph is strengthened greatly. If our actual natures are the only possible natures that could exist, then the set of morally worthy objects of desire and the morally permissible means for obtaining those objects is concretely fixed. Modality thus reinforces Spinoza's quasi-realism. There are no moral absolutes—there are no moral truths or facts that hold in all possible worlds. This is in keeping with moral anti-realism. Yet there is a set of moral truths or facts that hold in the only world that could possibly exist. This is consistent with moral realism.

Admittedly, the grounds for Spinoza's realism are different from Blackburn, who is driven away from straightforward moral realism by what Mackie called the "queerness" of moral values.[42] As Blackburn writes, realist theorizing "worries too little about the curious place that moral and modal commitments have, about what notion of truth can be appropriate to them, about why it matters, and about how the commitments blend with others that we have."[43] Because he is so impressed by the queerness of moral commitments, Blackburn cannot see how they can be straightforwardly real in the way that scientific commitments are. Spinoza is not moved to a quasi-realist position because he regards the moral domain as anomalous from other domains. To the contrary, Spinoza thinks that all of nature is always and everywhere the same (IIIPref). Rather, Spinoza embraces a quasi-realist stance with regard to moral values because of his non-cognitivism, prescriptivism, and modal theory.

Moving on, let me come to the second consideration in support of the claim that Spinoza seeks to enjoy the trappings of realism without being committed to a realist ontology. I see every indication of Spinoza's desire to preserve ordinary phenomena. Consider this remarkable passage:

> To perceive these two, the *true* and the *false* rightly, we shall begin with the meaning of the words, from which it will be plain that these are only extrinsic denominations of things and are not attributed to things except metaphorically. But since ordinary people first invent words, which afterwards are used by the Philosophers, it seems desirable for one seeking the original meaning of a term to ask what it first denoted among ordinary people—particularly where we lack other causes that could be used to investigate that [meaning], causes drawn from the nature of language.[44]

Here Spinoza enjoins us to start with common speech when investigating the nature of truth and falsity. Because the words used by philosophers were first

---

[42]See, e.g., Mackie (1977), p. 38.

[43]Blackburn (1993), p. 58.

[44]*Cogitata Metaphysica*, I.vi.3 (trans. Curley).

invented by ordinary people, we must consider their original meaning before we can hope to construct theories about those words.

To be sure, Spinoza is talking about truth, not morality. Moreover, he closes the excerpt by saying it is especially important to deal with the lexical origins of words "where we lack other causes that could be used to investigate" their meaning. Still, I think this tendency to preserve ordinary discourse remains in the works of the mature Spinoza, including those parts of the works dealing with ethical issues. One passage from IVPref will have to prove my point:[45]

> As far as good and evil are concerned, they also indicate nothing positive in things, considered in themselves, nor are they anything other than modes of thinking, or [*sive*] notions we form because we compare things to one another . . .
>
> But though this is so, still we must retain these words. For because we desire to form an idea of man, as a model of human nature which we may look to, it will be useful to us to retain these words with the meaning I have intended.

Where Blackburn tried to help himself to the trappings of realism by seeking to show how sentences involving moral propositions could possess truth predicates even though there should be no "fact" of the matter supporting them, Spinoza's basis for realism is different. He argues instead that moral discourse has a use-function. Moral terms may not indicate anything "positive in themselves." Nevertheless, they ought to be retained because they help us to understand what it is to be a good human being.

While I could further expand my case for Spinoza's quasi-realism, I shall forebear from doing so and instead return to the central topic of this paper, which is connecting Spinoza to natural law ethics. Suppose that Spinoza's ethics are quasi-realist in the foregoing sense. Then he thinks that moral judgments (1) lack truth-values and (2) are desires or other pro-attitudes. He also holds (3) a causal account of moral experience and (with this) (4) the values we assign to objects outside of ourselves are determined by our causal interaction with them. Moreover, (5) the modality of his metaphysics provides a reason for both denying the absoluteness of moral values and affirming the necessity of the moral values that govern us in the world we inhabit. Finally, (6) he wants to retain ordinary moral practice without necessarily accepting a moral ontology.

Given points (5)–(6), I see him continuing to use "ought" in a moral manner. That is, the "ought" found in those passages of Spinoza's writings touching on practical matters is a moral "ought." In this respect, Spinoza's ethics are consonant with the Stoics. So, for example, when Spinoza says that we ought to perfect our intellect,[46] he is issuing a truly moral imperative. It is analogous in two

---

[45]See also *Ethics* DefAffXXExp (pp. 535–36 of Curley's translation).

[46]For another passage, see *TTP* IV, paragraph seven.

respects to the Stoic imperative that we ought to become one with our natures as rational beings: firstly, both Spinoza and the Stoics issue moral imperatives to conform to our natures; secondly, both parties conceive of our natures as ultimately rational.

Points (5)–(6) are the "realist" part of "quasi-realism." So it is unsurprising that Spinoza's theory would be closest to the Stoics at this location. The "quasi" part arises in points (1)–(4). Taken together, they have the effect of forcing a deflationary concept of "ought" on Spinoza. Still, (5–(6) are enough of an anchor that the prescriptivism of the ought cannot be completely uprooted.

Providence

In the previous section, I dealt with the structure and normativity of Spinoza's moral system, especially those parts that explicitly invoke natural laws. I showed that the use of natural laws in Spinoza is highly similar to that in Stoicism. This is significant, for if there should be natural laws in Spinozism but they were not central to his ethics, then a major gulf would separate him from the Stoics (and other natural law theorists), who do make the laws central to their ethics. So both systems think of morality as intrinsically involving laws of nature.

In addition, I argued that Spinoza and the Stoics take the injunctions issued by the laws to be moral injunctions. When the laws command that an action ought to be performed, both parties take the ought to be prescriptive and not descriptive. Admittedly, they interpret the ought differently, with the Stoics giving it a more robust reading. The key point, however, is that they agree in thinking that statements of obligation are more than just statements of what is necessary.

In this section, I move on to a new topic: providence. While I found nontrivial overlap between Spinoza and the Stoics in the previous section, here I shall find significantly fewer affinities between the two systems. Let me begin with the Stoics.

1. Stoics were famous in antiquity for their providentialism:

> [It] is unnecessary to show that this mighty structure of the world does not endure without some one to guard it, and the assembling and the separate flight of the stars above are not due to the workings of chance; that while bodies which owe their motion to accident often fall into disorder and quickly collide, this swift revolution of the heavens, being ruled by eternal law, goes on unhindered, producing so many things on land and sea, so many brilliant lights in the sky all shining in fixed array; that this regularity does not belong to matter moving at random.[47]

[47]Seneca, *On providence*, I.1–2 (trans. John W. Basore in *Seneca: Moral Essays*, vol. 1 (London: Heinemann, 1928)).

According to Stoicism, the universe and all its inhabitants are governed by *Nous* (or *Zeus*). *Nous* is a causal principle that is immanent or in-dwelling in the cosmos itself. Through its constant presence and actions, *nous* maintains the order of the universe. *Nous* maintains this order partially by ensuring that all events and all things in the universe have an aim or goal. Because the aim or goal given to each thing comes from *nous*, it is certain that those aims or goals are good. By its actions in coordinating all members of the universe, *nous* ensures that the universe as a whole is good. Indeed, because *nous* is the source or, perhaps better, the nature of value itself, and given that *nous* always acts in keeping with its own nature, it follows of necessity that those things it lends its value to are more than good: they are the best. In Stoicism, then, we find the earliest known version of the idea of the best of all possible worlds. It is the best possible world because of God's providence.[48]

It is important to see how Stoic providentialism informs their natural law theory. It is not that Stoic providentialism is exhausted by natural law. While it is true that *nous* gave us the natural law out of his concern to ensure the perfect order and goodness of the world, *nous* through its providentialism does much more besides this: it causally acts to keep the world going; it sets the ends which the world will attain; and so on. The law that *nous* gives us to follow is but a minor sub-set of the totality of the rational ordering which steers the universe.

2. Commentators rarely treat Spinoza's views on providence.[49] Whatever the reason for this, it cannot be because Spinoza had no views. To the contrary, he discusses providence many times, from the early *Short Treatise* to his mature masterpieces, the *Ethics*, and the *TTP*. It is not necessary for me to introduce all of the texts. Instead, I will focus on those which are most relevant.

The texts can be divided into two groups: those which set out positive doctrine versus those which are critical of providence. Taking the positive doctrine first, there are two themes which Spinoza stresses. One of these is set out in the *Short Treatise*: providence is "nothing but that striving we find in both the whole of Nature and in particular things, tending to maintain and preserve their being."[50] Spinoza had a penchant for co-opting tradition. Here we find him co-opting traditional terminology. As we have seen with the Stoics, providence traditionally meant the concern that God exhibited for his creation. In Spinoza's system, the only way that God could be concerned[51] for the world is through the laws of nature by which he governs it. The principal law of nature—what Argument One above called "the Supreme Law"—is *conatus*:

---

[48] I shall not quote multiple sources for these well-known claims. A wealth of material is collected in Susanne Bobzien, *Determinism and Freedom in Stoic Philosophy* (Oxford: Clarendon Press, 1998), pp. 45–47.

[49] A recent exception is Genevieve Lloyd. See her *Providence Lost* (Cambridge, MA: Harvard University Press, 2008), esp. Chapter 6. Lloyd also has an extensive discussion of the Stoics; see esp. Chapter 3.

[50] *Short Treatise*, I.v.

[51] To be clear, the concern that God has here is not a feeling. It is just a necessary interest in the world.

namely, ensuring that the whole as a whole and all parts thereof strive to remain in existence.

As Spinoza puts forth his conception of providence, he also attempts to co-opt the traditional distinction between universal and special providence. This distinction was advanced by many previous thinkers, including some close to Spinoza's world, such as Goclenius[52] and Calvin.[53] Ordinarily, universal providence is taken to refer to God's governance of the entire universe, while special providence is the care God has for the well-being of particular humans. As Spinoza understands the two notions, universal providence is "that through which each thing is produced and maintained insofar as it is a part of the whole of Nature" while special or particular providence is "that striving which each particular thing has for the preservation of its being insofar as it is considered not as a part of Nature, but as a whole." I shall return to Spinoza's use of this distinction momentarily but first I want to introduce the other piece of positive doctrine.

This appears in, e.g., Ep. 19, where Spinoza asserts that God's providence "is identical with his will."[54] Around this stage of his life, Spinoza was formulating his mature views on the will. He denies both freedom of the will (in the sense of being able to choose between two or more equally available options) and a faculty of will (there are just individual acts of will). One's will is ultimately just one's desire. Given the foregoing, we can gloss Ep. 19 as saying that providence is nothing more than God's desire. Since a being's desire is just his *conatus*, God's providence proves to be his striving to remain in existence.

Now let me briefly mention Spinoza's criticisms of providence. His main critique is the ignorance and laziness inevitably accompanying the notion. Thus he writes in *Ethics* IApp,

> And they[55] say that God has created all things in an orderly way, without realizing that they are thus attributing human imagination to God—unless perchance they mean that God, out of consideration for the human imagination [*humanae imaginationi providentem*], arranged all things in the way that men could most easily imagine. And perhaps they will find no obstacle in the fact that there are any number of things that far surpass our imagination, and a considerable number that confuse the imagination because of its weakness. (trans. Shirley.)

---

[52]For Goclenius, see his *Conciliator philosophicus* (first published 1609; reprint Hildeshiem: Georg Olms: 1980), pp. 323ff.

[53]For an overview of both the primary and secondary literature on Calvin's views on the distinction between universal and special providence, see Charles Partee, *Calvin and Classical Philosophy* (Leiden: Brill, 1977), esp. Chapter 9.

[54]Shirley translation, p. 808.

[55]The "they" here refers to those who suppose that God acts for an end, specifically, and that he exhibits providential concern for his creation, more generally.

Providence is a substitute for hard thinking. People make recourse to providence because they want to maintain certain beliefs. As one commentator has written, providence "turns out to be nothing but a refuge, a sanctuary for human ignorance. The truth is that all things happen of necessity . . . Not only does [Spinoza's] God not act out of concern for human well-being, this is a God who does not act for 'ends' at all."[56] It is plain that Spinoza has no patience for providence by this stage of his life, which may explain why the Appendix to Part I is the only place in the *Ethics* where he uses the word.

Now return to Spinoza's version of the distinction between universal and special providence. This distinction is advanced at a time when Spinoza takes providence seriously. Even so, the critique of providence from *Ethics* IApp is presaged here. Special providence is usually taken to be those actions that God undertakes on behalf of individual members of the universe. Spinoza thinks this means that special providence must take individuals to be wholes whose conditions for existence and action can be severed from their surroundings. As such, the notion is absurd because it overlooks the embeddedness of individuals in a larger system. No individual member of the universe is a whole in the sense supposed by special providence.

The upshot is that even when Spinoza takes providence seriously, he departs in significant ways from traditional theories of providence. For him, there is only one kind of providence, universal providence. Special providence is based on an impossibly naïve mereology.

3. It is time to bring together Spinoza and the Stoics. As intimated in subsection 1 of this section, Stoic providentialism is central to their natural law doctrine. Because of God's concern for the world and its inhabitants, he brought forth the natural law so they could flourish. There is a way in which Spinoza's writings on providence—at least from early in his career—echo this. In the *Short Treatise*, providence is described in terms of *conatus*. As we learned in the previous section, *conatus* is the supreme law of nature. So in his early writings, what Spinoza says about providence bears a formal resemblance to the Stoics.

But that is in his early writings. By the time of the *Ethics* and the *TTP*, he utterly abandons the connection between providence and the law of nature. Now providence has become a refuge for the narrow-minded and/or stupid. It is perhaps for this reason that Spinoza ceases to link providence to natural laws.[57]

One final point. In Stoicism, the natural law is an expression of God's will. It is his command for how we are to act. Because Spinoza occasionally associates

---

[56]Lloyd (2008), pp. 204–5.

[57]I ought to acknowledge that Spinoza does raise providence more often in the *TTP*, some twenty times by my counting. The theological orientation explains why he should do so. Outside of theology, Spinoza has no patience for providence by the end of his life. Thus he does not use the word or a cognate term once in the *TP*.

the natural law with the divine will, there is overlap between the two systems on this important issue. The difference is that Stoics (and other natural law theorists) take natural laws to be literal decrees of the divine being. Such is not the case for Spinoza. Though he may speak of God's will in some places, God does not really have a will—he has a desire to remain in existence.

Conclusions

Throughout his life, Spinoza maintained a deep interest in natural laws. I have not introduced situational factors that are doubtless relevant to explaining his interest in them. These factors include the general flourishing of natural law ethics in the sixteenth and seventeenth centuries, as well as Spinoza's very substantial knowledge of key natural law theorists, such as Suárez, Grotius, and Hobbes. Because my focus has been on the more analytical question of how his ethics compares to natural law ethics, I have not attempted to contextualize Spinoza. Doubtless, we could learn more about his relation to the natural law by studying what he knew and made of the works of such men as Grotius.[58]

Still, while I have not addressed Spinoza's motivation for engaging natural law ethics, I hope to have made some progress toward understanding how certain aspects of his moral system compare to the equivalent aspects of the natural law, especially as articulated by the Stoics. At the same time, I hope to have provided convincing arguments concerning the range of possible interpretations that can be made of both Spinozism and the natural law itself.[59]

[58]Garrett (2003–4) goes further than anyone I know in connecting Spinoza to the historical natural law tradition of his day.

[59]An early version of this chapter was presented at a Spinoza conference sponsored by the Texas A&M University Department of Philosophy in September 2011. I am grateful to all present for their feedback. I am also grateful to Jonathan Jacobs for his invitation to write the essay and for his helpful comments on the penultimate draft.

{ 9 }

Agent Centeredness and Natural Law

PERFECTIONISM, IMMANENCE, AND TRANSCENDENCE

Douglas B. Rasmussen and Douglas J. Den Uyl

For, corresponding to each of our trained faculties, there is a special form of the noble and the pleasant, and perhaps there is nothing so distinctive of the good or ideal man as the power he has of discerning these special forms in each case, being himself, as it were, their standard and measure.

—Aristotle, *Nicomachean Ethics, Bk. III. Ch. 4. 1113a30–33*

That which doth assign unto each thing the kind, that which doth moderate the force and power, that which doth appoint the form and measure of working, the same we term a Law.

—Richard Hooker, *The Laws of Ecclesiastical Polity, Bk. 1, Ch. 2.1*

It may seem that the term "natural law" is univocal, but there are in fact different approaches to the subject of natural law that render the term referentially diverse. "Natural law" to the contemporary ear would, no doubt, evoke the idea of a scientific description of a natural process. Those exposed to philosophy might associate the term, however, with some medieval doctrine having to do with God's commands as understood by the power of reason alone. This last understanding of "natural law" itself differs from a more modern conception that sees "natural law" as referring to regularized patterns of social interaction conducive to grounding norms of social cooperation.[1] In addition, how one works with the various terms may affect one's understanding of "natural law." For example, with respect to the term "nature," a universe in which final causality is posited will give one a different conception of nature from one in which

[1]See, for example, the "Natural Law and Enlightenment Classics Series" series, Knud Haakonssen general editor, Liberty Fund Books, http://www.libertyfund.org/encollection.html, where none of the authors are medieval and most social theorists.

only efficient causes are allowed. The classical and modern natural law traditions may divide on just this point. Moreover, the appeal to nature has also grounded the natural *rights* tradition, yet there has been a long dispute about whether doctrines of modern natural rights are in any way connected to, or compatible with, the preceding classical natural law tradition.[2] The pre-modern natural law tradition is commonly said to posit "objective" right, while the natural rights approach is said to posit "subjective" right.[3] In the former case one is referring to general truths of human nature that give rise to universal rules of obligation. In the latter case, one tends to be speaking of individuals obligating themselves only by acts of will and choice. Though that dichotomy gives us a way of separating the two traditions, some contemporary thinkers, such as John Finnis, have sought to blend them and to argue for their inherent compatibility.[4]

Yet besides some sort of general naturalism, what seems to go unquestioned through all these various interpretations and divisions connected to the topic of natural law are two points: first, the norms connected to natural law are tied to human nature, and those that characterize the *classical* natural law tradition are derived from human nature, specifically the agent's own[5] inherent tendencies towards fulfilling natural potentialities whose completion marks the perfection of the agent and the measure of right conduct. We might say that because of this focus on the individual agent's nature, classical or traditional (we use these terms interchangeably here) natural law purports to be fundamentally agent centered. Secondly, the modern era, by contrast to the classical, is characterized by the abandonment of this agent centered focus in favor of one whose norms are grounded elsewhere. If there is modern natural law theory, the focus has been upon human social interaction rather than agent perfection. Beginning perhaps with Hobbes's list of natural laws in Chapters 14 and 15 of *Leviathan,* the agent's own perfectibility is ignored or denied as a factor in the determination of those laws. Rather, principles grounded in a particular perspective on the

---

[2]For a summary of these issues see Ralph McInerny, "Natural Law and Human Rights," *American Journal of Jurisprudence*, Vol. 36, 1991. McInerny identifies the focus of our project here when he says, "A difficulty that faces both the natural law and natural rights traditions is the accessibility of human nature which is the vehicle of claims of either obligation or right," p. 14 n. 21.

[3]See in this connection A.P. d'Entreves, *Natural Law* (London: Hutchinson University Library, 1970). D'Entreves refers to the change to natural rights as one which puts the "accent" on the individual and which rationalizes and secularizes natural law. This identifies an important element of our thesis, as we shall see below.

[4]John Finnis, *Natural Law and Natural Rights* (Oxford: Clarendon Press, 1980). We also discuss this issue in Douglas B. Rasmussen and Douglas J. Den Uyl, *Norms of Liberty: A Perfectionist Basis for Non-Perfectionist Politics* (University Park, Pennsylvania: Pennsylvania State University Press, 2005), pp. 62–75.

[5]Although there is a definite individualistic character to the perfection process, this does not mean or entail an atomism or disconnection from others or one's environment. Traditionally, other orientedness is a necessary feature of the perfection of an individual human agent.

nature of social interaction define the norms for agents. The perspectives and assumptions of different modern thinkers may change, but the lack of agent centeredness remains.[6] The idea of grounding moral norms generally, and thus natural law in particular, in terms of what is perfecting of the agent's own nature alone therefore seems essentially classical. Consequently, our use of the term "agent centered" here refers to this perfectionist understanding of the basis for normative principles. Agent centeredness in this sense, as our first point suggests, seems to be the province of the classical tradition of natural law, while absent from any significant theorist of the modern era, as suggested by our second point. We intend to challenge both these assumptions.

In the former, and perhaps more controversial of the two claims, we concentrate our attention upon Aquinas. It seems to us at least arguable that Aquinas represents the central statement of the classical natural law tradition. As such, we shall first show how agent centeredness is indeed found in Aquinas's philosophical anthropology. However, we shall also show that agent centeredness has little if anything to do with the source of natural law for Aquinas. This is because the norms of natural law derive not from the nature of the individual agent, but from God, though they may be applied *to* the agent. Thus, despite appearances, the agent centeredness found in Aquinas is highly problematic. Fundamentally, Aquinas's doctrine is not agent centered, but rather God centered. Of course, this tension between agent centeredness and God centeredness is later appreciated and "corrected" by Spinoza. Rather than employing transcendence which moves natural law away from the agent, Spinoza gives us agent centeredness through immanence. As it turns out, then, there is after all an important modern thinker whose ethics is agent centered. This is surprising in itself, since Spinoza's attacks on teleology, hylomorphism, and final causality would seem to put him outside of a perfectionist agent centered ethics. We shall discover, however, that Spinoza does have his own strong form of agent centeredness, though we shall also mention some aspects of his doctrine which, like Aquinas's, pull away from it. Agent centeredness in Spinoza, however, does not seem to issue in what one would normally think of as natural law. Consequently, the upshot of our overall argument is, on the one hand to sever any necessary connection between agent centeredness and the Thomistic version of classical natural law, while on the other to begin to explore the scope of the normative implications—and limitations—of agent centeredness itself, if indeed there is more than one form of it. We hope, in other words, to call into question the easy association of agent centered ethical frameworks with natural law, both because agent centeredness may neither be its source nor be restricted to a particular philosophical tradition. In the long

[6]Of course, it does not follow from this that there cannot be any overlap in the specific norms recommended by each approach. Moreover, elements of each approach can be found in the other. For example, classical natural law theory develops principles based upon the nature of social interaction, and modern natural rights doctrines often appeal to what is natural to acting agents.

run our question is whether agent centeredness can be a sufficient framework for a moral and political theory or whether it is inherently fraught with one or more of the tensions we identify below?[7] If nothing else, the sorts of issues we examine with our thinkers in what follows should have some bearing on what needs to be considered in today's debates over the nature and foundations of virtue ethics and perhaps ethics generally considered.

FOUNDATIONS OF AQUINAS'S NATURAL LAW ETHICS

There are seven interrelated points that need to be made to understand the essential underpinnings of Aquinas's conception of natural law. First, Aquinas's view of natural law could be said to involve a commitment to what is today called "natural goodness," but it is a *non-reductive*, naturalistic account of goodness. In other words, goodness is based on or determined by the nature[8] of a thing, but it is not simply the properties of a thing. For example, the goodness of a strawberry is not merely one of a cluster of properties belonging to it. Rather, it is a result of those properties in virtue of which the strawberry is said to be mature or complete—that is, actual as compared with just potential. Thus, to say that a strawberry is good is not to say that it just *is* red, juicy, and sweet. Rather, it is good *because* it is red, juicy, and sweet—that is, because these properties reveal its maturity, completion, or actuality. Henry B. Veatch expressed Aquinas's view as follows:

> To use some stock examples from the literature, a strawberry is said to be a good one, because it is sweet, red, juicy, etc., or a man is a good man, because he has good judgment, has the courage of his convictions, is fair-minded, etc. And why should being sweet, red, and juicy constitute grounds for calling a strawberry good, or having good judgment, the courage of convictions, etc. be grounds for calling a man good? The answer is that it is precisely the fully developed, perfect strawberry that has such properties; or, analogously, it is only the man of reason and judgment, of courage and justice, who approximates to what a human being might be or could be, and who in this sense has really actualized the full potentialities of being human. In other words, the logic of the consequential or supervenient character of goodness or value becomes clear. Thus a thing is said to be good because it has properties *a, b*, and *c*. And why should *a*, *b*, and *c* make such a thing good? It is simply because *a*, *b*,

[7]We have sought elsewhere to make agent centeredness the basis of a political theory and have used it also as a vehicle for criticizing both classical and new natural law theories. See *Norms of Liberty*, Ch. 8 especially.

[8]"Nature" is understood in an Aristotelian sense. The nature of a thing is the answer to the question "What is it?" and it is also the principle (or determinate set of potentialities) in terms of which the change and development of a thing are explained.

> and *c* are characteristics of that thing in its full actuality or perfection, and to be good means to be actual as over against being merely potential. And so it is that our definition of goodness not only takes cognizance of the fact that goodness is anything but a simple property of the ordinary kind, but also makes it intelligible just why and in what sense goodness is a supervenient property.[9]

Goodness thus strongly supervenes on natural properties for Aquinas. In other words, something's goodness can be dependent on its being a, b, and c but without that goodness being identical with being a, b, and c. Goodness is derived from these properties, but is not reducible without remainder to them.

Second, goodness is an ontological and relational property, and as such is found throughout all of reality in the relation of the actual to the potential. It is hence not subsumable under any single category or genus. Goodness is thus a transcendental—it applies across all the categories and various ways of being. It is to be understood in an analogical manner.

Third, since goodness is not only a transcendental property but also a supervenient one for Aquinas, it is not possible to define goodness, if we understand a definition in terms of *per genus et differentiam*.[10] Thus, there is a sense in which Aquinas's approach to goodness could agree with G. E. Moore regarding goodness being indefinable. However, it is also the case that Aquinas would insist that goodness have an ontological ground in the sense that it is understood to be based on, and derived from, a thing's nature—that is, the relationship of actuality to potentiality.

But there is even more to Aquinas's view, and this brings us to our fourth point: a thing's goodness consists not only in its actuality but also in this actuality being what is desirable and thus the object of desire for that thing.

> The essence of goodness consists in this that it is in some way desirable. Hence the Philosopher says . . .: "*Goodness is what all desire.*" Now it is clear that a thing is desirable only in so far as it is perfect; for all desire their own perfection. But everything is perfect so far as it is actual. Therefore it

---

[9] *For An Ontology of Morals: A Critique of Contemporary Ethical Theory* (Evanston, IL: Northwestern University Press, 1971), pp. 109–110. Of course, strawberries, like many other things in nature, can be changed and developed by humans for their own purposes, and thus in turn can be judged good or bad in those terms. But there remains nonetheless a difference between what is a good strawberry for humans and what is good for a strawberry as such, or to be precise, a strawberry plant. Further, if the analogy between a strawberry and a human being is to work, then it must be emphasized that human rationality is the mode in which human potentialities are actualized. There is nothing passive about human self-actualization. See also Anthony J. Lisska, *Aquinas's Theory of Natural Law: An Analytic Reconstruction* (Oxford: Clarendon Press, 1996), who follows Veatch in taking this approach to Aquinas.

[10] See Veatch, *For An Ontology of Morals*, 106 n. 8. This is the sense of indefinability that Panayot Butchvarov develops in *Skepticism in Ethics* (Bloomington and Indianapolis: Indiana University Press, 1989), pp. 61 and 115–22. See also Butchvarov, "That Simple, Indefinable, Nonnatural Property Good," *The Review of Metaphysics* 36 (1982): 51–75.

> is clear that a thing is perfect so far as it exists; for it is existence that makes all things actual. . . . Hence it is clear that goodness and being are the same really. But goodness presents the aspect of desirableness, which being does not present. (*Summa Theologiae* [hereafter *ST*], I, 5.1.)[11]

For Aquinas, a thing's potentiality is a kind of appetite or desire for its relevant perfection or actuality. Thus, though this appetitive power—*appetitus*—might be found primarily in the unique potentialities and capacities of living things,[12] it was regarded as being coextensive with potentiality in general, even if only understood in an analogical manner.[13] For Aquinas, there is an appetite for completion, perfection, actuality, and thus goodness, everywhere and in everything. Whether it is necessary to view the desire for actuality on such a cosmic scale is a matter of how one understands final causality.[14] We need not consider this question here, because what is crucial to see is that for Aquinas the goodness of a thing is not only its actuality as it exists in relation to its

---

[11]Unless otherwise indicated, translations used are from *The "Summa Theologica" of St. Thomas Aquinas*, literally translated by Fathers of the English Dominican Province, second and revised edition, 1920: http://www.op.org/summa/.

[12]As Aquinas states: "The soul, however, has both knowing and appetitive powers. *Good* expresses the correspondence of being to the appetitive power, for, and so we note in the *Ethics*, the good is 'that which all desire.' *True* expresses the correspondence of being to the knowing power, for all knowing is produced by an assimilation of knower to the thing known. . . ." *The Disputed Questions On Truth* (hereafter *DQT*), Vol. I, trans. Robert W. Mulligan, S.J. (Chicago: Henry Regnery, 1952), 1.1, Reply, p. 6. For a contemporary thinker who stresses the fundamental importance of life to these considerations, see Philippa Foot, *Natural Goodness* (Oxford: Clarendon Press, 2001).

[13]Goodness is after all a transcendental property for Aquinas. Here we are also following Veatch's account of Aquinas. See *For Ontology of Morals: A Critique of Contemporary Ethical Theory*, p. 113 n18. Veatch references *DQT*, Vol. III, trans. Robert W. Schmidt, S.J., (Chicago: Henry Regnery, 1954), 21.1, p. 7 and Reply in 21.2, pp. 10–11, as supporting this reading.

[14]This question involves not only the issues of what it means to say that teleology is ultimately naturally or supernaturally based but also, if it is ultimately naturally based, what is its scope. For example, does it pertain to all natural beings or only to living things? Following Philippa Foot and others, it has been suggested that natural teleology is fundamentally grounded in the nature of living things and so teleology is no longer cosmic but of more limited scope. We think this view has great plausibility, but there is another possibility, suggested by David S. Oderberg, worthy of mention. It is to understand natural teleology or natural function broadly—that is, as being applicable to anything that has a natural specific activity (usually in the context of larger events or processes)—but then to note that the kind of teleology or function that has normative significance is one that is due to causes and effects within one and the same being (immanent causation), but not from causes and effects belonging to different beings (transient causation). Hence, it is only to living things that teleology has value or normative significance. "Stones and electrons might have functions but they cannot flourish, or behave better or worse, rightly or wrongly, or be harmed, satisfied, or possess any of the fundamental normative states belonging to subjects of immanent causation, that is living things. There is no mere continuum here, but a point at which nature is carved at the joints. Yet the normative functions of living things are as real as the nonnormative functions of everything else in the cosmos. Natural goodness is as real as natural viscosity, natural harm as natural radioactivity." David S. Oderberg, "The Metaphysical Foundations of Natural Law" in Holger Zaborowski, ed., *Natural Moral Law in Contemporary Society* (Washington, DC: The Catholic University of America Press, 2010), 64–65. See also Oderberg, "Teleology: Inorganic or Organic," in A. M. González, ed., *Contemporary Perspectives on Natural Law* (Aldershot, UK: Ashgate, 2008), 259–79.

potential but also as it exists as the object and measure of a thing's strivings and endeavors.

The fifth point to grasp, then, about the basis of Aquinas's view of natural law is that the notion of desire ultimately employed in his account is not merely psychological but metaphysical. It is an expression of final causality. The terminus of a thing's potentiality is to be understood, then, not only in terms of attaining something actual but also in terms of attaining something desirable, and as such is something at which a thing naturally aims.[15] A thing's nature is not only what it is but also its end or *telos*, and it is in that regard the standard for determining whether it functions well or poorly.[16]

In terms of Plato's *Euthyphro*, being an object of desire is not merely the result of being desired. The goodness of a thing is indeed desired and thus can never be considered apart from its relationship to the appetitive powers of a thing, but its goodness is not the mere result of being desired. This leads us to the sixth point regarding Aquinas's view of natural law.

Aquinas states that "law is a rule and measure of acts. . . ." (*ST,* I–II, 90.1). In its most fundamental sense, "law" means for Aquinas a measure,[17] a standard, or a rule, and these terms are to be understood as referring to something one sets down to measure or evaluate something else—specifically, a thing or its actions. Hence, to speak of natural law is to hold that it is the nature of a thing that provides the measure, standard, or rule for judging it or its actions. Further, since the nature of a thing is for Aquinas also its *telos* or final cause, a thing's nature is the first principle of all its actions, and thus "rule" can also be understood as directing action towards that end. Moreover, this entire process develops directly out of the ontological structure of potentiality and actuality, because a thing's nature can be understood as being a potentiality ordered to its actuality. As Veatch succinctly put the matter, "natural law is nothing but this order of potency to act."[18] Thus, for a thing to actualize its nature is for it to attain its end or fulfill its function. It is for it to act in accordance with its own inner law. It is the nature of a thing that is the law in this fundamental and seemingly agent centered sense.

This sense of "law" implies a distinction between the origin of law and the law itself—that is, as a measure, standard, or rule. There is a sense in which "law" can be retained even if the general philosophical consensus is that there is insufficient

---

[15]*DQT*, I, 1.1, p. 6.

[16]For Aquinas, of course, there is more than just the natural order of things and thus the ultimate and final object of desire—that which provides fulfillment, perfection, and actuality to a human being—is God. See *Summa Contra Gentiles* (hereafter *SCG*), Bk III, Chs. 37–40, 47–48, 51–63: http://dhspriory.org/thomas/ContraGentiles.htm

[17]R. J. Henle, S.J. observes that "measure is . . . a quantitative measure. . . . However, it is extended to qualitative things as well. Aristotle, for example, extended it to any kind of standard. St. Thomas refers to Aristotle's discussion of measure as the conception of measure which he himself is using." *The Treatise on Law*, edited, translated, and commentary by R. J. Henle, S.J. (Notre Dame: Notre Dame University Press, 1993), pp. 59–60, paragraph 288.

[18]Henry B. Veatch, *For An Ontology of Morals*, p. 123.

evidence to justify believing that God exists and is a lawgiver.[19] The basic sense of "law" for Aquinas is not command.

The seventh point, then, to get clear regarding Aquinas's view of natural law, is that it is not some version of divine command theory, if by such a theory we mean that the goodness or the obligatory character of a course of conduct is determined solely by its being commanded or willed by God. It is important to recall in this regard that Aquinas had an intellectualist conception of God, and hence God's commands are not arbitrary. According to Anthony Kenny, "Aquinas follows Augustine in locating in the divine mind the paradigms on which creatures are modelled: they are the divine ideas. Because God is a simple undivided being, these ideas are not really distinct from his essence, and they do not depend in any way upon his will. Creation according to the ideas is free, but not the existence of the ideas in the first place."[20] Also, Aquinas held that the Decalogue belonged to the natural law and that God could not dispense from it or grant permission to act against it. "For Aquinas the entire Decalogue is part of the natural law, flowing from the divine essence and governed by the ideas."[21] God can neither make 2 + 2 = 5 true nor torturing babies for fun legitimate.[22] God commands or wills what is true and good; what is true and good is not determined by merely what God commands or wills.

Of course, Aquinas also translates "rule and measure of human acts" into "dictates of reason" in article 1 of *The Treatise on Law*, but this does not mean that reason (be it speculative or practical) creates or constructs the standard by which human actions are measured. Reason, at least human reason, is understood to function in Aquinas's account of natural law within the context of metaphysical realism.[23] Reason discovers the standard or law for judging human conduct by understanding the human good, and this is grounded in human nature. Reason's dictates are, then, ultimately a matter of what *is* (that is, human nature teleologically understood).

Though we will later have more to say about the basics of Aquinas's approach to natural law, we can for now say that it is critically dependent on the following

---

[19]To say this is, of course, not to say that anything could exist without God for Aquinas. It is only to note that one can consider the nature of a thing as the measure or rule—that is, as the law for its manner of operation—without considering its ontological dependence on God.

[20]Anthony Kenny, "Seven Concepts of Creation," *Aristotelian Society Supplementary Volume* 78.1 (2004): 89.

[21]Ibid., p. 90. James M. Gustafson notes that "for Thomas it is the *mind* of God in which the natural moral law and the revealed law in the Bible participate that grounds objective ethics theologically. The mediation of the ultimate ground of ethics for Thomas is through continuities and relationships that persist through laws, and not through the immediacy of a direct command." *Ethics from a Theocentric Perspective, Volume Two: Ethics and Theology* (Chicago: University of Chicago Press, 1984), p. 46. But also see *ST*, I-II, 94.5.

[22]*SCG*, II, 25.

[23]Metaphysical realism holds (1) that there are beings that exist and are what they are independent and apart from our cognition and (2) that we can come to know, though not without great difficulty, both the existence and nature of these beings.

metaphysical principles: the ontological structure of potentiality and actuality; things having natures; our ability to know the existence and nature of these things; and the thoroughly teleological character of reality. It is in the very idea of a thing's potentiality being ordered to its actuality that we find what could be called the "ontological pull" of both the actual and the desirable. Aquinas's view entails, then, a commitment to what also could be called "ontological goodness."

AQUINAS AND NATURAL MORAL LAW

The teleological character of reality provides the ontological pull of goodness. Such a pull is fundamental to Aquinas's view of human nature and thus to his approach to ethics as well. Accordingly, ethics begins for Aquinas by noting that every human being has an inherent potentiality for perfecting themselves. This potentiality is expressed in their natural desire (or strong disposition) for happiness or self-perfection. Even though humans might have a vague or even a mistaken understanding of their good, they have this natural orientation for it.[24] Freedom of the will is thus not radical for Aquinas but set within the context of human nature teleologically considered. Human beings cannot live other than as human beings; and so in what the actualization of this basic potentiality consists is not merely a matter of choice. They do not have freedom with regard to their ultimate end or its general character. Nonetheless, there is freedom of the will for Aquinas, and this is understood as a series of particular human actions that actualize this potentiality. Human beings must select the means by which to achieve their ultimate end or good or perfection, and this is where individual human agency is of central importance to the living of a good life. Such living cannot be predetermined by theoretical knowledge of ethical goodness alone but depends in the final analysis on the moral act of an individual—that is, the individual's own thinking, choosing, and acting.

We will have more to say about the role of the individual in the moral act in the next section, but it is necessary to note that the teleological character of human nature also provides the context for ethical reasoning. For Aquinas, the first principle of practical reasoning and natural moral law is: "Good is to be done and pursued; and evil is to be avoided" (*ST,* I–II, 94.2). This statement does not tell one in what human perfection ultimately consists or what is good in particular cases but rather only reports the implicit principle upon which human conduct is based. It is the principle of action for human beings

[24]"The will naturally tends toward its ultimate end; for every man naturally desires happiness. And all other volitions are caused from this natural volition, since whatever a man desires is wished on account of an end. Therefore, the love of the good, which man naturally desires as an end, is a natural love, but the love derived from this, of a good loved for the sake of the end [in other words, the love of a means to an end], is an elective [free] love." *ST,* I, 60.2. Translation with interpolations is from Vernon J. Bourke, *Ethics: A Textbook in Moral Philosophy* (New York: Macmillan Co., 1951), pp. 27–28.

understood teleologically. Just as the principle of non-contradiction is grasped implicitly in our apprehension and understanding of anything, so as well is the first principle of natural moral law grasped in our planning of any action. It is implicit in our decision to do or not do anything. Without such a principle, human conduct is unintelligible, because there would be nothing for which such conduct would be ultimately performed. Furthermore, without it, there could be for Aquinas no ultimate moral determination of human conduct. As Aquinas states:

> For, every agent acts for the sake of an end, and this [an end] has the formal nature of the good. So, the first principle in practical reason is that which is based on the *formal* nature of the good, which is: the good is that which all seek after. (*ST,* I–II, 94.2.)[25]

It is important to emphasize, however, that Aquinas here is speaking of the formal character of the good, that is, as an end, and not saying that this first principle is sufficient for determining what is good (or evil) or what ought (or ought not) to be done.[26]

This first principle could be stated in other ways: "Lead a life of virtue," "Be the kind of person you ought to be," "Perfect yourself," or even "Be true to yourself,"[27] but these statements still only note other ways of speaking of human perfection, they do not tell one what it is or how to achieve it. However, Aquinas does add that "all other precepts of natural law are based on this [the first principle of natural moral law]; so that whatever practical reason naturally apprehends as a human good (or evil), belongs to the precepts of the natural law as something to be done or avoided . . . hence it is that all those things to which man has a natural inclination, are naturally apprehended by reason as being good, and consequently as objects of pursuit, and their contraries as evil, and objects of avoidance" (*ST,* I–II, 94.2). This statement encompasses two claims:

1. As we come to know in what human perfection consists (that is, as we apprehend basic "generic" goods), then we have a more specific understanding of human perfection; and so attaining a particular good (or avoiding a particular evil) is a particularization of this most general first-principle.
2. Yet this is not to say that we derive a more specific understanding of human perfection (and what ought to be done) by simply unpacking a priori the first principle of natural law. Rather, the basic generic goods that constitute human perfection are themselves also non-discursively

---

[25]This is Bourke's translation, *Ethics*, p. 189.

[26]Vernon J. Bourke, "Is Thomas Aquinas a Natural Law Ethicist?" *The Monist* 58.1 (January, 1974), p. 57.

[27]Most of these alternative formulations are taken from Milton A. Gonsalves, *Fagothey's Right & Reasons: Ethics in Theory and Practice*, 9th ed., (Upper Saddle River, NJ: Prentice Hall, 1989), p. 117.

> or non-inferentially known from our understanding of human beings. As we come to know in what the basic potentialities of human beings consist, then we also know what the goods of human perfection are. Goodness is the actual as compared to the potential, and so for Aquinas knowledge of the basic generic goods is both self-evident and based on human nature.[28]

AGENT CENTEREDNESS IN AQUINAS

Aquinas notes that self-preservation, sexual union, care of one's children, knowledge, religion, and sociality are among the basic generic goods that compose human perfection.[29] Moreover, Aquinas speaks of the four cardinal virtues—prudence, justice, temperance, and fortitude—as major constituents of the human good.[30] Human perfection is thus an inclusive (or comprehensive) good for Aquinas, since it is constituted by basic generic goods and virtues.

Aquinas gives priority to prudence among these cardinal virtues, because it is upon prudence (or right reason) that the others rest.[31] As Ralph McInerny notes:

> The human good, man's ultimate end, is complex, but the unifying thread is the distinctive mark of the human, namely, reason. . . . [For example], a man does not simply have an instinct for self-preservation which must be pursued at all costs. He recognizes life as a good and devises ways and means of securing it in shifting circumstances. Since it is not the only good there is, it cannot take automatic precedence over all other constituents of human good.[32]

The intellectual virtue of prudence (or right reason) supplies the insight into the contingent and the particular that makes human perfection an integral whole—that is to say, prudence supplies the unifying thread. As Aquinas states:

---

[28]There is for Aquinas nothing incompatible with knowledge being self-evident and based on the nature of things. For a defense of this view, see Henry B. Veatch, *Two Logics*: *The Conflict between Classical and Neo-Analytic Philosophy* (Evanston, Illinois: Northwestern University Press, 1968).

[29]See *ST*, I–II, 94.2. For an account of the various lists of basic drives and inclinations from psychological and anthropological literature, see Thomas Davitt, S.J., "Basic Values in Law: A Study of the Ethico-legal Implications of Psychology and Anthropology," *Transactions of the American Philosophical Society* (New Series—Volume 58, Part 5, 1968).

[30]*ST*, I–II, 61.

[31]"Prudence is the principal of all the virtues simply." *ST*, I–II, 61.2, Reply to Objection 1. "Prudence is the virtue which commands." *ST*, I–II, 61.3. "Now in the genus of human acts the highest cause is the common end of all human life, and it is this end that prudence intends." *ST*, II–II, 47.2.

[32]Ralph McInerny, *Ethica Thomistica: The Moral Philosophy of Thomas Aquinas*, revised ed. (Washington, D.C.: The Catholic University Press of America, 1997), p. 46. (This revised edition does not include McInerny's critical reflections on the views of Germain Grisez and John Finnis that were present in the earlier, 1982 edition, but as McInerny states in the preface of this revised edition, "I have come to think this is not the place to do that . . . [but] this is not a recantation" [xi]. We will very soon use some material from these critical reflections in the earlier edition.)

> Prudence directs the moral virtues not only in the choice of means, but also in appointing the end. Now the end of each moral virtue is to attain the mean in the matter proper to that virtue, which mean is appointed according to the right reason of prudence. . . . (*ST*, I–II, 66.3, Reply to Objection 3.)[33]

This virtue turns a speculative or abstract understanding of human perfection into a reality—that is, into a concrete activity where right reason shapes and forms the potentialities of a human being into their proper actualization for the individual.[34]

Even if we interpret Aquinas as holding that there is an objective hierarchy of the basic generic goods based upon features of human nature, this does not mean that one may act directly against one of the basic generic goods for the sake of another. Such a hierarchy does not require the reduction of goods lower on the natural scale to be mere instruments for the sake of higher ones. It is perfectly possible for the goods that compose human perfection to be ends in themselves and not merely instruments. Again, as McInerney states:

> Both Thomas and Aristotle take that perfection of rational activity they call contemplation to be objectively the highest. Neither man thinks that anyone could devote himself exclusively to contemplation, however. The human good remains complex and irreducible to the well-performing of any single type of rational activity.[35]

It is through the exercise of prudence that the various goods and virtues of human perfection are given their proper emphasis or weighting.[36] This requires

---

[33]Daniel Mark Nelson observes that "we participate in the natural law both rationally and appetively. Our knowledge of the good in either mode, however, is general or abstract. The first principle of practical reason, or the first principle of natural law, does not tell us which goods in particular to pursue or how to pursue them. And our inclinations are only toward the general kinds of goods with which our various powers are concerned. In order to pursue appropriate goods, and in order to act reasonably with respect to our inclinations, we are dependent on the virtues under the direction of prudence, which is right reason about how to act." *The Priority of Prudence: Virtue and Natural Law and the Implications for Modern Ethics* (University Park, Pennsylvania: Pennsylvania State University Press, 1992), p. 107.

[34]"For there is a certain natural disposition demanded by the human species, so that no man can be without it. And this disposition is natural in respect of the specific nature. But since such a disposition has a certain latitude, it happens that different grades of this disposition are becoming to different men in respect of the individual nature." *ST,* I–II, 51.1.

[35]Ralph McInerny, *Ethica Thomistica: The Moral Philosophy of Thomas Aquinas*, (Washington, D.C.: The Catholic University Press of America, 1982), p. 59. Also, for a further discussion of human good as an inclusive or comprehensive good, see McInerny, "Ethics," *The Cambridge Companion to Aquinas*, ed. Norman Kretzmann and Eleonore Stump (Cambridge: Cambridge University Press, 1993), p. 211.

[36]"The truth of practical intellectual virtue, if we consider it in relation to things, is by way of that which is measured; so that both in practical and in speculative intellectual virtues, the mean consists in conformity with things. But if we consider it in relation to the appetite, it has the character of a rule and measure. Consequently the rectitude of reason is the mean of moral virtue, and also the mean of prudence—of prudence as ruling and measuring, of moral virtue, as ruled and measured by that mean. In like manner the difference between excess and deficiency is to be applied in both cases" (*ST,* I–II, 64.3).

that attention be given to the particular and contingent circumstances in which an individual acts. Natural law ethics for Aquinas thus does not provide a formula or recipe by which the mean is determined. That is delegated to prudence, and here we find the essence of the measure (or the "law") for natural law ethics.

Prudence is the excellent use of practical reason, and it is through prudence that human perfection for an individual attains its appropriate concrete form. But practical reason is not automatic or mindless.[37] It must be initiated by the individual. So, not only is the human good found in the perfection of the individual human being, but the very character of human perfection is itself a self-directed activity. Human perfection is achieved, maintained, and enjoyed by the individual human being's exercise of right reason.[38] It is active, not passive. Thus, in making the virtue of prudence central to the ethical life, Aquinas has put the individual human being at the center of the process of perfection.

The self-directed dimension of Aquinas's account of human perfection is not always fully appreciated, however. A major reason for this is that the term in English that designates the genus to which prudence, along with all the other cardinal virtues, belongs is a certain kind of *habit*.[39] However, this term fails to convey the nature of prudence, as well as the other virtues, that constitute the self-perfecting life. It suggests that perfection could be merely the repetition of "appropriate"[40] acts without either thought or choice. Indeed, it even suggests an operation that is automatic or mechanical. But nothing could be further from the meaning that is intended by Aquinas, for the virtues epitomize what is free and voluntary. For Aquinas, the term for the genus to which prudence and the other cardinal virtues belong is the Latin word, *habitus*. A *habitus* is a quality of essential steadiness or readiness, and in humans this quality is a state of character that results from (and is maintained by) thought and choice.[41] Thus, the genus to which prudence and the other cardinal virtues belong are operations that are not simply habitual. A virtuous individual has the state of character that leads to virtuous acts, but this character exists, and these acts only become appropriate, through the agent's *own exercise* of right reason. Living virtuously or excellently is in its very essence a matter of human agency—a personal achievement. A virtuous individual knows, desires, and chooses to live virtuously.

---

[37]Aquinas states that "man is the master of his actions through his reason and will; whence too, the free-will is defined as 'the faculty and will of reason'" (*ST,* I–II, 1.1).

[38]This process involves, of course, the moral virtues.

[39]*ST*, II–I 55.4.

[40]But even here, we can only speak of "appropriate" acts as those that would be so *if* they were chosen.

[41]See Yves R. Simon, *The Definition of Moral Virtue*, ed. Vukan Kuic (New York: Fordham University Press, 1986), pp. 55–61 and 71–79 as well as his discussion of *habitus* in his work, *An Introduction to the Metaphysics of Knowledge*, trans. Vukan Kuic and Richard J. Thompson (New York: Fordham University Press, 1990), pp. 159–60. Finally, see Clifford G. Kossel, S.J., "Thomistic Moral Philosophy in the Twentieth Century," *The Ethics of Aquinas*, ed. Stephen J. Pope (Washington, D.C.: Georgetown University Press, 2002), pp. 393–94.

It would seem then that Aquinas holds an agent centered approach to human perfection, if he holds (a) that human perfection is an inclusive or comprehensive good that is constituted by basic generic goods and virtues; (b) that it is only through the overall guiding virtue of prudence that human perfection is given appropriate concrete form for some individual; (c) that the individuality of a human being is critical to the determination of this appropriate concrete form; and (d) that human agency or self-direction is vital to the excellent use of practical reason. If these conditions hold, then human perfection for Aquinas is not ultimately based in simply the actions or intentions of the individual human being but rather in a way of being for a human being—a *habitus*—that is itself grounded in the self-directed activity of prudence. However, if any of these conditions do not hold then his ethics would not be agent centered.

DE-CENTERING THE INDIVIDUAL HUMAN AGENT

We have in no way reached the final word regarding Aquinas's ethical theory. There is much more to the story, and it goes to the very heart of Aquinas's thought. Indeed, there are four basic considerations that work against interpreting him as holding an agent centered approach to human perfection.

First, Aquinas makes it quite clear that contrary to what has so far been noted, the virtue of prudence is not the center point of his ethical theory,[42] for prudence is concerned with means only and never with the end. "It does not belong to prudence to appoint the end, but only to regulate the means" (*ST,* II–II, 47.6). Rather, it is the natural capacity of practical reason—the intellectual *habitus* of *synderesis*[43] or natural reason[44]—that appoints the end to moral virtues,[45] and thus *the mean* that prudence appoints to moral virtues is now no

[42]See James F. Keenan, S. J., "The Virtue of Prudence (IIa IIae, qq. 47–56)," *The Ethics of Aquinas*, pp. 259–71 for a helpful account of this issue.

[43]"Now, just as there is a certain habitus of the human soul, whereby it knows the principles of the speculative sciences, which we call the understanding of principles, so, too, there is in it a certain natural habitus concerning things to be done, which are the natural principles of the natural moral law; and this habitus pertains to synderesis." *De Veritate*, 16.1, Reply. This translation is from Bourke, *Ethics*, p. 192.

[44]"Natural reason known by the name of 'synderesis' appoints the end to moral virtues." *ST,* II–II, 47.6, Reply to Objection 1.

[45]"The end concerns the moral virtues, not as though they appointed the end, but because they tend to the end which is appointed by natural reason. In this they are helped by prudence, which prepares the way for them, by disposing the means. Hence it follows that prudence is more excellent than the moral virtues, and moves them: yet 'synderesis' moves prudence, just as the understanding of principles moves science." Ibid., Reply to Objection 3. Nelson interprets this passage as showing that the function of synderesis is only to explain how we begin to reason practically, not to provide content for our moral deliberation. See *The Priority of Prudence*, p. 97. Yet, it is evident that Aquinas links the precepts of the natural law with the generic goods that natural reason (synderesis) apprehends. On this last point, see Thomas S. Hibbs, "Interpretations of Aquinas's Ethics Since Vatican II," *The Ethics of Aquinas*, pp. 416–17.

longer identified as the end. Instead the end is set by the precepts of the natural law, and "whatever practical reason naturally apprehends as a human good (or evil) belongs to the precepts of the natural law" (*ST,* I–II, 94.2)—that is to say, the above-mentioned basic "generic" goods and their contraries. "So in the practical reason, certain things pre-exist, as naturally known principles, and such are the ends of the moral virtues. . . ." (*ST*, II–II, 42.6). Thus, prudence's role is relegated strictly to the determination of the means to these ends.[46]

The place of prudence in Aquinas's ethical theory is illustrated in his thorough analysis of the operations of the moral act found in the *Summa Theologiae*, I–II, Q. 8–17.[47] Overall, Aquinas describes this process of thinking, choosing, and acting as proceeding in an orderly fashion: "First there is the apprehension of the end; then the desire of the end; and then the counsel about the means to the end; and then the desire of the means" (*ST,* I–II, 15.3). It is clear from his analysis that the intellectual act of prudence does not determine the end. It does not discover the concrete, determinate form of the end in the particular and contingent.[48] Instead, it is confined to seeking the instantiation of the generic goods that synderesis has already apprehended as determining the ends of practical reason.

Second, the precepts of the natural law are grounded in the eternal law in which human nature participates.[49] As Aquinas states, "the natural law is nothing else than the rational creature's participation of the eternal law," (*ST,* I–II, 91.2) and the eternal law is, of course, the set of paradigms or archetypes, which are analogous to Plato's world of Forms, that are found as the divine ideas in the mind of God.[50] As Aquinas states:

> Just as in every artificer there pre-exists a type of the things that are made by his art, so too in every governor there must pre-exist the type of the order of those things that are to be done by those who are subject to his

[46]Also, it should at least be noted that Aquinas holds that since the function of prudence is to arrange things to their ends, divine providence can be understood as prudence (*ST*, I, 22.1). Indeed, Daniel Westberg in *Right Practical Reason* (Oxford: Clarendon Press, 1994) holds, as Fergus Kerr observes in *After Aquinas: Versions of Thomism* (Oxford: Basil Blackwell, 2002), that there is "a certain analogy between divine providence and the habitual practice of the prudent human being" (p.123). Yet, this analogy "seems not to do much work" (ibid.) in the *Summa Theologiae*, Kerr further observes.

[47]See Vernon J. Bourke, *St. Thomas and the Greek Moralists* (Milwaukee, Wisconsin: Marquette University Press, 1947), pp. 15–16 and also Bourke's *Ethics: A Textbook in Moral Philosophy*, Ch. 3, pp. 57–120 for a useful outline of Aquinas's analysis. Further, see John Finnis, *Aquinas: Moral, Political, and Legal Theory* (Oxford: Oxford University Press, 1998), p. 71.

[48]Douglas J. Den Uyl, *The Virtue of Prudence* (New York: Peter Lang, 1991), p. 90.

[49]It is through synderesis that human beings participate in the eternal law. See *DQT,* II, 16.1, pp. 300–08.

[50]Anthony J. Lisska, *Aquinas's Theory of Natural Law*, p. 92. But this should not be taken to mean that God is subject to the eternal law, because "things pertaining to the Divine Nature or Essence are not subject to the eternal law, but are the eternal law itself" (*ST*, I–II, 93.4). Or, as Fergus Kerr states: "God and the eternal law are identical." *After Aquinas*, p. 107.

> government. And just as the type of the things yet to be made by an art is called the art or exemplar of the products of that art, so too the type in him, who governs the acts of his subjects, bears the character of a law, provided the other conditions be present. . . . Now God, by His wisdom, is the Creator of all things in relation to which He stands as the artificer to the products of his art. . . . Moreover He governs all the acts and movements that are to be found in each single creature. . . . Wherefore as the type of the Divine Wisdom, inasmuch as by It all things are created, has the character of art, exemplar or idea; so the type of Divine Wisdom, as moving all things to their due end, bears the character of law. Accordingly the eternal law is nothing else than the type of Divine Wisdom, as directing all actions and movements. (*ST,* I–II, 93.1.)

God, as the simple act of existence (pure being),[51] is for Aquinas not only the cause of all being but also the source of the specification of the beings who share in existence, and this is achieved through God's creative act by means of the divine ideas in his intellect. These ideas are not only that through which being and the other transcendentals (for example, truth and goodness) become specified, but also they are the exemplars that individual beings imitate.[52] Further, since these ideas are from God's intellect, the imitation of these ideas results "because of the intention of an agent who antecedently determines the end himself" (*DQT*, I, 3.1, p. 14.) That is to say, the teleological character of all of existence and that of the nature of every being thus comes from the creative act of God. This is the ultimate source for the desire or appetite that all beings have for their perfection. Finally, a being's nature is "known better by means of the species in the divine mind than it could be known by means of its own essence. . . ." (*DQT*, I, 3.1, p. 142). The divine idea in which a being participates is thus a "more real" example of its nature than its own.[53]

To summarize this second consideration, it may be said then that the divine ideas are the measure of the truth of all things, and through natural reason's knowledge of them, they are as well the measure of a being's goodness and thus of a human being's own perfection. The standard or measure for the ends that constitute the law for the ethical life is the divine idea of human being in which the natures of individual human beings participate.[54] This is the standard for

[51]*ST*, I, 3.4.

[52]"The idea of a thing is form which a thing imitates" (*DQT*, I, 3.1, p. 140).

[53]For a helpful account of these points, see James Michael Jacobs, "The metaphysics of morals in Thomas Aquinas: The transcendentals as the foundation for natural law ethics" (January 1, 2002). *ETD Collection for Fordham University*. Paper AAI3045128. http://fordham.bepress.com/dissertations/AAI3045128

[54]"That which is said to be of a certain sort by participation is said to be such only in so far as it has a certain likeness to that which is said to be such by essence" (*SCG*, I, 40.3).

human perfection—that is, the basis for the mean that constitutes an individual's perfection—and not the concrete, determinate nature of individual human beings themselves.[55] *Aquinas's ontological goodness then involves more than Aristotle's relation of potentiality to actuality in individual beings but also the actuality that God's creative act of existence provides through divine ideas which ground the law for these beings.*

Third, not only is the divine idea of human being the standard for individual human perfection for Aquinas but also human perfection in itself is not measured *ultimately* in human terms. Vernon Bourke provides us with insight here, and he does this by means of a comparison between Aristotle and Aquinas.

> But Aristotle never thought of the order of moral reason as St. Thomas did. There is completely lacking, in the original Aristotelianism, the ordering of free human acts to an *objectively real*, ultimate end. Aristotle's man looks only to subjective [that is, individual] self-perfection: his God has nothing to do with human acts.[56]

Bourke is basing this comparison on a distinction Aquinas makes regarding two ways of speaking of the ultimate end: "First, as being the thing itself; secondly, as the attainment thereof. These are not, of course, two ends, but one end, considered in itself, and in its relation to something else" (*ST,* I–II, 11.3, Reply to Objection 3). The interesting question, of course, is whether our ability to speak of or consider such an end apart from its relation to something else requires that it exist in such a manner. Moreover, there is the question of whether such an end can only be objective if it bears no intrinsic relation to something else, and finally, there is the question of whether an ultimate natural end may not be essentially relational (and then ultimately only in relation to the actions of some living agent[57]). Thus, when it comes to human beings, could. not the objectively real, ultimate end for a human being have its source or ground in the very nature of the individual human being?

We shall put these concerns aside, however, because our point is simply that for Aquinas human perfection is not ultimately an individual engaging in those activities that make it complete or actual, and thus good, but rather it is in the individual possessing or attaining the perfect good, which is something other than the individual human being. As Aquinas states, "man is not the supreme good" (*ST* I–II, 2.5). Full and final human perfection is thus found only in an objectively real end that is itself transcendent. That is to say, it is only in an end

[55]Jacobs makes the point nicely: "The creature, as individuated by matter and endowed with individual potentiality, is to be evaluated by the extent to which it actualizes its potentiality and achieves the fullness of being specified by the divine idea." "The metaphysics of morals in Thomas Aquinas: The transcendentals as the foundation for natural law ethics," pp. 111–12.

[56]Bourke, *St. Thomas and the Greek Moralists*, p. 27 (emphasis in the original). Bourke understands "subjective" to mean "individual" here; hence, our interpolation.

[57]We are thinking here of Philippa Foot's *Natural Goodness*, *op. cit*., pp. 5 and 25–37.

that bears no intrinsic relation to the individual human being.[58] As Aquinas states:

> It is impossible for any created good to constitute man's happiness. For happiness is the perfect good, which lulls the appetite altogether; else it would not be the last end, if something yet remained to be desired. Now the object of the will, i.e. of man's appetite, is the universal good; just as the object of the intellect is the universal true. Hence it is evident that naught can lull man's will, save the universal good. This is to be found, not in any creature, but in God alone; because every creature has goodness by participation. Wherefore God alone can satisfy the will of man, according to the words of Ps. 102:5: "Who satisfieth thy desire with good things." Therefore God alone constitutes man's happiness. (*ST*, I–II, 2.8.)

Thus, the performance of excellent activities—whether they consist in attaining the proper mean of practical reasoning or the truths of speculative knowledge—will not do for human perfection. Bourke puts this bluntly, "The *objective* ultimate end is not anything which belongs to the nature of the human soul."[59] Only God will do, for only God is the objectively real ultimate end.

Fourth, human beings cannot by their own efforts in this life attain or possess the perfect good, which for Aquinas means we cannot through our own cognitive powers know God's essence in and through itself.

> Imperfect happiness that can be had in this life, can be acquired by man by his natural powers, in the same way as virtue, in whose operation it consists. . . . But man's perfect Happiness . . . consists in the vision of the Divine Essence. Now the vision of God's Essence surpasses the nature not only of man, but also of every creature. . . . Every knowledge that is according to the mode of created substance, falls short of the vision of the Divine Essence, which infinitely surpasses all created substance. Consequently neither man, nor any creature, can attain final Happiness by his natural powers. (*ST*, I–II, 5.5.)

Thus, human knowledge of what God is must be attained by something other than a natural process. Knowing the essence of God is a supernatural event, and

---

[58]This must be so for Aquinas, because the finitude of human capacities would militate against the perfect goodness of this objectively real, ultimate end. Moreover, the very notion that human beings are made in the image of God helps to confirm this very point. "Now it is manifest that in man there is some likeness to God, copied from God as from an exemplar; yet this likeness is not one of equality, for such an exemplar infinitely excels its copy. Therefore there is in man a likeness to God; not, indeed, a perfect likeness, but imperfect. And Scripture implies the same when it says that man was made "to" God's likeness; for the preposition "to" signifies a certain approach, as of something at a distance" (*ST*, I, 93.1). Also, Aquinas states that the image of God "exists in man as in an alien nature, as the image of a king is in a silver coin" (Ibid., Reply to Objection 2).

[59]Bourke, *Ethics,* pp. 34–35 (emphasis in the original).

it can only be attained through God's assistance.[60] In saying this we are referring not only to the beatific vision that happens in the next life, but we are also noting that Aquinas infuses the natural moral virtues of prudence, temperance, fortitude, and justice with the theological virtues of faith, hope, and charity. "These virtues are called Divine, not as though God were virtuous by reason of them, but because of them God makes us virtuous, and directs us to Himself" (*ST*, I–II, 62.1, Reply to Objection 2). These virtues direct us to God by assisting us in beginning our eternal life. Without these virtues we cannot be brought to God.

There are then four basic considerations that work against understanding Aquinas's account of natural moral law as agent centered. (1) The end of the moral life is not set by prudence determining the proper concrete form of the worthwhile life for some individual, but instead is set by the generic goods that synderesis apprehends. (2) The standard or measure for the ends that constitute the ethical life is the divine idea of human being in which the natures of individual human beings participate and not the determinate natures of individual human beings themselves. (3) Human perfection is not *ultimately* an individual engaging in those activities that make it complete or actual, and thus good, but rather it is in the individual possessing or attaining the perfect good, which is something other than the individual human being—namely, God; and (4) we cannot attain our perfection through our own self-directed acts. We require God's assistance.

AGENT CENTEREDNESS IN SPINOZA

In general terms it would appear that no two thinkers could be further apart than Aquinas and Spinoza. In the first place there is Spinoza's famous rejection of final causality:

---

[60]This is not to say that acting virtuously in this life is not a necessary means to this knowledge of God (*ST*, I–II, 5.7 and 62.3). Indeed, F. C. Copelston, S.J., argues that *if* one understands *beatitudo* not as the ultimate end but as the activity by which the ultimate end is possessed (that is, knowledge of God), then one "cannot justifiably make a dichotomy between human moral conduct on the one hand and the glory of God on the other. . . . God is glorified by the highest possible development of man's potentialities as a rational being, and every moral act of man has therefore intrinsic value. But this is not to say that they have value purely atomistically, so to speak; they have intrinsic value within the total context of man's movement towards his final end, which is in concrete fact, though not by necessity of nature, the supernatural possession of infinite good." *Aquinas* (Harmondsworth, Middlesex, England: Penguin Books, 1955), p. 211. Yet such actions on our part can never be sufficient, for the object of this activity is nonetheless (and must be for Aquinas) different from the activity of pursuing it. Thus the extent an agent centered ethics of perfection can be understood in terms of an unachievable goal is most problematic, to say the least. Moreover, the claims that the desire for knowledge of God results from an inherent potentiality of individual human beings and that such knowledge is perfective of them are by no means evident, if one seeks to establish these claims on the basis of human nature alone. Though his concerns are different than ours, Denis J. M. Bradley states the problem nicely: "One can have either a Thomist theology illegitimately calling itself a moral philosophy or one can have a Thomist moral philosophy, purportedly derived from Aquinas, that is no longer authentically Thomistic because it cannot incorporate the only ultimate end recognized by Aquinas." *Aquinas on the Twofold Human Good: Reason and Human Happiness in Aquinas's Moral Science* (Washington, DC: Catholic University Press, 1996), p. 495.

> Nature has no fixed goal and . . . all final causes are but figments of the human imagination. . . .
>
> This doctrine of Final Causes turns nature completely upside down, for it regards as an effect that which is in fact a cause, and vice versa. . . .
>
> Again, this doctrine negates God's perfection; for if God acts with an end in view, he must necessarily be something that he lacks. (E1App.)[61]

Such comments in themselves would seem to unravel any attempt to reconcile Spinoza with the Aristotelian/Thomist tradition, for without teleology the act/potency framework that defines the tradition is lost as well. In addition, it would seem that without the act/potency framework and teleology, "goodness" would be unable to be an attribute of the nature of things and thus have ontological import. In this connection too, Spinoza apparently rejects the ontological character of goodness when he tells us, "as for the terms 'good' and 'bad,' they likewise indicate nothing positive in things considered in themselves, and are nothing but modes of thinking" (E4Pref.).[62] Without ontological goodness it would further seem that the heart of natural law would be removed, for if nothing else, natural law is the idea that nature provides the measure for evaluating the presence or absence of goodness. Indeed, how could a system where "nothing in nature is contingent, but all things are from the necessity of the divine nature determined to exist and to act in a definite way" (E1P29) allow for normativity at all? The idea that what is, must be, holds out little hope for anything normative, since what ought to be the case presupposes that things could be otherwise. And in particular, the denial of free will (E2P48) would appear to rule out ethical conduct for humans. On the face of it, then, to enter Spinoza's world seems to dramatically close the door on the world of Aristotle and Aquinas.[63] It is not that we shall be showing in what follows that Spinoza

---

[61]Quoted texts are from Samuel Shirley's *Spinoza Complete Works* (Indianapolis: Hackett Publishing Co. 2002). However, we have checked the phrasing against the Curley edition (Edwin Curley *The Collected Works of Spinoza* (Princeton NJ: Princeton University Press, 1986)) and consulted the Latin when necessary. The following standard protocol will be used for citing texts: "E" *Ethics* (followed by Arabic numeral for part and internal references); "Ep"—*Letters,* "TP"—*Political Treatise* (followed by a Roman numeral for the chapter, and Arabic for the paragraph), "TTP"—*Theological-Political Treatise* (followed by a Roman numeral for the chapter).

[62]Spinoza has a confusing array of definitions of good and bad. Compare, for example, E3P39Schol. with E4Def. 1&2 (which definitions are different from what is said just before them in the preface). More on this below.

[63]There is, of course, the famous and important study by Harry Wolfson (*The Philosophy of Spinoza: Unfolding the Latent Processes of His Reasoning*, Cambridge, MA: Harvard University Press, 1934) that shows much the opposite, that is, it ties Spinoza squarely into some of the central philosophical traditions that precede him including the Aristotelian one. However, despite the connections to Aristotelianism, Wolfson says little about Aquinas. There are not many sustained comparisons between the two thinkers. For one such, see Guy Stephen Blakemore, "Recovering the Soul: Interpreting Baruch Spinoza's Doctrine of Mind-Body Identity in the Light of Thomas Aquinas's Metaphysical Theory of Form and Matter," Doctoral Thesis, University of Tennessee Knoxville, May 2007.

retreats from the positions just ascribed to him. Rather what qualifications we may make upon those positions will be in the service of indicating that Spinoza has an agent centered doctrine of value nonetheless. And since our overall thesis concerns the way in which agent centeredness is the critical variable as a foundation for natural law, Spinoza may qualify as a figure within the classical natural law tradition.

The subject of teleology in Spinoza has been a source of significant controversy in Spinoza scholarship,[64] and we shall not endeavor to resolve that issue here. However teleology fares in general terms, there are features of Spinoza's thought that at least bear a resemblance to certain understandings of it and which are central to the agent centered themes we are exploring. As we saw earlier, Spinoza rejects "final causes" and argues that "good" and "bad" are not to be found in the nature of things. He is not, however, averse to talking about "perfection" (*perfectio*). The most obvious use of this concept is to claim that God produces everything with perfection (E1P33Schol.2). God produces everything perfectly. For Spinoza "reality" and "perfection" mean the same thing (E2Def.6), and God is all reality (E1P15). This connection between God and "perfection" does not, however, prevent Spinoza from elsewhere speaking of things other than God in terms of their degrees of perfection. The mind, for example, "can undergo considerable changes, and can pass now to a state of greater perfection, now to one of less perfection . . ." (E3P11Schol.). Moreover, pleasure *and* pain are themselves conceived within a framework of perfection: "pleasure (*laetitia)* is man's transition from a state of less perfection to a state of greater perfection. Pain (*tristitia)* is man's transition from a state of greater perfection to a state of less perfection" (E3Def. Of Emotions 2&3). These definitions of pleasure and pain are followed by this comment:

> I say "transition," for pleasure is not perfection itself. If a man were to be born with the perfection to which he passes, he would be in possession of it without the emotion of pleasure. This is clearer in the case of pain, the contrary emotion. For nobody can deny that pain consists in the transition to a state of less perfection, not in the less perfection itself, since man

[64]Jonathan Bennett's account of teleology is a good place to start examining the issue (*A Study of Spinoza's Ethics* (Indianapolis: Hackett Publishing Co. 1984) Ch. 9. For a brief survey of the issue see, Charles Jarrett, *Spinoza: A Guide for the Perplexed*, (New York: Continuum International Publishing Group, 2007), Ch. 7, especially 116–19 as well as Charles Jarrett, "Teleology and Spinoza's Doctrine of Final Causes," in *Desire and Affect: Spinoza as Psychologist*, Yirmiyahu Yovel (ed.) (New York: Little Room Press, 1999). For a good discussion coming down on the side of Spinoza not having final causality, but which also draws comparisons to Aquinas, see John Carriero, "Spinoza on Final Causality" in Daniel Garber and Steven Nadler, eds., *Oxford Studies in Early Modern Philosophy* (Oxford University Press, 2005), vol. 2, pp. 105–47. It is clear to us that Spinoza wished to avoid final causality in his accounts of agency, but whether he succeeds or not is an issue we cannot address here. The broader philosophical question of whether agent centeredness requires teleology is also something we cannot attempt to answer here but has motivated us in doing this study.

> cannot feel pain insofar as he participates in any degree of perfection. (E3Def. Of Emotions Def. 3 Explication.)[65]

Not only does the foregoing passage allow us to conceive of conditions that are closer or farther away from conditions of perfection, but the movement towards or away from certain ways of being is reminiscent, if nothing else, of talk about movement towards or away from ends. For in the Aristotelian tradition, movement towards ends in accord with our nature is thought to be movement towards perfection, whereas movement towards ends not in accord with our nature is movement towards imperfection. Moreover, with perfection being reality itself, we seem in the last clause where Spinoza speaks of "any degree of perfection" not too far from the ontological idea of being as goodness in the sense Aquinas sometimes uses it. That is to say, as a condition whose state is "better" or "good" relative to its alternative of non-existence, being is good simply because non-existence cannot be "good," since non-existence cannot be anything.[66] Being (or reality) is similarly "perfection" for Spinoza. For Aquinas "better" or "good" in a valuational or normative setting connects analogically to the ontological sense just mentioned. A good state of being carries with it somehow "more reality" than lesser states of being. Similarly for Spinoza in the passage above, the state of being per se is regarded as a perfection of some type, leaving open the question of how the term might be used in a valuational context.[67] We shall see in a moment that perfection in the human case for Spinoza refers to a power of activity that can be either enhanced or diminished (*actus quo hominis agendi potentia*). In this respect "goodness" is a strictly valuational term for Spinoza requiring a valuer even if "perfection" is not. In any case, Spinoza wants to ensure that "reality" is a term used independently of any valuer, and the term "goodness" when applied to reality simply confuses that issue to Spinoza's mind.

What ties the ontological understanding of perfection in Spinoza to a valuational one is power. In principle, power, reality, and perfection are all interchangeable concepts in Spinoza. Yet because people can transition to or from states of perfection, we might speak of the ability to do so in terms of increasing or decreasing forms of power. For our purposes here, the power involved is the endeavor of something to persist in its own being—what Spinoza calls "conatus" (E3P6&7). As particular things we "express in a definite and determinate way the

[65]Spinoza, in what appears to be a direct rejection of the Aristotelian tradition, notes "nor can we say that pain consists in the privation of greater perfection, for privation is nothing, whereas the emotion of pain is an actuality."

[66]This brief account is obviously made without reference to God whose choice to put things in existence may, for Aquinas, contribute to the understanding of "good" here.

[67]Perfection may be less analogical in Spinoza than goodness is in Aquinas depending on how differently their respective understanding of states of being may be. In a universe where "things" are radically different in character one would expect more expansive degrees of analogy between them than in a universe where everything is pretty much the same.

power of God" (E3P6Proof), and this expression takes the form of an endeavor to persist in our own being. This conatus turns out to be our essence (E3P7). When thinking of our essence, we can refer to ourselves either in terms of mind or body; but when both are taken together the conatic endeavoring is called "appetite" (*appetitus*) by Spinoza. Appetite is "nothing else but man's essence" (E3P9Schol.). In short, we have a "definite and determinate" way of being that constitutes the sort of thing we are. Our being is manifest through acts of endeavoring that strive to preserve what we are. It turns out that we can do this endeavoring either well or badly. This process of endeavoring in a certain way, both in accordance with our "definite and determinate" way of being, and in an effort to sustain that way of being, thus establishes the framework within which we can come to define "success" and "failure." *That is, the essence of what we are turns out to be the measure of whether we are acting well or badly.*

The "emotions" or affects (*affectus*) are a good place to see how this process of living well or badly might operate, because with appetite as our essence our perspective will be in the language of endeavoring rather than achievement.[68] So whereas in the Aristotelian tradition the language is one of achieving or not achieving ends, for Spinoza the language is one of ever greater or less forms of endeavoring. And unlike the typical description of the Aristotelian model, the problem here is not one of using reason to moderate or control the appetites. Yet similarly to Aquinas, reason *is* a form of appetite for Spinoza (E3P9), so the moral problem for him is engendering the right sort of endeavoring, and not a process of checking or moderating appetite. This is not to say Spinoza does not sometimes speak in a very similar fashion. The opening lines of E4, for example, read, "I assign the term 'bondage' to man's lack of power to control and check the emotions. For a man at the mercy of his emotions is not his own master but is subject to fortune, in whose power he so lies that he is often compelled, although he sees the better course, to pursue the worse" (E4Pref.). Yet the "checking of the emotions" is not one of reason simply blocking or diminishing certain forms of emotional expression, but rather one of altering the way in which those emotions get expressed (e.g., E4P7Cor.). Appetite remains throughout.

As is well known, the point of Spinoza's ethics is to bring us to freedom, making bondage the chief "bad." Bondage is the wrong form of endeavoring, whereas freedom is the right form; both forms of endeavor will be discussed below. In the meantime, it is worth noting that Spinoza actually has three characterizations of the good (and bad), all of which are jointly meant to help us understand the difference between bondage and freedom.[69] The first and most

---

[68] For some accounts of both *conatus* and its connection to the affects, see *Desire and Affect,* Sections I and II.

[69] A fuller account of this is to be found in Den Uyl, *God, Man, and Well-Being: Spinoza's Modern Humanism* (New York: Peter Lang, 2008), Ch. 4.

basic instance of goodness connects it to pleasure (and badness to pain): "by 'good' I understand here every kind of pleasure and furthermore whatever is conducive thereto. . . . By 'bad' I understand every kind of pain" (E3P39Schol.). Not much later he defines "good" as "that which we certainly know to be useful (*utile*) to us," and "bad" as "that which we certainly know to be an obstacle to our attainment of some good" (E4Defs.1&2). In reference to these two definitions, Spinoza tells us to see the end of his own Preface to Part 4 which precedes these definitions. There he tells us "I shall mean by 'good' that which we certainly know to be the means for our approaching nearer to the model of human nature that we set before ourselves, and by 'bad' that which we certainly know prevents us from reproducing the said model" (E4Pref.). In general, what is useful to us will be what helps us approach more closely to the model of human perfection Spinoza has in mind. This, of course, is certainly reminiscent of Aristotle's moral exemplar and bears at least a procedural similarity to the movement towards or away from ends in a traditional teleological account. Like Aristotle, Spinoza would have us look not simply to abstract notions of human perfection, but at least initially to concrete human actors if we can find them. But of course the question that immediately arises is what sort of model is Spinoza considering here?

Whatever that model may be,[70] we know that movement towards or away from it is connected to perfection and highly agent centered: "men are more perfect or less perfect insofar as they are nearer to or farther from this model" (E4Pref.). And the movement to greater or lesser perfection is to "conceive [one's] power of activity, insofar as this is understood through his nature, to be increased or diminished" (E4Pref.). So to sum up to this point some of these various components, we are striving to preserve our own being which is a "definite and determinate" form of being in a way that will increase our power of activity. Pleasure is a sign we are moving in the right direction, while pain a sign we are moving in the wrong one. Pleasure and pain, however, must themselves be understood in light of a model of human perfection that measures whether those signs are accurately pointing in the right direction. Those signs point in the right direction if they accompany an increased power of activity. Now since pleasure—even when it is misleading—is always a form of perfection relative to pain, since it increases our endeavoring in a certain direction, we must finally be able to distinguish what truly enhances our power of activity from what may only seem to do so. Here is where the final characterization of the good comes

[70]There is some controversy about how to read this model. See in this connection, Matthew J. Kisner, *Spinoza on Human Freedom: Reason, Autonomy and the Good Life* (Cambridge: Cambridge University Press, 2011) Ch. 8. Kisner argues that the "model" Spinoza has in mind is not one of the completely free person moved only by adequate ideas, but includes elements of passivity. We regard the model as a benchmark in the movement towards or away from perfection, rather than as the measure of that perfection itself. Whether that requires passivity we shall leave undiscussed here.

in (the first two being pleasure and utility): the good is finally found in agents who are active, rather than passive, and the degree of activity is a function of the degree to which one acts from one's own nature alone.

To act from one's own nature is the essence of virtue for Spinoza.[71] It is tied directly to the degree of one's power: "by virtue and power I mean the same thing; that is . . . virtue, insofar as it is related to man, is man's very essence, or nature, insofar as he has power to bring about that which can be understood solely through the laws of his own nature" (E4Def. 8). To be virtuous then is to be active; to be active is not to be driven by forces outside of our nature, for that is to make us passive. If we want to be virtuous, we should act solely through the laws of our own nature. If we do that, we are active. And if we are active, we are powerful; passivity is a diminishment of our power with the outer limit of that diminishment being death. As we learn from the Preface to Part 4 and elsewhere in Spinoza's *Ethics*, the chief obstacle to activity is our emotions, because they are generally signs of passivity rather than activity. Notice, however, that whether we are speaking of activity or passivity here, the focus is entirely agent centered.

We have reached a point in our discussion where we need to ask the simple question of what exactly is activity and passivity and why are emotions Spinoza's focus? Spinoza answers as follows:

> I say that we are active when something takes place, in us or externally to us, of which we are the adequate cause; that is . . . when from our nature there follows in us or externally to us something which can be clearly and distinctly understood through our nature alone. On the other hand, I say we are passive when something takes place in us, or follows from our nature, of which we are only the partial cause. (E3Def. 2.)

We must thus be the adequate cause of what we do or effect to be active. We are passive insofar as we are inadequate or partial causes, which here means it is unclear to us exactly why and how we are doing what we are doing. Our emotions can increase or decrease our power of endeavoring (E3Def. 3), but we are generally passive with respect to them, because emotions are essentially "confused ideas," which is to say we are moved by them without fully understanding what we are doing. They seem to move us rather than us them. To be an adequate cause, however, means that any effect "can be clearly and distinctly perceived through the said cause" (E3Def. 1). To be the adequate cause of events within our environment, therefore, means to understand what, how, and why we are endeavoring the way we are within it. We are active in our world

[71]It is important here to say acting *from* one's own nature as opposed to acting *according to* one's own nature as seems common in the Aristotelian tradition. Virtue is an act of self-expression for Spinoza, not an act of conformity. We have chosen with Shirley to retain the word "emotion" throughout rather than the more accurate "affect" because it helps express this point more clearly.

when we are the adequate cause of what we do within it. By contrast, to guide ourselves by emotion is generally to endeavor with only partial or incomplete understanding of what we are doing and why. Knowledge is power for Spinoza, and successful, i.e., powerful, action is an indication of knowledge. It is also what it means to be virtuous.

Though emotions are chiefly passive for Spinoza, there are also active emotions, and they are the ones connected to reason (E4Appendix#3; E5P7, 25, 26). The pleasure that accompanies them might be described as feelings of efficacy we have when we are doing something well or successfully. Active emotions are forms of appetition imbued with understanding by the agent of the agent's actions and environment. The project of ethical life then is rather simple: it is to replace passivity with activity; passive emotions with active ones; ignorance with knowledge. If we do this, we will be efficacious actors within our environment, that is, powerful or virtuous ones. Being active, however, requires that we act from our nature which, for Spinoza, is human nature. As is evident from our mention of the importance of being an adequate cause and the role of clear and distinct ideas, reason is a central feature of human nature. It is the sort of "appetite" we must develop if we are to act from our nature and be active.

Spinoza's doctrine, as one might expect, can become rather complex as one builds upon the components we have identified above. We cannot pretend to flesh out even a small portion of the details applicable to that framework, such as what is implied by a life of reason or to discuss such questions as to whether this doctrine must issue in a kind of intellectualism.[72] The elements that concern us most, however, have been surveyed above and summed up by Spinoza himself in the following way:

> Desires that follow from our nature in such a way that they can be understood through it alone are those that are related to the mind insofar as the mind is conceived as consisting of adequate ideas. The other desires are related to the mind only insofar as it conceives things inadequately; and their force and increase must be defined not by human power but by the power of things external to us. So the former always indicate our power, the latter our weakness and fragmentary knowledge.
>
> Our active emotions, that is, those desires that are defined by man's power, that is, by reason, are always good; the other desires can be either good or evil. (E4Appendix 2&3)

From the foregoing discussion it is evident that like the Aristotelian tradition, the valuational use of the good in Spinoza is tied to our nature as a measure of the success or lack thereof in attaining the good. As such we find passages like

[72]See Den Uyl, *God, Man And Well-Being.*, pp. 59–65 for a discussion of this issue which argues against such a conclusion. The issue is dealt with much more extensively in Michael LeBuffe, *From Bondage to Freedom: Spinoza on Human Excellence* (New York: Oxford University Press, 2010), passim.

the following that, if one did not know otherwise, could easily be thought to come from a thinker within the Aristotelian tradition:

> In so far as a thing is in agreement with our nature, to that extent it is necessarily good. . . . Hence it follows that the more a thing is in agreement with our nature, the more advantageous [*utilior*] it is to use, that is, the more it is good; and conversely, the more advantageous a thing is to us, to that extent it is more in agreement with our nature. (E4P31Dem&Cor.)

Spinoza's discussion is thus agent focused in two ways: first, the agent's self-development is the object of the ethical theory, and secondly, the good is a function of that development and not a function of social conditions, mere conformity to rational rules, or the exercise of purported obligations. Spinoza's is a thoroughly immanentized ethics because it seeks to internalize all dimensions of value as features of the agent's endeavors rather than as objects of an agent's aspirations. This effort to thoroughly integrate value is filtered through and measured, as we have seen, in terms of the agent's nature.

SPINOZA AND NATURAL LAW

Spinoza is not normally considered to be a part of the natural law tradition.[73] If, however, agent centeredness is a critical component of that tradition, then perhaps Spinoza should be welcomed into it. Earlier we referenced a passage from Aquinas that we will cite here, since we take it to be a highly representative statement of the ontological foundations of classical Natural Law as it is typically understood. This passage can serve us well in considering Spinoza's own qualifications for being a part of the natural law tradition.

> Because in man there is first of all an inclination to good in accordance with the nature which he has in common with all substances: inasmuch as every substance seeks the preservation of its own being, according to its nature: and by reason of this inclination, whatever is a means of preserving human life, and of warding off its obstacles, belongs to the natural law. Secondly, there is in man an inclination to things that pertain to him more specially, according to that nature which he has in common with other animals: and in virtue of this inclination, those things are said

[73]A discussion of Spinoza on law that still has value can be found in Huntington Cairns, "Spinoza's Theory of Law," *Columbia Law Review* 48.7 (Nov. 1948): 1032–48. Cairns notes that "in its most abstract or absolute sense the word law means, he [Spinoza] says, that in virtue of which things of the same species act in a certain determinate manner" (p. 1037). Cairns offers comparisons between Aquinas and Spinoza, noting similarities and differences. At one particular point he separates them on human law over the common good (p. 1038), arguing that Spinoza does not make reference to this as a standard for human law. Our own perspective is that it is less the issue of the common good than the limitations Spinoza places on the ends of the state that separates them. (But Cairns seems to take what he said back later on p. 1044, but not for the reasons we would suggest.)

> to belong to the natural law. . . . Thirdly, there is in man an inclination to good, according to the nature of his reason, which nature is proper to him: thus man has a natural inclination to know the truth about God, and to live in society: and in this respect, whatever pertains to this inclination belongs to the natural law. (*ST,* I–II, 94.2)

What is remarkable about this passage is that there is really nothing in it with which Spinoza would disagree. Indeed, we could imagine Spinoza saying just such things himself based upon the passages we have already witnessed.[74] No doubt much of the reason Spinoza could agree with this passage is that the passage itself makes no normative claims nor requires commitment to a particular ethical theory. But the passage does more than not just violate some doctrine of Spinoza's; its most striking feature is that, much like Spinoza does himself, the passage sees humankind as expressing directly forces of nature and uses that as a basis for speaking about natural law. In addition, the passage recognizes that the particular type of being a thing is will determine the appropriate rules of action for that being. In this respect the passage confirms a definite agent centeredness. But what are we to make of the term "natural law" that Aquinas repeatedly uses? Here it might be worthwhile to look at what Spinoza has to say about law:

> The word law, taken in its absolute sense, means that according to which each individual thing—either all in general or those of the same kind—acts in one and the same fixed and determinate manner, this manner depending either on Nature's necessity or on human will. A law which depends on Nature's necessity is one which necessarily follows from the very nature of the thing, that is, its definition; a law which depends on human will, and which could more properly be termed a statute (*ius*), is one which men ordain for themselves and for others with a view to making life more secure and more convenient, or for other reasons. (TTP 4 "Of the Divine Law.")

From this passage there could indeed be parallels between Aquinas's "inclinations" and Spinoza's "fixed and determinate manner," where the latter represents that conatus each individual thing has to preserve and extend itself. But Spinoza's determinism pushes us to read "fixed and determinate" more rigidly than we would Aquinas's thwartable "inclinations." That understanding would tend to move Aquinas's "natural law" to the side of "human will" in Spinoza's scheme of things, except that "human will" is a locution closer to what Aquinas would call positive law than to natural law. The match between our two thinkers thus does not seem to be exact. We believe, in fact, that Aquinas's "natural law" has a parallel in Spinoza, but is of such a different nature due to its dependency

[74]We removed a few of the particulars from this passage from Aquinas. We have no reason to believe Spinoza would disagree with most of these either, but it is the philosophical point that interests us and these specific examples may distract from it.

upon transcendence that it is fair to say that if Aquinas's doctrine is the paradigm natural law doctrine, Spinoza is not a natural law theorist.

If natural laws in Aquinas are dictates of reason meant to serve as normative guides for our conduct, Spinoza would seem to be supporting just this notion when he says, "therefore the best course we can adopt . . . is to conceive a right method of living, or fixed rules of life, and to commit them to memory and continually apply them to particular situations that are frequently encountered in life, so that our casual thinking is thoroughly permeated by them and they are always ready to hand." (E5P10Schol.)[75] Here we see something akin to the classical notion of prudence where universal principles are applied to varying particulars as a way of ordering our conduct. However, we believe that this way of appreciating Spinoza's comments is at least somewhat misleading. This particular passage is part of a proposition where Spinoza is speaking about ways in which an individual might better order his or her mind and conduct. It is not a passage about deriving fixed rules of life generally and for everyone, at least in the way we would ordinarily understand it. Indeed, it does not follow from this passage that the fixed rules for one person will be the same as that of another. The "rules" as one finds them here, and elsewhere in Spinoza, are more like orientations, maxims, attitudes, or traits of character than they are universally precise prescriptions for right and wrong action. In this particular proposition, for example, we are told to "concentrate on that which is good in every single thing . . . so that in so doing we may be determined to act always from the emotion of pleasure." This sort of advice is to be sharply contrasted with rules that one either conforms to or violates and with respect to which one's actions are determined to be good or bad. If one does not look to the good in things, one has perhaps violated a "rule" as Spinoza uses the term here, but not in the sense we normally understand rules or, more importantly, in the sense that the natural law tradition has tended to formulate its prescriptions.[76]

Rather than provide us with an ethics of rules, Spinoza instead offers us rather open-ended advice on the appropriate development of character, emotional

---

[75] Curley italicizes the "or" where it appears just before "fixed rules of life." We are unclear as to the reasons for this, but it seems only to enhance our point.

[76] For a look at the way natural law is often cashed out see: Thomas J. Higgins, *Man as Man: The Science and Art of Ethics*, rev. ed. (Milwaukee, Wisconsin: Bruce Publishing, 1958), p. 122; Thomas E. Davitt, *Ethics in the Situation* (New York: Appleton-Century-Crofts, 1970), Part Two, pp. 107–226, and even John Finnis, *Aquinas*, Ch. 5, pp. 132–86, *op. cit*. See also, Nelson's discussion of the "standard interpretation" of natural law and its account of the formulation of moral prescriptions in *The Priority of Prudence*, *op. cit*., Ch. 1, "The Natural Lawyers' Interpretation," pp. 1–26. Alternatively, some of the principles Aquinas advocates might also be of this advisory nature as well as would be consistent with classical ethics generally. Kisner, *op. cit.*, Ch. 6, wants to link Spinoza directly to the natural law tradition through E4P18Schol. Kisner's somewhat Kantian rendering of "reason's dictates" runs contrary to our reading here and seems to us to truncate this particular proposition unnecessarily. Nonetheless, we would agree that "natural law" for Spinoza would have to be less than the inexorable laws of nature and more than the contingent dimension of many human positive laws.

health, and attitudinal orientations that will lead to successful conduct. The sort of ethics Spinoza therefore presents is a practical exemplar model, and not a rule model. In this respect it is one reminiscent of Aristotle's definition of virtue, which calls upon us to look to the person of practical wisdom.

> For since we desire to form the idea of a man which we may look to as a model of human nature, we shall find it useful to keep these terms ["good" and "bad"] in the sense I have indicated. So in what follows I shall mean by 'good' that which we certainly know to be the means for our approaching nearer to the model of human nature that we set before ourselves, and by 'bad' that which we certainly know prevents us from reproducing the said model. Again, we shall say that men are more perfect or less perfect in so far as they are nearer or further from this model. For it is important to note that when I say that somebody passes from a state of less perfection to a state of greater perfection, and vice versa, I do not mean that he changes from one essence or form to another . . . but that we conceive his power of activity, in so far as this is understood through his nature, to be increased or diminished. (E4Pref.)

Here the modality is one of nearer and farther rather than conforming or not conforming, as one would have with rules or laws. And when one looks throughout the *Ethics* for rules, what one typically finds instead are descriptions of virtues and vices, positive and negative emotional orientations, matters that serve our advantage, and recommendations about which dispositions are appropriate for which situations (e.g., E4P42–58). The sort of ethics that measures the moral worth of an action according to its conformity to a rule or command is almost entirely missing. Such an approach to ethics is to be expected from a thoroughly immanentized and highly agent centered ethics, because the measure of good or bad, perfection or imperfection, would refer primarily to the agent's own character or circumstances and not the rule to which the agent is to conform. If the conclusions of our earlier discussion of Aquinas are correct, Spinoza "corrects" the rule and command tendency of the transcendent turn in natural law, and its inevitable movement away from the agent, by his insistence on immanence. Thus, instead of drawing forth dictates of reason, Spinoza's ethics is an encouragement to what the agent's reason would dictate.

Both thinkers would ground the natural law as it applies to humans in reason. Spinoza, for example, is clear that "true virtue is nothing other than to live by the guidance of reason" (E4P37Schol.1). Yet a failure of virtue for Spinoza is not an intellectual failure of some sort, but actually a form of weakness or passivity on the part of the agent. Spinoza continues, "Weakness consists solely in this, that a man suffers himself to be led by things external to himself and is determined by them to act in a way required by the general state of external circumstances, not by his own nature considered only in itself." In acting from within one's own nature one is distanced from the "general state of external circumstances." This distance is important, for it may suggest another divergence from the natural law tradition. If we consider once again the passage on law cited earlier, we seem to be given a choice between the inexorable laws of nature or the contingent laws of man. It is no accident that Spinoza connects the latter with "making life more secure and more convenient." Unlike the natural law tradition which would tend to merge the moral improvement of individuals with a social and political mission to ensure such improvement, Spinoza tells us that "the purpose of every society and state is secure and comfortable living" (TTP Ch.III) (security and convenience) and not our moral perfection: "simplicity and integrity of spirit are not inspired in men by the command of laws or by public authority, and it is quite impossible to make anyone blessed by force or legal enactments" (TTP Ch.VII). Spinoza then rather sharply distinguishes the political from the moral, giving the state a rather limited and specific role. Security and comfort are perhaps necessary for the moral life, but they are not descriptions of it and are for the sake of unvirtuous as much as the virtuous.[77]

We believe it is not simply coincidental that a strongly agent centered doctrine would have a light touch when it comes to generalized prescriptions or that what is generalized would have more to do with the conditions for moral conduct than that conduct itself. Dictates issuing from God Himself can hardly be more applicable to some than others or be applicable in different ways to different people. The best one could allow for would be variations based upon varying circumstances. In Spinoza's case, however, when he says something such as "his own nature considered only in itself," one has every reason to believe that each one of us separately has a distinct nature, if for no other reason than one's conatus is not shared: "the conatus whereby each thing endeavors to preserve its own being is defined solely by the essence of the thing itself . . .; given this essence alone, and not from the essence of any other thing, it necessarily follows . . . that everyone endeavors to preserve his

[77]Spinoza's political and social philosophy is, of course, a subject for extended treatment well beyond what can be provided here. For a further explanation of this reading of Spinoza's politics, see Den Uyl, *God, Man and Well-Being*, *op. cit*. Ch. 1, and for our perspective on Spinoza's place in the history of political thought, see Rasmussen and Den Uyl, *Norms of Liberty op. cit*., Ch. 3. It would certainly be a mistake to infer from our comments that Spinoza does not have things to say of an ethical nature about social life. One need only consult E4P36, 37, and 40. But we believe that even if one does not accept our reading of Spinoza on these matters, one will not find much of a prescriptive nature that resembles the prescriptions of the natural law tradition. For an alternative less individualist reading of Spinoza in political theory, but one which would agree that "the 'true purpose of the law' concerns the achievement of self-legislation, the formulation of 'a rule of life' with the end in view to expand the range of human power," (p. 172) see for example Nancy K. Levene, *Spinoza's Revelation: Religion, Democracy, and Reason* (Cambridge: Cambridge University Press, 2004) Ch. 3. In this connection see also Moira Gatens and Genevieve Lloyd, *Collective Imaginings: Spinoza, Past and* Present (London: Routledge, 1999), Chs. 4 and 5. There are now, of course, numerous studies devoted in whole or part to interpreting Spinoza's political and social theory. A good bibliography of such works along with works on other aspects of Spinoza's thought can be found in Jarrett, *Spinoza: A Guide for the Perplexed*, *op. cit*.

own being" (E4P25Dem).[78] It is thus not simply agent centeredness but self-directedness that defines the being of each of us. As separate centers of power, the language of harmony, cooperation, and coordination as a function of the open-ended interplay of those powers seems more appropriate than relations determined by rules. For Aquinas the realm of natural law would lie between that of positive human law and eternal law. Whatever counterpart to natural law there is in Spinoza, our point has been that the nature of the prescriptions would look different directly in proportion to the degree of agent centeredness the doctrines possess.

DE-CENTERING THE AGENT

It would be mistaken for us to leave the impression that Spinoza, unlike Aquinas, has a thoroughly agent centered doctrine. Although we believe that the transcendent dimension in Aquinas is a force drawing away from agent centeredness and that Spinoza's move towards immanence avoids those tendencies, Spinoza is not without his own de-centering dimensions. One need only recall Spinoza's famous "worm in the bloodstream" example to realize that in the Spinozistic universe agent centeredness may be a distorted perspective rather than the central one (Letter 32). The worm in the bloodstream "would regard each individual particle [in the blood] as a whole, not a part, and it would have no idea as to how all the parts are controlled by the overall nature of the blood and compelled to mutual adaptation as the overall nature of the blood requires." Passages such as this one suggest that what appears to be a central location of agency may not be as centralized as appearances suggest. Indeed, as is well known, in a doctrine such as Spinoza's where there is only one substance and individuals are but modes of that substance, the natural pull of such a system is likely to be away from agent centeredness. For it is not just that the agent (in this case the worm) is a single thing within a much larger system, but rather that the very "singleness" of the thing cannot be understood apart from components of the larger system that influence its behavior.

A good illustration of our last point comes with regard to E2Def.7 and in the lemmas and axioms following E2P13. Just prior to that proposition (E2P11), for example, we are told that "the actual being of the human mind is basically nothing else but the idea of an individual actually existing thing," which by E2P13 turns out to be "a definite mode of extension," i.e., our bodies. And as we further learn from the scholium to this proposition, to understand the mind we need to understand its object, namely the human body. So, Spinoza goes on

---

[78]Spinoza just a few propositions later begins to talk about our commonality as well. The propositions seem to us to neither be in contradiction or tension, provided that one does not read out the individuality we are emphasizing here. That, as we shall see below, may be one of the issues that pulls Spinoza away from his agent centeredness.

to give a description of what amounts to a characterization of individuality materially understood. Central to that description is Lemma 1: "bodies are distinguished from one another in respect of motion and rest, quickness and slowness, and not in respect of substance." This lemma and the ones to follow are themselves predicated upon E2Def.7: "by individual things I mean things that are finite and have a determinate existence. If several individual things concur in one act in such a way as to be all together the simultaneous cause of one effect, I consider them all, in that respect, as one individual." Hence our bodies are not substantial individual things but themselves composed of parts in motion and rest which retain a certain relationship to one another. Moreover, "the human body is composed of very many individual parts of different natures, each of which is extremely complex" (Lemma 7 Postulate 1). So long as those relationships between the parts remain the same, or proportionately the same, we have the "same" individual: "the individual thing so composed retains its own nature . . . provided that each constituent part retains its own motion and continues to communicate this motion to the other parts" (Lemma 7). Once the proportion of the parts is altered or the motion changes, then we no longer have the same "individual."

The upshot of all this for our purposes, since this is a complex matter in Spinoza which cannot be fully addressed here, is that locating "agency" in Spinoza may not be such a simple matter.[79] From the brief glimpse we have provided, one can see that as all beings are themselves a collection of "parts" within a larger collection of "parts" where one draws the line as to what constitutes an individual may be a matter of some dispute or arbitrariness. Moreover, given the definition of individuality just noted, individuality may be relative to an effect making it different for different effects. Some, for example, have regarded groups and states to be individuals because they can be the "cause of one effect."[80] It seems clear that the Aristotelian hylomorphism that Aquinas at least partially adopts, where the formal cause organizes matter, gives one a more circumscribed individuality than we find here, however infused that account may be with divinity.

[79]Agency would seem a simpler matter if individuals were substances, but as Wolfson notes, "man, then, as a whole is not a substance, nor are his soul and body taken individually, substances. Man is a combination of two modes." (Wolfson, *op. cit., p. 41 Vol. II*). For a classic discussion of some of these matters, see Hans Jonas, "Spinoza and the Theory of Organism" in Marjorie Grene, ed., *Spinoza: A Collection of Critical Essays* (Garden City, New York: Anchor Books, 1973), pp. 259–78, especially sections III–V. One also might consult Alan Gabbey, "Spinoza's natural science and methodology" pp. 168ff, and Michael Della Rocca, "Spinoza's metaphysical psychology," pp. 192ff both articles of which are in Don Garrett, ed., *The Cambridge Companion to Spinoza* (Cambridge: Cambridge University Press, 1996). See also Michael Della Rocca, *Spinoza*, (New York: Routledge 2008), pp. 106ff, 147ff. Finally, one might want to consult Olli Koistinen, "Spinoza on Action" in Olli Koistinen, ed., *The Cambridge Companion to Spinoza's Ethics*, (Cambridge: Cambridge University Press, 2009), pp. 166–87.

[80]Most prominently in this regard is Alexandre Matheron, *Individu et Communauté chez Spinoza* (Paris: Les editions de Minuit, 1968). For the contrary position with respect to the state see Lee C. Rice and Douglas J. Den Uyl, "Spinoza and Hume on Individuals," *Reason Papers* 15 (Summer 1990): 91–117.

Yet we suppose it could be said that Spinoza's individuals are equally infused with God, perhaps more so. After all, Spinoza tells us that "particular things are nothing but affections of the attributes of God; that is, modes wherein the attributes of God find expression in a definite and determinate way" (E1P25Cor.). Moreover, for Spinoza

> God is the cause not only of the coming into existence of things but also of their continuing in existence, or, to use a scholastic term, God is the cause of the being of things. For whether things exist or do not exist, in reflecting on their essence we realise that this essence involves neither existence nor duration. So it is not their essence that can be the cause of either their existence or their duration, but only God, to whose nature alone existence pertains. (E1P24Cor.)

If we add to all this the notion that "God is the efficient cause not only of the existence of things but also of their essence" (E1P25), the pull towards divinity seems as strong in Spinoza as in Aquinas. The differences come with respect to what we make of immanence in Spinoza versus transcendence in Aquinas and also what we are to make of their respective understandings of "essence."[81] We may wish to connect essence in Spinoza with *conatus* as seems suggested by E3P7&8. Here there is a kind of unitary persistence in a form of being where the "parts" retain their relative motions and proportions and where the agent can produce a variety of effects upon the environment in ways that cannot be understood through external causes alone.[82] But here again we move too far afield, for we can hardly begin a full discussion of Spinoza's concept of essence here, since over the years interpretations have ranged from idealism to mechanistic materialism. We have, nonetheless, sufficiently indicated that Spinoza's substantial monism will raise issues about where individuality, of the sort required for a concept of agent centeredness, will lie. In the end, therefore, we face somewhat similar challenges to those faced when looking at Aquinas, and perhaps for the same reasons. Namely, we face the challenge of squaring a strongly agent centered ethical framework with a God centered universe. However true that challenge may be with respect to our two thinkers, from what we have seen in our discussion above, it does appear to be the case that God centeredness in Spinoza has weaker *normative* implications than it does in Aquinas, even if it has equal importance ontologically. A brief, somewhat speculative note, therefore, needs to be made about this last claim, since that claim ties us back to "natural law."

[81] Blakemore notes correctly that Spinoza does not see the existence/essence distinction as implying transcendence as Aquinas does. Blakemore, *op. cit.*, p. 228.

[82] A useful discussion of many of these points can be found in Eric Schliesser, "Spinoza's Conatus as an essence preserving, attribute-neutral immanent cause: Toward a New Interpretation of Attributes and Modes" in Keith Allen and Tom Stoneham, eds. *Causation in Modern Philosophy* (Routledge Advances in the History of Philosophy, 2011). See also Blakemore, *op. cit.*, pp. 237ff which includes comparison of Spinoza's *conatus* and Aquinas's hylomorphism.

The claim would appear to be contradicted by Spinoza's fifth book of the *Ethics* and by an intellectualist tradition of reading Spinoza as advocating retirement from ordinary life for the life of contemplation of God's nature as the best or truly active life. Spinoza's own biography alone would suggest the latter reading, but even if we devoted ourselves to it, there is nothing about that reading which really challenges agent centeredness. Indeed the language of that interpretation supports it. Instead, we would like to make one point about why the fifth book of the *Ethics*, which admittedly has always been something of a mystery to interpret, may actually suggest a strong form of agent centeredness.

In E5 Spinoza speaks again of the three levels of knowledge he first discusses in E2P40Schol.2. There we learn that the lowest level of knowledge concerns the manipulation of symbols and the imagination. The second level, which Spinoza calls reason, involves "common notions and adequate ideas of the properties of things." Finally, however, there is a third level of knowledge that Spinoza calls intuition (*scientia intuitiva*) which "proceeds from an adequate idea of the formal essence of certain attributes of God to an adequate knowledge of the essence of things." We need not trouble ourselves of what to make of all this to notice some interesting comments Spinoza makes in E5. First he tells us that "the more we understand particular things, the more we understand God" (E5P24). We are also reminded that "the highest conatus of the mind and its highest virtue is to understand things by the third kind of knowledge" (E5P25). Consequently, Spinoza can tell us that,

> he who knows things by this third kind of knowledge passes to the highest state of human perfection, and consequently is affected by the highest pleasure, this pleasure being accompanied by the *idea of himself and his own virtue.* Therefore from this kind of knowledge there arises the highest possible contentment. (E5P27Dem; emphasis added.)

It seems possible, therefore, on the basis of passages such as these, coupled to the point noted earlier that the object of human mind is the body (E2P13), that at least one of those particular things we come to know by the third kind of knowledge, and arguably the most important, is our own selves. Spinoza seems to confirm this somewhat later when he tells us that "the more each man is advanced in this kind of knowledge, the more clearly conscious he is of himself and of God, that is, the more perfect and blessed he is" (E5P31Schol.). For our purposes here, therefore, remarks such as these suggest that in the end God does not pull us out of ourselves for Spinoza but rather more into ourselves, thus emphasizing a kind of agent centeredness.[83] Perhaps in those aspects of

---

[83]For a discussion of the issue of self-knowledge in Spinoza as it relates to the passages referenced here (as well as others), one might look at Michael LeBuffe, *op. cit.*, Ch. 11. See also Aaron V. Garrett, *op. cit.*, Ch. 7. In addition, it is useful to look at Charlie Huenemann, "Epistemic autonomy in Spinoza," in Charlie Huenemann, ed., *Interpreting Spinoza: Critical Essays* (Cambridge: Cambridge University Press, 2008), pp. 94–110.

Stoicism rooted in the Socratic maxim to "know thyself," we find a follower in Spinoza. Rather than issuing in "common notions" of reason, "natural law" for Spinoza culminates in a rather extreme form of agent centeredness.

CONCLUSION

If we understand an agent centered ethics to be a species of perfectionism in which the individual human being is both the agent and the object of the perfection process, then it can be fairly said that in the final analysis natural law ethics (at least as found in Aquinas) is not such an ethics.[84] Even more, not only is it not an agent centered ethics in this sense, but there is an uneasy tension between the agent centered side and what is contributed by the divine. This latter issue applies to both our thinkers, and the tendency in both may be a pulling away from agent centeredness. However, transcendence in Aquinas raises the question of what exactly agent centeredness is contributing to natural law ethics, and the answer to this has not been solved by contemporary natural law ethicists.[85] Spinoza may not succeed in bringing agent centeredness back to the fore, but immanence does imply that whatever qualifies as agent centeredness must constitute a source for any norms associated with perfectionism as connected to the agent. This is not clear with transcendence. If nothing else, our examination of Spinoza challenges the ethical naturalism carried forward from antiquity by at least some medieval thinkers by insisting on clarification of the extent to which naturalism ultimately matters ontologically. More generally, though, the problem of agent centeredness, where the pulls away from it as discussed above are God centered, may face similar pressures in more contemporary theories making no reference to God. In these theories individuals are seen as conditioned by society, culture, biology, gender, history, and the like,

[84]We hasten to note that we are sympathetic with any account of Aquinas's ethics that sees him as making the exercise of prudence by the individual human being central. Moreover, we believe that there are valid points to be made against holding that Aquinas has a merely mechanical or deductive view of how prudence functions. However, we are not convinced that such accounts ultimately win the day. We say this not because we deny that Aquinas's view of prudence might not turn out to be highly nuanced but because we do not see how prudence can have the principal function in an ethics that makes the eternal law the ultimate measure for human perfection and a transcendent perfect good the ultimate aim.

[85]This problem is not alleviated by the so-called new natural law theory advanced by John Finnis and Germain Grisez, for despite their attempts to free Thomistic natural law ethics from its metaphysical underpinnings and provide a larger role for individual human beings in fashioning a flourishing life, they nonetheless fail to recognize fully the importance of the individual as the agent and object of self-perfection. They fail because (1) they seek to replace the insight of individuals (that is, prudence) in determining *the mean* for human conduct with self-styled principles of practical reasonableness and (2) they regard individual human beings as mere placeholders or loci for human goods whose individual natures play no *moral* role in providing human goods with determinate character. Indeed, they ignore the central facet of an agent centered ethics—namely, that human goods are only actual, determinate, and valuable in relation to the lives and because of the choices and efforts of individual human beings. See our criticism of their attempts in *Norms of Liberty*, *op. cit.*, pp. 184–94.

rather than by God. From the perspective of these later theories the viability of an agent centered ethical naturalism could be regarded as of antiquarian interest only. We believe, by contrast, that focusing on the issue of agent centeredness in our two thinkers actually helps highlight the philosophical issues that need to be confronted with any naturalistic ethics. Specifically, do the substitutes for God just enumerated relieve any of the tensions we have identified in our discussion of Aquinas and Spinoza, and which directions in alleviating those tensions seem most plausible in light of the two significant philosophical systems we have examined here? The exercise might also remind us of possible alternatives to some contemporary fashions.

{ BIBLIOGRAPHY }

Adams, M., "The Structure of Ockham's Moral Theory," *Franciscan Studies* 46, (1986) 1–35.

———, "Ockham on Will, Nature and Morality," in *The Cambridge Companion to Ockham*, ed. P. Spade (Cambridge: Cambridge University Press, 1999), 245–72.

Adams, Marilyn McCord, "Ockham on Will, Nature, and Morality," in *The Cambridge Companion to Ockham*, Ed. Paul Vincent Spade, (Cambridge: Cambridge University Press, 1999), 245–72.

Albo, Joseph, *Sefer ha-'Ikkarim (Book of Principles)*, edited and translated by Isaac Husik. 4 vols. (Philadelphia: The Jewish Publication Society, 1929).

Algra, K., "Stoic Theology," in *The Cambridge Companion to the Stoics*, ed. B. Inwood (Cambridge: Cambridge University Press, 2003), 153–78.

Altmann, Alexander. "Saadya's Conception of the Law." *Bulletin of the John Rylands Library* 28, (1944) 3–24.

Annas, J., *The Morality of Happiness* (Oxford: Oxford University Press, 1993).

———, "Virtue and Law in Plato," in *Plato's Laws: A Critical Guide*, ed. Christopher Bobonich (Cambridge: Cambridge University Press, 2010), 71–91.

Anselm, *Opera omnia*, 6 vols, ed. F. S. Schmitt (Edinburgh: Nelson, 1946–61).

Aquinas, *Selected Writings of Aquinas,* ed. Ralph McInerny, (New York: Penguin, 1999).

Aquinas, *Summa Theologiae,* excerpted in *Introduction to Saint Thomas Aquinas,* ed. by Anton C. Pegis, (New York: The Modern Library, 1948).

Aquinas, *The Disputed Questions On Truth*, Vol. I, trans. Robert W. Mulligan, S.J. (Chicago: Henry Regnery, 1952).

———, *The Disputed Questions On Truth*, Vol. III, trans. Robert W. Schmidt, S.J. (Chicago: Henry Regnery, 1954).

———, *Disputed Questions on the Virtues in General*, ed. Ralph McInerny (South Bend, IN: St. Augustine Press, 1999).

———, *Sententia libri ethicorum, prefatio*. Translation by Charles I. Litzinger. (Chicago: Henry Regnery, 1966); also Rome. Leonine Edition, 1969.

———, 1995–1998. *Summa Theologiae*, I–II, QQ. 90–98. "Treatise on Law," Found in Lisska, 1996–98. *Aquinas's Theory of Natural Law*.

———, *De veritate*.

———, *Summa Contra Gentiles*, http://dhspriory.org/thomas/ContraGentiles.htm.

———, *The "Summa Theologica" of St. Thomas Aquinas*, literally translated by Fathers of the English Dominican Province, second and revised edition, 1920, http://www.op.org/summa/.

———, *Super Epistolam ad Romanos Lectura*. In *Super Epistolas S. Pauli Lectura* Taurini: Marietti, 1953.

———, *The Treatise on Law*, ed., trans., and commentary by R. J. Henle, S.J. (Notre Dame: Notre Dame University Press, 1993).

Aristotle, *Nicomachean Ethics*, Second Edition, trans. T. Irwin (Indianapolis: Hackett Publishing Company, 1999).

Ayers, Michael, "Locke versus Aristotle on Natural Kinds." *Journal of Philosophy*. 78 (5), 1981, 247–72.

Bellow, Saul, *More Die of Heartbreak* (New York: Morrow, 1987).

Betegh, G., "Cosmological Ethics in the *Timaeus* and Early Stoicism," *Oxford Studies in Ancient Philosophy* 24, (2003) 273–302.

Bett, R., "Beauty and its Relation to Goodness in Stoicism," in D. Sedley and A. Nightingale (eds.) *Ancient Models of Mind: Studies in Divine and Human Rationality* (Cambridge: Cambridge University Press, 2010).

Bennett, Jonathan, *A Study of Spinoza's Ethics* (Indianapolis: Hackett Publishing, 1984).

Blackburn, Simon, *Essays in Quasi-Realism* (Oxford: Oxford University Press, 1993).

Blakemore, Guy Stephen, "Recovering the Soul: Interpreting Baruch Spinoza's Doctrine of Mind-Body Identity in the Light of Thomas Aquinas's Metaphysical Theory of Form and Matter," Doctoral Thesis, University of Tennessee Knoxville, May 2007.

Bobonich, Christopher, "Persuasion, Freedom, and Compulsion in Plato's *Laws*," *Classical Quarterly* 41 (1991), 365–88).

———, *Utopia Recast: Plato's Later Political Philosophy* (Oxford: Oxford University Press, 2002).

Bobzien, Suzanne, *Determinism and Freedom in Stoic Philosophy* (Oxford: Clarendon Press, 1998).

Boler, John. "Aquinas on Exceptions in Natural Law." In *Aquinas's Moral Theory: Essays in Honor of Norman Kretzmann*, 161–92. Edited by Scott MacDonald and Eleonore Stump (Ithaca, NY: Cornell University Press, 1999).

Bourke, Vernon, *Ethics: A Textbook in Moral Philosophy (*New York: Macmillan, 1951).

———, *The Pocket Aquinas* (New York: Washington Square Press, 1960).

History of Ethics (Garden City, NY: Doubleday and Company, 1968).

———, "Is Thomas Aquinas a Natural Law Ethicist?" *The Monist* 58.1 (January, 1974).

———, *St. Thomas and the Greek Moralists* (Milwaukee, Wisconsin: Marquette University Press, 1947).

Bradley, Denis J. M., *Aquinas on the Twofold Human Good: Reason and Human Happiness in Aquinas's Moral Science* (Washington, DC: Catholic University Press, 1996).

Brown, Eric, "The Emergence of Natural Law and the Cosmopolis," in *A Companion to Ancient Greek Political Thought*, ed. Stephen Salkever (New York: Cambridge University Press, 2009), 331–63.

Butchvarov, Panayot, *Skepticism in Ethics* (Bloomington and Indianapolis: Indiana University Press, 1989).

Butchvarov, Panayot, "That Simple, Indefinable, Nonnatural Property Good." *The Review of Metaphysics* 36, (1982).

Bychkov, Oleg, "'Aesthetic' Epistemology: Parallels between the Perception of Musical Harmony and the Cognition of Truth in Duns Scotus," in Ludger Honnefelder and others (ed.), *Johannes Duns Scotus 1308–2008: Investigations into his Philosophy*, Archa Verbi, Subsidia, 5 (Münster: Aschendorff; St Bonaventure, NY: Franciscan Institute Publications, 2010), 345–56.

———, "*Decor ex praesentia mali*: Aesthetic Explanation of Evil in the Thirteenth-Century Franciscan Thought," in *Recherches de Théologie et Philosophie médiévales*, 68, (2001) 245–69.

———, "What does Beauty have to do with the Trinity? From Augustine to Duns Scotus," *Franciscan Studies*, 66, (2008) 197–212.

Cairns, Huntington, "Spinoza's Theory of Law," *Columbia Law Review* 48.7, (Nov. 1948).
Carriero, John, "Spinoza on Final Causality," *Oxford Studies in Early Modern Philosophy*, eds. Daniel Garber and Steven Nadler (Oxford University Press, 2005, Vol. 2).
Centrone, Bruno, "Platonism and Pythagoreanism in the Early Empire," in *The Cambridge History of Greek and Roman Political Thought*, eds. Christopher Rowe and Malcolm Schofield (Cambridge: Cambridge University Press, 2000), 559–84.
Cessario, Romanus, O. P. "Why Aquinas Locates Natural Law within the *Sacra Doctrina*." In *St. Thomas Aquinas and the Natural Law Tradition: Contemporary Perspectives*, 79–93. Edited by John Goyette, Mark S. Latkovic, and Richard S. Myers (Washington, D.C.: The Catholic University of America Press, 2004).
Cicero, Marcus Tullius, *The Treatises of M.T. Cicero: On the Nature of the Gods; On Divination; On Fate; On the Republic; On the Laws; and On Standing for the Consulship*. Translated and edited by Charles Duke Yonge, (London: Henry G. Bohn, 1853).
Coleman, Janet, *A History of Political Thought: Vol. Two: From the Middle Ages to the Renaissance* (Oxford: Blackwell, 2000).
Cooper, J., "Eudaimonism and the Appeal to Nature in *The Morality of Happiness*," *Philosophy and Phenomenological Research* 55, (1995) 587–98.
———, "Stoic Autonomy," in *Knowledge, Nature and the Good: Essays on Ancient Philosophy* (Princeton: Princeton University Press, 2004, 204–44).
———, "Chrysippus on Physical Elements," in *God and Cosmos in Stoicism*, ed. R. Salles (Oxford: Oxford University Press, 2009).
Copleston, F. C., S.J., *Aquinas*, Harmondsworth (Middlesex, England: Penguin Books, 1955).
Copleston, Frederick, *A History of Medieval Philosophy* (New York: Harper and Row Publishers, 1974).
Crisp, R., "Socrates and Aristotle on Happiness and Virtue," in *Plato and Aristotle's Ethics*, ed. R. Heinaman (Aldershot: Ashgate, 2003), 55–78.
Cross, Richard, "Duns Scotus on Goodness, Justice, and What God Can Do," *Journal of Theological Studies*, 48, (1997) 48–76.
———, *Duns Scotus, Great Medieval Thinkers* (New York and Oxford: Oxford University Press, 1999).
———, "Christocentrism and Theological Methodology in Duns Scotus," in *Giovanni Duns Scoto: Studie e ricerche nel VII Centenario della sua morte, in onore di P. César Saco Alarcôn*, 2 vols., ed. Martín Carbajo Núñez (Rome: Antonianum, 2008, II, 109–31).
Crowe, M., *The Changing Profile of the Natural Law* (The Hague: Nijhoff, 1977).
Curley, Edward, "The State of Nature and Its Law in Hobbes and Spinoza," *Philosophical Topics*, vol. 19:1 (1991).
Curran, Charles, *The Catholic Moral Tradition Today: A Synthesis* (Washington, D.C.: Georgetown University Press, 1999).
Daston, Lorraine and Michael Stolleis, eds., *Natural Law and Laws of Nature in Early Modern Europe: Jurisprudence, Theology, Moral and Natural Philosophy*. (Farnham, UK: Ashgate Publishing Limited, 2008).
David, Joseph E. "Maimonides, Nature and Natural Law." *Journal of Law, Philosophy and Culture*, Vol. V, No. 1, (2010) 67–82.
Davidson, Herbert A. "Maimonides's *Shemonah Peraqim* and Alfarabi's *Fusūl al-Madanī*," *Proceedings of the American Academy for Jewish Research* 31 (1963) 33–50.

Darwall, Stephen, "The Foundations of Morality," in *The Cambridge Companion to Early Modern Philosophy*, ed. Donald Rutherford (Cambridge: Cambridge University Press, 2006).

Davitt, Thomas E., S.J., "Basic Values in Law: A Study of the Ethico-legal Implications of Psychology and Anthropology," *Transactions of the American Philosophical Society* (New Series—Volume 58, Part 5, 1968).

———, *Ethics in the Situation* (New York: Appleton-Century-Crofts, 1970).

d'Entreves, A.P., *Natural Law* (London: Hutchinson University Library, 1970).

Den Uyl, Douglas J., *God, Man, and Well-Being: Spinoza's Modern Humanism* (New York: Peter Lang, 2008).

———, *The Virtue of Prudence* (New York: Peter Lang, 1991).

Diogenes Laertius, *Lives of the Philosophers* VII. 85–87, trans. R.D. Hicks (Cambridge, MA: Harvard University Press).

Dobbs-Weinstein, Idit. *Maimonides and St. Thomas on the Limits of Reason*. (Albany, NY: State University of New York Press, 1995).

Dodds, E.R., *Plato: Gorgias (*Oxford: Oxford University Press, 1959).

Donagan, A., *The Theory of Morality* (Chicago: University of Chicago Press, 1977).

Duns Scotus, *De primo principio*, ed. Allan B. Wolter (Chicago: Franciscan Herald Press, 1982).

———, *The Examined Report of the Paris Lecture: Reportatio I-A*, 2 vols, eds. Allan B. Wolter and Oleg Bychkov (St. Bonaventure, NY: Franciscan Institute, 2004–8).

———, *Opera omnia*, 12 vols, ed. L. Wadding (Lyon, 1639).

———, *Opera omnia*, ed. C. Balić and others (Vatican City: Vatican Polyglot Press, 1950).

Dworkin, Ronald, *Taking Rights Seriously* (Cambridge, MA: Harvard University Press, 1978).

———, "Interview," in Bryan Magee, *Men of Ideas*, 240–60 (New York: Viking Press, 1978).

———, "'Natural' Law Revisited." *The University of Florida Law Review*. 34 (2), 1982, 165–88.

———, "Liberalism" In *A Matter of Principle*. 181–204. (Cambridge, MA: Harvard University Press, 1984).

———, *Law's Empire*. (Cambridge, MA: Belknap Press of Harvard University Press, 1986).

Dyck, A., *A Commentary on Cicero*, De Legibus (Ann Arbor: The University of Michigan Press, 2004).

Efron, Noah J. "Nature, Human Nature, and Jewish Nature in Early Modern Europe." *Science in Context* 15 (2002) 29–49.

Eschmann, Thomas, OP., "Introduction," *On Kingship* (Toronto: The University of Toronto Press, 1949; 1982).

Efros, Israel. "Maimonides Arabic Treatise on Logic Introduction." *Proceedings of the American Academy for Jewish Research* 34 (1966) 155–60.

Farrell, Patrick, O.P., "Sources of St. Thomas' Concept of Natural Law," *The Thomist* 20 (1957): 237–94.

Finnis, John, *Natural Law and Natural Rights* (Oxford: Oxford University Press, 1980).

———, *Natural Law and Natural Rights*, (Oxford: Clarendon Press, 1982).

———, *Fundamentals of Ethics*. (Oxford: Oxford University Press, 1983).

———, *Aquinas: Moral, Political and Legal Theory* (Oxford: Oxford University Press, 1998).

Foot, P., "Moral Beliefs," *Proceedings of the Aristotelian Society* 59 (1958) 83–104.

Foot, Philippa, *Virtues and Vices and Other Essays in Moral Philosophy* (Oxford: Blackwell, 1978).

———, "Does Moral Subjectivism Rest on a Mistake?" In *Logic, Cause and Action*, ed. Roger Teichmann, 107–24. (Cambridge: Cambridge University Press, 2000).

Natural Goodness. (Oxford: Clarendon Press, 2001).

Forschner, M., "Zur aktualität der Stoischen Ethik," in O. Reverdin and B Grange (eds.) *Aspects de la philosophie hellénistique, neuf exposés suivis de discussions* (Vandoeuvres-Geneva: Fondation Hardt, 1986), 325–59.

Fox, Marvin. "On the Rational Commandments in Saadia's Philosophy: A Reexamination." In *Modern Jewish Ethics: Theory and Practice*, edited by Marvin Fox (Columbus: Ohio State University Press, 1975), 175–87.

———, "Maimonides and Aquinas on Natural Law." In *Interpreting Maimonides: Studies in Methodology, Metaphysics, and Moral Philosophy* (Chicago: University of Chicago Press, 1990), 124–51.

———, "The Nature of Man and the Foundations of Ethics: A Reading of Guide 1.1–2." In *Interpreting Maimonides: Studies in Methodology, Metaphysics, and Moral Philosophy* (Chicago: University of Chicago Press, 1990), 152–98.

Frankena, William K., "Spinoza's New Morality: Notes on Book IV," in *Spinoza: Essays in Interpretation*, ed. Maurice Mandelbaum and E. Freeman (LaSalle, IL: Open Court, 1975).

Frede, M., "The Stoic Conception of Reason," in *Hellenistic Philosophy*, vol. 2., ed. K. Boudouris (Athens: International Association for Greek Philosophy, 1994, 50–63.

———, "On the Stoic Conception of the Good," in *Topics in Stoic Philosophy*, ed. K. Ierodiakonou (Oxford: Oxford University Press, 1999), 71–94.

Fuller, Lon, *The Morality of Law* (New Haven, CT: Yale University Press, 1964).

Gabbey, Alan, "Spinoza's Natural Science and Methodology," *The Cambridge Companion to Spinoza*, ed. Don Garrett (Cambridge: Cambridge University Press, 1996).

Galston, Miriam. "The Purpose of the Law According to Maimonides," *The Jewish Quarterly Review* 69, no. 1 (Jul. 1978), 27–51.

Garrett, Aaron, "Spinoza as Natural Lawyer," *Cardozo Law Review*, vol. 25:2 (2003–4).

Gatens, Moira and Lloyd, Genevieve *Collective Imaginings: Spinoza, Past and* Present (London: Routledge, 1999).

Gérard Sondag, "The Conditional Definition of Beauty by Scotus," *Medioevo* 30 (2005), 191–206.

Gill, C., "The Stoic Theory of Ethical Development: In What Sense is Nature a Norm?," in J. Szaif and M. Lutz-Bachmann (eds.) *Was ist das für den Menschen Gute?* (Berlin: Walter de Gruyter, 2004), 101–25.

Goerner, E. A. "Response to Hall," *Political Theory* 18, 4 (1990): 650–55.

Golding, Martin, *The Philosophy of Law* (Englewood Cliffs, NJ: Prentice-Hall, 1975).

———, "Aquinas and Some Contemporary Natural Law Theories." *Proceedings of the American Catholic Philosophical Association*. 48 (1974) 238–47.

Gonsalves, Milton A., *Fagothey's Right & Reasons: Ethics in Theory and Practice*, 9th ed. (Upper Saddle River, NJ: Prentice Hall, 1989).

Goodman, Lenn, "Judaism and Natural Law," unpublished manuscript.

Gourinat, J. "The Stoics on Matter and Prime Matter: "Corporealism" and the Imprint of Plato's *Timaeus*', in *God and Cosmos in Stoicism*, ed. R. Salles (Oxford: Oxford University Press, 2009), 46–70.

Grafhoff, Gerd. "Natural Law and Celestial Regularities from Copernicus to Kepler." In *Natural Law and Laws of Nature in Early Modern Europe: Jurisprudence, Theology, Moral and Natural Philosophy*, edited by Lorraine Daston and Michael Stolleis, 143–62. (Farnham, UK: Ashgate Publishing Limited, 2008).

Gustafson, James M., *Ethics from a Theocentric Perspective, Volume Two: Ethics and Theology* (Chicago: University of Chicago Press, 1984).

Haakonssen, Knud, General Editor, "Natural Law and Enlightenment Classics Series" series, Liberty Fund Books, http://www.libertyfund.org/encollection.html.

———, *Natural Law and Moral Philosophy* (Cambridge: Cambridge University Press, 1996).

———, "Divine/natural law theories in ethics," in *The Cambridge History of Seventeenth-Century Philosophy*, vols. 1–2, ed. Daniel Garber and Michael Ayers (Cambridge: Cambridge University Press, 1998).

———, "Natural Law," in L. Becker and C. Becker, (eds.) *Encyclopedia of Ethics*. (New York: Routledge, 2001), 1205–12.

Haldane, John, "Natural Law and Ethical Pluralism." In *Faithful Reason*, ed. John Haldane, 129–51 (London: Routledge, 2004).

———, "Realism with a Metaphysical Skull" (with response by Putnam). In *Hilary Putnam: Pragmatism and Realism*, eds. J. Conant and Urszula Zeglen, 97–104. (London: Routledge, 2002).

———, "Thomistic Ethics in America." *Logos* 3 (4), (2000), 150–68.

Hall, J., "Plato's Legal Philosophy," *Indiana Law Journal* 31 (1956), 171–206.

Hall, Pamela M. "Goerner on Thomistic Natural Law." *Political Theory* 18, 4 (1990): 638–49.

———, *Narrative and Natural Law: An Interpretation of Thomistic Ethics*. Notre Dame, IN: University of Notre Dame Press, 1994.

Hansen, Mogens Herman, *The Athenian Democracy in the Age of Demosthenes* (Oxford: Blackwell, 1991).

Harman, Gilbert, *The Nature of Morality* (New York: Oxford University Press, 1977).

Harris, Errol E., "Spinoza's Treatment of Natural Law," in *Spinoza's Political and Theological Thought*, ed. C. de Deugd (Amsterdam/Oxford/New York: North-Holland Publishing Company, 1984).

Hart, H. L. A., *The Concept of Law* (Oxford: Oxford University Press, 1961).

Haskins, Charles Homer, *The Renaissance of the Twelfth Century* (Cambridge, MA: Harvard University Press, 1927).

Harvey, Warren Zev. "A Portrait of Spinoza as a Maimonidean." *Journal of the History of Philosophy* 19 (1981): pp. 151–72.

Hauerwas, Stanley, *The Peaceable Kingdom: A Primer in Christian Ethics* (Notre Dame, IN: University of Notre Dame Press, 1983).

Hentschke, A.B., (*Politik und Philosophie bei Plato und Aristoteles* (Frankfurt, 1971).

Hibbs, Thomas S., "Interpretations of Aquinas's Ethics Since Vatican II," *The Ethics of Aquinas*, ed. Stephen J. Pope (Washington, D.C.: Georgetown University Press, 2002).

Higgins, Thomas J., *Man as Man: The Science and Art of Ethics*, rev. ed. (Milwaukee, Wisconsin: Bruce Publishing, 1958),

Hittinger, Russell, "After MacIntyre: Natural Law Theory, Virtue Ethics and *Eudaimonia.*" *International Philosophical Quarterly* 29 (4): (1989), 449–61.

Hitz, Zena, "Plato on the Sovereignty of Law," *A Companion to Greek and Roman Political Thought*, ed. Ryan K. Balot (Malden, MA: Wiley-Blackwell, 2009), 367–81.

Horsley, R., "The Law of Nature in Philo and Cicero," *The Harvard Theological Review* 71, 1978, 35–59.

Huenemann, Charlie, "Epistemic autonomy in Spinoza," *Interpreting Spinoza: Critical Essays*, ed. Charlie Huenemann (Cambridge: Cambridge University Press, 2008).

Hyman, Arthur. "Spinoza's Dogmas of Universal Faith in the Light of their Medieval Jewish Background." In *Biblical and Other Studies*, edited by Alexander Altmann, 183–95. (Cambridge, MA: Harvard University Press, 1966).

Ibn Pakuda, Bahya, *The Book of Direction to the Duties of the Heart*, trans. Menahem Mansoor (Oxford: Littman Library of Jewish Civilization, 2000).

Ingham, Mary Beth, "Duns Scotus, Morality, and Happiness: A Reply to Thomas Williams," *American Catholic Philosophical Quarterly*, 74, 2000, 173–95.

———, "Duns Scotus' Moral Reasoning and the Artistic Paradigm," in Leonardo Sileo (ed.), *Via Scoti: Methodologica ad mentem Joannis Duns Scoti*, 2 vols (Rome: Antonianum, 1995), II, 825–37.

———, "Letting Scotus Speak for Himself," *Medieval Philosophy and Theology*, 10, (2001) 173–216.

Inwood, B., *Ethics and Human Action in Early Stoicism* (Oxford: Oxford University Press, 1985).

———, Review of Annas, *The Morality of Happiness*; *Ancient Philosophy* 15, 1995, 647–65.

———, "Rules and Reasoning in Stoic Ethics," in *Topics in Stoic Philosophy*, ed. K. Ierodiakonou (Oxford: Oxford University Press, 1999), 95–127.

Inwood, B. and L. Gerson, eds., *The Stoics Reader* (Indianapolis: Hackett Publishing Company, 2008).

Irwin, Terence, The *Development of Ethics*, vol. 1 (Oxford: Oxford University Press, 2007).

———, *The Development of Ethics*, vol. 2 (Oxford: Oxford University Press, 2008).

———, "Stoic and Aristotelian Conceptions of Happiness," in *The Norms of Nature: Studies in Hellenistic Ethics*, eds. M. Schofield and G. Striker (Cambridge: Cambridge University Press, 1986), 205–44.

———, "Virtue Praise and Success: Stoic Criticisms of Aristotelian Virtue," *Monist* 73, 1990, 59–79.

———, "Socratic Paradox and Stoic Theory," in *Companions to Ancient Thought 4: Ethics*, ed. Stephen Everson (Cambridge: Cambridge University Press, 1998a), 151–92.

———, "Stoic Inhumanity," in *The Emotions in Hellenistic Philosophy*, eds. J. Sihvola and T. Engberg-Pederson (Dordrecht: Kluwer Academic Publishers: 1998b), 219–41.

———, (forthcoming) "Nature, Law and Natural Law," in *Oxford Handbook of the History of Ethics*, ed. R. Crisp (Oxford: Oxford University Press).

———, "Morality as Law and Morality in the *Laws*," in *Plato's Laws: A Critical Guide*, ed. Christopher Bobonich (Cambridge: Cambridge University Press, 2010), 92–107.

Jacobs, James Michael, "The Metaphysics of Morals in Thomas Aquinas: The Transcendentals as the Foundation for Natural Law Ethics" (January 1, 2002). *ETD Collection for Fordham University*. Paper AAI3045128. http://fordham.bepress.com/dissertations/AAI3045128.

Jacobs, Jonathan. "Judaism and Natural Law." *The Heythrop Journal* 50, issue 6 (Nov. 2009) 930–47.

———, *Law, Reason, and Morality in Medieval Jewish Philosophy: Saadia Gaon, Bahya ibn Pakuda, and Moses Maimonides*. (Oxford: Oxford University Press, 2010).

Jaffa, Harry. *Thomism and Aristotelianism* (Chicago: University of Chicago Press, 1950).

Jarrett, Charles, *Spinoza: A Guide for the Perplexed* (New York: Continuum International Publishing Group, 2007).

———, "Teleology and Spinoza's Doctrine of Final Causes," in *Desire and Affect: Spinoza as Psychologist*, ed. Yirmiyahu Yovel (New York: Little Room Press, 1999).

Jonas, Hans, "Spinoza and the Theory of Organism," *Spinoza: A Collection of Critical Essays*, ed. Marjorie Grene (Garden City, New York: Anchor Books, 1973).

Jordan, Mark D., *The Invention of Sodomy in Christian Theology* (Chicago: University of Chicago Press, 1997).

Jospe, Raphael, *Jewish Philosophy in the Middle Ages*, (Boston: Academic Studies Press, 2009).

Kasher, A. and J. Levinger. *Sefer Yesha'yahu Lebovits: Kovets Ma'amarim 'Al Haguto Velikhevodo*, (Tel Aviv: Tel Aviv University Press, 1997).

Katz, Jacob. *Exclusiveness and Tolerance: Studies in Jewish-Gentile Relations in Medieval and Modern Times*, (New York: Schocken Press, 1962), 175–81.

Keenan, James F., S. J., "The Virtue of Prudence (IIa IIae, qq. 47–56)," *The Ethics of Aquinas* ed. Stephen J. Pope (Washington, D.C.: Georgetown University Press, 2002).

Kellner, Menachem, *Maimonides on Judaism and the Jewish People*, (Albany, NY: State University of New York Press, 1991).

———, *Maimonides's Confrontation with Mysticism*, (Oxford: The Littman Library of Jewish Civilization, 2006).

Kenny Anthony, *Aquinas on Mind (*London: Routledge, 1993).

———, "Seven Concepts of Creation," *Aristotelian Society Supplementary Volume* 78.1 (2004).

Kerford, G., "What Does the Wise Man Know?," in *The Stoics*, ed. J. Rist (Berkeley: University of California Press, 1978), 125–36.

Kerr, Fergus, *After Aquinas: Versions of Thomism* (Oxford: Basil Blackwell, 2002).

Kidd, I., *Posidonius*, 3 vols; (Cambridge: Cambridge University Press, 1988).

King, Peter, "Scotus' Rejection of Anselm: The Two Wills Theory," in *Johannes Duns Scotus 1308–2008: Investigations into his Philosophy*, Archa Verbi Subsidia, 5, eds. Ludger Honnefelder and others (Münster: Aschendorff, 2011), 359–78.

Kisner, Matthew J., *Spinoza on Human Freedom: Reason, Autonomy and the Good Life* (Cambridge: Cambridge University Press, 2011).

Klosko, George, *The Development of Plato's Political Theory* (London: Methuen, 1986)

Koistinen, Olli, "Spinoza on Action," *The Cambridge Companion to Spinoza's Ethics*, ed. Olli Koistinen (Cambridge: Cambridge University Press, 2009).

Koester, H., "Nomos Physeos: The Concept of Natural Law in Greek Thought," in *Religions in Antiquity*, ed. J. Neusner (Leiden: Brill, 1968), 521–41.

Koistinen, Olli, Biro, John, "Introduction," in *Spinoza*: *Metaphysical Themes*, ed. Koistinen and Biro, 3–10 (Oxford: Oxford University Press, 2002).

Kossel, Clifford G., S.J., "Thomistic Moral Philosophy in the Twentieth Century," *The Ethics of Aquinas*, ed. Stephen J. Pope (Washington, D.C.: Georgetown University Press, 2002).

Kraut, R., *Aristotle on the Human Good* (Princeton: Princeton University Press, 1989).

———, "Aristotle on the Human Good: An Overview," in *Aristotle's Ethics: Critical Essays*, ed. N. Sherman (Lanham: Rowman and Littlefield, 1999), 79–104.

Kretzmann, Norman, *The Metaphysics of Theism* (Oxford: The Clarendon Press, 2001).

Kretzmann, N., and Eleonore Stump, "Being and Goodness." In *Being and Goodness: The Concept of the Good in Metaphysics and Philosophical Theology*, ed. Scott MacDonald, 98–128 (London: Routledge, 1991).

Laks, André, "Legislation and Demiurgy: On the Relationship between Plato's *Republic* and *Laws*," *Classical Antiquity* 9 (1990), 209–29.

———, "The *Laws*," in *The Cambridge History of Greek and Roman Political Thought*, ed. Christopher Rowe and Malcom Schofield, (Cambridge: Cambridge University Press, 2000), 258–92.

Leaman, Oliver, *An Introduction to Medieval Islamic Philosophy*, (Cambridge: Cambridge University Press, 1985).

———, *Moses Maimonides*. (London: Routledge Press, 1990).

LeBuffe, Michael, *From Bondage to Freedom: Spinoza on Human Excellence* (New York: Oxford University Press, 2010).

Lee, Patrick, "Is Thomas's Natural Law Theory Naturalist?" *American Catholic Philosophical Quarterly*, LXXI. # 4, (1997), 567–88.

Lerner, Ralph. "Natural Law in Albo's *Book of Roots*." In *Ancients and Moderns: Essays on the Tradition of Political Philosophy in Honor of Leo Strauss*, edited by Joseph Cropsey (New York: Basic Books, Inc., 1964), 132–47.

Levene, Nancy K., *Spinoza's Revelation: Religion, Democracy, and Reason* (Cambridge: Cambridge University Press, 2004).

Levine, Michael P. "The Role of Reason in the Ethics of Maimonides: or, Why Maimonides Could Have Had a Doctrine of Natural Law Even if He Did Not." *The Journal of Religious Ethics* 14, no. 2 (Fall 1986), 279–95.

Lichtenstein, Aharon. "Does Jewish Tradition Recognize an Ethic Independent of Halakha." In *Modern Jewish Ethics: Theory and Practice*, edited by Marvin Fox, pp. 62–88. (Columbus: Ohio State University Press, 1975).

Lisska, Anthony J., *Aquinas's Theory of Natural Law: An Analytic Reconstruction*, (Oxford: The Clarendon Press, 1996).

———, "Finnis and Veatch on Natural Law in Aristotle and Aquinas." *The American Journal of Jurisprudence*. 36: (1991) 55–71.

———, "Review of *Fundamentals of Ethics*," by John Finnis. *New Blackfriars* 65(768), (1984) 288–90.

Lloyd, Genevieve, *Providence Lost* (Cambridge, MA: Harvard University Press, 2008).

Lombard, Peter. *Sententiarum Quatuor Libri*. http://www.Franciscan archive.org/lombardus /opera/ls2–30.html.

Long, A.A., "Aristotle's Legacy to Stoic Ethics," *Bulletin of the London University Institute of Classical Studies* 15, (1968), 72–85.

———, "Greek Ethics after MacIntyre and the Stoic Community of Reason," *Ancient Philosophy* 4, (1983) 77–101.

———, "The Stoics on World Conflagration and Everlasting Recurrence," *Southern Journal of Philosophy* 23, (1985) 13–37.

———, "Stoic Eudaimonism," *Proceedings of the Boston Area Colloquium in Ancient Philosophy* 4, (1989) 77–101.

———, and D. Sedley, *The Hellenistic Philosophers*, vol. 2; (Cambridge: Cambridge University Press, 1987).

Lorberbaum, Menachem. *Politics and the Limits of Law: Secularizing the Political in Medieval Jewish Thought*. (Stanford, CA: Stanford University Press, 2001).

De Lubac, Henri. *Mystery of the Supernatural*. Translated by Rosemary Sheed (New York: Herder and Herder, 1967).

Lutz, C., *Musonius Rufus: The Roman Socrates* (New Haven: Yale University Press, 1947).

MacIntyre, Alisdair, *After Virtue* (South Bend, IN: University of Notre Dame Press, 1981).
———, *Dependent Rational Animals: Why Human Beings Need the Virtues* (Chicago, IL: Open Court, 1999).
———, "Natural Law as Subversive: The Case of Aquinas," *Journal of Medieval and Early Modern Studies* 26.1 (1996) 61–83.
———, "Politics, Philosophy and the Common Good." In Kelvin Knight. *The MacIntyre Reader*. 235–53 (Notre Dame, IN: University of Notre Dame Press, 1998).
———, *Three Rival Versions of Moral Enquiry* (London: Duckworth, 1990).
———, *Whose Justice? Which Rationality?* (Notre Dame: University of Notre Dame Press, 1988).
Magee, Bryan, *The Great Philosophers* (Oxford: Oxford University Press, 1998).
Mackie, J.L., *Ethics: Inventing Right and Wrong* (Harmondsworth: Penguin, 1977).
Maguire, J.P., "Plato's Theory of Natural Law," *Yale Classical Studies* 10 (1947), 151–78.
Maimonides, Moses. *The Code of Maimonides*. Translation of *Mishneh Torah*. 14 vols. (New Haven: Yale University).
———, "Commentary on the Mishnah. Introduction to Helek: Sanhedrin, Chapter Ten." In *A Maimonides Reader*, edited by Isadore Twersky (New York: Behrman House, 1972, 387–400).
———, "Eight Chapters [introduction to commentary on Mishnah Avot]." In *Ethical Writings of Maimonides*, translated by Charles Butterworth and Raymond L. Weiss, pp. 60–104. (New York: New York University Press, 1975).
———, *Guide of the Perplexed [Arabic: Dalâlat al-hâirîn; Hebrew: Moreh Nevukhim]*. Translated by Shlomo Pines. 2 vols. Chicago: University of Chicago Press, 1963; Translated into Hebrew by Michael Schwartz. 2 vols. (Ramat Aviv, Israel: Tel Aviv University Press, 2002).
———, "Kings and Wars." In *A Maimonides Reader*, edited by Isadore Twersky (New York: Behrman House, 1972, 117–215).
———, "Laws Concerning Character Traits." In *Ethical Writings of Maimonides*, translated by Raymond L. Weiss (New York: Dover, 1975, 27–58).
———, *Mishneh Torah: Book of Knowledge*. Edited and translated by Moses Hyamson. (Jerusalem: Boys Town Jerusalem Publishers, 1962).
———, "Treatise on the Art of Logic." Edited and translated by Israel Efros. *Proceedings of the American Academy for Jewish Research* 8 (1938): English sec. pp. 1–65; Hebrew and Arabic section pp. 1–136; 1966. "Maimonides's Arabic Treatise on Logic," Proceedings of the American Academy of Jewish Research. 34: pp. 155–60 [English]; 34: pp. 1–42 [Arabic].
Markus, R.A., "The Latin Fathers," in *The Cambridge History of Medieval Political Thought: c. 350–c. 1450*, ed. J. H. Burns (Cambridge: Cambridge University Press, 1988), 92–122.
Matheron, Alexandre, *Individu et Communauté chez Spinoza* (Paris: Les editions de Minuit, 1968).
Maurer, Armand A., *Medieval Philosophy* (New York: Random House Publishing Company, 1962).
McInerny, Ralph, *Ethica Thomistica: The Moral Philosophy of Thomas Aquinas* (Washington, D.C.: The Catholic University Press of America, 1982).
———, "Natural Law and Human Rights," *American Journal of Jurisprudence*, Vol. 36, 1991.

———, *Aquinas on Human Action* (Washington, DC: Catholic University of America Press, 1992).
———, *Ethica Thomistica: The Moral Philosophy of Thomas Aquinas*, revised ed. (Washington, D.C.: The Catholic University Press of America, 1997).
———, "Ethics," *The Cambridge Companion to Aquinas*, ed. Norman Kretzmann and Eleonore Stump (Cambridge: Cambridge University Press, 1993).
———, On-line Review of *Aquinas's Theory of Natural Law. The Medieval Review*. http://hdl.handle.net/2027/spo.baj9928.9801.010, 1998.
Menn, S. "Physics as a Virtue," *Proceedings of the Boston Area Colloquium in Ancient Philosophy* (1995) 11, 1–34.
Meyer, Susan Sauvė, "Plato on the Law," in *A Companion to Plato*, ed. Hugh H. Benson (Oxford: Blackwell, 2006), 373–87.
Milbank, John. *Theology and Social Theory: Beyond Secular Reason* (Malden, MA: Blackwell, [2006], c1990).
Miller, Fred D. Jr., "Plato on the Rule of Reason," *The Southern Journal of Philosophy* 43 (2005), 50–83.
———, "The Rule of Reason in Plato's *Statesman* and the American *Federalist*," *Social Philosophy & Policy* 24:2 (2007) 90–129.
———, "Aristotle's Philosophy of Law," in *A History of the Philosophy of Law from the Ancient Greeks to the Scholastics*, eds. Fred D. Miller, Jr., and Carrie-Ann Biondi (Dordrecht: Springer, 2007), 79–110.
Miller, Jon, "Stoics, Grotius and Spinoza on moral deliberation," in *Hellenistic and Early Modern Philosophy*, ed. Jon Miller and Brad Inwood (Cambridge: Cambridge University Press, 2003).
Mitsis, P. and J. DiFilippo, "Socrates and the Stoic Natural Law," in *The Socratic Tradition*, ed. P. Vander Waerdt (Ithaca: Cornell University Press, 1994), 252–71.
Mitsis, P., "The Stoic Origin of Natural Rights," in *Topics in Stoic Philosophy*, ed. K. Ierodiakonou (Oxford: Oxford University Press, 1999), 153–77.
Möhle, Hannes, *Ethik als scientia practica nach Johannes Duns Scotus: Eine philosophische Grundlegung*, Beiträge zur Geschichte der Philosophie und Theologie des Mittelalters, N.F., 44 (Münster: Aschendorff, 1995).
Möhle, H., "Scotus's Theory of Natural Law," in Williams, ed., *Cambridge Companion*, 312–31.
Montagnes, B. "Autonomie et dignité de l'homme" *Angelicum* 51 (1974) 186–211.
Morris, Thomas V., "Duty and Divine Goodness," *American Philosophical Quarterly*, 21, (1984) 261–68.
Morrow, Glenn R., "Plato and the Law of Nature," in *Essays in Political Theory Presented to George H. Sabine*, eds. M. R. Konvitz and A. E. Murphy (Ithaca, NY: Cornell University Press, 1948), 17–44.
———, "The Demiurge in Politics: The *Timaeus* and the *Laws*," *Proceedings of the American Philosophical Association* 27 (1953–4), 5–23.
———, *Plato's Cretan City* (Princeton: Princeton University Press, 1960; repr. 1993).
Murphy, Mark. (2008) "The Natural Law Tradition in Ethics," in *The Stanford Encyclopedia of Philosophy*, ed. E. Zalta, retrieved from http://plato.stanford.edu/archives/fall2008/entries/natural-law-ethics/.
Nagel, T., *The View from Nowhere* (Oxford: Oxford University Press, 1989).

Nelson, Daniel Mark, *The Priority of Prudence: Virtue and Natural Law and the Implications for Modern Ethics* (University Park, Pennsylvania: Pennsylvania State University Press, 1992).

Nelson, Everett J. 1967. "Metaphysical Presuppositions of Induction." Presidential Address, 1967 meetings of the Western Division of the American Philosophical Association. *Proceedings and Addresses of the American Philosophical Association, 1966–68*, 19–33. Yellow Springs, OH: American Philosophical Association.

Newlands, Samuel, "The Harmony of Spinoza and Leibniz," *Philosophy and Phenomenological Research*, vol. LXXXI, no. 1 (July 2010), pp. 64–104.

Niebuhr, Reinhold. "Christian Faith and Natural Law." In *Love and Justice: Selections from the Shorter Writings of Reinhold Niebuhr*, 46–54. Edited by D. B. Robertson (Philadelphia: Westminster Press, [1992], c1957).

Novak, David. *The Image of the Non-Jew in Judaism: An Historical and Constructive Study of the Noahide Laws*, (Toronto: The Edwin Mellen Press, 1987).

———, "Natural Law, Halakhah, and the Covenant." In *Contemporary Jewish Ethics and Morality: A Reader*, edited by Elliot N. Dorff and Louis E. Newman (Oxford: Oxford University Press, 1995), 35–58.

———, "Jewish Ethics and Natural Law." *The Journal of Jewish Thought and Philosophy* 5, issue 2, (Dec. 1996) 205–17.

———, *Natural Law in Judaism*. (Cambridge: Cambridge University Press, 1998).

Nussbaum, Martha Craven. *Aristotle's De motu animalium (*Princeton, NJ: Princeton University Press, 1978).

———, *The Fragility of Goodness*. Cambridge: Cambridge University Press, 1986).

———, "Non-Relative Virtues." In *The Quality of Life*, Eds. Martha Nussbaum and Amartya Sen, 242–69 (Oxford: Clarendon Press, 1993).

———, *Frontiers of Justice* (Cambridge, MA: The Belknap Press of Harvard University Press, 2006).

———, "Constitutions and Capabilities: 'Perception' Against Lofty Formalism." *The Harvard Law Review: The Supreme Court Edition*. (2007), 10–97.

Oakley, Francis, *Natural Law, Laws of Nature, Natural Rights: Continuity and Discontinuity in the History of Ideas*, (New York: Continuum International Publishing Group Inc., 2005).

Ober, Josiah, *Mass and Elite in Democratic Athens: Rhetoric, Ideology, and the Power of the People* (Princeton, NJ: Princeton University Press, 1989).

O'Connor, Daniel John. *Aquinas and Natural Law* (London: MacMillan, 1968).

Oderberg, David S., "The Metaphysical Foundations of Natural Law," *Natural Moral Law in Contemporary Society*, ed. Holger Zaborowski (Washington, DC: The Catholic University of America Press, 2010).

———, "Teleology: Inorganic or Organic," *Contemporary Perspectives on Natural Law*, ed. A. M. González (Aldershot, UK: Ashgate, 2008).

Osborne, Thomas M., "Ockham as a Divine—Command Theorist." *Religious Studies*, (2005) Vol. 41.

Ostwald, Martin, *From Popular Sovereignty to the Sovereignty of Law* (Berkeley, CA: University of California Press, 1986).

Owens, Joseph, "Aristotle and Aquinas." *The Cambridge Companion to Aquinas*, Eds. Norman Kretzmann and Eleonore Stump, 38–59 (Cambridge: Cambridge University Press, 1993).

Pangle, Thomas, *The Laws of Plato* (Chicago: University of Chicago Press, 1988).

Partee, Charles, *Calvin and Classical Philosophy* (Leiden: Brill, 1977).

Pines, Shlomo. "Truth and Falsehood Versus Good and Evil," In *Studies in Maimonides*, edited by Isadore Twersky, pp. 95–157. (Cambridge, MA: Harvard University Press, 1990).

Plato, *The Laws of Plato*, trans. Thomas Pangle (Chicago: University of Chicago Press, 1988).

———, *Complete Works*, ed. John M. Cooper (Indianapolis: Hackett, 1997), 1318–16.

Porter, Jean, *Natural and Divine Law* (Grand Rapids, MI: Eerdmans, 1999).

———, *Natural and Divine Law: Reclaiming the Tradition for Christian Ethics* (Ottawa: Novalis; Grand Rapids, MI: Eerdmans, 1999).

———, "Natural Law as a Scriptural Concept: Theological Reflections on a Medieval Theme," *Theology Today* 59, 2 (2002): 226–41.

———, *Nature as Reason: A Thomistic Theory of Natural Law* (Grand Rapids, MI: W. B. Eerdmans, 2005).

Railton, P., "Moral Realism: Prospects and Problems," in W. Sinnott-Armstrong and M. Timmons (eds.) *Moral Knowledge?* (Oxford: Oxford University Press, 1996), 49–81.

Ramelli, I. *Hierocles the Stoic:* Elements of Ethics, *Fragments, and Excerpts* (Atlanta: Society of Biblical Literature, 2009).

Rasmussen, Douglas B. and Den Uyl, Douglas J., *Norms of Liberty: A Perfectionist Basis for Non-Perfectionist Politics* (University Park, PA: Pennsylvania State University Press, 2005).

Rhonheimer, Martin. "The Cognitive Structure of the Natural Law and the Truth of Subjectivity," *The Thomist* 67 (2003) 1–44.

Rice, Lee C. and Den Uyl, Douglas J., "Spinoza and Hume on Individuals," *Reason Papers* 15, Summer 1990.

Riley, Patrick, *The Philosophers' Philosophy of Law from the Seventeenth Century to Our Days* (Dordrecht: Springer, 2009), 6.

Rocca, Michael Della, "Spinoza's Metaphysical Psychology," *The Cambridge Companion to Spinoza* ed. Don Garrett (Cambridge: Cambridge University Press, 1996).

———, *Spinoza* (New York: Routledge, 2008).

Rogers, Eugene F., Jr., "The Narrative of Natural Law in Aquinas's Commentary on Romans 1," *Theological Studies* 59 (1998), 254–76.

Ross, James, "Justice is Reasonableness: Aquinas on Human Law and Morality," *The Monist*, Vol. 58, No. 1, 1974, 86–103.

Rudavsky, T.M. *Maimonides* (Malden, MA: Wiley-Blackwell Press, 2010).

Rutherford, Donald, *Leibniz and the Rational Order of Nature* (Cambridge: Cambridge University Press, 1995).

———, "Spinoza's Conception of Law: Metaphysics and Ethics," in *Spinoza's Theological-Political Treatise: A Critical Guide*, ed. Yitzhak Y. Melamed and Michael A. Rosenthal (Cambridge: Cambridge University Press, 2010).

Ryan, Columba, "The Traditional Concept of Natural Law," in *Light on the Natural Law*, ed. Iltud Evans, 13–37 (Baltimore: Helicon Press, 1965).

Rynhold, Daniel. *An Introduction to Medieval Jewish Philosophy*, (London: I.B. Taurus Publishers, 2009).

Saadiah ben Joseph al-Fayyumi Gaon. *The Book of Beliefs and Opinions*. Translated by Samuel Rosenblatt. (New Haven: Yale University Press, 1948).

Sayre-McCord, Geoffrey, "The Many Moral Realisms," in *Essays on Moral Realism*, ed. Sayre-McCord, 1–23 (Ithaca: Cornell University Press, 1988).

Schliesser, Eric, "Spinoza's Conatus as an Essence Preserving, Attribute-Neutral Immanent Cause: Toward a New Interpretation of Attributes and Modes," *Causation in Modern Philosophy*, eds. Keith Allen and Tom Stoneham, Routledge Advances in the History of Philosophy, 2011.

Schneewind, J. B., *The Invention of Autonomy* (Cambridge: Cambridge University Press, 1998).

Schofield, Malcolm, *Plato: Political Philosophy* (Oxford: Oxford University Press, 2006).

———, *The Stoic Idea of the City* (Cambridge: Cambridge University Press, 1991).

Schwartzschild, Stephen. "Do Noachites Have to Believe in Revelation?" *The Jewish Quarterly Review* 52, no. 4 (Apr. 1962): 297–308; Continued in 53, no. 1 (Jul. 1962), 30–65.

Sedley, D., "The Origins of Stoic God," in D. Frede and A. Laks (eds.) *Traditions of Theology (*Leiden: Brill, 2002), 41–83.

Seneca, *Moral Essays*, vol. 1, trans. John W. Basore (London: Heinemann, 1928).

Shellens, Max, "Aristotle on Natural Law," *Natural Law Forum* 4 (1959), 72–100.

Sidgwick, H., *Outlines of the History of Ethics* (London: Macmillan, 1892).

———, *The Methods of Ethics* (London: Macmillan, 1907).

Sigmund, Paul, "Law and Politics," in The *Cambridge Companion to Aquinas*, eds. Norman Kretzmann and Eleonore Stump, 217–31 (Cambridge: Cambridge University Press, 1993).

Simon, Yves R., *The Definition of Moral Virtue*, ed. Vukan Kuic (New York: Fordham University Press, 1986).

———, *An Introduction to the Metaphysics of Knowledge*, trans. Vuka Kuic and Richard J. Thompson (New York: Fordham University Press, 1990).

Southern, R. W., *Scholastic Humanism and the Unification of Europe*, Vol. One (Oxford: Blackwell, 1995).

Spinoza, *The Collected Works of Spinoza*, ed. Edwin Curley (Princeton, NJ: Princeton University Press, 1986).

———, *Spinoza Complete Works*, ed. Samuel Shirley (Indianapolis: Hackett Publishing Co. 2002).

Stalley, R.F., "Persuasion in Plato's *Laws*," *History of Political Thought* 15 (1994), 157–77.

Steinberg, Justin, "Spinoza's Political Philosophy," *The Stanford Encyclopedia of Philosophy* (Spring 2009 Edition), ed. Edward N. Zalta, http://plato.stanford.edu/archives/spr2009/entries/spinoza-political/.

Stolleis, Michael. "The Legitimation of Law through God, Tradition, Will, Nature and Constitution." In *Natural Law and Laws of Nature in Early Modern Europe: Jurisprudence, Theology, Moral and Natural Philosophy*, edited by Lorraine Daston and ——— pp. 45–56. (Farnham, UK: Ashgate Publishing Limited, 2008).

Strauss, Leo. *Natural Right and History* (Chicago: University of Chicago Press, 1950).

Strickman, H. Norman and Arnold M. Silver. *Ibn Ezra's Commentary on the Pentateuch: Exodus (Shemot)*. Vol. 2. (New York: Menorah Publishing Company, Inc., 1996).

Striker, G., "Antipater, or the Art of Living" in M. Schofield and G. Striker (eds.) *The Norms of Nature* (Cambridge: Cambridge University Press, 1986), 185–204.

———, "The Origins of the Concept of Natural Law," *Essays on Hellenistic Epistemology and Ethics* (Cambridge: Cambridge University Press, 1996), 209–20.

Stump, Eleonore and Norman Kretzmann, "Being and Goodness," in Scott MacDonald, Editor, *Being and Goodness: The Concept of the Good in Metaphysics and Philosophical Theology*. 98–128 (Ithaca, NY: Cornell University Press, 1991).

Sturgeon, N. "Ethical Intuitionism and Ethical Naturalism," in *Ethical-Intuitionism: Reevaluations*, ed. P. Stratton-Lake (Oxford: Oxford University Press, 2003), 184–211.

———, "Ethical Naturalism," in *The Oxford Handbook of Ethical Theory*, ed. D. Copp (Oxford: Oxford University Press, 2006), 91–121.

Sweeney, Eileen C. "From Determined Motion to Undetermined Will and Nature to Supernature in Aquinas," *Philosophical Topics*, 20, 2, Fall 1992, 189–214.

Syse, Henrik, *Natural Law, Religion, & Right* (South Bend, IN: St. Augustine's Press., 2007).

Tierney, Brian. 1997. *The Idea of Natural Right: Studies in Natural Right, Natural Law and Church Law: 115–162* (Atlanta, GA: Scholars Press, 1997).

Torrell, Jean-Pierre. "Nature et grâce chez Thomas d'Aquin," *Revue Thomiste* 101, 2001, 167–202.

Toulmin, Stephen, *An Examination of the Place of Reason in Ethics* (Cambridge: Cambridge University, 1950).

Tuck, Richard, *Natural Rights Theories* (Cambridge: Cambridge University Press, 1979).

Tugwell, Simon, "Aquinas: Introduction," in Tugwell, *Albert and Thomas: Selected Writings*. 201–351 (New York: Paulist Press, 1988).

Twersky, Isadore, ed. *A Maimonides Reader*, (New York: Behrman House, 1972).

———, ed. *Introduction to the Code of Maimonides (Mishneh Torah)*, (New Haven: Yale University Press, 1980).

Vander Waerdt, P., "Zeno's Republic and the Origins of Natural Law," in *The Socratic Tradition*, ed. P. Vander Waerdt (Ithaca: Cornell University Press: 1994), 272–308.

Veatch, Henry B., *For An Ontology of Morals: A Critique of Contemporary Ethical Theory* (Evanston, IL: Northwestern University Press, 1971).

———, *Human Rights: Fact or Fancy*? (Baton Rouge, LA: Louisiana State University Press, 1986).

———, *Swimming Against the Current in Contemporary Philosophy*. (Washington, DC: Catholic University of America Press, 1990).

———, *Two Logics*: *The Conflict between Classical and Neo-Analytic Philosophy* (Evanston, Illinois: Northwestern University Press, 1968).

Vogt, K. *Law, Reason, and the Cosmic City: Political Philosophy in the Early Stoa* (Oxford: Oxford University Press, 2008).

Watson, G., "The *Natural Law* and Stoicism," in *Problems in Stoicism*, ed. A. Long (London: Athlone Press, 1971), 216–38.

Westberg, Daniel, *Right Practical Reason* (Oxford: Clarendon Press, 1994).

White, N., "The Basis of Stoic Ethics," *Harvard Studies in Classical Philology* 83, (1979) 143–78.

Whiting, J. (2002) "*Eudaimonia*, External Results, and Choosing Virtuous Actions for Themselves," *Philosophy and Phenomenological Research* 65: 270–90.

William of Ockham. *Reportatio*. Found in Syse, Chapter II, passim.

———, *In I and III Sententiarum*. Found in Syse Chapter II, passim.

Williams, Bernard. *Shame and Necessity* (Berkeley, CA: University of California Press, 2nd ed. 2008).

Williams, Thomas, "How Scotus Separates Morality from Happiness," *American Catholic Philosophical Quarterly*, 69 (1995), 425–45.

———, "Reason, Morality, and Voluntarism in Duns Scotus: A Pseudo-Problem Dissolved," *The Modern Schoolman*, 74 (1997), 73–94.

———, "The Unmitigated Scotus," *Archiv für Geschichte der Philosophie*, 80 (1998), 162–81.

———, "A Most Methodical Lover? On Scotus's Arbitrary Creator," *Journal of the History of Philosophy*, 38 (2000), 169–202.

———, "From Metaethics to Action Theory," in *The Cambridge Companion to Duns Scotus*, ed. Williams, 332–51.

———, "The Divine Nature and Scotus's Libertarianism," http://shell.cas.usf.edu/~thomasw/The%20Divine%20Nature%20and%20Scotus%27s%20Libertarianism.pdf.

———, ed., *The Cambridge Companion to Duns Scotus* (Cambridge: Cambridge University Press, 2003).

Wilson, Catherine. "From Limits to Laws: The Construction of the Nomological Image of Nature in Early Modern Philosophy." In *Natural Law and Laws of Nature in Early Modern Europe: Jurisprudence, Theology, Moral and Natural Philosophy*, edited by Lorraine Daston and Michael Stolleis, pp. 13–28 (Farnham, UK: Ashgate Publishing Limited, 2008).

Wolfson, Harry, *The Philosophy of Spinoza: Unfolding the Latent Processes of His Reasoning* (Cambridge, MA: Harvard University Press, 1934).

Wolter, Allan B., *Duns Scotus on the Will and Morality* (Washington, DC: Catholic University of America, 1986).

———, "The Unshredded Scotus: A Response to Thomas Williams," *American Catholic Philosophical Quarterly*, 77 (2003), 315–56.

{ INDEX }